ADVANCES IN
LIBRARY ADMINISTRATION
AND ORGANIZATION

Volume 15 • 1997

ADVANCES IN LIBRARY ADMINISTRATION AND ORGANIZATION

Editors: DELMUS E. WILLIAMS
Dean, University Libraries
University of Akron

EDWARD D. GARTEN
Dean of Libraries and Information Technologies
University of Dayton

VOLUME 15 • 1997

 JAI PRESS INC.

Greenwich, Connecticut   *London, England*

ISBN: 0-7623-0371-9

CONTENTS

INTRODUCTION

If one were to ask any manager in a library or other not-for-profit setting to list the vexing issues in his or her environment, it is likely that issues relating to program assessment, the development of a competent and dedicated workforce, and the rationalization of the organizational structure to meet the changing needs of the program would rank at the top of that list. Measuring the quality of library services has been discussed often in our profession, and new models are continually being developed to help those who lead our organizations better understand how we are doing. Personnel issues are also discussed often in our business as we try to assess how the skills that library workers bring to their jobs match the needs of our organizations and then develop programs that can address mismatches when they occur. And every manager worth his or her salt is looking for an organizational structure that will optimize the way we apply the resources that we have to the tasks we are expected to perform. All three issues are important as libraries and those who lead them try to cope with a rapidly changing environment.

The nine papers in this volume focus on these three issues. Marilyn Domas White begins by addressing how we might more effectively assess service quality. She describes SERVQUAL, a methodology that has some promise for providing a simple, intuitive way to determine how our organizations are doing. SERVQUAL uses a simple formula that defines quality as performance minus expectation and then develops and applies an instrument to determine how well service programs live up to that standard. White's piece is followed by an analysis of Ohio's "Measuring Library Services" Project written by Connie Van Fleet and Frances Haley. Van Fleet and Haley are working under the auspices of the Ohio Library Council and the State Library of Ohio to standardize measures to be used in assessing the quality of public libraries. The project focuses on developing standard definitions of library services that can be matched across libraries, determining what measurements best indicate the effectiveness of activities, and then deciding exactly what needs to be counted for those measurements to be made.

Elizabeth Plummer's paper provides a transition from a focus on measures to a concentration on the people providing services. She is still interested in the quality of service, but her focus is on the role of staff training on the service program. She reports the results of a survey on the use of customer service training programs in academic libraries. Plummer's premise is that libraries cannot assume that employees come to their jobs with an understanding of what constitutes good customer service or that staff and librarians will continue to interact effectively with patrons over time unless the library provides training and other kinds of reinforcement for their best efforts.

Mary Bushing looks at personnel from a different angle. While many people have written over the years about the need for professional training for librarians, Bushing has reached the conclusion that many public libraries in smaller communities in this country are unlikely to attract people with the MLS for their libraries. As a result, she concludes that we must begin to appreciate the contribution made by people who come to libraries without this credential, to assess their needs and to welcome and nurture them as colleagues if we as a profession are truly committed to providing universal library service of a high quality. Ray McBeth then follows with a more philosophical piece, exploring new rules for the management of organizations and those who work within them in an information age.

The volume ends with a series of papers on library structure. Edward O'Hara offers a summary of a series of case studies in elite liberal arts colleges in which he explores the impact of the introduction of new technologies on their structures. Kathleen Webb and Kerrie Moore follow with a discussion of the process used to reorganize the library at the University of Dayton by using a process that emphasized the need for the staff and faculty to actively participate in determining how their organization could be made more client-centered. They also discuss the application of the Work Environment Scale (WES) to measure the succes of the reorganization. Christine Kollen, Nancy Simons and Jennalyn Tellman then discuss efforts at the University of Arizona to develop split positions designed to create more varied and interesting job assignments. And, finally, Hweifen Weng explores the relationship between the organizational structure of libraries, the technologies they use, and the performance of those organizations.

The editors believe that there are a number of pieces in this volume that can be of use to any manager. In keeping with the traditions of this series, the pieces range from serious research studies to more practical discussions of how organizations solve very real problems. But each offers its own unique contribution to library managers' attempts to understand what it is they are about, what new ideas are on the horizon, and where they might go in their quest for a better way to do business.

Delmus E. Williams
Co-editor

MEASURING SERVICE QUALITY
IN LIBRARIES

Marilyn Domas White

INTRODUCTION

As service organizations, libraries have much to gain from marketing research oriented to marketing services, not goods. The service sector is the fastest growing sector of the American economy. Over the last few decades, considerable research has been conducted to understand what distinguishes services from goods and the factors to be considered in providing services so that firms can maintain their competitive edge and market share. "Competitive edge" and "market share" are foreign terms for libraries, where the price of a transaction is often invisible to the client since the library is subsidized through taxes or organizational support. But, as libraries face increased competition from other areas of the information service industry, such as vendors of electronic databases or electronic document delivery services, they will have to think more like their counterparts in other areas of the service sector to maintain a viable role with their client groups.

Advances in Library Administration and Organization,
Volume 15, pages 1-35.
Copyright © 1997 by JAI Press Inc.
All rights of reproduction in any form reserved.
ISBN: 0-7623-0371-9

Even without recourse to service marketing research, libraries have long been concerned with evaluating the quality of the services that they provide (e.g., Baker and Lancaster 1991; Orr 1973). In recent research, White, Abels, and Nitecki (1994) identified approximately 29 service attributes considered as measures of service quality in 17 studies of library services. Many of these are comparable to service quality dimensions described in the service marketing literature, such as responsiveness, including timeliness of response (Dalton 1992; Griffiths and King 1992; Whitehall 1992), tangibles, such as neatness of the physical facilities (Budd and DiCarlo 1982; D'Elia and Walsh 1985), level of knowledge and skill of the staff (Baker and Lancaster 1991; Dalton 1992), and the staff's willingness to help (Baker and Lancaster 1991; Budd and DiCarlo 1982). Most of the library studies addressed only one service, such as an online search service or a document delivery service.[1]

The growing use of total quality management (TQM) and continual quality improvement (CQI) in libraries has created considerable interest in measuring service quality from the client's perspective (Buchanan and Marshall 1995, 1996; Dalton 1992; Riggs 1992; Shaughnessy 1993). Several library-related publications about service quality have been published within the last few years, providing a variety of perspectives on service quality (e.g., Hernon and Altman 1996; Shaughnessy 1996; St. Clair 1997). Some of them refer to service marketing concepts and approaches. In several cases, researchers have devised programs and/or instruments for measuring the quality of services, some of which are based on user judgments or input (American Library Association, Reference and Adult Services Division 1995; Cronin 1985; Hernon and Altman 1996; Van House, Weil and McClure 1990; Van House and others 1987).

This paper has two major objectives: first, to explain an approach widely used in service marketing to measure service quality and second, to show the usefulness of this approach by analyzing and comparing the results of several studies assessing the service quality of library services through this approach. In the first section, this paper clarifies several key service marketing concepts that are applicable to libraries. The second section discusses approaches used in service marketing to measure service quality, emphasizing the performance minus expectations approach. It also describes SERVQUAL, an instrument that has been used for over ten years to measure service quality in a wide range of service organizations, including libraries, and describes a variant of this which has been developed for use in special libraries. The third section discusses the findings of several library-related studies that have used the SERVQUAL instrument or the Modified SERVQUAL, SLA Version. This discussion compares the findings not only among these studies, but also, in some parts of the analysis, with those from other types of service organizations. The fourth section summarizes the findings and makes some recommendations regarding measuring service quality in libraries.

The Modified SERVQUAL, SLA Version, and results from its implementation in two special libraries are presented for the first time; the results of the public library and academic library studies in the third section are drawn from the literature, with some re-analyses or modifications as noted to allow for comparison.

Key Service Marketing Concepts

Service quality is a major factor that clients consider in purchasing services, either with their time or with money. Other factors, such as cost, being equal, clients will opt for the best quality service. *Service quality* is a complex, multi-faceted concept, but basically it is a measure of the "goodness" of a service as seen from the client's perspective. In an early library-related article, Orr (1973) characterizes it as the response to the question: "How good is the service?" (p. 316). More recently, Boyce, Meadow and Kraft (1994) define quality for an information system as "conformity to requirements" (p. 12). Hernon and Altman (1996) emphasize that service quality is based on a customer's judgment, not on the service provider's: "If customers say there is quality service, then there is. If they do not, then there is not" (p. 6). As defined by marketing researchers, service quality is not customer satisfaction, although they recognize the relationship between satisfaction judgments and perception of service quality. *Customer satisfaction* is a judgment based on one use, that is, the reaction to a specific encounter. In comparison, *service quality* is a more enduring, generalized judgment derived from multiple encounters. A client may discount an occasional unsatisfactory transaction and still consider service quality good.

Services differ significantly from *goods*, and these differences need to be addressed in measuring the quality of services. First, goods are tangible. A service, on the other hand, is a performance or an act, and thus intangible. Second, because goods are often produced to meet specific, objectively measured standards or guidelines, they have great consistency within product lines. Significant deviations of a product from the standards usually result in rejection by producers because they know that consumers value the predictability of being able to purchase the same item and anticipate its characteristics. Dependent on the interaction between the client and the service provider, services, even of the same type, or provided by the same individual, have greater variation. Third, with goods, production is separate from consumption; and corrections or modifications to the goods can occur between the two actions. From the customer's point of view, production is essentially a private process. The customer appears only at the final stage and sees only the finished product. With services, the customer is often present throughout the service encounter. He sees the progression of the service and perhaps even participates in several different stages. The process is public, at least to the provider and the client. Services, then, differ from goods in three important ways; they are characterized by:

- Intangibility
- Heterogeneity
- Inseparability of production and consumption (Parasuraman, Zeithaml and Berry 1985; Lovelock 1991).

Measuring Service Quality in Service Marketing

One approach has dominated service quality measurement in service marketing research for the last 10 to 15 years: the performance-minus-expectations (P-E) approach.[2] This approach views service quality as the gap between performance and expectations. It is based on disconfirmation theory, which is also a dominant approach to measuring customer satisfaction. According to disconfirmation theory as it is applied in service marketing, a client approaches a service with several expectations. After the service encounter, he compares actual performance with his expectations, which are either confirmed or disconfirmed. If performance matches his expectations, the expectations are confirmed; if performance is higher than expectations, they are positively disconfirmed; if performance is lower than expectations, they are negatively disconfirmed. One reason this approach has become pre-eminent is that a flexible instrument exists to measure service quality based on this approach.

SERVQUAL was developed in 1988 by Parasuraman, Zeithaml and Berry to measure service quality (see also Parasuraman, Zeithaml and Berry 1991, 1994a). Previously these authors had developed a gaps model, which focused on several service gaps that affect service quality.[3] The SERVQUAL instrument emphasizes the "expected service-perceived service gap."

In SERVQUAL the client responds to the same 22 questions twice: first, to establish his expectations for the *ideal or excellent* service; second, to get his perceptions of the *actual* service that is provided. Each response is scored on a 7-point Likert scale. Difference scores are computed by subtracting the score for expectations from the perception scores, so scores can range from -6 to +6. The higher the score, not considering the sign, the greater the difference between perception and expectations. A negative sign indicates that expectations are higher than perceptions; a positive sign indicates that perceptions are higher than expectations.

Service quality is a multidimensional concept. The 22 questions in SERVQUAL relate to five dimensions: Tangibles, Reliability, Responsiveness, Assurance, and Empathy. Table 1 presents definitions of these dimensions.[4] The basic 22 questions are often coupled with questions which judge overall service quality, rank these dimensions by importance, and/or provide demographic data about the respondents.

Table 1. Service Quality Dimensions Covered in SERVQUAL

Dimension	Definition
Tangibles	The appearance of physical facilities, equipment, personnel, and communication materials.
Reliability	The ability to perform the promised service dependably and accurately.
Responsiveness	The willingness to help customers and to provide prompt service.
Assurance	The knowledge and courtesy of employees and their ability to convey trust and confidence.
Empathy	The provision of caring, individualized attention to customers.

Note: The dimensions are arranged in order of their appearance on SERVQUAL.

Source: Zeithmal, et al. (1990).

The most important criticisms of SERVQUAL have focused on:

- the scale's theoretical base (Cronin and Taylor 1992, 1994);
- the number and generic nature of the dimensions (Carman 1990);
- the validity of difference scores as data (Babakus and Boller 1992; Brown, Churchill and Peter 1993; Carman, Churchill and Brown 1993);
- its length (Cronin and Taylor 1992); and
- the ease of administration and data analysis (Cronin and Taylor 1992; Ennew, Reed and Binks 1993).

The authors have refuted these criticisms to a large extent,[5] however, and SERVQUAL has become widely used because of its flexibility and adaptability to specific service organizations.

An alternative approach to measuring service quality is the performance-based approach, which eliminates any consideration of expectations and simply bases judgment about service quality on the clients perception of performance. Research has generally shown a closer correlation between results using this approach and overall assessment of performance quality or evidence of the client's actions based on that assessment, such as recommending the service to a friend. SERVPERF is a variant of SERVQUAL used with this approach; it includes the same questions as SERVQUAL but omits the expectations segment (Cronin and Taylor 1992, 1994).

A major strength of the P-E approach, which is shown in the next large section, is its diagnostic capability. Based on scores computed from the SERVQUAL questionnaire, a service organization can discover the service characteristics that a client values (Expectations), can determine the client's perception of service along those same characteristics (Perceptions), and can measure the differences between expectations and perceptions. A library staff, for example, may discover that they are prioritizing empathy, when the client considers that minimally important, or, conversely, discover that they are not prioritizing promptness of response, which the client values highly. The strength of the performance-based approach, that is, its greater accuracy in measuring service quality, is offset by its lack of a diagnostic capability. In an operational setting, since SERVPERF is essentially a subset of SERVQUAL, it is still possible to replicate its results by using the Perceptions data alone from SERVQUAL.

In recent research, White et al. (1994) tested the appropriateness of SERVQUAL for use in special libraries and developed a modified version for special libraries. They were especially concerned about the correspondence between the underlying dimensions in SERVQUAL and values clients mention in connection with library services. In their initial data-gathering, which addressed this question, they conducted interviews with focus groups of special library users. In the process, they discovered considerable commonality between the service qualities considered important by library clients and those covered by SERVQUAL and noted some specific library-related behavior that indicated these aspects. After incorporating the latter into SERVQUAL, they obtained feedback on a preliminary version of their modified instrument in a half-day interactive session with 15 special librarians from a broad range of special libraries. The questionnaire was further modified slightly, based on the librarians' input, and then tested with clients in two special libraries. This research project was funded by the Special Libraries Association (SLA).

A copy of the questionnaire generated from this project, the Modified SERVQUAL, SLA Version, is included in Appendix A. This questionnaire differs from SERVQUAL in that four questions were added (Questions 5, 14, 15, 26) and wording for three questions was modified significantly (Questions 4, 9, 18). In addition to these relatively important changes, the wording was revised, as done in many studies using SERVQUAL, to reflect a library setting. Because this article is the first publication of the instrument, Appendix B also includes directions for computing the various scores which can be determined from this questionnaire, many of which are used in the following analysis.

Using SERVQUAL in Library Settings

Several studies have used SERVQUAL or its variant, the Modified SERVQUAL, SLA Version, in libraries (Hebert 1993, 1994; Nitecki 1995a, 1995b, 1996; White and Abels 1995; White et al. 1994). The data discussed in this section are drawn from three major studies which are summarized in Table 2. The special library data have been re-analyzed for this paper to show the results by individual library and to provide new analyses.

Table 2. Summary Characteristics of Three Studies

Characteristic	Hebert	White et al.	Nitecki
Date	1993	1994	1995
Version of SERVQUAL used	SERVQUAL	Modified SERVQUAL, SLA Version	SERVQUAL
Type of library	Public libraries (38)	Special libraries (2)	Academic library (1)
Type of service	Interlibrary loan	Services not differentiated	Interlibrary loan, Reference, Reserve circulation
Purpose	To investigate the "quality of interlibrary borrowing services from …: the library perspective based on fill rate and turnaround time and the customer perspective based on expectation disconfirmation." (Hebert 1993, Abstract)	"To develop a data-gathering instrument which can be used to derive customer satisfaction measures about information services," (White et at. 1994, p. 3) modifying or adapting if possible, techniques and instruments used in service marketing.	To "examine the transferability to an academic library setting of the SERVQUAL instrument …" (Nitecki 1995a, p. 4)
Sample	Total=130	Total=142 (L1=84; L2=58)	Total=343 (ILL=139; Reference=95; Reserve=109)

Note: For the row, "Type of Library," the number in parentheses indicates the number of libraries. The sampling technique for each study is described in text.

Sources: Hebert (1993, 1994); Nitecki (1995a, 1995b, 1996); White et al. (1994).

Modification of SERVQUAL

In using SERVQUAL each researcher modified the questionnaire somewhat. In the expectations portion, Hebert's (1994) statements referred to "a public library that you would like to use" (pp. 13-14). Four statements (4, 5, 8, 15) varied significantly from SERVQUAL characteristics, although they were consistent with the dimension's objectives; one (18) varied slightly. Nitecki (1995a) kept the original SERVQUAL wording, inserting as necessary the name of the specific library and/or service. The modifications incorporated into the Modified SERVQUAL, SLA Version, used in the special libraries, were more substantial and have already been described in a previous section. Since both Nitecki and White et al. (1994) were primarily concerned with assessing the appropriateness of the questionnaire for use in particular settings, they allowed respondents to indicate "no basis to judge" for each statement in the perceptions section. Normally this would not be done in administering either of these questionnaires. The version of the Modified SERVQUAL, SLA Version included in Appendix A does not include this modification. The non-responses in this section affected the computation and reporting of difference scores.

Sample of Respondents

Hebert (1994) recruited individuals who had used a public library in the previous 12 months to participate in a contrived situation. In the situation, an individual client approached a librarian indicating that a specific book was not in the library. If the librarian did not offer interlibrary loan, the client eventually asked specifically about the service. The situation ideally continued until the library provided the book through interlibrary loan (ILL), although some encounters stopped earlier. Each client completed the expectations portion of a modified SERVQUAL before the encounter and the perceptions portion after the encounter.

Her methodology creates some validity problems with the data. The expectation responses may indeed be representative of public library users' expectations for ILL, although she makes no reference to attempting to locate library clients who had actually used ILL services before. The performance responses, on the other hand, are intentionally structured to measure satisfaction with the contrived service encounter. As such, the instrument is being used to measure *satisfaction*, not *service quality*. As noted earlier, the latter is formed over many service encounters. Another problem relates to the validity of data based on contrived, instead of real encounters. The extent to which satisfaction in a contrived situation that does not represent the client's actual information need represents satisfaction in an actual situation is unknown. It seems likely that, if a client actually needs a book, not receiving it may create a more negative reaction than simply not receiving a book requested as part of an experiment.

For special libraries, White et al. (1994) drew a random sample of library clients from a list of clients who had used the special libraries several times over a 1 to 2 month period preceding distribution of the questionnaire. The lists were provided by the librarian in each of the two libraries. Each sample was drawn separately. No attempt was made to stratify on the basis of use of a particular service, primarily because special library clients are likely to use several different services and may even receive these at the same service point, so they may not always differentiate among services. Asking them to evaluate only one service when services are clustered and inter-related would confound the results.

Nitecki (1995a), on the other hand, felt that clients of a large academic library could differentiate among the services. The services were provided at different locations and were sufficiently different that even clients who used more than one service were not likely to confuse them. She also thought that the services were sufficiently different that clients might alter their expectations accordingly. Her sample was drawn systematically from clients who had completed a service transaction during a specified 8-week period (slightly longer for reference); there was no duplication in the samples across the client groups.

Plan of Analysis

The emphasis in the analysis is on showing the diagnostic capability inherent in the P-E approach, especially as developed in SERVQUAL and in the Modified SERVQUAL, SLA Version. The analysis addresses the following questions:

1. What dimensions or aspects of service do clients prioritize?
2. What particular service features or characteristics reflecting these dimensions do clients prioritize?
3. How well do libraries perform both on the specific service features or characteristics and on the more generalized dimensions?
4. How well do libraries' performances match the priorities of their clients?
5. How do the results from this P-E approach relate to other judgments of quality? In comparison, how do the results derived from performance alone relate to other judgments of quality?

In answering these questions, the analysis compares the results of the library studies and relates the findings of the library studies to those of similar studies in other service organizations. As Nitecki (1996) points out, "No comparative norms exist to interpret the importance of any of these score values across academic libraries. Rather, the focus of service quality is on the local situation" (p. 186). On the other hand, the use of SERVQUAL has showed striking similarities in clients' expectations, if not always perceptions, across different types of services. While it is realistic to believe that perceptions of quality may vary across institutions, it would be useful to know (a) if the expectations of library clients are similar to those of clients of other services, and (b) within the library setting, if these expectations differ by type of library or by type of service within a library or type of library. This analysis of experiences in connection with three types of libraries and several types of services provides some tentative answers to these questions. The developers of SERVQUAL suggest its use in several different types of comparative studies.[6]

The analysis draws on scores computed from data in SERVQUAL or the Modified SERVQUAL, SLA Version. These scores are defined and the methods for computing them are indicated in Appendix B.

In the analysis, for White et al. (1994), results are presented for each special library and, for Nitecki (1995a, 1995b, 1996), for each service. In subsequent tables and analysis, the studies are referred to as Hebert, White/L1, White/L2, Nitecki/ILL, Nitecki/Reference, and Nitecki/Reserve. The results disaggregated by special library are new; the original report presents results based only on combined data.

Relative Importance of Dimensions

In judging service quality, what dimensions or aspects of the service do clients prioritize? In these studies the clients were asked to assess the relative importance of the service dimensions by allocating 100 points across summary statements describing the five dimensions (see the Feature Importance question in the Modified SERVQUAL, SLA Version, Appendix A). If each dimension were considered equally important, it would receive 20 points.[7]

The relative rankings of the dimensions are amazingly consistent, both within the library studies and in comparison with studies from several other service organizations. This consistency is a strong argument for viewing libraries as

Table 3.   Relative Importance of Service Dimensions

| | Libraries | | | | | | | |
| | Hebert | White | | Nitecki | | | | |
Dimension	ILL	L1	L2	ILL	Ref	Res	Combined	Service Organizations
Tangibles	12	13	11	9	10	9	11	11
Reliability	35	33	36	39	26	35	34	32
Responsiveness	20	24	22	23	25	24	23	23
Assurance	20	18	18	17	22	19	19	19
Empathy	14	13	12	13	18	13	14	17

Notes: The numbers in each column do not always add up to 100 exactly because of rounding. The Combined column shows the average points allocated for each dimension in the combined library studies. Data in the service organizations represent aggregated results of research done in five service organizations (insurance companies, banks, and a telephone company) during the refinement of SERVQUAL in 1991 (n = 1936). (Parasuraman et al. 1991). Both Nitecki and Hebert report similar, but slightly different, comparisons for service organizations (n = 1936), based on data presented in Zeithmal, Parasuraman and Berry (1990, pp. 28-29). They note 22 for responsiveness and 16 for empathy.

Sources: Hebert (1994, Table 4, p. 16); White, Computed from original data; Nitecki (1995a, Table 24, p. 152). For Hebert and Nitecki, data were rounded for comparison.

service organizations, like myriad other service organizations. As Table 3 shows, regardless of the type of library and/or service being considered within the library, the subjects in the library studies ranked Reliability first, then Responsiveness, Assurance, Empathy, and, finally, Tangibles. Reliability addresses the dependability and accuracy of the service; Responsiveness deals more with promptness and willingness to help; Assurance relates to the client's trust and confidence; Empathy is concerned with caring, individualized attention; and Tangibles with physical facilities. Their ranking parallels the ranking found in studies of other service organizations (Table 3, Service Organizations column). Library users and users of many other services prioritize the same qualities.

Even the range of points allocated per dimension is remarkably similar across the studies. In the library studies, for all dimensions but Reliability, the difference between the high and low allocations ranged from 4 to 6 points. For Reliability, this difference among the point allocations for the middle four studies is 3 points, but two studies are outliers: a high of 39 points for Nitecki's ILL study, and a low of 26 points in Nitecki/Reference. The scores for other service organizations (last column) fall within the high/low range for libraries in each dimension. Clients of other service organizations rate Empathy slightly higher than those in most of the library studies, but not as high as Nitecki's reference service clients.

Nitecki's study, which assessed the importance of these dimensions to clients of different services within the same library, found some variation across the services, not in the ranking, but in the relative weights. Reference clients prioritize Reliability, Responsiveness, and Assurance more equally, with only four percentage points variance across the dimensions, and attach more importance to Empathy than the ILL or reserve service clients. These findings would be more remarkable if the clients were the same across the services, but different clients rated each service. Nevertheless, as she points out, this anomaly merits additional study (Nitecki 1995a, p. 194, 1996, p. 188).

Both Hebert and Nitecki studied ILL, which permits comparisons across libraries for a similar service. That comparison shows that ILL clients of both academic libraries and public libraries prioritize the same dimensions, both in rank and in the weights attached to them. Differences ranged from 1 (Empathy) to 4 points (Reliability).

Individual Item Analysis

In SERVQUAL and Modified SERVQUAL, SLA Version, each dimension is addressed by four to six statements. These statements or items operationalize the dimension, that is, make it more specific through statements about service characteristics that reflect that particular dimension. The dimensions themselves are never referred to by name. Instead they are addressed indirectly

Table 4. Statements Relating to the Reliability Dimension
(Modified SERVQUAL, SLA Version

No.	Statement
E6	When employees of excellent special libraries promise to do something by a certain time, they will do so.
E7	When clients have a problem, excellent special libraries will show a sincere interest in it.
E8	Excellent special libraries will perform the service correctly the first time.
E9	Excellent special libraries will provide services during stated hours.
E10	Excellent special libraries will maintain accurate records, for example, circulation or catalog records.

Notes: The statement is phrased as it occurs in the Expectations section. The E preceding each number indicates Expectations section.

through the expectations and perceptions statements and through statements briefly summarizing each dimension in the Feature Importance question. The service characteristics described in the statements related to each dimension should be more real to the client than vague statements about the broad dimension. That increased tangibility should result in more reliable and valid assessments. Table 4 shows, for example, the statements that relate to the dimension of Reliability.

For Modified SERVQUAL, SLA Version, the questionnaire statements or items are grouped into the following dimensions:

Tangibles	5 items	Items 1-5
Reliability	5 items	Items 6-10
Responsiveness	6 items	Items 11-16
Assurance	4 items	Items 17-20
Empathy	6 items	Items 21-26

The questionnaire, like SERVQUAL, is designed to measure *normative* expectations, that is, the expectations clients *would* have of an excellent special library, so the high scores are not surprising. This perspective differs from a *prescriptive* one in which respondents are asked to indicate what an excellent special library *should* have. None of the items is expressed using the word "should."

Table 5 shows the mean expectation, perception, and difference scores for each study by item. Table 6 groups these items into ranges of scores.

For expectation and perception scores, the analysis follows the same pattern: it identifies and discusses the general level of the scores and indicates variations across the studies by looking both at the percentage falling within certain ranges

Table 5. Mean Expectation, Perception, and Difference Scores for the Three Studies

No.	Hebert E	P	DS	White/Library 1 E	P	DS	White/Library 2 E	P	DS	Nitecki/ILL E	P	DS	Nitecki/Reference E	P	DS	Nitecki/Reserve E	P	DS
							Tangibles											
1/1	3.46	5.08	1.62	6.13	5.21	-.88	6.24	5.65	-.60	3.61	4.78	.68	4.29	5.51	1.16	3.57	4.72	.96
2/2	3.98	5.21	1.23	4.89	4.51	-.44	4.59	6.19	1.61	3.64	4.58	.76	4.67	5.42	.74	4.05	4.93	.79
3/3	4.08	5.61	1.53	4.81	5.54	.67	4.48	6.48	1.95	3.86	5.36	1.29	4.78	5.48	.71	3.77	4.90	.89
4/4	4.67	5.15	.45	6.13	4.85	-1.27	5.83	5.62	-.23	4.11	4.57	.22	4.61	5.05	.28	3.81	4.51	.41
-/5				6.39	5.40	-1.05	6.79	6.04	-.74									
							Reliability											
5/6	6.12	5.13	-.99	6.56	5.62	-.94	6.62	6.00	-.62	6.69	5.67	-.96	6.51	5.44	-.65	6.74	4.56	-1.61
6/7	6.51	5.19	-1.32	6.39	5.69	-.68	6.40	6.34	-.05	6.71	5.66	-.90	6.79	5.50	-1.25	6.75	4.59	-1.78
7/8	6.38	4.47	-1.91	6.13	5.57	-.48	6.28	6.16	-.12	6.44	5.56	-.87	6.17	5.41	-.64	6.51	4.48	-1.75
8/9	6.17	5.14	-1.03	6.57	6.45	-.08	6.52	6.45	-.07	6.68	5.58	-.98	6.57	5.62	-.65	6.72	4.83	-1.38
9/10	5.77	5.51	-.26	6.27	5.78	-.48	6.45	5.65	-.98	6.28	5.12	-.54	6.28	4.64	-.77	6.33	3.56	-1.42
							Responsiveness											
10/11	5.63	4.53	-1.28	5.92	5.02	-.88	5.98	5.72	-.24	5.95	4.46	-1.28	6.17	4.89	-.77	6.21	4.49	-1.00
11/12	5.91	5.31	-.60	6.20	5.60	-.64	6.48	6.02	-.47	6.54	5.67	-.90	6.50	5.52	-.94	6.63	4.78	-1.74
12/13	6.35	5.45	-.90	6.40	5.78	-.62	6.67	6.19	-.48	6.72	6.02	-.68	6.81	5.60	-1.18	6.72	4.75	-1.89
13/14	5.82	5.50	-.32	5.69	5.36	-.29	5.88	5.71	-.17	6.04	5.75	-.33	5.95	4.94	-.97	6.08	4.43	-1.55
-/15				6.05	5.03	-1.04	6.11	5.43	-.70									
-/16				6.43	5.68	-.76	6.62	5.89	-.69									

(continued)

13

Table 5. (Continued)

No.	Hebert			White/Library 1			White/Library 2			Nitecki/ILL			Nitecki/Reference			Nitecki/Reserve		
	E	P	DS	E	P	DS	E	P	DS	E	P	DS	E	P	DS	E	P	DS
							Assurance											
14/17	5.50	5.08	-.42	6.01	5.44	-.59	6.24	6.09	-.18	6.26	5.62	-.67	6.19	5.42	-.70	6.04	4.45	-1.52
15/18	5.88	5.53	-.35	5.46	5.63	-.29	5.62	6.12	.21	6.02	5.96	-.18	6.14	5.56	-.52	6.12	5.46	-.72
16/19	6.15	5.87	-.28	6.20	5.49	-.72	6.34	6.26	-.09	6.21	5.97	-.24	6.44	5.73	-6.91	6.23	5.01	-1.21
17/20	6.66	5.44	-1.22	5.95	5.43	-.54	6.14	5.98	-.13	6.25	5.69	-.59	6.56	5.42	-1.11	6.63	4.40	-2.04
							Empathy											
18/21	5.55	5.38	-.17	5.70	5.88	.22	6.16	6.37	.18	6.20	5.83	-.36	6.26	5.67	-.55	6.01	4.80	-1.10
19/22	6.36	5.52	-.84	5.49	5.99	.41	5.76	5.72	.07	6.14	4.87	-1.32	6.28	5.26	-1.02	6.30	5.12	-1.10
20/23	5.55	5.40	-.15	5.62	5.84	.20	6.00	6.28	.25	6.12	5.71	-.41	6.33	5.56	-.77	6.03	4.78	-1.19
21/24	5.81	5.09	-.72	6.02	5.77	-.34	5.91	6.27	.25	6.29	5.84	-.43	6.28	5.35	-.80	6.34	4.56	-1.25
22/25	5.99	4.46	-1.53	5.74	5.50	-.24	5.95	5.67	-.25	6.10	5.48	-.53	6.20	5.20	-.98	6.04	4.39	-1.24
-/26				5.87	5.51	-.34	6.24	5.77	-.33									

Notes: In the first column the first number refers to the statement on the statement on the SERVQUAL/SLA modification, which has 26 statements. E refers to Expectations, P to Perceptions of performance, and DS to Difference score (P-E). The average expectation score and standard deviation, ranked in descending order according to the mean, are: White/L1: 6.08 (SD .547); Nitecki/Reference: 6.00 (SD .73); White/L2: 5.96 (SD .45); Nitecki/Reserve: 5.89 (SD 1.04); Nitecki/ILL: 5.86 (SD 1.02); Hebert: 5.65 (SD .86). The average perception score and standard deviation, ranked in descending order according to the mean, are: White/L2: 6.0 (SD .29); White/L1: 5.52 (SD .39); Nitecki/ILL: 5.44 (SD .49); Nitecki/Reference: 5.22 (SD .38); Nitecki/Reserve: 4.66 (SD .36). The average difernce score and standard deviation, ranked in ascending order according to the mean, are: White/L2: -.10 (SD .47); Hebert: -.43 (SD .94); White/L1: -.47 (SD .47); Nitecki:ILL: -.54 (SD .68); Nitecki/Reference: -.83 (SD 1.51); Nitecki/Reserve: -1.02 (SD .92). A negative difference score indicates that expectations exceed perceptions. In the White and Nitecki studies, because respondents were allowed to indicate "no basis to judge" for each statement, the number of responses varied for perception and expectation scores. Difference scores can be computed only for pairs of expectation and performance scores. The total number of pairs varied across the statements. Data for Nitecki's studies were rounded to 2 instead of 3 places after the decimal for comparative purposes.

Sources: Hebert (1994, Table 2, p. 14); Nitecki (1995a, Table 10, p. 116 for Expectations; Table 11, p. 118 for Perceptions; Table 14, p. 125; for Difference Scores; White/L2, Computed from original data).

of scores and at the average score for each study. The analysis also discusses the variation among the scores for each study. Then it discusses the five statements ranked lowest and highest, emphasizing those ranked similarly by more than half the studies.

Expectations

The clients generally had high expectations for almost all items; in the combined studies expectations on 86 percent of the items were ranked 5 or above on a 7-point scale. Most of these were concentrated at 6 or above (66%). In the individual studies, the percentage of scores 6 or above on the expectation items ranged from 36 percent (Hebert) to 82 percent (Nitecki/Reserve). As a rule, most of the lower expectation scores (below 5) were for items related to the Tangibles dimension (see Dimension Score analysis).

For the White and Nitecki studies, the average expectation scores are very similar; the range covers only .22 of a point, from 5.86 (Nitecki/ILL) to 6.08 (White/L2). The average expectation score in Hebert's study (5.65) fell .21 below the lowest Nitecki study, indicating that, comparatively, public library ILL clients had lower expectations than academic or special library clients, regardless of the type of service. The low rating may be due to the service rather than to the type of library; both interlibrary loan studies had the lowest expectations. Nevertheless, the scores in all studies differ by less than half a point. Within a study, the degree of variation across scores, measured by the standard deviation, was tighter for the White studies, approximately half a point; at the other extreme, for Nitecki's Reserve and ILL studies, it was over a point (see note in Table 5).

The individual expectation statements were ranked by their average score to determine the five items ranked lowest and highest for each study. In comparing these polar items across studies, an arbitrary figure of inclusion in at least four studies (67%) was used as a threshold for indicating strength of agreement among the studies on a particular statement. The statements ranked high by more than two-thirds of the studies are identified by number, content and service dimension; the statements ranked in fewer studies are identified by number and service dimension. The number of unique statements included among each ranked group is also identified.

Eleven statements were mentioned among the lowest-ranked statements. The studies agreed significantly in ranking the Tangibles statements lowest; four to six studies considered them least important (Nos. 1/1, 2/2, 3/3, 4/4). In comparison with other service characteristics, the respondents in these studies considered it less important that libraries have modern equipment, visually appealing physical facilities, neat-appearing librarians or that service-related printed materials be clearly written and visually appealing. No other items were ranked lower by four or more studies. The seven other statements included

Table 6. Distribution of Mean Expectation, Perception, and Difference Scores for Individual Items in the Three Studies

Range	Hebert ILL Number, % age	White L1 Number, % age	White L2 Number, % age	White ILL Number, % age	Nitecki Reference Number, % age	Nitecki Reserve Number, % age	Total Number, % age
			Expectation Scores				
6.0-6.99	8 36.4%	15 57.7%	17 65.4%	17 77.3%	17 77.3%	18 81.8%	92 65.7%
5.0-5.99	10 45.5%	9 34.6%	7 26.9%	1 4.5%	1 4.5%		28 20.0%
4.0-4.99	2 18.2%	2 7.7%	2 7.7%	1 4.5%	4 18.2%	1 4.5%	12 8.6%
3.0-3.99	2 18.2%			3 13.6%		3 13.6%	8 5.7%
			Perception Scores				
6.0-6.99		1 3.8%	15 57.7%	1 4.5%			17 12.1%
5.0-5.99	19 86.4%	23 88.5%	11 42.3%	16 72.7%	19 86.4%	3 13.6%	91 65.0%
4.0-4.99	3 13.6%	2 7.7%		5 22.7%	3 13.6%	18 81.8%	31 22.1%
3.0-3.99						1 4.4%	1 .7%

16

Difference Scores

.01-.49	8 [1] 36.4%	12 [3] 46.2%	18 [5] 69.2%	7 [1] 31.8%	1 [1] 4.6%	1 [1] 4.6%	47 [12] 33.6%
.5-.99	5 22.7%	11 [1] 42.3%	6 23.1%	12 [2] 54.6%	15 [2] 68.2%	4 [3] 18.2%	53 [8] 37.9%
1.0-1.49	5 [1] 22.7%	3 11.5%		3 [1] 13.6%	5 [1] 22.7%	9 40.9%	25 [3] 17.9%
1.5-1.99	4 [2] 18.2%		2 [2] 7.7%			7 31.8%	13 [4] 9.3%
2.0-2.49						1 4.6%	1 .7%
[2.5-6.49]							
6.5-6.99					1 4.6%		1 .7%

Notes: Within each type-of-score section, the percentages are computed per study, that is, the percentages within a column within a section total to 100 percent. The last column totals the scores across the studies and gives the total percentage for each range of scores across all studies. Total n per type of score = 140: 22 items per column per type of score for Hebert and Nitecki, 26 items for White, whose data are based on the 26-item Modified SERVQUAL, SLA Version. Total difference scores in the range, disregarding the sign, are reported; the percentages reported in this section are based on these figures. Most of these are negative; the number in brackets following the total represents the total positive scores in that range. There is a total of 27 positive difference scores across all studies. For difference scores, no entries fell between 2.5 and 6.49 in any study.

17

in the lowest-ranked statements were dispersed across the dimensions (Reliability: No. 10/11; Responsiveness: 13/14; Assurance: 14/17, 15/18; Empathy: 18/21, 19/22, and 20/23).

Ten statements were included among the highest-ranked statements. There was also significant agreement among the highest-ranked items with five or more studies ranking the same four statements. Three relate to the Reliability dimension (Nos. 5/6, 6/7, 8/9): the clients prioritized library staff's meeting deadlines, showing a sincere interest in the clients' problems, and performing the service correctly the first time. The last relates to Responsiveness (No. 12/13): they prioritized the staff's being willing to help clients. Special library clients in both libraries prioritized the library's providing access to the information the client needs (No. -/16, only on the Modified SERVQUAL, SLA Version). The five other statements included in the highest-ranked statements were dispersed, like the lowest-ranked statements, across the dimensions (Tangibles: -/5; Reliability: 7/8; Responsiveness: 11/12; Assurance: 17/20; and Empathy: 19/22).

Perceptions

The perceived level of library performance found in these studies was generally high but not as high as the clients' level of expectations. Most perception scores were concentrated between 5 and 5.99 (65%) and an additional 22 percent rated in the 4 range. The clients scored libraries 6 or above on only 17 statements (12%); most of these occurred in White/L2.

The average perception scores were not as similar as the average expectation scores across the studies, however (see note in Table 5). With the exception of Hebert's study, client expectation scores had been very similar. Based on average perception scores, the clients' perception of performance in four libraries was also very similar, ranging only .3 point of each other between 5.22 and 5.52. But these four scores were framed by a high and low outlier. The outliers differed between themselves by 1.34 points; between each one and its nearest other score by .5 or over. In comparison among the studies, White/L2, with an average perception score of 6.0, performed markedly better than the others and Nitecki/Reserve, with a score of 4.66, performed poorer than the others. Within a study, the scores were relatively consistent as measured by the standard deviation, which ranged from .27 for Nitecki/Reference to .49 for Nitecki/ILL.

The same method used for determining and comparing the statements with the lowest and highest expectation scores was followed for perception scores (see previous section). There was less agreement among the lowest-ranked perception statements than among the comparable expectation items. A total of twelve statements were ranked but only four were mentioned in four or more studies. The four statements ranked lowest by at least four studies fell into three dimensions: Tangibles: 1/1, 4/4; Responsiveness: 10/11; and Empathy: 22/25. The clients considered the modernity of the equipment, the intelligibility and visual appearance of printed materials explaining services, accurate records, and convenient operating hours less important than other service characteristics. The other eight statements ranked lowest by at least one study ranged across the dimensions: Tangibles: 2/2; Reliability: 7/8, 9/10; Responsiveness: 13/14; Assurance: 14/17, 17/20; Empathy: 19/22.

Fourteen statements were mentioned in the highest-ranked group, but only two were ranked highly in at least four studies (16/19, 18/21):

P16/19[8]   Employees of XYZ Special Library are consistently courteous with clients (Assurance).

P18/21   XYZ Special Library gives clients individual attention (Empathy).

The other twelve statements (Tangibles: 2/2, 3/3; Reliability: 6/7, 8/9, 9/10; Responsiveness: 10/11, 12/13; Assurance: 15/18; Empathy: 19/22, 20/23, 21/24, 22/25) were again distributed across all other dimensions. Clients in both special libraries thought they were almost always able to contact an appropriate person for the service (No. -/15); this statement is unique to the Modified SERVQUAL, SLA Version, so agreement by both libraries constitutes total agreement.

Difference Scores

The high expectations for so many items make it difficult for any but truly excellent libraries to score positively in the difference scores,[9] which are based on both perceptions and expectations of performance. Difference scores, computed by subtracting the expectations score from the perceptions score for each item, mask the level and show discrepancies between performance and expectations.

In considering the magnitude of the differences between expectations and perceptions of performance, 101 (72%) of the average difference scores were minimal, averaging less than a point on a 7-point scale. The other 39 (28%) showed greater differences, with all but one ranging from 1 to almost slightly more than 2 points (2.04). They are more problematic. The one difference score of 6.91 (Nitecki/Reference No. 16/19) is a real anomaly.[10] From a diagnostic standpoint, the second group of scores indicates areas in which libraries should consider making modifications. Depending on the direction of the gap, and in most cases, these were negative scores, the libraries can either: (a) raise or lower the level of client expectations; (b) modify their performance to try to meet client expectations; and/or (c) take efforts to indicate the existing level of performance clearly to clients so that perceptions of performance change. It is important to note that SERVQUAL and Modified SERVQUAL, SLA

Version do not actually measure performance quality, merely the clients' perceptions of performance; reality and perceptions may not always agree. Of the 14 difference scores of one-and-a-half or more points, 10 were negative scores. Most of these occurred in Nitecki's reserve study and ranged across Reliability, Responsiveness, and Assurance.

Of the total of 140 difference scores in all studies, 113 were negative. The remaining 27 positive scores were scattered across the studies, ranging from 4 (all but White/L2) to 7 (White/L2) per study. Of the 27, 19 (70%) were for statements related to the Tangibles dimension. Only 3 of these occurred in the special library studies, where clients' expectations for modernity of equipment, the clarity of writing and visual appeal of material prepared by the library, and the organization of facilities were generally quite high, sometimes markedly higher than in the other studies. But only the two special libraries scored positively on statements related to the other dimensions. In both special libraries, the staff performed better than expected in Empathy-related items, for example, giving clients individual and personal attention and treating clients' requests confidentially. In White/L2, the clients' perceptions that the library had their interests at heart exceeded expectations.

In Hebert, White/L1, White/L2, and Nitecki/ILL, the average difference score was about half a point or less (Table 4, Note). In the other studies, the average difference score was almost a point. The standard deviations were greatest for Hebert, Nitecki/Reference, and Nitecki/Reserve, indicating that the individual difference scores varied more.

Table 7. Mean Dimension Scores for the Three Studies

Dimension	Hebert			White/Library 1			White/Library 2		
	E	P	DS	E	P	DS	E	P	DS
Tangibles	4.05	5.26	1.20	5.59	6.00	-.59	5.67	5.10	.40
Reliability	6.19	5.08	-.57	6.45	6.12	-.53	6.38	5.82	-.37
Responsiveness	5.93	5.15	-.68	6.29	5.80	-.71	6.12	5.41	-.46
Assurance	6.05	5.48	-.77	6.08	6.11	-.54	5.90	5.50	-.05
Empathy	5.85	5.17	-1.10	6.00	6.01	-.01	5.74	5.75	-.05
	Nitecki/ILL			Nitecki/Reference			Nitecki/Reserve		
Tangibles	3.80	5.37	.74	4.60	5.37	.72	3.81	4.77	.76
Reliability	6.57	5.52	-.85	6.45	5.32	-.79	6.62	4.40	-1.59
Responsiveness	6.31	5.48	-.80	6.36	5.24	-.97	6.40	4.61	-1.55
Assurane	6.19	5.81	-.42	6.34	5.53	-2.31	6.27	4.83	-1.37
Empathy	6.18	5.55	-.61	6.27	5.41	-.82	6.15	4.73	-1.18

Notes: The *mean dimension score* is the average score of all items corresponding to a particular dimension. As noted, it is computed for expectations (E), perceptions (P), and difference scores (DS). A negative difference score indicates that expectations exceed perceptions.

Sources: Hebert (1994, Table 5, p. 17 for DS); Nitecki (1995a, Table 9, p. 114 for E); E and P for Hebert and P and DS for Nitecki were computed from mean item scores in Table 5. White dimension scores were computed from original data. Scores were rounded as necessary for comparison.

Dimension Scores

The *mean dimension score* is the average score of all items relating to that dimension. It is computed separately for expectations, perceptions, and the difference scores.[11] It is possible to compute a weighted dimension score by weighting the dimension score by the expectation score, but that score is not used in the analysis in this paper (see Appendix B).

Table 7 shows the mean dimension scores for each study.[12] When the dimensions were ranked according to the mean dimension scores based on expectations, the rankings correlated very closely with the subjects' judgments of the relative importance of the dimensions based on allocating 100 points across the dimensions (See the earlier section on Relative Importance of Dimensions). Deviations occurred in only two studies (Hebert, White/L1) when two dimensions ranked sequentially based on the mean expectation dimension scores shared the same rank on the basis of allocation of points. This consistency in client judgments on two forms of a question is a good indicator of the internal validity of the SERVQUAL instrument.

Considering the mean dimension score based on *difference* scores, in all but White/L2, the libraries exceed expectations on only the Tangibles dimension. On the other four dimensions, the participants in these studies generally regarded the libraries as deficient. The mean difference scores, albeit negative, were minimal in White/L1 for Empathy and in White/L2 for Empathy and Assurance. Excluding the Tangibles dimension, the range per dimension across the studies was slightly more than a quarter of a point (-.63 for Empathy to -.91 for Assurance). Within each dimension, consistency was less (S.D. .38 (Responsiveness) to .81 (Assurance) than it was for dimension scores based on either perceptions or expectations. For Assurance, for example, the scores across the studies ranged from -.05 (White/L2) to -2.31 (Nitecki/Reference).

Within a dimension, the dimension scores based on *expectations* were relatively similar across the studies, except for Tangibles. Library clients, regardless of the type of service or type of library, had similar high expectations for Reliability, Responsiveness, Assurance, and Empathy. But among these dimensions there was some range in the average dimension score. The average dimension score per dimension was over six points, ranging from 6.03 (Empathy) to 6.44 (Reliability). In addition, the scores within each dimension across the studies were relatively consistent. Standard deviations ranged from .15 (Reliability) to .21 (Empathy). The Tangibles dimension was clearly different, with an average dimension score of 4.59 (S.D. .81) and a range of 3.8 and 3.81 for Nitecki/ILL and Nitecki/Reserve respectively to 5.67 for White/L2. In general, clients from the special libraries had markedly higher expectations for Tangibles than clients in other libraries.

Considering dimension scores based on *perceptions*, the mean dimension scores for all dimensions were lower than the scores based on expectations but relatively close across the dimensions, within about a quarter of a point of each other. They ranged from 5.28 (Responsiveness) to 5.54 (Assurance). Despite the fact that expectations for the Tangibles dimension varied widely across the studies, as noted above, perceptions of how the libraries performed on this dimension did not vary widely (S.D. .41) in comparison with the consistency in other dimensions. Within each dimension, however, there was generally about twice as much variation in the scores across the studies as there had been in dimension scores based on expectations. The standard deviations ranged from .40 (Responsiveness) to .60 (Reliability).

Both Nitecki (1995a) and White et al. (1994) report reliability coefficients (Cronbach's alphas) for the dimensions to measure the internal consistency among items within each dimension, thus assessing the questionnaires' reliability. In White's study, the reliability coefficients were computed for the combined data from both libraries. For special libraries, the scores ranged from .66 for Reliability to .84 for Responsiveness.[13] The alphas were lower than for SERVQUAL as tested in several other service organizations, but comparable to Nitecki's range. For other service organizations, they ranged from .80 to .93 (Parasuraman et al. 1991, p. 423). In Nitecki (1995a), the alphas were computed for the combined data from all services; they ranged from .69 for Tangibles to .86 for Reliability. The higher the score, the greater the consistency among statements within each dimension.

Relationship between SERVQUAL and Other Measures of Quality

All three studies related SERVQUAL or Modified SERVQUAL, SLA Version findings to other measures of quality as a check on the validity of the questionnaire findings. The measures of quality varied as follows:

Hebert   Client's satisfaction with ILL
Client's willingness to recommend the service
Client's attitude about the library
Libscore, based on factors related to turnaround time and fill rate (Hebert 1994, pp. 12-15)
White   Client's perception of overall quality of the library[14]
Nitecki   Client's perception of overall quality of the library
Client's experiencing problem with service during previous year
Client's satisfaction with resolution of problem
Client's determination if information received was valuable
Client's willingness to recommend the service (Nitecki 1995a, pp. 71-74).

For both special libraries White found statistically significant correlations for all dimensions between dimension difference scores and the overall quality measure. Across the two libraries the correlations ranged from .32 (Tangibles, White/ L1) to .62 (Responsiveness, White/L2). In both libraries, the correlations between the Tangibles scores and the overall quality measure were lower, but still significant at at least the .004 level. Correlations of .53 (statistically significant at the .0001 level or above) occurred for the Responsiveness and Assurance scores in White/L1 and for all dimensions besides Tangibles in White/L2. The correlations with dimension perception scores were higher, ranging from .52 (Assurance, White/L2) to .74 (Responsiveness, White/L1) (all statistically significant at .0001 or higher). Unlike the findings based on dimension difference scores, Tangibles scores correlated at levels comparable to the other dimensions.

In Hebert (1994), the mean difference score was -.43 (S.D. .94), the mean perception score was 5.22 (S.D. 1.76). The mean difference score for each dimension was determined in this paper (see Table 7); correlations with the mean dimension scores were not reported by Hebert. The correlations between the difference scores and the quality measures ranged from .49 for the Libscore to .80 for satisfaction with ILL. Correlations between perception scores and the quality measures were slightly higher and ranged from .54 with the Libscore to .85 with attitude about the library. All correlations were significant at the .001 level (Hebert 1994, p. 15).

In Nitecki (1995a), across the services, correlations between difference scores for each dimension and overall measure of quality ranged from .17 (Tangibles, Nitecki/ILL) to .78 (Responsiveness, Nitecki/Reference). All correlations were significant at the .001 level with the exception of Tangibles, significant at the .05 level. Correlations with perception scores alone were slightly higher, ranging from .40 (Tangibles, Nitecki/ILL) to .80 (Reliability, Nitecki/Reserve).

The extent to which difference scores correlate with service quality varies across the library studies, as it has in studies in other service organizations. In the library studies, correlations range from .17 (Tangibles, Nitecki/ILL) to .8 (Hebert). Parasurman et al. (1991) found a smaller range of correlations (and a lower high correlation) of .57 to .71 across five companies (insurance companies, banks, and a telephone company).

Nitecki's other quality-related variables have only nominal-level responses (yes/no), so she used pooled variance *t*-tests or separate variance t-tests, as necessary, to check the relationship between the other measures, and the overall SERVQUAL score. She found that, based on the combined scores for all studies, clients' difference scores are negatively related to the clients' having had a problem with the service during the previous year and not being satisfied with its resolution and positively related to the clients' considering the information provided valuable and their willingness to recommend the service. These findings are significant at at least the .006 level (Nitecki 1995a, pp. 146-150). But not all of these findings are statistically significant for the individual services. Those that are statistically significant are: experience with a problem (all services); resolution of the problem (none); information considered valuable (all services); and willingness to recommend (only Nitecki/Reserve).

The correlations between different scores from the SERVQUAL or Modified SERVQUAL, SLA Version questionnaires and other measures of quality highlight the debate between P-E and the performance-based approaches to measuring service quality. Certainly the results show that the SERVQUAL *difference* scores correlate with overall measures of quality. SERVQUAL difference scores, then, seem to be good predictors of the quality of library service. Nitecki's insignificant service-specific findings for some overall measures may be confounded by the use of nominal data, which may mask nuances in judgment or simply indicate a problem with the quality measures.

Critics of SERVQUAL and proponents of SERVPERF have indicated that the predictive power of perception scores alone, which measure only performance, is generally higher (Brown, Churchill and Peter 1992; Cronin and Taylor 1994; Peter, Churchill and Brown 1993). This finding was evident in both White and Nitecki's studies: correlations between an overall measure of quality and perception scores alone were higher than for the difference scores. Correlations ranged from .40 (Tangibles, Nitecki/ILL to .80 (Reliability, Nitecki/Reserve), averaging .12 higher per dimension. For the same studies mentioned above, Parasuraman et al. (1991) had similar findings, with correlations increasing to a range of .72 to .81.

CONCLUSION

This paper shows that the performance-minus-expectations approach widely used in service organizations as seemingly disparate as auto repair shops to accounting and banking services can be used effectively in library settings. Comparisons between the expectations of library clients in several studies and clients of other organizations show that priorities were remarkably similar across service dimensions both in terms of the rankings of particular dimensions and of the relative weights assigned to them.

As the comparative results in the third section indicate, library clients place less emphasis on the Tangibles of services, such as the appearance of the physical facilities or the neatness of the staff, and more on Reliability and Responsiveness. Reliability, with its emphasis on the dependability and accuracy of services, is shown, for example, in the staff's performing the service correctly the first time and meeting deadlines. Responsiveness focuses on the staff's willingness to help and prompt service; it includes factors such as the clients always being able to contact an appropriate person. Assurance, defined as the "knowledge and courtesy of employees and their ability to convey trust and confidence" (see Table 2), and Empathy, which stresses giving caring, individual attention to customers, occupied a middle position in most studies. Reference service clients were the exception and seemed to weight Responsiveness almost equal to Reliability. They also placed more emphasis on Empathy than other library service clients. The expectations were often quite high; performance was often high, too, with most of the studies showing performance at the level of 4 or 5 on a 7-point scale for many specific dimension-related service characteristics. Only in special libraries was performance ranked 6 or above.

In general, the clients' perception was that libraries' performance did not match the clients' expectations except in the Tangibles dimension, where expectations were lower. A high percentage of the difference scores related to other dimensions—Reliability, Responsiveness, Assurance, and Empathy—were negative. Although most of these scores were relatively low and probably not reflective of significant problems, some showed differences of one-and-a-half or more points. Almost all of these negative large difference scores appeared in one academic library study. From an operational standpoint, the large, negative scores indicate problems that need to be addressed.

The clients showed some unanimity on even the specific statements operationalizing each dimension considered lowest and highest for both expectations and perceptions, although the agreement was stronger among the expectations statements.

In addition to analyzing and comparing the results of the application of SERVQUAL in several library studies, this study also points out that, in all of these studies the correlation between performance, as measured only in the Perceptions section of SERVQUAL (i.e., the equivalent of SERVPERF), is higher than it is for SERVQUAL. This finding is similar to that found in several other service-industry-related studies. Proponents of performance-based measurement argue that these findings alone favor measuring service quality directly.

Measuring service quality should not be an end in itself, however, but part of an overall program of quality improvement based on achieving greater congruency between the service and the demands and expectations of the client group. With this objective, the P-E approach, which is the basis for SERVQUAL and its variant, the Modified SERVQUAL, SLA Version, seems to be a better choice for measuring service quality. Not only does it measure the service quality, but it also provides vital information about the client's priorities and expectations of the service and a means for measuring the gaps between those expectations and the perception of the service organization's performance. In an era when cost-effectiveness is essential, libraries can then target improvement efforts to areas where adjustments or modifications are most needed and would have the greatest impact on clients. Both SERVQUAL and its variant, Modified SERVQUAL, SLA Version, are easy to administer and interpret. They can be used easily to measure changes over time, across client groups, and across services. If results are reported, it may be possible to establish benchmarks which allow libraries to compare their results with those of similar institutions.

APPENDIX A

Modified SERVQUAL, SLA Version

Expectations Section

Directions: Based on your experiences as a client in special libraries or information centers, please think about the kind of special library that would deliver excellent quality information service—the kind you would like to use. Indicate the extent to which you think such a special library would possess the feature described by each statement. If you think a feature is not at all essential for excellent special libraries, circle the number "1." If you consider a feature absolutely essential for excellent special libraries, circle "7." If your feelings are less strong, circle one of the numbers in the middle. There are no right or wrong answers—the number should truly reflect your expectations regarding special libraries that would deliver excellent quality of service.

		Not essential						Absolutely essential
E1	Excellent special libraries will have modern equipment.	1	2	3	4	5	6	7
E2	Physical facilities at excellent special libraries will be visually appealing.	1	2	3	4	5	6	7
E3	Employees of excellent special libraries will be neat-appearing.	1	2	3	4	5	6	7
E4	In excellent special libraries, materials associated with services will be clearly written and visually appealing.	1	2	3	4	5	6	7
E5	The facilities of excellent special libraries will be well-organized.	1	2	3	4	5	6	7
E6	When employees of excellent special libraries promise to do something by a certain time, they will do so.	1	2	3	4	5	6	7
E7	When clients have a problem, excellent special libraries will show a sincere interest in it.	1	2	3	4	5	6	7
E8	Excellent special libraries will perform the service correctly the first time.	1	2	3	4	5	6	7
E9	Excellent special libraries will provide services during stated hours.	1	2	3	4	5	6	7
E10	Excellent special libraries will maintain accurate records, e.g. circulation or catalog records.	1	2	3	4	5	6	7

		Not essential						Absolutely essential
E11	Employees of excellent special libraries will tell clients exactly when services will be performed.	1	2 3 4 5 6					7
E12	Employees of excellent special libraries will give prompt service to clients.	1	2 3 4 5 6					7
E13	Employees of excellent special libraries will always be willing to help clients.	1	2 3 4 5 6					7
E14	Employees of excellent special libraries will never be too busy to respond to client requests.	1	2 3 4 5 6					7
E15	In excellent special libraries, clients will always be able to contact an appropriate person.	1	2 3 4 5 6					7
E16	Excellent special libraries will provide access to the information the client needs.	1	2 3 4 5 6					7
E17	The behavior of employees of excellent special libraries will instill confidence in clients.	1	2 3 4 5 6					7
E18	Clients of excellent special libraries will feel their transactions will be held confidential.	1	2 3 4 5 6					7
E19	Employees of excellent special libraries will be consistently courteous with clients.	1	2 3 4 5 6					7
E20	Employees of excellent special libraries will have the knowledge to answer client questions.	1	2 3 4 5 6					7
E21	Excellent special libraries will give clients individual attention.	1	2 3 4 5 6					7
E22	Excellent special libraries will have operating hours convenient to all clients.	1	2 3 4 5 6					7
E23	In excellent special libraries employees will give clients personal attention.	1	2 3 4 5 6					7
E24	Excellent special libraries will have the clients' best interests at heart.	1	2 3 4 5 6					7
E25	The employees of excellent special libraries will understand the specific needs of their clients.	1	2 3 4 5 6					7
E26	In excellent special libraries, physical access to the services will be convenient for all clients.	1	2 3 4 5 6					7

Perceptions Section

Directions: The following set of statements relate to your perceptions about XYZ Special Library. For each statement, please show the extent to which you believe XYZ Special Library has the feature described by the statement. Circling a "1" means that you strongly *disagree* that XYZ Special Library has that feature, and circling a "7" means that you strongly *agree*. You may circle any of the numbers in the middle that show how strong your feelings are. There are no right or wrong answers—all we are interested in is a number that best shows what you think about XYZ Special Library service.

		Strongly disagree						Strongly agree
P1	XYZ Special Library has modern equipment.	1	2	3	4	5	6	7
P2	Physical facilities at XYZ Special Library are visually appealing.	1	2	3	4	5	6	7
P3	Employees of XYZ Special Library are neat-appearing.	1	2	3	4	5	6	7
P4	In XYZ Special Library, materials associated with services are clearly written and visually appealing.	1	2	3	4	5	6	7
P5	The facilities of XYZ Special Library are well-organized.	1	2	3	4	5	6	7
P6	When employees of XYZ Special Library promise to do something by a certain time, they do so.	1	2	3	4	5	6	7
P7	When clients have a problem, XYZ Special Library shows a sincere interest in it.	1	2	3	4	5	6	7
P8	XYZ Special Library performs the service correctly the first time.	1	2	3	4	5	6	7
P9	XYZ Special Library provides services during stated hours.	1	2	3	4	5	6	7
P10	XYZ Special Library maintains accurate records, e.g. circulation or catalog records.	1	2	3	4	5	6	7
P11	Employees of XYZ Special Library tell clients exactly when services will be performed.	1	2	3	4	5	6	7
P12	Employees of XYZ Special Library give prompt service to clients.	1	2	3	4	5	6	7

		Strongly disagree						Strongly agree
P13	Employees of XYZ Special Library are always willing to help clients.	1	2 3 4 5 6					7
P14	Employees of XYZ Special Library are never too busy to respond to client requests.	1	2 3 4 5 6					7
P15	In XYZ Special Library, clients are always able to contact an appropriate person.	1	2 3 4 5 6					7
P16	XYZ Special Library provides access to the information the client needs.	1	2 3 4 5 6					7
P17	The behavior of employees of XYZ Special Library instills confidence in clients.	1	2 3 4 5 6					7
P18	Clients of XYZ Special Library feel their transactions are held confidential.	1	2 3 4 5 6					7
P19	Employees of XYZ Special Library are consistently courteous with clients.	1	2 3 4 5 6					7
P20	Employees of XYZ Special Library have the knowledge to answer client questions.	1	2 3 4 5 6					7
P21	XYZ Special Library gives clients individual attention.	1	2 3 4 5 6					7
P22	XYZ Special Library has operating hours convenient to all clients.	1	2 3 4 5 6					7
P23	In XYZ Special Library employees give clients personal attention.	1	2 3 4 5 6					7
P24	XYZ Special Library has the clients' best interests at heart.	1	2 3 4 5 6					7
P25	The employees of XYZ Special Library understand the specific needs of their clients.	1	2 3 4 5 6					7
P26	In XYZ Special Library, physical access to the services is convenient for all clients.	1	2 3 4 5 6					7

Feature Importance Question

Directions: Listed below are five features pertaining to special libraries and the services they offer. Please allocate a total of 100 points among the five features according to how important you think each feature is. The more important you think a feature is, the more points you should allocate to it. Please ensure that the points you allocate add up to 100.

Points   Features

_____ 1.   The appearance of the special library's physical facilities, equipment, personnel, and communications materials.

_____ 2.   The ability of the special library to perform the promised service dependably and accurately.

_____ 3.   The willingness of the special library to help clients and provide prompt service.

_____ 4.   The knowledge and courtesy of the special library's employees and their ability to convey trust and confidence.

_____ 5.   The caring, individualized attention the special library provides its clients.

Personal Information

Directions: Now, a few questions about yourself and your overall perception of the library's services.

1. How frequently do you use the XYZ Special Library? (Check the one that best characterizes your use.)

    _____ At least once a day   _____ Several times a month
    _____ Several times a week   _____ About once a month
    _____ About once a week   _____ Several times a year

2. Gender: _____ Female _____ Male

3. Overall, how do you rate the quality of the services at XYZ Special Library?
    _____
    (Rate from 1 to 10 with 10 as the highest quality.)

APPENDIX B

Guidelines for Computing Scores Derived from Modified SERVQUAL, SLA Version

The scores covered in this section are based on the statements contained in the Expectations and Perceptions sections of the Modified SERVQUAL, SLA Version. Occassionally the statement will be referred to by the type of statement, referring to expectation statement or perception statement. Average scores can be determined on several different bases:

- the individual respondent
- dimension
- all respondents

Note that the respondents can be grouped by other variables, such as gender or frequency of use of the service. The scores for multiple respondents, however grouped, are computed analogously to the scores for all respondents.

Expectation Score per Statement per Respondent

Perception Score per Statement per Respondent

Simply accept the number of the circled score. The numbers should range from 1 to 7. If a score is missing, code it as missing. If computations are being done manually or with an electronic spreadsheet, it may be useful to use an alphabetic code, for example, "x," so that it is clear that data are missing as computations are done. If computations are being done using SPSS or another statistical package, code missing data as 0 or 9 and designate those numbers as indicating missing data. If the latter is not done, the numbers will be used in computation and result in spurious results.

Computed Scores

1. *Difference score per statement per respondent* (Difference scores are sometimes referred to as the SERVQUAL score.)

For each statement for each respondent, subtract the expectation score from the performance score. Answers should range from -6 to +6. Scores which are positive indicate that the perception was greater than expectations; negative scores indicate that expectations were greater than perception. Each respondent should have 26 difference scores, one for each statement. If either score is missing, it is not possible to compute the difference score for that statement, and the difference score should be noted as missing accordingly.

2a. *Average expectation score per respondent.*
2b. *Average perception score per respondent.*
2c. *Average difference score per respondent.*

In this situation, the individual respondent is the focus, not all respondents. For each respondent, sum all statement scores of one type and divide by 26 (i.e., the number of statements). If an individual score is missing, reduce the number of statements accordingly.

3a. *Average expectations score per statement* (*across all respondents*).
3b. *Average perceptions score per statement* (*across all respondents*).
3c. *Average difference score per statement* (*across all respondents*).

The purpose here is to identify the average score of each type across respondents. For each type of statement, sum all scores and divide by the number of respondents. If data are missing, reduce the number of respondents accordingly.

4a. *Average expectation score per dimension per respondent.*
4b. *Average perception score per dimension per respondent.*
4c. *Average difference score per dimension per respondent.*

The statement are numbered from 1-26 in each section. The statements for each dimension are follows:

Dimension	Statement	Total statements
Tangibles	1-5	5
Reliability	6-10	5
Responsiveness	11-16	6
Assurance	17-20	4
Empathy	21-26	6

For each type of statement, sum the statement scores pertaining to the dimension and divide by the total number of statements in that dimension (3d column above). If a statement score is missing, reduce the total number of statement scores in that dimension accordingly.

5a. *Average expectation score per dimension (across all respondent).*
5b. *Average perception score per dimension (across all respondent).*
5c. *Average difference score per dimension (across all respondent).*

Compute the average score per dimension per respondent (see 3a, 3b, 3c). Then sum all average scores per dimension per respondent and divide by the number of respondents. If data are missing, reduce the number of respondent accordingly.

ACKNOWLEDGMENTS

The research underlying a portion of this paper was funded by the Special Libraries Association. This paper benefits from discussions with Eileen G. Abels, College of Library and Information Services, University of Maryland, Danuta A. Nitecki, Associate University Librarian, Yale University, and Roger S. White, Congressional Research Service, Library of Congress. Both Abels and Nitecki actively participated in the SLA-funded research project which resulted in the Modified SERVQUAL, SLA Version. The author is also grateful to the staff and clients of the special libraries who tested the Modified SERVQUAL, SLA Version, and to the special librarians and special library clients who participated in the early stages of its development.

NOTES

1. D'Elia and Walsh's study (1985) is an exception, covering quality and availability of the collection, physical facilities, library staff, and convenience of hours.

2. Information in this section is addressed more comprehensively in White and Abels (1995).

3. The gaps model focuses on several service gaps that affect service quality: between customers' and management perceptions of service expectations (Gap 1); between management perceptions of customers' expectations and service-quality specifications (Gap 2); between service-quality specifications and actual service delivery (Gap 3); and between actual service delivery and what is communicated to customers about it (Gap 4). The quality gap (Gap 5) can be closed by reducing the four internal gaps found within the management of a service organization. See Zeithaml, Parasuraman and Berry (1990).

4. See Berry, Zeithaml and Parasuraman (1990). Based on interview data, the authors identified ten dimensions: Tangibles, Reliability, and Responsiveness, Communication, Competence, Courtesy, Credibility, Security, and Understanding/knowing the customer. In developing the scale, overlaps in the factors or dimensions were eliminated to leave the five dimensions noted in Table 1 (Parasuraman, Zeithaml and Berry 1988, 1991).

5. For reactions by SERVQUAL's developers to the criticisms, see Parasuraman, Berry and Zeithaml (1991, 1993, 1994a, 1994b).

6. Zeithaml, Parasuraman, and Berry (1990) suggest a range of uses for SERVQUAL: monitoring clients' expectations and perceptions over time; comparing a firm's scores with those of competitors; "examining customer segments with differing quality perceptions" (p. 178); and assessing the perceptions of internal customers, that is, employee/users of a service, about services provided by another department in the same firm. The latter is similar to White's studies, in which the clients and library staff were both employees of the same firm.

7. In the questionnaire, the dimensions are never identified by one word to avoid as much as possible confounding the results by any connotations the respondents may attach to that particular word. In the point allocation question (Feature Importance question in the Modified SERVQUAL, SLA Version) the respondent can easily compare the dimensions. In the perceptions/expectations statements, the respondent evaluates manifestations of the dimensions, and no connections are made between specific statements and the dimensions although statements relating to each dimension are grouped.

8. The statements are phrased as they appear in the Perceptions section, as denoted by the P preceding the number of the statement. XYZ denotes the name of the library.

9. A difference score is sometimes referred to as a SERVQUAL score.

10. Nitecki makes no comments in her dissertation or either article about the extraordinary difference between this figure and the other difference scores. Nitecki (personal communication, August 17, 1996) subsequently verified its accuracy.

11. See Appendix B for computation directions. Normally a dimension score is computed from the disaggregated data; however, in this paper, for Hebert's study (1994), where the data were not available and mean dimension scores for expectations and perceptions were not included in her published article, they were derived from the aggregated data presented in Table 2 (p. 14). Nitecki's data were rounded for comparative purposes.

12. Both White et al. (1994) and Nitecki (1995a) did a factor analysis based on combined data from all respondents in their studies and did not find the same five factors as Parasuraman et al. had in previous studies. The factors correspond to the dimensions. Nitecki, for example, found evidence of a three-factor structure instead of the original five dimensions. For the special library data, a 6-factor solution better explained the expectations scores; a 13-factor solution explained 95 percent of the variance in the perceptions data, but the first factor explained about 50 percent of the variance. These results raise the question of the constancy of the underlying dimensions in SERVQUAL and are consistent with the findings of several other studies using modified versions of SERVQUAL. The number of factors found in studies using the original SERVQUAL, including Nitecki, varies from two (Babakus and Boller 1992) to eight (Carman 1990). Although Nitecki (1995b, 1996) does not report dimension scores in her published articles, she does compute them

in her dissertation (1995a, p. 114). White et al. (1994) did not report dimension scores in their original study. See White et al. (pp. 25-31) for a more thorough explanation of their findings.

13.   White et al. (1994, pp. 25-26). In this study, the reliability coefficients were also calculated for SERVQUAL items only (excluding the new items in the Modified SERVQUAL, SLA Version) for the combined data from both libraries. As noted in the text, the alphas for both versions are lower than for SERVQUAL as tested in several other service organizations. In the three dimensions where items had been added—for Tangibles and Responsiveness, alphas for the Modified SERVQUAL were slightly higher; for Empathy, the original SERVQUAL items showed slightly greater consistency. The differences between the two library-related versions were minimal.

14.   White et al. (1994, pp. 31-33). See the third question in the Personal Information Section of Modified SERVQUAL, SLA Version for the wording of the original question (Appendix A).

REFERENCES

American Library Association, Reference and Adult Services Division, Evaluation of Reference and Adult Services Committee. 1995. *The Reference Assessment Manual*. Ann Arbor: Pierian Press.

Babakus, E. and G. W. Boller. 1992. "An Empirical Assessment of the SERVQUAL Scale." *Journal of Business Research* 24: 253-268.

Baker, S. L. and F. W. Lancaster. 1991. *The Measurement and Evaluation of Library Services*, 2nd edition. Arlington, VA: Information Resources Press.

Berry, L., V. A. Zeithaml and A. Parasuraman. 1990. "Imperatives for Improving Service Quality." *Sloan Management Review* 32: 29-38.

Boyce, B. R., C. T. Meadows and D. H. Kraft. 1994. *Measurement in Information Science*. San Diego, CA: Academic Press.

Brown, T. J., G. A. Churchill, Jr. and J. P. Peter. 1993. "Improving the Measurement of Service Quality." *Journal of Retailing* 69: 127-139.

Buchanan, H. S. and J. G. Marshall. 1995. "Bench Marking Reference Services: An Introduction." *Medical Reference Services Quarterly* 14: 59-73.

————. 1996. "Bench Marking Reference Services: Step-by-Step." *Medical Reference Services Quarterly* 15: 1-13.

Budd, J. and M. DiCarlo. 1982. "Measures of User Evaluation of Two Academic Libraries." *Library Research* 4: 71-84.

Carman, J. M. 1990. "Consumer Perception of Service Quality—An Assessment of the SERVQUAL Dimensions." *Journal of Retailing* 66: 33-55.

Cronin, J. J., Jr. and S. A. Taylor. 1992. "Measuring Service Quality: A Reexamination and Extension." *Journal of Marketing* 56: 55-68.

————. 1994. "SERVPERF versus SERVQUAL: Reconciling Performance-based and Perceptions Minus-expectations of Service Quality." *Journal of Marketing* 58: 125-131.

Cronin, M. J. 1985. *Performance Measurement for Public Services in Academic and Research Libraries*. Washington, DC: Association of Research Libraries.

Dalton, G. M. E. 1992. "Quantitative Approach to User Satisfaction in Reference Service Evaluation." *South African Journal of Library and Information Science* 60: 89-103.

D'Elia, G. and S. Walsh. 1985. "Patrons' Uses and Evaluation of Library Services: A Comparison Across Five Public Libraries." *Library and Information Science Research* 7: 3-30.

Ennew, C. T., G. V. Reed and M. R. Binks. 1993. "Importance-performance Analysis and the Measurement of Service Quality." *European Journal of Marketing* 27: 59-70.

Griffiths, J. M. and D. King. 1991. *A Manual on the Evaluation of Information Centers and Services*. Neuilly-sur-Seine, France: AGARD.

Hebert, F. 1993. *The Quality of Interlibrary Borrowing Services in Large Urban Public Libraries in Canada*. Unpublished doctoral dissertation, University of Toronto, Toronto, Canada.

————. 1994. "Service Quality: An Unobtrusive Investigation of Interlibrary Loan in Large Public Libraries in Canada." *Library and Information Science Research* 16: 3-21.

Hernon, P. and E. Altman. 1996. *Service Quality in Academic Libraries*. Norwood, NJ: Ablex Publishing Corporation.

Lovelock, C. H. 1991. *Services Marketing*. Englewood Cliffs, NJ: Prentice Hall.

Nitecki, D. A. 1995. *An Assessment of the Applicability of Servqual Dimensions as Customer-based Criteria for Evaluating Quality of Services in an Academic Library*. Unpublished doctoral dissertation, University of Maryland, College Park.

————. 1996. "Changing the Concept and Measure of Service Quality in Academic Libraries." *Journal of Academic Librarianship* 22: 181-190.

————. 1995. "User Expectations for Quality Library Services Identified Through Application of the SERVQUAL Scale in an Academic Library." Pp. 53-66 in *Proceedings of the Seventh National Conference of the Association of College and Research Libraries*, edited by R. AmRhein. Pittsburgh, PA: Association of College and Research Libraries.

Orr, R. H. 1973. "Measuring the Goodness of Library Services: A General Framework for Considering Quantitative Measures." *Journal of Documentation* 29: 315-332.

Parasuraman, A., V. A. Zeithaml and L. L. Berry. 1994. "Alternative Scales for Measuring Service Quality: A Comparative Assessment Based on Psychometric and Diagnostic Criteria." *Journal of Retailing* 70: 201-230.

————. 1985. "A Conceptual Model of Service Quality and its Implication for Further Research." *Journal of Marketing* 49: 41-50.

————. 1993. "More on Improving Service Quality Measurement." *Journal of Retailing* 69: 140-147.

————. 1994. "Reassessment of Expectation as a Comparison Standard in Measuring Service Quality: Implication for Further Research." *Journal of Marketing* 58: 111-124.

————. 1991. "Refinement and Reassessment of the SERVQUAL Scale." *Journal of Retailing* 67: 420-450.

————. 1988. "SERVQUAL: A Multiple-item Scale for Measuring Consumer Perception of Service Quality." *Journal of Retailing* 64: 12-40.

Peter, J. P., G. A. Churchill, Jr. and T. J. Brown. 1993. "Caution in the Use of Difference Scores in Consumer Research." *Journal of Consumer Research* 19: 655-662.

Riggs, D. 1992. "Strategic Quality Management in Libraries." Pp. 93-105 in *Advances in Librarianship*, edited by I. P. Gooden. New York: Academic Press.

St. Clair, G. 1997. *Total Quality Management in Information Services*. New Providence, NJ: Bowker Saur.

Shaughnessy, T. W. 1993. "Bench Marking, Total Quality Management, and Libraries." *Library Administration and Management* 7: 7-12.

————. ed. 1996. "Perspectives on Quality in Libraries [Special Issue]." *Library Trends* 44(3).

Van House, N. A., B. T. Weil and C. R. McClure. 1990. *Measuring Academic Library Performance: A Practical Approach*. Chicago: American Library Association.

Van House, N. A. 1987. *Output Measures for Public Libraries*, 2nd edition. Chicago: American Library Association.

White, M. D., E. G. Abels and D. Nitecki. 1994. *Measuring Customer Satisfaction and Quality of Service in Special Libraries*. [unpublished technical report]. College Park, MD: University of Maryland, College of Library and Information Services.

White, M. D. and E. G. Abels. 1995. "Measuring Service Quality in Special Libraries: Lessons from Service Marketing." *Special Libraries* 86: 36-45.

Whitehall, T. 1992. "Quality in Library and Information Service: A Review." *Library Management* 13: 23-35.

Zeithaml, V. A., A. Parasuraman and L. L. Berry. 1990. *Delivering Quality Service: Balancing Customer Perceptions and Expectations*. New York: The Free Press.

CLARITY, CONSISTENCY, AND CURRENCY:
A REPORT ON THE OHIO "MEASURING LIBRARY SERVICES" PROJECT

Connie Van Fleet and Frances Haley

THE OHIO CONTEXT

State of Ohio Public Libraries

There are 250 tax supported Ohio public library systems with a total of 700 service outlets, serving the state population of 11,150,506 (*Statistics* 1996). In 1995, Ohio public libraries held over forty-one million volumes and were responsible for over 133 million circulations. The Library and Local Government Support Fund (LLGSF, a percentage of the state income tax) contributes just over 69 percent of library income, with other taxes (usually local) accounting for just over 20 percent and other income nearly 11 percent. The average LLGSF distribution to public libraries was $28.57 per capita;

Advances in Library Administration and Organization,
Volume 15, pages 37-62.
Copyright © 1997 by JAI Press Inc.
All rights of reproduction in any form reserved.
ISBN: 0-7623-0371-9

library income per capita (from all sources) averages $41.40, well above the national average for public library support (*Statistics* 1996). Median total revenue from all sources in 1995 was $542,970; median LLGSF revenue was $439,993 (*Statistics* 1996).

While averages are indicative of advanced and well-supported public libraries, the systems are widely divergent in terms of population served, staff, and funding. The diversity in administrative structure, funding, holdings, circulation, and staff is typical of the public library environment in many states. Recognition of the range of resources (both monetary and personnel) was a key factor in the structure and outcome of the measurement project.

The smallest library in terms of funding and circulation is Alger, one of six libraries in a county of 31,558 people; the largest, Cincinnati, is a single library system with forty-one branches serving a county population of 863,908. In 1995, Alger's only tax revenue derived from the LLGSF ($32,432), with approximately $2,000 from other sources. Cincinnati received over forty-one and a half million dollars in LLGSF funds and an additional four and one half million dollars from other sources (*Statistics* 1996).

In 1995, the median number of volumes held by Ohio public libraries was nearly 64,500 and the state median circulation was nearly 188,000. While lowest ranked Zanesfield had just over 10,000 volumes, the Public Library of Cincinnati and Hamilton County held well over four and one half million. Actual circulation totals ranged from Alger's 5,200 to Cincinnati's 12,167,291. The Gratis library, which employed the fewest full time staff (.58 FTE) was open only 12 hours per week; Cincinnati, which employed the greatest number of staff, was open 73 hours per week and employed nearly 693 FTE (*Statistics* 1996).

Diversity in level of automation exists as well. A survey undertaken in early 1995 identified 110 systems already part of an automated consortium (or with circulation greater than one million), 69 libraries that were automated but not part of a consortium, and 80 libraries (nearly one-third of the 250 public library systems in Ohio) that were not automated (Byerly 1996).

Patron Use and Satisfaction

Use and satisfaction measures indicate that Ohio public libraries are effective in serving patrons. A National Center for Education Statistics (1997) survey on use of public library services by households found that Ohio was among the six states reporting higher than average use of public library services in both the previous month (53% of households in Ohio as compared to 44% of U.S. households) and previous year (70% of Ohio households as compared to 65% of U.S. households.) Fifty-seven percent of Ohioans responding to a statewide poll reported visiting the public library monthly or more frequently, with 82.5 percent of those surveyed indicating that they had visited the public library at least once during the previous year (*State-wide* 1996). Eighty-two per cent of those surveyed rated their public library as excellent or good, a much higher approval rating that they gave to public schools (48.4% excellent or good), road and highways (38.5% excellent or good), or mental health services (34.4% excellent or good).

Measurement Activities

Library directors and administrators have long been involved in local and national measurement activities. Currently, there are two systems for gathering and analyzing statistics on a statewide basis. The State Library of Ohio requires a statistical report from each public library. Based largely on Federal State Cooperative System elements, it may also include questions about service areas of local interest. The Standards Task Force, Library Development Committee of the Ohio Library Council, has developed a set of standards that incorporate many of the output measures, as well as additional statistics. Typically, a standard will set a given level of performance on an output measure. Reporting is on a voluntary basis. Results are compiled and analyzed by the Ohio Library Council executive staff, who publish a report indicating the number of libraries responding and the number who meet the standard, typically fewer than half.

IMPETUS FOR THE MEASUREMENT PROJECT

Several factors compelled Ohio librarians to look at measurement of public library services: increased use of planning and resource allocation techniques that rely on comparative data; emphasis on state level planning precipitated by state funding, the Ohio Public Libraries Information Network, and standards revision; and recognition of the impact of electronic information delivery, whether through the Ohio Public Library Information Network (OPLIN) or local resources.

Planning and Resource Allocation Based on Comparative Data

Consistently defined, gathered, and reported data are essential to planning and evaluation. Ohio library administrators are concerned about the inconsistency with which traditional measures are gathered and concerned about their validity for benchmarking and other comparative procedures. In addition, they recognize that derived measures, such as the outcome measures upon which their standards are based, are weakened by poor data that serve as the basis for their calculations. They need measures that are self-evidently relevant and persuasive to lay bodies for budget presentations and public relations. State funds (the Local Library Government Support Fund) are distributed to each county on a predetermined basis. However, distribution of funds to systems within each county is often based on statistical performance, with heavy reliance on circulation figures. Many libraries supplement state funds with local tax levies and monies from other sources, and measures that present an accurate and complete picture of library service are essential for justification of additional funding.

State Level Planning Perspective

Ohio public libraries are rapidly moving toward state level planning and development. Because base funding for public libraries throughout the state comes from a state fund, librarians are compelled to think in terms of a patron population that extends beyond the local city or county and to offer service to any resident of the state. This move has led to statewide planning and development efforts focused through the Ohio Library Council and The State Library of Ohio and to unparalleled cooperative agreements among libraries in the form of regional systems and automated consortia with shared catalogs and fully reciprocal lending arrangements. For patrons who use one of the consortia libraries, the administrative boundaries are transparent. Other patrons of the state hold cards from several library systems. OPLIN, the Ohio Public Library Information Network, was established with a state budget allocation of $12.85 million and will be maintained by state level funding separate and in addition to the LLGSF (Byerly 1996). Planning and evaluation of OPLIN is undertaken from a broad, state level perspective, although local level data will be made available to individual library systems.

Public library standards are phrased in terms of service to the citizens of Ohio, not local residents (Standards Task Force 1996). The revision of these standards offers an additional impetus for a project that examines, defines, and clarifies measurement and data gathering procedures.

Electronic Information Delivery Mechanisms

New delivery mechanisms are being developed as technology becomes more advanced and widely available. It is critical to determine ways to assess the use and impact of electronic service delivery. The ready availability of electronic services has focused attention on measurement of traditional services, as librarians fear that provision of online and remote services will precipitate a decline in traditional measures and create a false impression that library services are no longer in demand. There does not, at this point, appear to be any documentary evidence of this phenomenon. In fact, there are many who argue that electronic delivery is simply an additional option, and that user preference and subsequent demand will dictate that libraries continue to offer an ever-expanding menu of format options and services. Nevertheless, whether one chooses to regard online collections and electronic reference as new services or new methods of delivering traditional information and materials services, there is an obvious and critical need to measure use of new delivery mechanisms in their own right if librarians are to provide a complete and compelling picture of library activity. Advances in technology and administrative structures that take advantage of computer networking make additional demands on library resources as patron expectations rise and demands for digitized information, computer access services, and specialized service provision grow. But there are, as yet, no statewide measures for use of such services. Relying solely on traditional measures in describing, evaluating, and planning for library service in a networked electronic information environment overlooks a rapidly growing, highly visible, and resource intensive area. The establishment of the Ohio Public Library Information Network provides immediate impetus for the development of measures of electronic service delivery.

Currently, many directors are concerned about evaluating and planning for the array of services that community-based planning requires. Programming and outreach services to groups and individuals are resource intensive, but a high priority for libraries that want to provide equitable service to all patrons and to make the library services visible and accessible.

THE "MEASURING LIBRARY SERVICES" PROJECT

"Measuring Library Services" is a response by the library community to the context and trends discussed above. It is the result of discussion about measures in groups throughout the state, with regional groups and chapters reporting concerns and possible projects to the Ohio Library Council (OLC). The project was a cooperative effort of the Council and The State Library of Ohio, based on a proposal developed by OLC and funded by a grant from the State Library.[1]

Project Goals

The purpose of the project is to develop measures that reflect the range of services provided by public libraries and that can be reported consistently and accurately by all Ohio public libraries. Measurement is understood to be "the process of ascertaining the extent or dimensions or quantity of something" (Lynch 1983).The objectives of the project are:

1. to identify the library services to be measured;
2. to recommend methods of measurement for all services identified; and
3. to recommend procedures for implementing and reporting new measures of service.

Existing methods of measuring and representing public library service are characterized by two weaknesses. First, locally reported traditional measures are subject to varying definition and inconsistent data gathering procedures, resulting in figures that are suspect when used for comparison or benchmarking. Recognition of this problem is not unique to Ohio. The Public Library Management Forum Standards Review Committee of the Illinois Library Association (1996, p. 4) identified problems that occurred when output measures were used "to measure quality or to compare one library to another." "Lack of agreement on what is a reference question" was one of these problems, and this lack of consistent definition was problematic throughout (Public Library Management Forum 1996). It would appear that while we are developing ever more complex measures that require increasing sophistication and resources to implement, we have not yet learned to define and count the most basic units of library service. This deficiency seemed an appropriate starting point for the project.

Further, traditional measures, while they have some intuitive validity for the public and for funding bodies, do not provide a comprehensive picture of public library service in a context that is at once moving to provide increased service in two expensive areas: electronic access and programming.

Procedure

The project was coordinated by Frances Haley (Executive Director, Ohio Library Council) and Connie Van Fleet (Center for the Study of Librarianship, School of Library and Information Science, Kent State University). Four task forces were formed, three to concentrate on different areas of library service and one to examine procedures and guidelines for the implementation of the project results. Each of these task forces— reference services; circulation (later renamed access services to highlight the expanded responsibility perspective of this group); programming and outreach; and implementation—was comprised of two co-chairs (one from a public library and one a consultant from The State Library of Ohio) and volunteers from the Ohio public library community. Consultants from The State Library of Ohio were appointed co-chairs to ensure a statewide perspective and provide continuity. A concerted effort was made to ensure that libraries from all areas of the state and of every size were represented by librarians whose major interest and expertise lay in their appointed area of responsibility (Task Force Memberships, Appendix A). The external consultant attended meetings of all groups to offer consistency, coordination, and information about national trends and evaluation research. Task forces were provided with pertinent literature reviews and bibliographies as requested. In addition to function-specific information, the literature reviews included examples of national measures and ways to define and operationalize them (American National Standards Institute 1983; Hallman 1981; National Center for Higher Education Management Systems 1977; Palmour, Bellassai and DeWath 1980; Van House et al. 1987).

Each task force met independently and task force chairs met as a steering committee on an intermittent basis to report progress, exchange information, and discuss issues. OLC's project coordinator provided direction and support services, pointed out opportunities and limitations for the group and its vision. The steering committee was provided with additional selected literature on measurement and evaluation to provide an overview of issues and approaches, including Curran and Clark (1989) on tying state aid to performance measures, Lynch (1983) on basic approaches to measurement, and Smith (1996) on uses and presentation of public library statistics.

The project gained support and enthusiasm beyond the task forces, and interested groups and individuals with complementary objectives made themselves available to provide information and perspectives. This was a critical element in the outcome of the project. Among those consulted were representatives of the Ohio Public Library Information Network, who met with the project team prior to OPLIN's selection of a serials vendor and relayed the group's recommendations for statistical reporting; data coordinator for The State Library of Ohio; a representative to the Federal State Cooperative System, who explained FSCS data elements and the manner in which they are derived; and the chair of the Public Library Standards Task Force, who reported on the standard revision process and timetable.

Criteria for Measures

The task forces were each given a set of criteria to use in developing a set of measures. The guidelines stipulated that to be included, a measure had to be:

1. *Meaningful.* The measure has intuitive validity for lay people, including funding bodies and the libraries' constituencies, as well as for library staff and administrators. The selected measure is useful in management processes that rely on charting internal trends and benchmarking using comparative figures from other Ohio libraries. The locus of discussion quickly emerged not as, "What *can* we measure?" but "What *should* we measure?"

2. *Standardized.* Every effort is made to conform to nationally recognized definitions and procedures when these are available. Conformity with the Federal State Cooperative System definitions (National Center for Education Statistics 1996), ANSI standards (American National Standards Institute, 1983), and *Output Measures for Public Libraries* (Van House et al. 1987) guidelines for data gathering have been incorporated when appropriate.

3. *Easily gathered.* Data gathering procedures are straightforward and require a relatively small commitment of resources. In recognition of the diversity of resources available to public libraries within the state and of the desirability of full reporting and cooperation, guidelines require that a selected measure be supported by data that can easily and consistently be gathered in even the smallest library. Those measures that are meaningful but require expensive or complex data gathering procedures were either eliminated or recommended for future projects requiring external expertise.

The final list of selected measures reflects two different approaches to data gathering. Some measures are actual annual totals; others are based on sample periods. Data for all measures based on samples are gathered during the same two sample weeks. The committee reached a compromise between consistency and flexibility. Librarians choose one week in February and one week in October for the sample weeks. Circulation statistics reported by a sample of Ohio libraries indicate that these are weeks during which library activity is at typical levels.

The methods of data gathering also vary. Some measures are based on manual tallies, completed by either staff or self-reported by patrons. Circulation and interlibrary loan figures are generally based on automated system reporting. Electronic access services are best measured by automated counting, and recommendations are made for vendor specifications. Recommendations for software protocols were also sent to the board of the Ohio Public Library Information Network.

4. *Quantitative.* Counts are perceived as a basic measure. They are more easily collected, data gathering procedures are more easily tracked, and results lend themselves to comparison more readily. Qualitative measures are meaningful, but are, by their very nature, subjective, and data are often inconsistent and difficult to compare across libraries. More complex quantitative measures, such as output measures, are often based on counts, but these measures are meaningful and reliable only if the basic counts from which they are calculated are characterized by consistent definition and reporting.

The task forces quickly and independently developed an administrative perspective. They were concerned with measures that represented the expenditure of resources and were particularly concerned with representing those activities that required staff time and effort.

ISSUES AND RESPONSES

Electronic Information Delivery Formats

One of the first issues to be resolved was the procedure for examining electronic information delivery. Essentially, there were two options: creation of a fifth task force to develop measures for counting the use of machine readable databases, computer equipment, and related services or integration of the responsibilities into the existing task forces. Task force discussions resulted in a decision to view computers as an additional delivery mechanism rather than a distinct service and to incorporate discussion of new formats and services into the respective responsibilities of the existing groups.

As a result, the circulation task force revamped itself as the access services task force, and identified three areas of service provision as being within its charge: "circulation," including both adult and juvenile circulation and interlibrary loan; "in-house use of library materials" (both print and electronic resources to produce materials for individual use) and "mediated remote access to library resources" (document delivery). Each of these areas was defined to address the provision of materials for individual use, whether a published print on paper source, an item that is printed on demand, or material downloaded to a disk.

The reference task force identified two distinct areas of reference service to be measured: "mediated reference services" (involving direct interaction with a library staff member, through whatever means) and "nonmediated reference services" (involving the use of the library's electronic resources without interacting with a staff member).

Programming and outreach included Internet presence in sections on "programming via the media" and "marketing efforts via media," and included the provision of adaptive technology in the section on "programming and outreach services to individuals." Other areas addressed by this task force were "programming," "institutional outreach," "volunteer services" and "literacy services."

Access Services

Those who study the measurement of public library service often assert that circulation is the most consistently gathered, most easily understood, and the most universally used measure of public library service (Goldhor 1987; Smith 1996). Smith contends that "Circulation has been the flagship library statistic for decades. ... [It] is perhaps the most reliable output measure of public library work" (Smith 1996, p. 42). But, while it may be that circulation is the most easily gathered and reliable measure, the access services task force identified a number of inconsistencies in the manner in which data concerning the circulation of library materials was collected and reported. In addition, the task force noted weaknesses in traditional reporting methods.

The circulation task force expanded its responsibility to include all of those services in which the library provides materials to users, whether in print or electronic format, and included the in-house use of materials and mediated remote access services, in addition to traditional circulation and interlibrary loan.

Access Services Literature Review Summary

A literature review completed for the access services task force revealed the following main points:

1. There are some nationally accepted definitions and procedures for gathering circulation and interlibrary loan statistics. ANSI Z39.7 (*American National Standard for Library and Information Sciences and Publishing Practices-Library Statistics*] (American National Standards Institute 1983), the Federal State Cooperative System (1996) administrative elements and definitions, and Smith's (1996) explanation of these provide an important foundation. The FSCS/NCES definitions use more current jargon and tend to be more inclusive; the ANSI standard definitions are more precise, but the language may need updating.

2. In-house use is generally felt to be a meaningful statistic, but it seems virtually impossible to define a procedure for consistent data gathering that results in a reliable and valid figure. Some authors assert that only non-circulating materials should be counted when determining in-house use (Smith 1996). Rubin (1986) provides the most comprehensive discussion of measuring in-house use of materials; Baker and Lancaster (1991) discuss the difficulty in obtaining in-house use data and discuss data-gathering technique. The simplest, and probably most universally employed definition and data-gathering procedure for in-house use of materials appears in *Output Measures for Public Libraries* (Van House et al. 1987).

3. It is critical to develop recommendations for measuring use of electronic resources, as few meaningful guidelines are extant. Some of these uses are within the library, some are through remote access. Some of the resources, such as CD-ROM databases are owned by the library; in some cases the library provides online access to materials and databases it does not own. At this point, it seems that the question has simply been whether or not a library provides such services. Researchers and academics seem more inclined to explore the quality of such services. Procedures include everything from simply counting the number of computers to having patrons complete questionnaires to in-depth analysis of individual searches.

4. Many authors assume that circulation statistics are consistent, comparable, and easy to gather because many libraries use automated systems (Goldhor 1987; Smith 1996). Discussion within the task force suggests that automation does not ensure consistency.

Access Services Issues

The access services task force brought to light a number of issues. These included deviation from standard practice, the manner in which items were counted, and inconsistency in interlibrary loan reporting. Generally, resolution was obtained by providing explicit interpretation of standard practice and by deferring to national definitions (FSCS).

Some librarians counted circulated items twice—once when checked out and once again when returned. Another library was reported as automatically renewing unreturned items on the due date. Clearly this is a deviation from standard practice. Less clear was the global renewal for bookmobile patrons whose stop was canceled. The first two practices are specifically addressed in definitions and counting rules; a recommendation is provided for the third.

Another problem arose in counting multiple item sets. The committee used a standard decision rule: items packaged together as a unit and generally checked out as a unit count as one physical unit—that is, one circulation. Problems will arise with libraries that have assigned individual bar codes to each part of a multiple item set, but this decision rule should offer the guideline for future cataloging as well as circulation.

Interestingly, interlibrary loan was an area of heated discussion. First, traditional aspects were addressed. The task force chose to count both interlibrary lending (the library's materials loaned to a different library) and interlibrary borrowing (another library's materials obtained and loaned to the library's own patrons). This was not in conformity with FSCS and State Library reporting guidelines, which define direct circulation as the sum of adult circulation, juvenile circulation, and interlibrary borrowing. The committee deferred to the recognized definition of total direct circulation as previously defined, and added a new measure—total circulation—which was the sum of total direct circulation plus the number of items loaned through interlibrary loan.

Automated consortia with shared cataloging presented opportunities for inconsistent reporting. Librarians in some consortia treated loans to other libraries in the consortium in the same manner as loans between branches of their systems—that is, they did not count any of the materials as interlibrary loans. Some libraries counted loans to other consortium libraries twice—once as circulation and once as interlibrary loans. There was a great deal of debate about the manner in which such transactions should be counted. Ultimately, for the sake of simplicity and consistency with national statistic gathering efforts, the task force relied on the traditional interlibrary loan definition (exchange of materials between libraries under different administrative units). As a result, loans to other libraries are counted as interlibrary loan with no distinction made between consortium member libraries or nonmembers. A general perception persists that national definitions do not always keep pace with changing administrative structures and Ohio practice.

Recognition that length of loan period is an intervening variable that could affect circulation figures led the task force to include this measure. It is actually designed to provide supplemental information to be used primarily in interpreting other data.

Debate over in-house use of materials arose in two areas. The first was whether or not to include in-house use of print materials, as this is an area in which it is notoriously difficult to gather consistent and reliable data. The task force opted to include the measure, using the definition and procedures from the output measures manual (Van House et al. 1987).

The second, and more difficult question, was framing a measure for in-house use of electronic resources and in differentiating circulation from reference functions. The circulation task force determined that provision of materials for individual use—printouts or disk copies—fell within the circulation area with its concentration on a physical, information carrying object. While it does not fit neatly into the definition of circulation—particularly the "loan with the expectation of return" clause, provision of materials through electronic access is an important indicator of use and service and will be increasingly important in planning for resource allocation. The task force provided an operationalized definition: "the number of times the print or download command results in printouts of abstracts, full text articles, citations, etc. from any database on patron workstations." While recognizing that an automated counting mechanism would be the most reliable and consistent method of data gathering, the group was concerned about cost and delay in implementing the measure. They developed an "Individual Electronic Resources Tally Sheet," which appears in the final report (Haley and Van Fleet 1996).

Reference Services

While researchers may conclude that circulation counts are "near perfect" (Goldhor 1987) and the "most reliable" (Smith 1996) of public library use statistics, no such illusions exist about the counting of reference questions. Yet, it has been asserted that while quantitatively, the loan of materials may be the most important function that public libraries serve, qualitatively it is the answering of reference questions (Goldhor 1987).

Reference Services Literature Review Summary

Proceeding from the assumption that the primary goal of the task force was to develop definitions and criteria for counting reference questions that could be applied in a consistent and relatively simple manner across libraries, a scan of the literature from about 1970 to the present was undertaken. Key points were:

Defining a "reference transaction" and a "reference question" appears to be a knotty problem. The first (and purportedly simplest) step in evaluating reference appears to be counting and categorizing reference questions. While much of the literature gives the impression that this step has been accomplished and we have moved on to more complex issues, such as evaluating reference process, determining accuracy, and exploring other measures of reference effectiveness, definition and categorization of reference questions remains ambiguous (Kesselman and Watstein 1987) and calls into question comparisons among libraries (Goldhor 1987; Curran and Clark 1989).

Problems occur when output measures are used "to measure quality or to compare one library to another" (Public Library Management Forum Standards 1996). McClure, one of the authors of *Output Measures for Public Libraries* (Van House et al. 1987), asserts that the measures were designed for internal use in public libraries and contends that "using output measures as a basis for standards and comparison is misleading at best, and down-right erroneous at worst" (Curran and Clark 1989). The authors specifically suggest that measures be chosen and modified to provide information that will help libraries meet their individually formulated goals and objectives. Nevertheless, the purpose of the manual is articulated as defining "a basic set of output measures that are ... comparable across libraries" (Van House et al. 1987, p. xviii). The authors, however, suggest a secondary purpose, which is "to provide some understanding of measurement in general so that readers know when and how they can (or cannot) expand, extend, and adapt" the measures (Van House et al. 1987, p. xviii). If output measures are to be used for comparative purposes, as with the Ohio Public Library Standards, they should be based on mutually understood and agreed upon basic counts.

Some definitions of reference transactions and types of data elements have been developed and are accepted nationally. (American National Standards Institute 1983, Federal State Cooperative System 1996, National Center for Higher Education Systems 1977, Smith 1996). While the National Center for Higher Education Management Systems is older, it provides some explicit definitions and includes databases as reference tools. Emerson (1984) discusses the ANSI standard, definitions, and issues. Smith's *Collecting and Using Public Library Statistics: A How-to-Do-It Manual for Librarians* (1996) begins with the FSCS (Federal State Cooperative System) definition and offers further discussion. Baker and Lancaster (1991) provide an overview of questions that may be asked in evaluating reference service, including a discussion of different categorizations of reference queries. Hallman's 1981 article on designing optical mark forms for reference statistics suggests types of data that may be collected. Because recording reference questions involves the human element, this measure is less reliable than circulation counts (Goldhor 1987). While there will always be some inconsistency when judgment is involved or when people perceive that some benefit will accrue to a certain interpretation of criteria, reliability can be enhanced through definition and process. The bottom line seems to be to clearly define what you want counted, provide complete criteria and examples of categories, provide training in application of the measures, monitor application for common misinterpretation or inappropriate application, and make it simple for people to comply. Baker and Lancaster (1981) assert that "The problem of data reliability can be alleviated somewhat by giving reference librarians precise instructions about which questions fall into each category. Definitions of categories should be contained on the data collection form whenever possible." Binkely and Eadie (1989) provide definitions and tally forms. Kesselman and Watstein (1987) provide an interesting case study and a practical methodology.

There is no consensus in current literature on reference evaluation. Much of the current literature explores the evaluation of reference services and reference personnel, looking at the reference process, methods of measuring accuracy, and factors other than accuracy that may influence effectiveness or efficiency in the reference transaction. Some researchers at this point want to move beyond output measures to outcome measures; that is, how library service affects the individual and society (*Report* 1996). Some argue for utility, not performance measures (Hernon 1987). But, attention to these issues is beyond the scope of this project, which is concerned with counting and measurement, not evaluation.

Electronic reference needs definition. Baker and Lancaster's chapter on database searching provides a starting point for discussion (1991). Three elements of electronic reference relate to the reference transaction and can be easily addressed within the framework of traditional statistics. One element is the use of a machine readable database to answer a reference query. The definitions of reference transaction provided by national bodies are flexible enough to include mediated database searching, whether locally-based (CDs) or requiring the use of remote sources (online). ANSI (1983) and the National Center for Higher Education Management Systems (1977) specifically include use of machine readable databases.

A second element in defining electronic reference involves the source of a reference query. Some libraries (mostly academic at this point) have accepted reference queries via e-mail (Abels 1996).

A third element of electronic reference provision focuses on holdings, access, and use. The National Commission on Library and Information Science survey emphasized issues, motivation, connectivity, and staff use of computer services. Direct patron service questions addressed types of services offered and whether or not a fee is charged and the type and quantity of equipment offered (Bertot et al. 1996). The State Library of Ohio reports on number of software packages held and circulated (*Statistics* 1996). Measures of the use of computer services and materials are still in the developmental stage.

Reference Services Issues

Reference service issues fell into three categories: incorporating elements related to electronic information services into those definitions and processes, bringing clarity to the definition of a reference question, and expanding scope to include nonmediated reference services.

To include electronic information sources, the task force relied on ANSI (American National Standards Institute 1983) definition of reference transaction: "an information contact that involves the use, recommendation, or instruction in the use of one or more information sources, or knowledge of such sources, by a member of the library staff. Information sources include (1) print and non-print materials; (2) machine-readable databases; (3) the library's own bibliographic records, excluding circulation records; (4) other libraries and institutions; and (5) persons both inside and outside the library" (emphasis added). It defined mediated references in terms of interaction of a staff member with a patron who has requested assistance, noting that such interaction can take several forms: in-person, telephone, mail, electronic mail, or FAX. These two definitions incorporate the critical elements of electronic reference service addressed above: use of machine-readable databases and source of inquiry.

Sections of counting rules and examples of reference questions by category were included to clarify definition and counting procedures. In addition to "information and/or resource queries," "reader's advisory," "referrals," and other traditional categories, "technology assistance and instruction" was included, with "Can you help me log on to the computer?" as an example. "Other" questions are counted as well, as this measure reflects a use of staff time and could be valuable in developing and understanding staffing patterns. Examples of "other" questions by category (rules and policies, mechanical, directional) provides a useful contrast to reference question examples and should assist in clarifying the differences between the two.

The task force noted that organizing and developing electronic resources, subscribing to database services, and purchasing and maintaining equipment were services that require substantial resource investment but are not reflected by traditional use measures. Determining patterns of independent use of information electronic resources is viewed as critical to planning and budget justification. Measures include "number of searches of OPAC (online public access catalog)," "number of searches of CD-ROM or other electronic database," "number of accesses of the library home page," and "number of accesses of the OPLIN home page" through the library's home page. No manual procedure is suggested for gathering this data; instead, recommendations are made for vendor specifications.

Programming and Outreach

As society becomes increasingly dependent on mass media and information technology, the demand for personalized, humanized information and services persists and intensifies. Community based planning provides the impetus for responsive services.

Programming and Outreach Literature Review Summary

Programming and outreach services involve a variety of activities, and the services that fall under that rubric may be widely varied. Heim (1982), in a comprehensive look at these activities, groups them under the umbrella of "stimulation to use." She offers two perspectives on outreach. Outreach may be defined as taking services outside of the library to individuals, groups, and institutions, or it may be defined as marketing library materials and services of any sort. Other authors provide discussion of issues in programming and specific elements and procedures for evaluation (Brown 1992; Trotta 1993; Van House 1987).

Programming and Outreach Issues

Issues of concern to this task force revolved around definitions of outreach, determining how to represent the various services, and ensuring ease of reporting. Final decisions were based on an examination of the literature cited above, an examination of the Ohio Public Library Standards (Standards 1996), and a discussion of current legislation that might affect service, in particular, the Americans with Disabilities Act of 1991.

A typology of services was delineated. Categories include programming offered within the library, programming and services provided outside of the library to individuals, groups, and institutions, volunteer services, literacy services and programs, use of media for programming and use of media for marketing. The first decision was whether to include programs held in the library but not sponsored by the library, which was resolved by including all programs provided in the library, whether sponsored by the library or not, and whether scheduled or not.

The next was a consideration of the dual definition of outreach: programming and marketing. Further discussion of Heim's (1982) article and an examination of the Ohio Public Library Standards (Standards Task Force 1996) resulted in the inclusion of checklists of media used for both activities. For ease of use, the checklists parallel those in the standards.

Another issue dealt with when numeric counts were necessary and when a simple checklist of provide/do not provide would be as effective. This facet of each measure was decided on a case-by-case basis, and the results are reflected in the final report. Generally number of participants in library sponsored programs, number of visits, number of institutions served, number of volunteers are requested. Checklists are provided for use of media and types of outreach activities. The most controversial count, partially because meaning was unclear and partially because of perceived difficulty in gathering the data, was population of institutions visited. Request for the count remains, with instructions to call the institutions for their official population count.

Selected Measures and Supporting Material

A checklist of the selected measures appears in Appendix B. The project report includes a handbook of measures, with a section for each of the three function task forces: access services, reference, and outreach and programming. Within each of these sections are subsections of those services. For instance, the access services section is divided into 3 subsections: circulation, in-house use of library materials, and mediated remote access. Each subsection follows the same outline. A brief overview is followed by a definition of the service. For example, "A circulation transaction is any transaction in which the patron assumes responsibility for library materials, generally to be used outside of the library, with the expectation of return of the material to the library. Circulation measures refer to total number of individual items circulated to patrons, not number of patrons who borrowed materials." A summary list of the selected measures is given (e.g., adult circulation), followed by definitions of the measures. In this case, adult circulation is defined as "the total number of items from your library's collection catalogued as adult materials, in all formats, circulated to any of your library's patrons during the previous year. This figure includes renewals." Counting rules follow: "Circulation transactions should be counted once only when the items are checked out or renewed; transactions occurring when items are returned and checked in should not be counted as circulation transactions." or "Each physical unit counts as one circulation, regardless of the number of items it contains. Items packaged together as a unit and generally checked out as a unite should be counted as one physical unit." Examples illustrating the rules are included. For instance, *Gone with the Wind* video, 2 tapes packaged together = 1 circulation; *Civil War Series* videos, 7 tapes packaged separately = 7 circulations. Each section concludes with procedures for data gathering and reporting. The complete subsection on "mediated reference" is provided with this article as an example of format and content (Appendix C).

Implementation

The implementation and accountability task force met on several occasions to discuss steps in ensuring the use of the new measures. The importance of feedback and the changing nature of the measures document were emphasized when the project was introduced to Ohio's public librarians with a panel presentation at the 1996 OLC Conference. The final report, consisting of the project description, handbook of measures, recommendations, and individual task force reports, has been distributed, with copies to be sent to the library director and board of each public library. Additional copies are available upon request from the OLC office.

The implementation task force recommended field testing of the measures, procedures, and instructions in sample libraries. Over a dozen libraries of different sizes and from different geographic regions have volunteered as test sites.

Upon completion of field testing, evaluation, and revision, a wider training program will be undertaken. Education and training play a critical role in ensuring that measures are applied in a consistent manner across the state. A variety of methods and venues should be utilized to permit broad participation. Those recommended include: regional workshops; Ohio Library Council conference workshops; regional training via the statewide interactive audiovisual network; and training by State Library of Ohio consultants. Educational programs should include instruction in the use and value of the resulting data, as well as "how-to" training in data gathering procedures.

Part of implementing the new measures will be to attempt to incorporate them, where possible, into the Ohio Public Library Report Form. The task force has worked with the State Library to review the current Report Form and prepare for integrating new changes to the form. Future meetings with the Public Library Standards Development Committee will ensure that the measures developed by the two groups support and complement one another. Reporting methods for OPLIN data will be developed as new methods for data gathering are implemented at the state network level.

RECOMMENDATIONS

The Measuring Library Services final report recognizes the project as an important first step in describing and evaluating public library service to the citizens of Ohio. The task force developed several recommendations that were beyond the scope of this project, but which may serve as the basis for future planning and development. These were:

1. *Keep the project moving.* Assign specific responsibility for field testing, evaluation, revision, and training and develop a reasonable timetable for these activities.
2. *Use professional development activities to provide context for the measures.* Include instruction in the value, use, and presentation of statistics as well as training in data gathering procedures. Measures of service should be directly related to pertinent Ohio Public Library Standards.

3. *Simplify reporting.* Incorporate measures into one of the two existing reporting venues, either The State Library of Ohio annual report forms or the Public Library Standards Committee survey.

4. *Develop automated data reporting procedures and software counting protocols using the recommendations of the access services and reference task forces.* Standardized automated reporting systems will ensure consistency, alleviate much of the data gathering burden, and accurately count electronic access services. An important component of this software development project is ensuring that all libraries, regardless of size or funding, will be able to install and utilize this software. OLC and The State Library of Ohio are natural partners in this project, due to the relative missions and expertise of the two organizations. OPLIN, which has already begun exploring software to evaluate its services, may be an appropriate partner in this activity as well.

5. *Develop a statewide electronic reporting mechanism.* Eliminating paper forms will also eliminate transcription errors, check reporting errors, and allow for more in-depth analysis at the state level.

6. *Develop and implement projects that evaluate public library service from a statewide perspective.* Ohio public libraries receive state funding and it is appropriate to conceptualize quality of service on a state level. Current statistics rely solely on aggregates of locally gathered and self-reported data. These can be supplemented with broader based, in-depth studies. Independently conducted projects employing sampling techniques offer the benefits of consistency, objectivity, expertise, and simplicity for local librarians. Resulting data would be reliable for state level planning and continuing education efforts, and could also serve to establish benchmarks for service at the local level.

The Future

A proposal addressing recommendations one through five as described above has been developed by the Ohio Library Council offices and submitted to The State Library of Ohio for funding. Specifically, the following activities are proposed: field testing, evaluation, and revision of the measures; professional development, including the development of a handbook for use in training; simplified reporting through sustained cooperation with the State Library of Ohio and the Standards for Public Libraries Task Force and through development of forms for reporting to the public; cooperation among the Ohio Library Council, The State Library, the Ohio Public Library Information Network, and representatives of the public library community to develop protocols for counting software which can be used on local computer equipment to facilitate data gathering and ensure that reporting is consistent; and development of protocols for a statewide electronic reporting mechanism.

Summary

The project team has fulfilled its charge in identifying measurable library services, developing procedures to measure them, and recommending procedures for implementation and reporting. The measures selected combine refined traditional measures with newly developed measures to provide a comprehensive representation of public library service in the modern context. Data can be gathered with reasonable facility in even the smallest library, the recommended procedure could be applied consistently, and the resulting information will be useful for either internal decision making or in representing the library to funding bodies and other constituencies. A second phase of the project will implement the recommendations of the first phase and result in simplified, consistent, and useful reporting of public library services in Ohio.

Additionally, the project has strengthened cooperative links with groups and individuals who share measurement concerns and who are vital to the effective implementation of the new measurement procedures: The State Library of Ohio; Ohio Public Libraries Information Network; the OLC Library Development Committee Public Library Standards Task Force, and the professional public library community. The State Library of Ohio has already shortened and simplified the public library statistical report form, and it is expected that cooperative efforts will continue. OPLIN personnel have negotiated statistical reporting mechanisms with their serials vendor and have sought input from the committee in working to develop statistical formats for reporting usage of other OPLIN services.

Recommendations for future projects, including establishing computer protocols for automated data gathering and developing alternative evaluation methods, were developed, and action has been taken to address these recommendations.

APPENDIX A

Task Force Membership

Access Services Task Force:

James H. Buchman, Co-chair, The State Library of Ohio
Ann Yankura, Co-chair, McKinley Memorial Library, Niles
Debby Anderson, Morley Library, Painesville
Sarah Brown, Mason Public Library
Greg Edwards, Public Library of Cincinnati and Hamilton County
Patrick Finan, Portage County District Library, Garrettsville

Cheryl Foote, Wellsville Carnegie Public Library
Alison Gibson, Union Township Public Library, Ripley
Lynn Stainbrook, Orrville Public Library
Bob Smith, Medina County District Library
Michael Wantz, Perry County District Library, New Lexington
Jeannine Wilbarger, Toledo-Lucas County Public Library

Reference Services Task Force:

Jay Burton, Co-chair, The State Library of Ohio
Judith Coleman, Co-chair, Columbus Metro Library
Susan C. Masirovits, Willoughby-Eastlake Public Library
Jeannie Pierson, Public Library of Cincinnati and Hamilton county
Bruce F. Pomerantz, Clermont County Public Library
Susan A. Steinke, Dayton and Montgomery County Public Library

Programming and Outreach Task Force:

Pat Lewis, Mary L. Cook Public Library, Waynesville
Cindy McLaughlin, The State Library of Ohio
Susan K. Barrick, Southwest Public Libraries
Nancy M. Foth, Toledo-Lucas County Public Library
Janice Kagermeier, Public Library of Cincinnati and Hamilton County
Jean A. Roberts, Lorain Public Library

Implementation and Accountability Task Force

Alan Hall, Co-chair, Public Library of Steubenville and Jefferson County
Bill Morris, Co-chair, The State Library of Ohio
Bescye Burnett, Cleveland Heights-University Heights Public Library
Susan Hagloch, Tuscarawas County Public Library
Keith Kuhn, Public Library of Cincinnati and Hamilton County

Project Coordinator: Frances Haley, Ohio Library Council
Project Consultant: Connie Van Fleet, Center for the Study of Librarianship, School of Library and Information Science, Kent State University

APPENDIX B

Recommended Measures

Access Services-Circulation

Adult circulation (*Actual annual total*)
Juvenile circulation (*Actual annual total*)
Interlibrary loan (ILL) borrowing (*Actual annual total*)
Total *direct* circulation. Sum of adult circulation + juvenile circulation +
    interlibrary loan borrowing. (*Actual annual total*)
Interlibrary loan (ILL) lending (*Actual annual total*)
Total circulation. Sum of total *direct* circulation + interlibrary loan lending
    (*Actual annual total*)
Length of normal loan period (in days)

Access Services - In-house Use

In-house uses of print resources. Number of items left on tables. (*Annual total
    extrapolated from two, one week samples*)
Uses of electronic resources to produce materials for individual use. Number
    of downloads, either to paper or disk (*Annual total extrapolated from
    two, one week samples. Count of number of downloads from patron-
    completed tally sheets x 26*)

Access Services - Mediated Remote Access

Mediated remote access transactions. Number of sources copied for direct
    document delivery. (*Annual total extrapolated from two, one week
    sample totals. Count of number of sources copied for direct document
    delivery to patrons x 26. Excludes interlibrary loan*)

Reference Services - Mediated Use

Reference transactions (*Annual total extrapolated from two, one-week sample
    periods. Librarian-completed tally of number of reference questions
    asked*)
Other informational (directional, mechanical, policy) transactions (*Annual
    total extrapolated from two, one-week sample periods. Librarian-
    completed tally of number of "other" questions asked.*)

Reference Services - Nonmediated Use

Number of searches (questions) conducted on the library's online public access
    catalog (*Actual annual total from automated reporting*)
Number of searches (questions) conducted on any of the library's CD-ROM
    or other electronic databases (*Actual annual total from automated
    reporting*)
Number of times the library's home page is accessed (*Actual annual total from
    automated reporting*)
Number of times the OPLIN home page is accessed (*Actual annual total from
    automated reporting*)

Programming and Outreach Services - Programming

Number of library sponsored programs, by type of program (*Actual annual
    total*)
Total attendance at library sponsored programs, by type of program (*Actual
    annual total*)
Total attendance at library sponsored juvenile programs (*Actual annual total*)
Number of programs held at library sponsored by nonlibrary organizations
    (*Actual annual total*)
Number of unscheduled meetings held in the library by nonlibrary
    organizations (*Actual annual total*)

Programming and Outreach Services - Outreach: Institutional Efforts

Number of institutions visited the previous year, by type of institution, for
    purpose of circulation (*Actual annual total*)
Population totals, by type of institution, for institutions visited the previous
    year for the purpose of circulation (*Populations reported by institutions,
    updated annually.*)

Programming and Outreach Services - Outreach: Individual Efforts

Provide/Do Not provide checklist of outreach efforts to individuals:
    Purchase of materials in alternative formats
    Borrow alternative formats from other libraries
    Have in-house adaptive equipment or software for print-handicapped or
    hearing-impaired patrons
    Provide mail or delivery service to homebound individuals
Number of individual patrons served annually through outreach deliveries
    (*Actual annual total*)

Programming and Outreach Services - Volunteers

Total number of volunteers (*Actual annual total*)
Number of teen volunteers (*Actual annual total*)
Number of senior volunteers (*Actual annual total*)
Total number of volunteer hours donated (*Actual annual total*)

Programming and Outreach Services - Literacy/Tutoring

Number of individuals provided literacy tutoring (*Actual annual total*)
Number of individual tutors serving in the library [*Actual annual total*)
Checklist, literacy services (*Check services provided in the previous year*)
    Space
    Train tutors
    Provide special or deposit collections
    Coordinate tutoring schedules
    Is library part of a literacy coalition?
    Checklist, programming via media (*Check media used in programming in the previous year*)

Programming and Outreach Services - Outreach/Programming via the Media

Checklist, programming via media (*Check media used in marketing in previous year*)

Programming and Outreach Services - Outreach/Marketing via the Media

Checklist, marketing via media (*Check media used in marketing in previous year*)

APPENDIX C

Reference Services - Mediated Service

Summary

Annual reference transactions
Annual other transactions

Mediated reference service occurs when a library staff member participates with a patron who has requested assistance. Staff participation with a patron can take several forms: in-person contact, a telephone contact, mail (letter) contact, electronic mail (E-mail) contact, or FAX contact.

A reference question is "an information contact that involves the use, recommendation, or instruction in the use of one or more information sources, or knowledge of such sources, by a member of the library staff. Information sources include: (1) print and non-print materials; (2) machine-readable databases; (3) the library's own bibliographic records, excluding circulation records; (4) other libraries and institutions; and (5) persons both inside and outside the library" (American National Standard for Library and Information Sciences and Related Publishing Practices 1983).

Measures

Reference Transactions: total number of reference questions asked during the previous year, as extrapolated from tally sheets during two, one-week sample periods.

Other Transactions (directional, mechanical, policy): total number of reference questions asked during the previous year, as extrapolated from tally sheets during two, one-week sample periods.

Counting Rules

All questions are counted, regardless of whether they are asked at the reference desk or at another location in the library.

Count each question, not number of patrons asking questions. If a patron asks more than one question, count each question separately.

Distinctions between reference and other questions can be determined using the lists of examples in "How to Count Reference Questions" and "How to Count Other Questions."

How to Count Reference Questions

Examples of Reference Questions

Listed below are types of questions and examples that are counted as reference questions.

General and ready-reference questions: "What's the capital of Alaska?" "How do you spell "Plethora?" "What is the address and phone number for the "American Border Collie Association?"

Information and/or resource queries: "I need information on applying for a small business loan." "Can you help me find a book on starting an aquarium?"

"Where do I get something to read about coaching youth soccer?" Homework and/or school related questions: "I have to do a report on a famous American inventor. Can you help me?" "My teacher wants me to write a paper on the state symbols of Ohio?" "Do you have anything about how to study for the GED?"

Research and in-depth questions: "Can you find a chart or something that has the past ten years Gross National Product figures for the United States?" "I need to compare a current presidential speech with the Gettysburg Address." "Where can I get a list of the casualty figures for these World War II battles?"

Reader's Advisory: "I love Stephen King books. Can you recommend any other authors similar to him?" "Can you recommend any good mysteries with female sleuths?"

Referrals: "Where could I go to arrange for a reading tutor?" "Do any organizations in town have information on businesses?"

Instruction: "How can I look up articles on the Olympics?" "How do I use the on-line catalog?" "Can you help me use this computer?" "How do I use the OPLIN Internet computer?"

Technology Assistance & Instruction: "Can you help me log on to the Internet?"

How to Count "Other" Questions

Examples of "Other" Questions

Some questions are not properly categorized as reference questions. Policy, mechanical, and directional questions should be counted under "other" questions.

Questions of Rules and Policies: "Are you open on Sundays?" "Do you allow caged birds in the library?" "How much are fines?"

Mechanical Questions on the Use of Machines: "How do you make a copy?" "Will you show me how to print this article?"

Directional Questions: "Where are the restrooms?" "Can you show me where the 633's are?" "Where are the videos?"

Procedures for Data Gathering and Reporting

All data collected for measures based on sampling is gathered during the same two weeks. Local libraries should select one week in February and one week in October. During each of the two sample weeks, use the "Reference Survey" to record the number of reference and "other" transactions. Staff should mark desk tally sheets each time either a reference or "other" transaction is completed. Compile the daily totals to a weekly total.

Combine the two weekly totals and multiply by 26 to calculate the annual in-house use total.

(Total of sample week 1 + total of sample week 2) x 26 = annual total

Report only the annual total as calculated. Do not report actual annual totals even if such data are available.

NOTE

1. Copies of the final project report, "Measuring LIbrary Services" are available from the Ohio Library Council, 35 East Gay Street, Suite 305, Columbus, Ohio 43215-3138.

REFERENCES

Abels, E. G. 1996. "The e-mail Reference Interview." *RQ* 35: 345-58.

American National Standards Institute, Inc. 1983. *American National Standard for Library and Information Sciences and Publishing Practices-Library Statistics.* ANSI Z39.7 - 1983. New York: American National Standards Institute, Inc.

Baker, S. L. and F. W. Lancaster. 1991. *The Measurement and Evaluation of Library Services.* Arlington, VA: Information Resources Press.

Bertot, J. C., C. R. McClure and D. L. Zweizig. 1996. *The 1996 National Survey of Public Libraries and the Internet: Progress and Issues. Final Report.* Washington, DC: Government Printing Office.

Binkely, D. and T. Eadie. 1989. *Wisconsin-Ohio Reference Evaluation at the University of Waterloo.* CALCUL Occasional Paper Series No. 3. Canadian Association of College and University Libraries.

Brown, B. J. 1992. *Programming for Librarians: A How-to-do-it Manual.* New York: Neal-Schuman.

Byerly, G. 1996. "Ohio: Library and Information Networks." *Library Hi Tech* 14(2-3): 245-254.

Curran, C. and P. M. Clark. 1989. "Implications of Tying State Aid to Performance Measures." *Public Libraries* 348-354.

Emerson, K. 1984. "Definitions for Planning and Evaluating Reference Services." Pp. 63-79 in *Evaluation of Reference Services,* edited by B. Katz and R. A. Fraley. New York: Haworth Press.

Federal State Cooperative System, National Center for Education Statistics. 1996. *Administrative Entity Data Element Definitions.* Washington, DC: Government Printing Office.

Goldhor, H. 1987. "An Analysis of Available Data on the Number of Public Library Reference Questions." *RQ* 27: 195-201.

Haley, F. and C. Van Fleet. 1996 *Measuring Library Services: a Joint Project of the Ohio Library Council and The State Library of Ohio.* Columbus, OH: Ohio Library Council.

Hallman, C. N. 1981. "Designing Optical Mark Forms for Reference Statistics." *RQ* 20: 257-264.

Heim, K. M. 1982. "Stimulation." Pp. 120-153 in *The Service Imperative for Libraries,* edited by G. A. Schlachter. Littleton, CO: Libraries Unlimited.

Hernon, P. 1987. "Utility Measures, Not Performance Measures, for Library Reference Service?" *RQ* 26: 449-459.

Kesselman, M. and S. B. Watstein. 1987. "The Measurement of Reference and Information Services." *The Journal of Academic Librarianship* 13: 24-30.

64   CONNIE VAN FLEET and FRANCES HALEY

Lynch, M. J. 1983. "Measurement of Public Library Activity: The Search for Practical Methods." *Wilson Library Bulletin* 57: 388-393.
National Center for Education Statistics, Office of Educational Research and Improvement, U.S. Department of Education. 1997. *Use of Public Library Services by Households in the United States: 1996. Statistics in Brief March 1997.* Washington: Government Printing Office.
National Center for Higher Education Management Systems. Dennis Jones, Project Director. 1977. *Library Statistical Data Base: Formats and Definitions.* Boulder, CO: National Center for Higher Education Management Systems.
Palmour, V. E., M. C. Bellassai and N. V. DeWath. 1980. *A Planning Process for Public Libraries.* Chicago: American Library Association.
Public Library Management Forum Standards Review Committee, Illinois Library Association. 1996. *Serving Our Public: Standards for Illinois Public Libraries.* Chicago: Illinois Library Association.
Report on the Library and Information Services Policy Forum on Impact of Information Technology and Special Programming on Library Services to Special Populations. 1996. Funded by the National Center for Education Statistics and Co-sponsored by the U.S. National Commission on Libraries and Information Science with the Cooperation of the Office of Library Programs and the National Institute on Postsecondary Education, Libraries, and Lifelong Learning. Alexandria, Virginia. May 20-21, 1996.
Rubin, R. 1986. *In-house use of Materials in Public Libraries.* Urbana: University of Illinois, Graduate School of Library and Information Science.
Smith, M. L. 1996. *Collecting and Using Public Library Statistics: A How-to-do-it Manual for Librarians.* New York: Neal-Schuman.
Standards Task Force, Ohio Library Development Committee, Ohio Library Council. Mary Pat Essman, Chair. 1996. *Standards for Public Library Service in Ohio. Draft document for discussion.* Unpublished report.
State-wide Library and Technology Issues: Preliminary Survey Data for the Ohio Library Council and The State Library of Ohio. Conducted by Terry Casey and Midwest Communications. 1996. Paper presented at the Ohio Library Council Conference, Columbus, Ohio.
Statistics of Ohio Libraries 1996. 1996. Columbus, OH: The State Library of Ohio.
Trotta, M. 1993. *Managing Library Outreach Programs: A How-to-do-it Manual for Librarians.* New York: Neal-Schuman.
Van House, N. A., M. J. Lynch, C. R. McClure, D. L. Zweizig and E. J. Rodger. 1987. *Output Measures for Public Libraries: A Manual of Standardized Procedures.* Chicago: American Library Association.

CUSTOMER SERVICE TRAINING IN OHIO ACADEMIC LIBRARIES

Elizabeth L. Plummer

The academic library's public image is crucial to its ability to fulfill its mission. How it is perceived by the board of trustees, the administration, the faculty, the students, and the public often influence budgetary decisions. The library staff, from the student assistants to the library director, decides what help the patron receives. If the staff is competent, friendly, and willing to listen, it will succeed. If all they do is sit behind their desks and appear unapproachable, it will not. To insure desired outcomes, public services staff must be sufficiently trained in how to operate the on-line catalog, the CD-ROM products, and the printers, must be able to answer reference and directional questions correctly, and must refer patrons to the proper department or person. To insure competence, training must be provided to these employees to insure that they can help patrons meet their information needs. This study is designed to determine how Ohio libraries implement customer service training programs to meet this need.

A literature review from 1984 to 1994 on the ERIC and Library Literature databases revealed that literature on customer service training was practically nonexistent. Since 1994, many books and articles have been published describing

Advances in Library Administration and Organization,
Volume 15, pages 65-101.
Copyright © 1997 by JAI Press Inc.
All rights of reproduction in any form reserved.
ISBN: 0-7623-0371-9

how to develop and implement customer service programs in various types of libraries. The term *customer service* has become very popular in private business circles. Broadly defined, customer service training is an attempt to prepare personnel and develop systems to be responsive to the needs and expectations of customers. By doing this, companies hope to make satisfied customers, thereby ensuring repeat business.

Businesses are redesigning training, job descriptions, procedures, and departments to deliver their products or services to customers quickly and efficiently. The goal is to deliver products and services right the first time so that customers will experience no aggravations. Schlesinger and Heskett (1991) explain the idea of putting customers first this way:

> Putting customers first means focusing on how and where they interact with the company. That, in truth, means focusing on the workers who actually create or deliver the things customers value—a spotless hotel room, a quick and easy refund, a fresh, inexpensive sandwich. In companies that are truly customer oriented, management has designed (or redesigned) the business to support frontline workers' efforts and to maximize the impact of the value they create. New job definitions and compensation policies are critical parts of the redesigned systems. The product is economic performance that is startling companies with the performance of traditional industry competitors (p. 77).

However, the term customer service does not appear in the ERIC or Library Literature databases from 1984 to 1995, although customer service appears in the ABI INFORM database (1971-1995) more than 9,000 times. This paper reflects a study of the training given public services staff members of academic libraries concerning how they respond to the patrons' requests and needs for information. For this study, the term *academic library* was restricted to libraries belonging to not-for-profit higher-education institutions. *Training* was defined as formal training programs in customer service offered to public service employees by library or institution administration. Customer service was defined as all contact with patrons by the public services staff. Included in this definition was directional assistance, telephone calls, written requests for assistance, reference help, and the many other contacts between the library's employees and patrons. *Patrons* were considered information seekers who visited the library building, who telephoned, or who sent correspondence by letter, fax machine, or electronic mail. *Public services staff* was defined as those library employees employed in the Circulation and Reference Services departments.

Studying the level of customer service training offered in academic libraries in the state of Ohio highlights the extent to which this training is available. It identifies the kind of training available, its content, and the audience for that training. In this age of budget cutbacks and academic libraries' having to more carefully justify expenditures, academic libraries must be perceived as friendly and accessible places where staff members are willing and helpful in meeting patrons' information needs. Learning what is actually happening in working with patrons will help libraries improve their efforts to satisfy patrons. This in turn, will help improve the library's public image, thus helping create and increase public support for library funding.

LIBRARY AND INFORMATION SCIENCE LITERATURE REVIEW

Very few articles and books are available in the literature of librarianship about training staff to provide good customer service, and a perusal of books on library personnel theory and practices revealed none that contained any information on the subject. The reason perhaps for this lack of literature may be the library profession's lack of awareness of the subject. Typical of this is a 1987 survey of the University of Rhode Island's library student employees and their supervisors (Vocino and Kellogg 1987). Student employees were important to the University of Rhode Island (URI) libraries as they are in all academic libraries, constituting about 75 percent of the workforce. In fact, they provided the primary staff for nights and weekends, given that on Saturdays, no professional librarian worked, and on Sundays, only one librarian and several clerical staff were available (pp. 7-8). Michael Vocino, Jr., Chair of Technical Services, and Martha H. Kellogg, Assistant Acquisitions Librarian at the University of Rhode Island Libraries looked at who the typical student employees were, and what the conditions of their employment were as perceived by the students themselves and the staff who hired, supervised, and trained them (p. 5). However, not one question was asked of the students about the training that was provided to them to prepare them to serve users and none were asked about problems experienced while working with the public. Staff members were asked to complete a questionnaire about the qualifications and skills of student employees they liked to hire. Skills such as typing, familiarity with computers, and familiarity with library systems such as OCLC, reference tools, and LC classification were mentioned, but interpersonal skills used in working with patrons and colleagues were not mentioned.

Another way to gauge customer service training given to staff members is through a study of student employee personnel manuals. The Association of Research Libraries, Office of Management Services (1991), surveyed their 119 member institutions about information desks, their staffing, their functions and how they relate to the other service points within the particular library (Flyer 172). Of the responding libraries, 43 percent offered informational services 80 percent to 100 percent of the time they were open. Librarians were rarely used to staff information desks; paraprofessionals were the predominant staffing at thirty-two libraries (p. 4). Training was mostly on-the-job (30, with 25 providing procedures manuals) (Flyer 172). One-on-one training and observation were also used. Very few libraries used either video presentations (five) and software for training (six) (p. 5). Training occurred in a short period of time, with 67 percent giving only one to two weeks of training before placing a person at the information desk (Flyer 172). No questions regarding customer service training were asked in the questionnaire.

However, several institutions returned training materials with their survey questionnaires, which helped illuminate the level of customer service training given library staff members. Approachability of staff members was stressed in these training materials; patrons are hesitant to approach someone whose head is buried in paperwork or who is engaged in telephone or personal contacts. If the staff member is helping someone else, the patron should be greeted and advised that he or she will be assisted shortly (Association, 1991, p. 41). Excellent listening skills were emphasized. It is important for staff members to understand the question the patron is asking. Communication barriers can result in a confused and frustrated patron (p. 144). Library acronyms such as OCLC, ILL, and library terminology, such as serials and databases should be dispensed with in favor of terms the patrons understand (p. 104). Employees were asked to empathize with irate patrons and try to solve their problem. Special skills for helping disabled patrons and patrons for whom English is a second language were also discussed. Guidelines for making referrals to the Reference Desk were outlined (pp. 106-107). The *Ohio State University Libraries Information/LCS Assistance Desk Manual: Policies and Procedures* advised that staff circulate among the on-line catalog terminals to see if any patrons needed assistance instead of sitting behind the desk (p. 141).

Norman Roberts and Tania Kann (1989) reported a survey of 52 university and polytechnic librarians in Great Britain and Scotland. Their survey sought information about forms of continuing education and training that were provided in their libraries (p. 109). Initially, questions were asked concerning induction (orientation) training for new employees. The content of these programs was defined as:

> those activities and classes of information which new entrants are required to be familiar with to carry out their duties effectively. At the most basic level, these may cover such practicalities as working conditions, location of departments, staff structures and duties. At a more general level induction programmes may include the role of the library in university or polytechnic contexts, the work of other departments and the teaching of specific skills. The transmission of such information may be undertaken through formal, systematized methods of teaching and demonstration, or informally, on a 'need to know' basis, or on a 'find out for yourself' basis, or through a combination of methods (Roberts and Kann 1989, p. 127).

Customer service training is not mentioned. It is also not mentioned as a form of education for librarians following orientation.

Rawlins (1982) reported on an experiment conducted at the University of Evansville in Indiana. Tests were made to determine whether student assistants trained using Computer Assistance Instruction (CAI) programs in circulation procedures were as well trained as student assistants in a control group who received training that relied on the traditional lecture and question-and-answer format (pp. 27-29). The format consisted of three to five frames of information on a computer screen; a question was presented which could be typed in by answering a question on the keyboard (p. 27). The topics covered included aspects of customer service such as how to refer a patron to reference, how to correctly handle telephone calls, how to take messages, and how to charge out books, but it did not include instruction regarding how to handle irate patrons. Results showed that students who completed computer-assisted instruction did better in a follow-up examination than those who were taught in the traditional way (Rawlins 1982, p. 27). In a follow-up to this study, Marvin C. Guilfoyle (1984) reported that the University of Evansville had extended computer-assisted instruction to student employees wishing to work in the periodicals' section of the library. Program topics included a general introduction to the entire library, use of the periodicals holding list, circulation procedures for nonprint materials, and the use of microforms and microform equipment. Training workers to help patrons was not mentioned. Guilfoyle wrote that the library was planning to use computer-assisted instruction to develop role-playing programs that would react to the specific responses of the trainee, and then branch into questions based on those responses. He did not mention if these role-playing programs were to be used to teach aspects of customer service (Guilfoyle 1984, p. 336).

Philippa Dolphin (1986) wrote of a series of video recordings that were used to promote social and communication skills for HERTIS, a technical and college library network based in Great Britain. HERTIS has over 250 staff members. New library assistants were required to attend six three-hour training sessions using these videos. Two of the sessions were devoted to interpersonal skills and dealing with awkward situations. In teaching these classes, Dolphin was appalled at the lack of suitable training packages available. To solve this problem, she developed 25 trigger video recordings. A trigger video comprised short episodes that were designed to stimulate or trigger a discussion. The triggers were grouped on the tape into episodes; librarians talking to patrons, patrons speaking to library staff, library staff talking to each other, and finally particular management problems being depicted. Participants worked in pairs or in a larger group analyzing the responses to and feelings about a particular episode. Dolphin said that each trigger generated at least 30 minutes of lively discussion. Participants cited an increased confidence in dealing with awkward situations at work and greater awareness of the various types of response and behavior. No follow-up research was conducted to see if this confidence and awareness translated into better customer service (p. 143).

In the Fall of 1988, Temple University's Central Library System initiated a program of library staff orientation and public service training designed to supplement the technical and job-specific training already received by employees (Arthur 1990, p. 5). Gwen Arthur, Coordinator of Reference Desk Services, reported on the development and implementation of the session of the public services training focusing on communication skill. After completing the session, staff should be able to: (a) determine patron needs through effective communication and either provide the service or refer the patron to someone who can; (b) greet and interact with patrons in ways which encourage patrons to ask for their assistance; and (c) react politely, patiently, and pleasantly when problems arise at the desk (p. 6). The customer service program was three hours long and was scheduled for three different dates during November and December, 1988. Since a person's level of education and administrative skill do not necessarily equate with that person's level of service skill, Arthur reported that all levels from clerk to paraprofessional to librarian and department head were asked to attend (pp. 4, 6). The program focused on six aspects of service: (a) importance of quality service; (b) components of service, including service strategy, systems, and customers; (c) teamwork; (d) communication skills, including image presentation; (e) sensitivity to customers, including responsiveness; and (f) complaint management, including remaining calm, allowing the customer to vent, asking questions, suggesting solutions, and taking action (p. 7). Arthur reported that the staff rated the program a 3.4 on a 4.0 scale, 4.0 being the most positive. They also indicated that many of the program's suggested strategies on how to work better with fellow staff, communicate with patrons, and deal with complaints, would be useful to them on the job and that they planned to apply some of them there (p. 10). Temple did not measure on-the-job performance as a follow-up to the service program. As of April 1990, the library had just initiated a library-wide performance evaluation program, part of which focused on service skills for public services staff. During the semester following the library-wide service training, the Reference and Information Services Department introduced a department program focused on positive communications skills. The Central Library Systems Staff Orientation committee was evaluating the public services program overall and considering ways to insure that skills and information presented during training were indeed learned and applied (Arthur 1990, pp. 11-12). Arthur did not report whether the service training sessions continued after the initial class.

In the 1990s, libraries experiencing budget reductions and the need to justify their existence to funding authorities have expressed more interest in customer service training for their employees. Three books were published in 1994 alone on how to develop and implement customer service programs in libraries. *Customer Service: A How-To Do-It Manual for Libraries* (1994) by Suzanne Walters offers a step-by-step approach for developing and instituting a customer service program. Her experience is mostly from a public library setting. Her tips and suggestions are very practical. Guy St. Clair's book, *Customer Service in the Information Environment* (1993), views customer service from a more theoretical framework. St. Clair, a past president of the Special Libraries Association, provides suggestions that are geared for special libraries. *Putting Service Into Library Staff Training* (1994) by Joanne M. Bessler combines theory and practicality in encouraging library managers to identify service ideas, transform these ideas into realistic goals, and guide both new and experienced staff in fulfilling these ideals even in the face of adversity. This book is suitable for all types of libraries. Listed below is a summary of the suggestions made in these three books:

1. Customer service is important because the library must compete with all sorts of information services. People will go elsewhere if the library cannot deliver quality goods and services. The way in which products or services are delivered is important enough that people are quite often willing to pay extra for them (St. Clair 1993, p. 13).
2. Customer service matters. The majority of unhappy patrons will never complain, but 90 percent will never come back and 13 percent will tell 20 or more people about their bad experience. It costs six times more to get a new customer than to retain an old one (Walters 1994, p. 1).
3. Twenty percent of the patrons account for 80 percent of the business. These people are strong advocates for the library. The loss of one can create an impact (Walters 1994, p. 2).
4. The commitment to customer service must come from the library director and the upper management of the library. That person must lead with vision, practice what he or she preaches, hold the employees accountable, empower employees, take risks, and commit to a long-term program. Customer service is not a quick fix (Walters 1994, p. 2). St. Clair (p. 55) says that customer service programs require a long-term commitment of perhaps three to five years. The initiation, design, and implementation of any formal customer service program require a major time commitment in the daily work life of the unit, requiring as much as 20 to 30 percent of staff time during the beginning stages. Later, not less than 10 percent and no less than 5 percent of staff time will be required to keep it operational.
5. Before the library can develop a customer service program, it must create an identity. What is the library's purpose? Who does it serve? If a mission statement has not been written, it should become the critical first step in this process. It should reflect the organization's goals and values, reality and also idealism. Staff members should be included in the process; they should be asked ways to gather patron and administrative ideas, as well as bringing their own. Ideas about patrons

should also be gathered, to include information about people who can provide financial support (governments, taxpayers, corporations, etc.), administrators, and users. What are their current needs and what are their expectations of the library? To obtain this information, the library should collect and analyze existing documents and data that describe the community, its composition and identity, and what it has historically wanted from its library. Key members of the above groups should be interviewed. Informal opinions can be solicited through a message board that allows self-posting of responses. Issues can be identified that attract a great deal of interest. Focus groups to discuss specific issues and challenges relating to the library's mission can also be helpful (Bessler 1994, p. 5).

6. Vacant positions should be designed to offer the opportunity to recruit individuals who possess excellent customer service skills. New employees should possess good oral communication skills, exhibit cooperation and teamwork, have problem-solving and decision-making skills, possess enthusiasm, have a high energy level, and be flexible and adaptable (Walters 1994, p. 35).

7. Management must first sell the library to its employees. Librarians and staff must understand that their suggestions and ideas are valued. They must believe that their jobs are important, and that the library is performing valuable services. Employees with low morale will not give good service. Customers will perceive the library has a quality organization if their experience matches their expectations (Walters 1994, p.15).

8. The library's culture must be changed. To encourage risk-taking, staff must be trained to provide patrons with good service even when it conflicts with library policy, to develop informed judgments, and to make decisions. Managers need to delegate decisions regarding service to customers to the line staff. Creating an atmosphere of autonomy and trust enables employees to feel important and respected. It also allows them to make mistakes (Walters 1994, p. 7).

9. Systems of accountability must be established. Walters (1994) suggested that job descriptions and performance-evaluation forms could be changed to describe and evaluate for levels of customer service. Systems for rewarding employees for providing good customer service and for reprimanding employees who do not provide good service also need to be incorporated into the program (Walters 1994, p. 98).

10. Reward and recognition programs should be designed so that they influence as many staff members as possible. Awards should be for heroic acts, consistent day-in-day-out behavior, and some team or departmental achievements that exemplify the internal or external customer service behavior the library wants to encourage. Rewards

could include both monetary and other forms of recognition such as spoken or written praise, an article in the library newsletter, praise in the presence of the boss, a prize parking space, time off, and or a trophy, book, or other token of gratitude (Walters 1994, p. 61).

Do academic libraries value employees who are motivated to provide good service to patrons? A study by Gillian Allen and Bryce Allen (1992) suggests that they do. They analyzed job advertisements received by the Graduate School of Library and Information Science at the University of Illinois at Urbana-Champaign between December 1, 1989 and September 1, 1990 (Allen and Allen 1992, p. 69). Questionnaires were sent to 120 people listed as contact persons in the advertisements. The ads were supplemented by ads from the CAREER LEADS section of issues of the *American Libraries* journal for the same time period. The contact people were asked to rank lists of selection criteria, personality variables, and methods for assessing the qualifications of job applicants for their relative importance. They were also asked to describe how they would evaluate service orientation in an applicant (p. 69). Service orientation, defined as:

the disposition to be helpful, thoughtful, considerate, and cooperative and represents an important aspect of nontechnical performance (that is, performance of activities not specifically related to the technical functions of librarianship which include the knowledge of reference tools or the ability to perform on-line services) (p. 69).

was ranked as the most important personality variable used as a selection criterion. The reference check was rated most important as a method of assessing qualifications. Contact people all reported using the interview as the primary method of evaluating service orientation in a job applicant (p. 75). Interestingly, personality testing was rated the least important of the methods for assessing job applicants, although service orientation as a personality characteristic had been ranked highly. Gillian Allen and Bryce Allen (1992) said that personality testing was a method of detecting these characteristics in job applicants. Their research showed that personnel directors valued service orientation in job applicants but that they were more likely to use the interview and reference check rather than personality testing to decide whether an applicant had that quality (p. 75).

In the literature reviewed, no follow-up research was identified that showed whether or to what extent training library employees in customer service leads to improved service for library patrons. Still, there is some evidence that suggests that customer service training leads to improved effectiveness in meeting patrons' expectations and needs. The Columbus, Ohio, Metropolitan Public Library was featured in an American Library Association tele-seminar held at their annual conference in 1994. The library has developed two training programs to give better customer service. The first is called CLASS (Customer Leaving Appreciated, Satisfied, and Sold). Statistics were not given regarding the effectiveness of this program. The second program is called STYLE (Service Techniques Yielding Library Effectiveness). This program is a commitment to reference accuracy. Staff members are trained to realize they are part of a team and are interdependent. Through unobtrusive reference surveys, the library has discovered that accuracy has increased. No actual statistics were cited (*Achieving Breakthrough* 1994).

There are no reliable statistics as to how many academic libraries provide customer service training to their employees. As mentioned previously, the Association of Research Libraries survey of member institutions in 1991 revealed 55 institutions offering some sort of training for paraprofessional and student staff in answering directional, informational, and holdings questions. Gwen Arthur (1994) reported of an electronic mail query over Library listservs LIBREF-L and LIBAD-MIN-L in Fall, 1992, asking academic librarians to report customer service training initiatives. Many reported customer service training programs, but Arthur failed to give any statistics about how many (pp. 219-220).

BUSINESS LITERATURE REVIEW

What can business literature reveal about customer service? Research studies have documented that good customer service is crucial to the success of an organization as it generates repeat business. In 1969, Philip Kotler and Sidney J. Levy expanded the theory of marketing to include nonbusiness organizations (pp. 10-15). Previously, marketing had been seen as the "task of finding and stimulating buyers for the firm's output" (p. 10). They postulated that marketing should be seen as, "the concept of sensitively serving and satisfying human needs" (p. 15). All organizations have products, services, ideas, and clients or consumers that they serve (p. 12). Marketing then is seen as that function of the organization that keeps in constant touch with the organization's consumers, discerns their needs, develops products or services that meet those needs, and builds a program of communication to express the organization's purpose (p. 15).

Implicit in this new definition of marketing is the idea that the organization must serve its patrons. A dilemma for service organizations that do not produce tangible products is posed by efforts to determine how one measures whether service is good or bad. In a manufacturing environment, precise specifications can be set for ensuring uniform quality; if these are not met, the product is rejected. In organizations that produce services, precise standards are hard to set. For those with a high labor component, performance often varies from producer to producer, from consumer to consumer, and from day to day. Their quality cannot be engineered and evaluated at the factory before delivery to consumers (Parsuraman, Berry and Zeithaml 1991, p. 253).

From 1983 until 1990, Berry, Zeithaml and Parsuraman (1990) conducted three studies on service quality (p. 38). The first survey sought to develop a model to measure service quality for organizations working in four industries: retail banking, credit cards, securities and brokerages, and product repair and maintenance. To find data for this model, they developed a survey instrument called SERVQUAL. Consumers' expectations and perceptions of a company were measured using focus groups, and 1,000 surveys of shoppers in a retail mall (Parsuraman, Berry and Zeithaml 1991, p. 257). Five dimensions of customer service were identified. A key finding of the focus groups was that service quality as defined by consumers is the discrepancy or gap between their perceptions and their expectations (p. 257). The researchers used this information to seek to identify the organizational gaps that led to discrepancies between consumers' perceptions and expectations of service. Interviews were conducted with 14 executives at four nationally known service companies in the four industries previously mentioned, and the researchers identified four organizational gaps that contributed to the service quality gap identified by consumers.

The second part of the research consisted of an empirical study Berry, Zeithaml and Parasuraman (1990) conducted to test their hypothesis of the five dimensions of customer service identified in the first survey (p. 38). Nearly 1,000 customers in the credit card, long-distance telephone, product repair, and retail banking sectors were surveyed. A comprehensive case study of one of the largest United States banks was also conducted. Managers and employees from these regions were interviewed individually and in focus groups. They also conducted a survey of bank customers (p. 38).

The third part of the study sought to validate the four organizational gaps between consumers' perceptions and expectations of customer service identified in the first study (Berry, Zeithaml and Parsaraman 1990, p. 38). To verify their hypothesis about potential causes of service quality problems, the authors conducted mail surveys of 1,936 customers, 728 contact personnel, and 231 managers in 89 separate field offices of five national service companies, two banks, two insurance firms, and a telephone company (Berry et al. 1990, p. 38). These surveys revealed five service imperatives necessary to improving service quality.

In the first survey, the researchers identified five customer service dimensions that consumers value: (a) *reliability*—the ability to perform the promised service dependably and accurately; (b) *responsiveness*—willingness to help customers and provide prompt service; (c) *assurance*—knowledge and courtesy of employees and their ability to convey trust and confidence; (d) *empathy*—caring, individualized attention the firm provides to customers; and (e) *tangibles*—physical facilities, equipment, and employees' personal appearance

(p. 261). The second survey validated their research that these customer service dimensions are important to consumers.

Four organizational gaps were postulated in the first survey to explain the gap between consumers' perceptions and expectations of customer service. They were:

1. Consumer Expectation-Management Perception Gap. Executives are unaware of critical consumer expectations or misread the importance of them. The example given by the researchers was that privacy and confidentiality in banking and securities brokerage transactions was extremely important to consumers, but executives in these industries seemed unaware of these expectations.

2. Management Perception-Service Quality Specification. The interviews revealed that, even in instances where management was aware of critical consumer expectations such as the need of the appliance repair and maintenance firms to promptly respond to appliance breakdowns, resource constraints, market conditions, and/or management indifference might prevent them from setting specifications to meet those needs.

3. Service Quality Specifications-Service Delivery Gap. Even when formal specifications were in place for performing services well, the actual performance fell short of those specifications. Executives mentioned as the cause of these problems the critical role of contact personnel and the wide variability of their performance, and the consequent difficulty in maintaining uniform standardized quality.

4. Service Delivery-External Communications Gap. One potential reason for poor perceptions of service quality by consumers is that their expectations are boosted by media advertising, sales presentations, and other communications to levels beyond a company's capability to deliver (Parasuraman et al. 1991, pp. 256-257).

By conducting large surveys of consumers, contact personnel, and managers of service-oriented companies in the third survey, the researchers sought to validate their hypotheses of the four organizational gaps that cause the gap between the desire to give excellent customer service and the actual performance of the service. Their research revealed that companies need to: (a) define the service role, (b) compete for talent (and use it), (c) emphasize service teams, (d) go for reliability, and (e) be great at problem resolution (p. 29).

It should be noted, however, that the above service imperatives do not themselves validate the service quality gaps hypothesized in the first article. Customer expectations and management perceptions that may contribute to service quality gaps were not defined. Also, criteria used to measure customer satisfaction were not explained.

Berry, Zeithaml, and Parsuraman's research is significant because it identified the aspects of good customer service that consumers value and the organizational problems companies have in meeting these expectations. Their findings provide a framework for organizations to develop plans on how to satisfy these customer service dimensions.

Azzolini and Lingle (1993) demonstrated that excellent internal customer service performance is crucial to the success of an organization (pp. 38-40). By internal customer service, they meant how the various departments (such as quality, research and development, and human resources) within an organization were serving each other. They tried to determine whether these departments support each other and work together, or whether there was rivalry, mistrust, animosity, and quarreling among them (p. 38). Surveying 841 managers and executives in 29 industries who were *Quality* magazine readers, the researchers found that 88 percent believed internal customer service was the key to company success (p. 38). A major improvement effort was reported to be undertaken by 76 percent of them.. Respondents were asked how customers would rate their overall service performance. Those that said they would be rated *excellent* or *above average* were 59 percent of the respondents, while 41 percent rated services received as *average* or *poor* (p. 39). Respondents were asked to classify their organizations in four ways: *industry leader, middle of the pack, up and comer,* and *follower.* These results were correlated with the results of the internal service improvement efforts of those who considered themselves "industry leaders" and "up and comers." Of these two groups, 74 percent and 71 percent respectively reported undertaking and being successful at internal service improvement. Those who were middle of the pack and followers only had 34 percent report service improvement efforts (p. 39).

Discussing the survey results, Azzolini and Lingle (1993) labeled those who rated their service as either excellent or as above average as leaders, and those who rated their service as average or poor as laggards. Leaders were shown to have a strategic plan followed by careful measurement of the five key organizational areas: work processes, structure, systems, culture, and capabilities (p. 40). These measurements identified misalignment with strategy and customer requirements. Leaders not only gave good service, but also received it from their internal suppliers. They viewed the parts of their organization as interdependent parts of a whole designed to provide for excellent customer/supplier relationships. The view taken was that all parts of the organization must prove service excellence (p. 40).

What are the attributes needed by customer-service people to accomplish their job successfully? Becker and Welling (1990) studied this question and reported their results (pp. 49-51). The authors derived a list of customer service attributes culled both from books and articles on customer service and from job analyses from their employer's database. From these sources, they developed two survey questionnaires, one for customers and one for customer service employees (p. 50). Respondents to both surveys were asked to rank each dimension on two scales, importance and proficiency. The importance scale asked about how important the dimension was to effective customer service. Rankings ranged from five (extremely important) to one (not important). The proficiency scale asked respondents to rank how well customer-service people use each dimension when they interacted. Responses varied again from five (always done well) to one (never done well) (p. 50). The second part of both surveys measured the impact of customer service on customers' decisions to do repeat business. The first question asked respondents to measure the impact of good service on their decision to do business again with the organization. On the five point scale, responses ranged from five (extremely great effect) to one (little or no effect). The second item asked respondents about whether they tell other people when they receive outstanding, adequate, or poor customer service." Response categories were, "never," "occasionally," and "frequently" (p. 50).

More than 1,300 customers from the United States, Canada, and Great Britain completed the customer survey. Nearly nine hundred customer service people from nine diverse organizations completed the customer service employee questionnaire (Becker and Welling 1990, p. 50). The results of the customers' survey revealed that customers rated all 17 dimensions between important and very important; means ranged from 3.56 to 4.10. On the proficiency scale, they ranked all but one dimension as rarely well done; means ranged from 2.54 to 3.24. All but 3 of the 17 dimensions showed a full point difference between average ratings for importance and proficiency (p. 50). In the importance segment of the customer service peoples' survey, the means ranged from 3.84 to 4.55. Proficiency ratings ranged from 3.16 to 3.66. Proficiency ratings were nearly one point lower than the importance ratings (p. 50). The customer service people ranked the importance of the 17 dimensions between important and very important, but ranked their own ability to perform the dimensions much lower. But even then, their proficiency rankings were higher than those given them by the customers.

The second part of the survey measured the impact of customer service on customers' decisions to conduct repeat business; the data revealed that 97 percent of customers and 83 percent of customer service people stated good customer service greatly affected peoples' decisions to do repeat business with an organization (Becker and Welling 1990, p. 51). When service was excellent, 57 percent of the customers reported telling others about it, while only 38 percent of customer service people believed customers talk frequently to others about excellent service. When service was considered poor, 65 percent of customers told others, while 75 percent of customer service employees perceived that customers told others of their bad experience (p. 51).

Becker and Welling concluded four principles from their research:

1. Service matters. Good customer service keeps customers coming back.
2. Organizations must monitor and evaluate the perceptions customers have of their customer service personnel. It is also important that they understand their own customer service peoples' views on the quality of customer service.
3. The job skills of customer service personnel need to be enhanced through training. The discrepancy between the importance and proficiency ratings on the surveys indicated this.
4. The list of customer service dimensions should serve as a criterion for selection and appraisal of customer service personnel (Becker and Welling 1990, p. 51).

This literature review clearly shows that no direct research has been done to show how the needs and priorities of patrons are handled in academic libraries. No study has been done to determine to what extent customer service has been incorporated into the operating philosophy of academic libraries. Work clearly needs to be done to determine if library systems operate efficiently to deliver excellent services to their patrons, whether these customers are satisfied and come back, what kinds of improvements in customer service may be needed and how best to effect these improvements.

Methodology

To support or disprove the hypothesis that academic libraries in the state of Ohio offer little or no customer service training to their public services staffs, a self-administered, anonymous questionnaire was mailed to 127 institutions listed in the Ohio section of the *1996 Higher Education Directory* (Rodenhouse 1996, pp. 271-288). Public services staff were defined as those library employees employed in the Circulation and Reference Departments. These institutions included two-year technical colleges granting associates' degrees, non-accredited Bible colleges, medical schools, graduate theological seminaries, four-year undergraduate institutions granting bachelors' degrees, and universities with both bachelors' degree and post-graduate degree programs. Excluded from consideration were for-profit institutions.

All these institutions have academic libraries and patrons who require assistance. Surveying different types of libraries gave a broader picture of the problem, and sampling a larger number of institutions allowed a sufficient response rate to make the survey results significant. The objectives were:

1. to test the hypothesis that little or no customer service training is given public services employees of academic libraries.

2. to determine if such training, if given at all, is given only to new employees.
3. to identify whether such training is offered to all public services employees; those with no seniority and those with many years of experience.
4. to determine the content of such training. Does it consist of verbal instruction from supervisors, communicating with colleagues, written materials, video tapes, role-playing, seminars, classroom instruction, materials to be studied independently or some combination of any or all of the above?

The questionnaire consisted of 16 questions with closed responses (Appendix A), and was organized in the checklist format. Many questions required a yes or no answer, but many asked the respondent to check all items in a list that might answer the question. Space for comments was not available, although several respondents did write brief notes. The survey was composed of two sections. One probed formal customer service training for new employees (new employee orientation). The other section sought information about training offered to employees who completed new employee orientation (continuing customer service training). Employees eligible for this training could have been employed from several weeks to many years. In both sections, the questions were similar, so the results were discussed together in the Data Analysis section.

Data Analysis

One hundred twenty-seven surveys were mailed. Of these, 87 were returned for a response rate of 68 percent. In two instances, comments were written on the survey forms, but the survey questions themselves were not answered. Findings are based on the data collected from 85 surveys. Libraries were asked if they offered formal programs of customer service training to staff of the public services department. It was assumed that this training would be offered to new employees. Formal programs of customer service training were reported by 43 (51%) libraries; 42 (49%) libraries said that they did not offer this training. Some confusion occurred about what formal meant. Several libraries wrote that they do train in customer service, but that it is not a prepared program but rather one-on-one instruction provided by the supervisor. Since no demographic information was solicited, it is hard to learn the reasons why this training is not offered in almost half of the libraries. One possible explanation is that only large and medium-sized libraries can afford this training, and libraries with small staffs and perhaps small budgets feel that this is a luxury that they cannot afford. Library directors with small staffs of one to five people might feel that they can teach their employees to be helpful and friendly without a formal program and that they can monitor staff performance themselves since they work closely with the staff. These issues require further study.

Table 1. Content Items

Content Items	New Employee Orientation 43 Responses		Continuous Customer Service Training—27 Responses	
	n	%	*n*	%
Library policies	42	98	23	85
Location of primary resources and services	40	93	16	59
Equipment training	37	86	19	70
Making referrals to other departments or employees	35	81	13	48
The library's mission	34	79	12	44
Telephone etiquette	32	74	12	44
Emergency Procedures	32	74	17	63
Employee demeanor	30	70	12	44
The employee's role in the library's mission	29	67	12	44
Dealing with irate or frustrated patrons	29	67	17	63
Complaint procedures	26	60	16	60
How to positively meet the customer's expectations	25	58	18	67
The role of the employee's department in the library's mission	21	49	7	26
Communication skills	20	47	12	44
Helping patrons with special needs	19	44	14	52
Problem solving skills	14	33	13	48
Treating staff as patrons	13	30	7	26
Other	4	9	5	12
None of the above	0	0	0	0

Libraries were also asked if their customer service training was available to public services staff after new employee training was finished. Of the 43 libraries that said they had formal customer service training programs, 27 (63%) libraries responded affirmatively. The majority of libraries with customer service training programs for new employee orientation do continue customer service training for employees with more seniority. Some who do not offer continuing programs may not feel it is necessary or have the funds to allow employees to upgrade or refresh their skills.

But, in any case, 27 (32%) of the 85 responding libraries offer continuing customer service training. Less than one-third of the employees with seniority in the responding libraries can participate in customer service training programs. If customer service training is offered, it is most often given to new employees, and, then, to a lesser extent, employees with seniority. Content that might be part of customer service training for new employees and for continuing programs was explored. The responses are shown in Table 1. Only those libraries that have formal customer service training responded. Multiple answers occurred, because libraries were asked to check all the items that applied.

Forty-two (98%) of 43 respondents said that their new employee orientation programs included instruction on library policies. Forty (93%) libraries provided information about the location of primary resources and services. Equipment training was the third item most often included in the training finding its way into the programs of 37 libraries (86%). Emergency procedures were taught by 32 (74%) of the libraries. Most of the responding libraries imparted information about the purpose and direction of the library. Thirty-four (74%) spoke about the library's mission, and 29 (67%) mentioned the employee's role in fulfilling that mission. Only 21 (49%) emphasized the role of the employee's department in that mission. Interpersonal skills training required for working in a library were also explored. Twenty (47%) libraries included communication skills in their training programs. It appears that these skills were covered under several different topics. Methods and procedures for making referrals to other departments or employees were taught by 35 (81%), and 32 (75%) instructed staffers in telephone etiquette. Employee demeanor (smile, patience, friendliness) was discussed by 30 (70%) libraries. Treating internal staff as patrons were listed by 13 (30%) libraries. Working in a library often requires dealing with irate or frustrated patrons and trying to solve their problem, but problem solving skills designed to deal with them were emphasized by only 14 (33%) libraries. However, problem solving was included in several other content areas. Training was provided in dealing with irate or frustrated patrons by 29 (67%) libraries, complaint procedures were taught by 26 (60%) libraries, how to positively meet the customer's expectations was stressed by 25 (58%) of the responding libraries, and 19 (44%) libraries reported training new employees how to help patrons with special needs.

Subjects covered in continuing customer service training programs were also studied. Their answers are also shown in Table 1. As with the new employee orientation programs, the topic covered most often was instruction in library policies. This was cited by 23 (85%) libraries. Next came equipment training with 19 (70%), and "how to positively meet customer's expectations" with 18 (67%) positive responses was third. The second item in the previous sentence was listed in the middle range of items for new employee orientation. Perhaps libraries feel that meeting customer's expectations is a harder level of communication skills training and is best attempted after preliminary communication skills training. In new employee orientation, teaching about the location of primary resources and services was second in importance, but only 16 (59%) libraries, thought this was important in continuing customer service training. Evidently, it is felt that employees should know the location of primary resources and services after new employee orientation has been completed and they have experience in working with materials. Training in interpersonal and problem solving skills predominated in continuing customer service training programs. As mentioned previously, how to positively meet customer's expectations was included by 18 (67%) libraries in this training; dealing with irate or frustrated patrons was rated as important by 17 (63%) libraries; sixteen (60%) responses dealt with complaint procedures; and helping patrons with special needs was included by 14 (52%) libraries. Making referrals to other departments or employees were listed by 13 (48%) libraries; twelve (44%) libraries each covered employee demeanor (smile, patience, friendliness), telephone etiquette, and communication skills; problem solving skills were stressed by 13 (48%) libraries, but only 7 (26%) libraries thought it necessary to include material on treating staff as patrons.

The emphasis placed on interpersonal skills and problem solving training changed from new employee orientation to continuing customer service training programs. Further customer service training beyond orientation focuses on the more difficult skills of helping irate or frustrated patrons and handling complaints. The new employee orientation programs stressed the library's mission, the role of the employee in that mission and the role of the employee's department in that mission. Continuing customer service training did not emphasize these items. Twelve (44%) libraries each mentioned the library's mission and the employee's role in that mission, while only seven (16%) libraries listed the role of the employee's department in that mission. The difference in emphasis might relate to the library administration's or instructor's assumption that employees with several months of employment are probably aware of the library's mission and their role in it. This assumption may or may not be true.

Libraries with formal customer service training programs were asked if they used prepared training materials in new employee orientation or in continuing customer service training. Prepared training materials are being used more for new employee orientation than for continuing customer service training. Of the 43 libraries, 27 (63%) used prepared training materials in new employee orientation. For continuing customer service training, 13 (48%) libraries used prepared training materials, and 13 (48%) did not use them. How libraries who do not use prepared training materials conduct customer service training was not studied. Libraries who responded that they used prepared training materials were asked to identify the type of training materials for new employee orientation and continuing customer service training. Since they were asked to check all the materials they used, multiple answers occurred. All libraries used written materials. Many supplemented the instruction with other mediums. The easy availability of written material on the subject may explain the heavy use of it. Videotapes were the most used audiovisual mediums. They were used more in continuing customer service training than in new employee orientation. There is a lack of awareness of current videotapes, audiotapes, and computer programs that provide instruction on the topic of customer service. All 27 (100%) libraries that used prepared training materials in new employee orientation reported that they used written materials. These were supplemented by four (15%) libraries where employees watched videotapes, one (3%) library that used audio tapes, and four (15%) libraries that used unspecified other materials. None instructed with computer programs. Those libraries with continuing customer service training programs reported 13 (100%) used written training materials. Supplementary materials included four (31%) with videotapes, four (31%) with unspecified other materials, two (15%) with audiotapes, and one (8%) with computer programs.

The type of instruction given was also explored for both new employee orientation and continuing customer service training. All who responded that they have formal programs of customer service training could answer these questions whether they used prepared training materials or not. They were asked to check all the formats they used, so multiple answers occurred. Of the 43 libraries having customer service training programs for new employee orientation, 40 (93%) provided individual training by the employee's supervisor while 23 of the 27 libraries offering continuing customer service training programs libraries did. Other methods of teaching in new employee orientation programs included classroom instruction used by nine (21%), while three (7%) used role-playing, and unsupervised instruction involving, written, audio, or video materials was provided by 16 (37%) libraries. Alternate instruction methods in continuing customer service training programs included classroom instruction used by 12 (44%) libraries, unsupervised instruction provided by eight (30%) libraries, computer-assisted instruction used by two (7%) libraries, and one library (4%) had their employees engage in role-playing. Most of the libraries rely on one-on-one instruction by the individual supervisor. Individual training by the supervisor was the most prevalent type of instruction for new employee orientation and continuing customer service training; a significant amount of instruction was also unsupervised. This may be due to the desire of the supervisor to have the employees study independently and then discuss with them what they have learned. More classroom instruction was provided in continuing customer service training than in new employee orientation. More groups of employees may be taught in continuing customer service training.

Respondents were asked who provided the customer service training during new employee orientation and continuing customer service training. They were asked to include everyone who provided the customer service training; multiple answers were possible. Of the 43 libraries with new employee orientation customer service training programs, 35 (81%) reported that the Circulation or Reference Department Supervisor provided the training. Human Resources/ Training inside the library was used by five (12%), and six (14%) used Human Resources/Training personnel from the parent institution. Outside consultants were listed by three (7%) libraries, and 11 (26%) checked other. Comments often mentioned the participation of the library director. Most of the training during new employee orientation is given by the new employee's immediate supervisor. In some libraries, it is supplemented by Human Resources/ Training of the library or parent institution.

Libraries with continuing customer service training reported that 21 (77%) of the 27 libraries had the Reference Department Supervisor provide the training. In 19 (70%) libraries, the Circulation Department Supervisor also provided instruction. For eight (30%) libraries, unspecified others provided the training, while seven (26%) hired outside consultants. Human Resources/Training personnel from the parent institution provided training for six (22%) libraries, and Human Resources/Training staff inside the library handled the program in four (15%) libraries. Most of the continuing customer service training given to public services employees is given by public services supervisors, the Circulation or Reference Department Supervisor. Many libraries (63%) did supplement this training by using outside consultants or the Human Resources/Training staff of the library or parent institution. Since demographic questions were not asked, it is difficult to detect how many libraries had Human Resources/Training departments that could help them.

Respondents were asked if customer service training for new employees as well as those receiving continuing customer service training was mandatory. Of the 43 libraries conducting customer service training for new employees, 39 (90%) replied that it was mandatory. Two (5%) said that it was optional, and two (5%) did not answer the question. Of the 27 eligible libraries giving continuous customer service training, 20 (74%) said that the training was mandatory. Seven (26%) reported that it was optional. The responses to both questions show that most of libraries with customer service training programs for new and regular employees require mandatory attendance.

All libraries that responded to the survey were asked whether funds were available for library staff members to seek further training outside the library system. Of the 85 responding libraries, 65 (76%) provide funds, while 19 (21%) did not. Three (3%) libraries did not answer the question. These data show that most of the academic libraries in the state of Ohio are committed to providing funds for outside training in customer service whether they have in-house customer service training programs or not.

Respondents were asked about who was involved in the formation of the customer service training programs. The library administration and professional librarians were identified by 26 (60%) libraries each. Department heads and support staff were mentioned by 19 (44%) libraries. A variety of other sources were mentioned as involved. The human resources department of the library was consulted by three (7%) libraries, as was the human resources department of the parent institution by three (7%) libraries. An outside consultant was hired by one (2%) library, and one (2%) used other departments of the institution. Unspecified other sources were used by two (7%) libraries.

It is not possible from this question to detect the ratio of Public Service Staff to Technical Services Staff input in the design of these programs.

SUMMARY AND CONCLUSION

The hypothesis that very few customer service training programs exist in academic libraries in the state of Ohio was not supported. Over 50 percent of the responding libraries said that they had formal programs of customer service training for new employees. Since demographic information was not solicited it is not known how the other half of the libraries encourage quality service for their patrons. Many respondents who did not have formal customer service training programs commented that they were small libraries with one to five employees and did not perceive the need for this type of training; informal customer service was provided by the library director. Others suggested that customer service training is a business model that is not applicable to nonprofit institutions such as academic libraries. This idea was expressed in a letter from a library director who chose not to complete the survey.

Over three-quarter (76%) of the responding libraries provide funds for training in customer service outside the library system. This includes many libraries who do not have formal internal customer service training programs. Why these libraries would pay to have their employees take this training and not have their own training programs is not known. One may speculate that with the day-to-day pressures of operating a library and perhaps cuts in funding levels, the library administration has not taken the time to develop a program of customer service training for its employees; it may also feel that it is not financially viable presently, or it may be waiting for an employee to take a course in customer service training and use that to help develop a program for their library. Less than two-thirds (63%) of the responding libraries that have formal programs of customer service training offered continuous customer service training to their employees beyond new employee orientation. This means that only one-third of all of the responding libraries' employees are receiving customer service training beyond new employee orientation. For employees with many years of service to the library, it would be beneficial to have them refresh and upgrade their customer service skills and learn about new or changing library policies, resources, and equipment. The majority (63%) of the libraries with formal customer service training for new employee orientation did perceive the need to offer customer service training to their employees with differing years of service. The rest (37%) have evidently not begun programs or do not see the need beyond new employee orientation.

The commitment to giving excellent service to the patrons is very important. Most of the libraries required customer service training to cement this commitment. For new employee training, the use of prepared training materials by 63 percent of the libraries suggests a desire for consistency and a structured program that does not change from teacher to teacher. In training beyond new employee orientation, the use of prepared training materials dropped to 50 percent of the libraries, showing a willingness by some libraries to allow the teachers to structure the training according to their wishes or the perceived needs of the trainees. A significant problem with not using prepared training materials is the lack of consistency in the training. Even with the same instructor, the nature of the instruction could vary from class to class. Employees may not have received the same training. This makes it difficult to measure the effectiveness of the training.

The data reveal that the Circulation or Reference Department supervisors perform most of the training for public services employees. It may be supplemented by Human Resources/Training personnel from the library or from the parent institution, or by outside consultants. Questions were not asked about the qualifications or training of the teachers. According to the survey results, most of the instruction is individual training given by the supervisor; classroom instruction, role-playing, computer-assisted instruction, and unsupervised instruction involving audio, written, or video materials are used to aid the supervisor's teaching. Having the employee's supervisor provide the customer service training could be beneficial since the supervisor can tailor the program to the needs of the department. Also, the supervisor is aware of the specific needs for customer service instruction relating directly to the job, because the supervisor is responsible for monitoring the performance of the employee in the work.

For new employee orientation, training covered basic information such as library policies, the location of primary resources and services, equipment training, and emergency procedures, and making referrals to other departments or employees. All these are essential in communications with patrons. A vision of the library's mission, the employee's role in fulfilling that mission, and the role of the employee's department in that mission was discussed. Basic skills of interpersonal communication such as telephone etiquette and employee demeanor (smile, patience, friendliness) were also taught. Over 50 percent of the libraries also provided training in dealing with irate or frustrated patrons (67%), complaint procedures (60%), and how to positively meet the customer's expectations (58%). It is significant that a substantial minority of libraries did not train their new employees to handle these situations. Often the students working at the Circulation desk, or the shelvers are the only library employees the patron meets. They may experience the patron's satisfaction or dissatisfaction with the library, and neglecting that training can cause pain.

Continuing customer service training emphasized library policies, equipment training, and emergency procedures; less attention was placed on the location of primary resources and services. Evidently, libraries believe that after the new employee orientation employees should know the location of primary resources and services. For many employees, this may not be true. If they work only in one department, they may not be aware of new resources and services in other departments. More emphasis was given to training in the more difficult interpersonal skills of meeting the customer's expectations, complaint procedures, and how to handle irate or frustrated patrons. Basic communications skills such as telephone etiquette and employee demeanor were de-emphasized as was information about the library's mission and the employee's role in that mission. This may be explained by the assumption of the instructors that employees with any length of service with the library should know this information. More libraries provided training to experienced employees on how to help patrons with special needs than in new employee orientation. The difference in content of the two training programs is attributed to the need in new employee orientation to impart basic information and skills. Instruction in more difficult communication skills is beneficial to employees who have had experience helping patrons with complaints or those who are angry or frustrated.

Assuming that employees in continuing customer service training already have basic communication skills such as telephone etiquette and employee demeanor may be faulty. These employees may never have received instruction in the library's methods of customer service and may be relying on their innate abilities. Instruction in basic communication skills should be included in the curriculum. Additionally, waiting until formal continuing customer service training to provide instruction in helping patrons with special needs may cause these patrons to receive inadequate service from untrained new employees. This instruction should also be required in the training curriculum.

The data revealed that only 74 percent of the libraries with new employee orientation customer service training programs instructed their employees in emergency procedures, although 98 percent taught about library policies. Of the libraries offering continuing customer service training programs, only 63 percent offered an orientation in emergency procedures. Since the Circulation or Reference Departments would probably be responsible for the evacuation of the library in case of a fire, tornado, or bomb threat, it is surprising that more do not offer this training. The Americans with Disabilities Act legislated that public institutions must provide access to their facilities for the mentally and physically challenged. It is surprising that only 44 percent of the libraries with new employee orientation training provided this instruction, while 52 percent of the libraries with continuing customer service training provided it. Demographic information was not included in this survey, so the number of libraries that are public or private institutions cannot be learned. It seems that all libraries do not provide teaching about how to help these customers if only to comply with the law.

Recent publications on the topic of customer service such as Suzanne Walter's *Customer Service: A How-To-Do- It Manual for Libraries* or Azzolini and Lingle's article, "Internal Service Performance" stress that a successful customer service program relies on employees giving the same high level of service to other employees that they do to give customers or patrons (Walters 1994; Azzolini and Lingle 1993). Only 30 percent of the libraries with new employee orientation and 26 percent of libraries with continuing customer service training included treating staff as patrons. Among the respondents, there might have been confusion about what this meant, or an assumption that this is normally expected of their employees.

Academic libraries in the state of Ohio in the decade of the 1990s have had to justify their existence. They have had to justify their needs for technology, staff, and materials. Central to their struggle is the duty to provide excellent service to their patrons. If patrons, who often are faculty, administration, and students, are happy, many will speak in favor of the library when budget cutbacks are proposed. Over one-half of the libraries in this survey have made a commitment to provide a consistent level of customer service through the training of Public services staff. They do not want to leave it to chance that a patron is treated well. A well-designed customer service training program can help provide this consistent level of quality service. Academic libraries that do not have formal customer service training programs should implement basic training programs concerning the library's mission, the employee's role in that mission, the role of the employee's department in that mission, library rules and procedures, location of resources, equipment training, emergency procedures, helping the disabled, and communication skills. This will lead to a consistency in the service given to the patrons of the library, but mechanisms need to be developed to measure whether customer service training is effective in improving the quality of service given and how it can be improved. Ways should be found to measure the quality of customer service given by a library employee, and this should be reflected in their performance appraisal. This combination of training and evaluation can do much to create the best possible service program.

APPENDIX A

Antioch University
Yellow Springs, OH 45387
Mr. Joseph J. Cali, College Head Librarian

Ashland University
401 College Avenue
Ashland, OH 44805
Mr. William B. Weiss, Director of the Library

Art Academy of Cincinnati
1125 St. Gregory St.
Cincinnati, OH 45202

Athenaeum of Ohio
6616 Beechmont Avenue
Cincinnati, OH 45230
Sr. Deborah Harmeling, Librarian

Baldwin-Wallace College
275 Eastland Road
Berea, OH 44017
Dr. Patrick Scanlan, Director of Library

Belmont Technical College
120 Fox Shannon Place
St. Clairsville, OH 43950
Ms. Pam Pollard, Dir. Learning Resource Ctr.

Bluffton College
280 W. College Avenue
Bluffton, OH 45817
Mr. Harvey Hiebert, Librarian

Bowling Green State University
Bowling Green, OH 43403
Dr. Linda S. Dobb, Dean of
   University Libraries

Bowling Green State University Firelands
College
901 Rye Beach Road
Huron, OH 44839
Mr. William W. Currie, Head Librarian

Capital University
2199 E. Main Street
Columbus, OH 43209
Dr. Albert F. Maag, University Librarian

Case Western Reserve University
University Circle
Cleveland, OH 44106
Mr. Ray Metz, Acting Director
   of the Libraries

Cedarville College
Box 601
Cedarville, OH 45314
Mr. Lynn A. Brock, Director of Library Services

Central Ohio Technical College
1179 University Drive
Newark, OH 43055
Ms. Louisa Strziuso, Head Learning Resource
Center

Central State University
Wilberforce, OH 45384
Mr. George T. Johnson, Librarian

Chatfield College
20918 State Rt. 251
St. Martin, OH 45118
Mr. Jack McKee, Librarian

Cincinnati Bible College and Seminary
22700 Glenway Avenue
Cincinnati, OH 45204
Mr. James H. Lloyd, Director of Libraries

Cincinnati College of Mortuary Science
3860 Pacific Avenue
Cincinnati, OH 45207

Cincinnati State Technical and Community College
3520 Central Parkway
Cincinnati, OH 45223
Ms. Kathryn O'Gorman, Dir. Learning Resources
   Center

Circleville Bible College
Box 458
Circleville, OH 43113
Mrs. Joanne Wolford, Librarian

Clark State Community College
570 E. Leffels Lane, Box 570
Springfield, OH 45501
Nancy H. Schwerner, Head Librarian

Cleveland College of Jewish Studies
26500 Shaker Boulevard
Beachwood, OH 44122
Mrs. Jean Lettosky, Chief Librarian

Cleveland Institute of Art
11141 East Boulevard
Cleveland, OH 44106
Ms. Christine Rom, Librarian

Cleveland Institute of Music
11012 East Boulevard
Cleveland, OH 44106
Ms. Jean Toombs, Director of the Library

Cleveland State University
East 24th and Euclid Avenue
Cleveland, OH 44115
Ms. Hannelore B. Rader, Director of Libraries

College of Mount St. Joseph
5701 Delhi Road
Cincinnati, OH 45233
Ms. Anne W. Chase, Director of
     Information Services

College of Wooster
Wooster, OH 44691
Dr. Damon Hickey, Director of the Library

Columbus College of Art and Design
107 N. Ninth Street
Columbus, OH 43215
Ms. Chilin Yu, Librarian

Columbus State Community College
Box 609
Columbus OH 43216
Ms. Linda K. Landis, Dean
     Educational Resources Center

Cuyahoga Community College
700 Carnegie Avenue
Cleveland, OH 44115
Mr. Douglas A. Fox, Asst.
     VP Educational/Technical Resources

The Defiance College
701 N. Clinton Street
Defiance, OH 43512
Mr. Edward S. Warner, Librarian

Denison University
Granville, OH 43023
Mr. David M. Pilachowski,
     Director of Libraries

Dyke College
112 Prospect Avenue
Cleveland, OH 44115
Dr. Donna R. Trivison, Director Library
     Resource Center

Edison State Community College
1973 Edison Drive
Piqua, OH 45356
Ms. Mary Beth Aust-Keefer, Dir. Library and
     Audio/Visual Services

Franciscan University of Steubenville
Steubenville, OH 43952
Mrs. Ruth Lloyd, Librarian

Franklin University
201 S. Grant Avenue
Columbus, OH 43215
Mr. Allyn K. Ehrhardt, Librarian

God's Bible School and College
1810 Young Street
Cincinnati, OH 45210

Hebrew Union College-Jewish Institute of
Religion
Central Office
3101 Clifton Avenue
Cincinnati, OH 45220
Dr. Herbert C. Zafren, Director of Libraries

Heidelberg College
Tiffin, OH 44883
Mr. Ed G. Krakora, Director of Library

Hiram College
Hiram, OH 44234
Dr. Patricia L. Basu, Head Librarian

Hocking Technical College
3301 Hocking Parkway
Nelsonville, OH 45764
Ms. Marge Kramer, Head Librarian

Jefferson Technical College
4000 Sunset Boulevard
Steubenville, OH 43952
Mrs Lois Rekowski, Dir. Library Services

John Carroll University
Cleveland, OH 44118
Dr. Gorman L. Duffett, Director of the Library

Kent State University
Kent, OH 44242
Dr. Don L. Tolliver, Dean University
   Libraries/Media Services

Kent State University Ashtabula Campus
3325 W. 13th Street
Ashtabula, OH 44004
Mr. Kim N. Cook, Library Director

Kent State University East Liverpool Campus
400 East 4th Street
East Liverpool, OH 43920
Ms. Susan M. Weaver, Library Director

Kent State University Geauga Campus
14111 Claridon-Troy Road
Burton Twp. OH 44021
Ms. Lilith R. Kunkel, Dir. Library

Kent State University Salem Campus
2491 S R 45 South
Salem, OH 44460
Ms. Lilith R. Kunkel, Dir. Library

Kent State University Stark Campus
6000 Frank Avenue NW
Canton, OH 44720
Ms. Judith Ohles, Library Director

Kent State University Trumbull Campus
4314 Mahoning Avenue NW
Warren, OH 44483

Kent State University Tuscarawas Campus
University Drive NE
New Philadelphia, OH 44663
Mr. G. Michael Kobulnicky, Librarian

Kenyon College
Gambier, OH 43022
Mr. Paul M. Gherman, Director of Libraries

Kettering College of Medical Arts
3737 Southern Boulevard
Kettering, OH 45429
Mrs. Ellen L. Rohmiller, Director of the Library

Lake Erie College
391 W. Washington Street
Painesville, OH 44077
Christopher Bennett, Librarian

Lakeland Community College
7700 Clocktower Drive
Mentor, OH 44060
Ms. Mary Jo Magner, Director Library

Lima Technical College
4240 Campus Drive
Lima, OH 45804
Dr. Mohamed Zehery, Head Librarian

Lorain County Community College
1005 N. Abi Road
Elyria, OH 44035
Mr. Z. Loranth, Dir. Library-Instructional
   Media

Marion Technical College
1467 Mt. Vernon Avenue
Marion, OH 43302

Malone College
515 25th Street NW
Canton, OH 44709
Mr. R. Stanford Terhune, Jr., Director of
    Library Services

Marietta College
Marietta, OH 45750
Ms. Sandra B. Neyman, College Librarian

Medical College of Ohio
P.O. Box 10008
Toledo, OH 43699
Mr. David Boilard, Director of Library

Methodist Theological School in Ohio
3081 Columbus Pike
P. O. Box 1204
Delaware, OH 43015
Dr. Paul Schrodt, Librarian

Miami University
Oxford, OH 45056
Ms. Judith A. Sessions, Dean and
    University Librarian

Miami University Hamilton Campus
1601 Peck Boulevard
Hamilton, OH 45011
Ms. Rebecca Zartner, Head Librarian

Miami University Middletown Campus
4200 E. University Boulevard
Middletown, OH 45042
Mr. Joseph Phillips, Director of Regional Campus
    Library

Mount Carmel College of Nursing
127 S. Davis Avenue
Columbus, OH 43222

Mount Union College
1972 Clark Avenue
Alliance, OH 44601
Mr. Robert R. Garland, Librarian

Mount Vernon Nazarene College
Martinsburg Road
Mount Vernon, OH 43050
Mr. Richard L. Schuster, Librarian

Muskingum Area Technical College
1555 Newark Road
Zanesville, OH 43701
Ms. Shana Fair, Librarian

Muskingum College
New Concord, OH 43762
Mrs. Robin G. Hanson, Director of Library

North Central Technical College
2441 Kenwood Cir. Box 698
Mansfield, OH 44901
Ms. Sherri L. Edwards, Librarian

Northeastern Ohio Universities College of
Medicine
P.O. Box 95
Rootstown, OH 44272
Ms. Jean W. Sayre, Director/Medical Librarian

Northwest State Community College
22-600 SR 34 Rt 1 Box 246a
Archbold, OH 43502
(vacant), Head Librarian

Northwestern College
1441 North Cable Road
Lima, OH 45805

Notre Dame College
4545 College Road
South Euclid, OH 44121
Ms. Karen Zoller, Director of Library

Oberlin College
Oberlin, OH 44074
Dr. Raymond English, Director of Libraries

Ohio College of Podiatric Medicine
10515 Carnegie Avenue
Cleveland, OH 44106
Mrs. Judy A. Cowell, Librarian

Ohio Dominican College
1216 Sunbury Road
Columbus, OH 43219
Ms. Trisha Morris, Librarian

Ohio Northern University
Ada, OH 45810
Mr. Paul M. Logsdon, Librarian

The Ohio State University Agricultural
   Technical Institute
Wooster, OH 44691

The Ohio State University
Columbus, OH 43210
Dr. William J. Studer, Director of Libraries

The Ohio University State Lima Campus
4240 Campus Drive
Lima, OH 45804
Dr. Mohamed H. Zehery, Librarian

The Ohio State University Mansfield Campus
1680 University Drive
Mansfield, OH 44906
Ms. Sherri L. Edwards, Head Librarian

The Ohio State University Marion Campus
1465 Mount Vernon Avenue
Marion, OH 43302
Mr. David G. Evans, Librarian

The Ohio State University Newark Campus
University Drive
Newark, OH 43055
Ms. Louisa Straziuso, Head Learning Resources
Center

Ohio University
Athens, OH 45701
Dr. Hwa-Wei Lee, Dean of Libraries

Ohio University Chillicothe Campus
Chillicothe, OH 45601
Mr. Stanley Planton, Head Librarian

Ohio University Eastern Campus
St. Clairsville, OH 43950
Ms. Patricia E. Murphy, Director of Library

Ohio University Lancaster Campus
1570 Granville Pike
Lancaster, OH 43130
Ms. Susan K. Phillips, Librarian

Ohio University Zanesville Branch
Zanesville, OH 43701
Mrs. Shana Fair, Librarian

Ohio Wesleyan University
Delaware, OH 43015
Ms. Kathleen L. List, Librarian

Otterbein College
Westerville, OH 43081
Mrs. Lois F. Szudy, Director of the Library

Owens Community College
30335 Oregon Road
P.O. Box 10000
Toledo, OH 43699
Mr. Thomas Sink, Director

Payne Theological Seminary
1230 Wilberforce Clifton Rd.
Wilberforce, OH 45384
Mr. Dale Balsbaugh, Head Librarian

Pontifical College Josephinum
7625 N. High
Columbus, OH 43235
Mr. Peter Veracka, Librarian

Rabbinical College of Telshe
28400 Euclid Avenue
Wickliffe, OH 44092

Saint Mary Seminary
28700 Euclid Avenue
Wickliffe, OH 44092
Mr. Alan Rome, Librarian

Shawnee State University
940 Second Street
Portsmouth, OH 45662
Ms. Teresa Midkiff,
    Dir. Library/Media Services

Sinclair Community College
444 W. Third Street
Dayton, OH 45402
Mrs. Virginia Peters, Dir. Learning
    Resources Center

Southern State Community College
200 Hobart Drive
Hillsboro, OH 45133
Mr. Louis Mays, Library Coordinator

Stark Technical College
6200 Frank Avenue NW
Canton, OH 44720

Terra State Community College
2830 Napoleon Road
Freemont, OH 43420
Ms. Mary Broestl, Librarian

Tiffin University
155 Miami Street
Tiffin, OH 44883
Miss Frances A. Fleet, Head Librarian

Trinity Lutheran Seminary
2199 E. Main St.
Columbus, OH 43209
Rev. Richard H. Mintel, Dir. Library Services

Union Institute
440 E. McMillan Street
Cincinnati, OH 45206

United Theological Seminary
1810 Harvard Boulevard
Dayton, OH 45406
Rev. Elmer J. O'Brien, Librarian

The University of Akron
The Buchtel Common
Akron, OH 44325
Dr. Delmus E. Williams, Dean University Libraries

University of Akron-Wayne College
10470 Smucker Road
Orrville, OH 44667
Mrs. Barbara Geisey, Librarian

University of Cincinnati
Cincinnati, OH 45221
Dr. David F. Kohl., Dean & University Librarian

University of Cincinnati-Clermont College
4200 Clermont College Drive
Batavia, OH 45103
Mr. Frederick Marcotte, Senior Librarian

University of Cincinnati-Raymond
Walters College
9555 Plainfield Road
Blue Ash, OH 45236

University of Dayton
300 College Park
Dayton, OH 45469
Dr. Edward D. Garten,
    Dir. University Libraries

The University of Findlay
1000 North Main Street
Findlay, OH 45840
Mr. Robert W. Schirmer, Head Librarian

University of Rio Grande
Rio Grande, OH 45674
Mr. J. David Mauer, Director of the Library

University of Toledo
2801 West Bancroft
Toledo, OH 43606
Mr. Leslie W. Sheridan, Dir.
    University Libraries

Urbana University
Urbana, OH 43078
Mr. Hugh Durbin, University Librarian

Ursuline College
2550 Lander Road
Cleveland, OH 44124
Ms. Betsey Belkin, Director of Library

Walsh University
3220 Easton Street NW
Canton, OH 44720
Mr. Daniel S. Suvak, Librarian

Washington State Community College
710 Colegate Drive
Marietta, OH 45750

Wilberforce University
Wilberforce, OH 45384
Mrs. Jean K. Mulhern, Chief Librarian

Wilmington College
Wilmington, OH 45177
Ms. Jennilou S. Grotevant, Library Director

Winebrenner Theological Seminary
Findlay, OH 45840
Dr. J. Harvey Gossard, Dir. of Library Services

Wittenberg University
Ward St Wittenberg Avenue
Springfield, OH 45501
(vacant), Director of the Library

Wright State University
Colonel Glenn Highway
Dayton, OH 45435
Mr. Arnold Hirshon, Director, University
Libraries

Wright State University Lake Campus
7600 State Route 703
Celina, OH 45822

Xavier University
Victory Parkway
Cincinnati, OH 45207
Dr. Jo Anne L. Young, Director of Libraries

Youngstown State University
Youngstown, OH 44455
Dr. David C. Genaway, University Librarian

APPENDIX B

Questionnaire

This questionnaire explores the training given public services staff. For the purpose of this questionnaire, *Public services staff* will be defined as those library employees who are employed in the Circulation and Reference departments. *Customer service* is defined as all contact with patrongs by the public services staff employees. Included in this definition would be directional assistance, telephone calls, written requests for assistance, reference help, and the many other contacts between the library's employees and patrongs. *Training* is defined as formal programs of instruction in customer service offered to public services staff by library or institution administration.

Please answer the following questions. Thank you for completing this questionnaire.

1. Is any formal customer service training offered by the library administration, branch, or department, to staff of public services departments? If not, please proceed to Question 15.

	n	%
_____ yes _____ no	YES 43	51%
	NO 42	49%

Customer Service Training during NEW Employee Orientation

2. Below is a list of content items that might be a part of customer service training for NEW employees. Please check all the items that are part of your training program.

	n	%
_____ the library's mission	34	79%
_____ the employee's role in that mission	29	67%
_____ the role of the employee's department in that mission	21	49%
_____ library policies	42	98%
_____ location of primary resources and services	40	93%
_____ emergency procedures	32	74%
_____ communications skills	20	47%
_____ making referrals to other departments or employees	35	81%
_____ telephone etiquette	32	75%
_____ employee demeanor (smile, patience, friendliness)	30	70%
_____ how to positively meet the customer's expectations	25	58%
_____ treating staff as patrons	13	30%
_____ dealing with irate or frustrated patrons	29	67%
_____ complaint procedures	26	60%
_____ helping patrons with special needs	19	44%
_____ equipment training	37	86%
_____ problem solving skills	14	33%
_____ other	4	9%
_____ none of the above	0	0%

3. Are prepared training materials used for this customer service training? If no, please proceed to question 5.

	n	%
_____ yes _____ no	YES 27	63%
	NO 15	35%
	N/A 1	2%

4. In what format are the prepared training materials? (Please check all that apply):

	n	%
_____ written	27	100%
_____ audio tapes	1	4%
_____ video tapes	4	15%
_____ computer programs	0	0%
_____ other	4	15%

5. What type of instruction is used: (Please check all that
    apply):   n   %
    _____ classroom instruction   9   21%
    _____ individual training by supervisor   40   93%
    _____ role-playing   3   7%
    _____ computer-assisted instruction   2   5%
    _____ unsupervised instruction involving written audio,   16   37%
              or video material,

6. Who provides the customer service training? (Please check all that
    apply):   n   %
    _____ Circulation or Reference Department supervisor   35   81%
    _____ Human Resources/Training inside library   5   12%
    _____ Human Resources/Training of parent institution   6   14%
    _____ outside consultant   3   7%
    _____ other   11   26%

7. Is the customer service training mandatory or optional?   n   %
    _____ mandatory _____ optional   MANDATORY 39   91%
                                               OPTIONAL 2   4.5%
                                                    N/A 2   4.5%

8. After new employee training is finished, is further customer service training
    available to Public Services staff employees? If no, please proceed to question
    15.   n   %
    _____ yes _____ no   YES 27   63%
                                                     NO 14   33%
                                                     N/A 2   4%

9. Below is a list of content items that might be a part of continuing customer
    service training for regular employees. Please check all the items that are part
    of your training program.   n   %
    _____ the library's mission   12   44%
    _____ the employee's role in that mission   12   44%
    _____ the role of the employee's department in that mission 7   16%
    _____ library policies   23   85%
    _____ location of primary resources and services   16   59%
    _____ emergency procedures   17   63%
    _____ communications skills   12   44%
    _____ making referrals to other departments or employees 13   48%
    _____ telephone etiquette   12   44%
    _____ employee demeanor (smile, patience, friendliness)   12   44%
    _____ how to positively meet the customer's expectations 18   67%
    _____ treating staff as patrons   7   26%
    _____ dealing with irate or frustrated patrons   17   63%
    _____ complaint procedures   16   60%
    _____ helping patrons with special needs   14   52%

_____ equipment training	19	70%
_____ problem solving skills	13	48%
_____ other	5	12%
_____ none of the above	0	0%

10. Are prepared training materials used for continuing customer service training? If no, please proceed to question 12.

	n	%
_____ yes _____ no	YES 13	48%
	NO 13	48%
	N/A 1	4%

11. In what format are the prepared training materials for continuing customer service training? (Please check all that apply):

	n	%
_____ written	13	100%
_____ audio tapes	2	15%
_____ video tapes	4	31%
_____ computer programs	1	8%
_____ other	4	31%

12. What type of instruction is used for continuing customer service training?

	n	%
_____ classroom instruction	12	44%
_____ individual training by supervisor	23	85%
_____ role-playing	1	4%
_____ computer-assisted instruction	2	7%
_____ unsupervised instruction involving written, audio, or video material	8	30%

13. Who provides the continuing customer service training? (Please check all that apply):

	n	%
_____ Circulation Department Supervisor	19	70%
_____ Reference Department supervisor	21	77%
_____ Human Resources/Training inside library	4	15%
_____ Human Resource/Training of parent institution	6	22%
_____ outside consultant	7	26%
_____ other	8	30%

14. Is the continuing customer service training mandatory or optional?

	n	%
_____ mandatory _____ optional	MANDATORY 20	74%
	OPTIONAL 7	26%

15. Are funds available for library staff members who wish to seek
     further training outside the library system?   n   %
     ———— yes   ———— no   YES 35   76.5%
                                                        NO 19   22%
                                                        N/A 1   1.5%

16. If your library has a formal customer service training program, who was
     involved in the formation of the program? (Please check all that apply):

		n	%
————	library administration	26	60%
————	department heads	19	44%
————	professional librarians	26	60%
————	support staff	19	44%
————	human resources department of library	3	7%
————	human resources department of parent institution	3	7%
————	other institution departments	1	2%
————	outside consultants	1	2%
————	other	2	5%

REFERENCES

Achieving Breakthrough Service in Libraries. 1994. [Videocassette]. Cambridge, MA: Kathleen
    Gilroy Associates.
Allen, G. and B. Allen. 1992. "Service Orientation as a Selection Criterion for Public Services
    Librarians." *Journal of Library Administration* 16(4): 67-76.
Arthur, G. 1990. *Customer Service Training for Public Services Staff at Temple University's
    Central Library System.* Unpublished microfiche, Temple University, Philadelphia.
————. 1994. "Customer Service Training in Academic Libraries." *The Journal of Academic
    Librarianship* 20: 219-222.
Association of Research Libraries. 1991. *Information Desks in ARL Libraries.* (Spec Kit 172).
    Washington, DC: Author.
Azzolini, M. C. and J. H. & Lingle. 1993. "Internal Service Performance." *Quality* 32: 38-40.
Becker, W. S. and Wellins, R. S. 1990. "Customer-service Perceptions and Reality." *Training and
    Development Journal* 44: 49-51.
Berry, L. C., Zeithaml, V. A. and A. Parasuraman. 1990. "Five Imperatives for Improving Service
    Quality." *Sloan Management Review* 29-38.
Bessler, J. M. 1994. *Putting Service into Library Staff Training.* Chicago: American Library
    Association.
Dolphin, P. 1986. "Interpersonal Skills Training for Library Staff." *Library Association Record*
    88: 134.
Guilfoyle, M. C. 1985. "Computer-assisted Training for Student Library Assistants." *Journal of
    Academic Librarianship* 10: 333-336.
Kotler, P. and S. J. Levy. 1969. "Broadening the Concept of Marketing." *Journal of Marketing*
    33: 10-15.
Parasuraman, A., Berry, L. L. and V. Zeithaml. 1991. "Understanding, Measuring and Improving
    Service Quality: Findings from a Multi-phase Research Program." Pp. 253-268 in *Service
    Quality: Multidisciplinary and Multinational Perspectives.* Lexington, MA: D.C. Heath.

Rawlins, S. M. 1982. "Technology and the Personal Touch: Computer-assisted Instruction for Library Student Workers." *The Journal of Academic Librarianship* 8: 26-29.

Roberts, N. and T. Konn. 1989. "Continuing Education and Training for Academic Library Staff." *Journal of Librarianship* 21: 109-128.

Rodenhouse, M. P. ed. 1996. *1996 Higher Education Directory*. Falls Church, VA: Higher Education Publications.

St. Clair, G. 1993. *Customer Service in the Information Environment*. New Jersey: Bowker Saur.

Schlesinger, L. A. and J. L. Heskett. 1991. "The Service-driven Service Company." *Harvard Business Review* 71-81.

Vocino, M., Jr. and M. H. Kellogg. 1987. *Student Employees in Academic Libraries*. Unpublished microfiche, University of Rhode Island, Kingston.

Walters, S. 1994. *Customer Service: A How-To-Do-It Manual For Librarians*. New York: Neal Schuman.

PROFESSIONALS WITHOUT DEGREES:
RURAL LIBRARIANS DEFINING THEMSELVES

Mary C. Bushing

BACKGROUND TO THE STUDY

The library profession is at the center of massive cultural, educational and economic change as the "information society" sorts out the implications of information as commodity, electronics as format, and professional specialization as criterion for excellence. Rather than libraries and librarians becoming less important, they appear to be gaining in both visibility and importance as they increasingly serve as intermediaries between the electronic technologies necessary to access information and the end-users of such information. This enabling function has further complicated the library environment and confused the role, function and identity of the librarian. The levels of service demanded by even the least sophisticated client are ever increasing. Librarians in academic, school, special and public libraries in the smallest as well as the largest communities or institutions must have advanced specialized skills and technological knowledge in addition to management and

Advances in Library Administration and Organization,
Volume 15, pages 103-164.
Copyright © 1997 by JAI Press Inc.
All rights of reproduction in any form reserved.
ISBN: 0-7623-0371-9

public relations abilities in order to make the most of the resources available to them. Libraries and librarians are at the center of the information age trying to keep pace with rapid changes in technology and the implications of the information explosion while sorting out their own roles and identities.

Libraries and the librarians who staff them have acquired a new prominence both because of the effects of technology and because of the expanding expectations of library users of all ages and educational backgrounds. Increasingly, smaller rural libraries are expected to be simply miniature versions of the most sophisticated research libraries. These libraries are no longer viewed as the traditional quiet and convenient popular reading centers they once were believed to be. Questions concerning the quality of services and the ability of staff to provide access to an ever-increasing and ever-changing body of information have arisen along with the increased expectations of the citizens of smaller communities. State libraries, library systems and consortia, the American Library Association (ALA), state and regional library associations, graduate library science program directors, and rural librarians themselves are struggling with continuing education delivery, certification, and quality content for rural librarians. The challenge is to provide continuing education and basic training that will enable rural librarians to develop their personal skills and abilities, along with professional identities, to assure their success in this more demanding environment. The efforts to improve the quality and delivery of educational opportunities to individuals working as rural librarians have been further complicated by the culture of the profession itself.

The issues embedded in efforts to educate, train and empower individuals working in rural libraries are complicated. Although a Master of Library Science (MLS) degree is considered by the profession to be the entry level credential for librarians, according to data from the U.S. Department of Education's National Center for Education Statistics (1994a), relating to 8,946 central libraries (not bookmobiles or branches), 57 percent are managed and operated by individuals without the professional entry level credential. In fact, because there are no ALA accredited baccalaureate programs in library science, these individuals not only do not have a masters degree in library or information science, they usually do not have any academic preparation for librarianship except their experiences as students and general library users.

While ALA has been accrediting library school programs since 1925, importance and control were added to the MLS requirement in 1951 when ALA issued the "Standards for Accreditation of Library Education Programs" and endorsed the Master of Library Science (MLS) degree as the first level of professional credentialing (American Library Association Planning Committee 1989). Since that time, the term *professional librarian* has meant one with such a degree. The accrediting structure for the MLS programs established a credentialing system based upon the attainment of a specific level (graduate) and type (library) of university degree. This requirement placed an emphasis upon the formal, theoretical, and specialized knowledge base of the profession rather than upon the practical, on-the-job knowledge which is what is known and observed by the public. The effect of this emphasis upon the formal graduate preservice model of preparation for librarianship has resulted in a caste system within the profession (Brugh and Beede 1976). The distinctions between those with the MLS degree and those without it have separated the "professional librarians" from the "others" who often serve as librarians in rural settings. The individuals without the MLS degree report feeling like "second class citizens" within the profession. They are reticent to get involved or to assert themselves within the profession because of prevailing attitudes despite the fact that they are the only librarians in almost half of the public libraries in the country.

While the profession of librarianship continues to require an MLS as the minimum level of preparation for sanctioned practice and recognition by other librarians, it is not now true, (nor has it ever been true in the United States), that the MLS is recognized by society as that which distinguishes librarians from others, nor is it recognized outside of the profession that such a degree is what qualifies an individual to practice librarianship (Miller 1989). As noted by Hanks (1991) when arguing for a new standard for professional entrance into librarianship, librarians with accredited MLS degrees did not hold a monopoly in the arena of practice at mid-century when the accreditation standards were implemented, and they have not been able to establish such a monopoly in succeeding years (p. 8). Many individuals without the MLS degree practice librarianship in the United States, particularly in schools and public libraries. Economic factors such as the fact that the small libraries and the communities they serve cannot afford to pay librarians with a masters degree (Vavrek 1989) complicate the situation.

Nancy Busch, in her 1990 study of recruitment and retention of rural librarians, said that it is necessary for the library and information profession to "increase its knowledge about those among its ranks who practice in the majority of the nation's public libraries" (p. 2), and it is these small libraries that constitute the largest segment of public library administrative units. Heasley and Preston (1989) note that the fact that more than 57 million people live in non-metropolitan America has helped to make the scope of the "rural librarian problem" more visible to the profession (p. 2). As a result, there has developed a realization that the preparation and education of these librarians must be more comprehensively addressed. There has been a growing awareness within the profession of the need to find practical solutions to the reality of rural librarianship. Terry Weech reported in 1980, when addressing public library standards and rural library services, that the area of adequate staffing for rural libraries was the third most frequently noted area of concern of state library agencies. While technology infrastructures may well be at the top of agency concerns now, technology issues are not separate from issues about adequate staffing for rural libraries but directly related to such human resource concerns.

The Meaning of Rural

Although rural libraries and librarians have been discussed for decades, agreement has still not been reached about what group of libraries constitute those that are rural. The information about these smaller libraries has not been consistently gathered and communicated until recently. Gradually, the national program for the collection of standardized statistics for public libraries through the National Center for Education Statistics in the U.S. Office of Education's Office of Educational Research and Improvement has greatly improved the quality, reliability and comparability of the statistics from all fifty states and the District of Columbia. The statistics generated through this data collection program have made the rural library situation more real and understandable because it provided the data required to compare the circumstances and resources available to residents of communities of all sizes in all parts of the country.

While this data is extremely valuable, rural libraries along with other rural service entities, have an identity problem because of the difficulty in determining a precise definition for the term *rural*. The difficulty in defining this term is not unique to this project. "The word rural lacks precision in everyday use because it is so comprehensive yet so imprecise" (Hobbs and Dillman 1982), and the definitions range across diverse disciplines from agriculture to psychology, and from demographics to social work. In 1982, rural psychologists Jeanine Bosak and Baron Perlman reviewed 178 sources in rural psychology and counseling literature in an attempt to determine the prevailing definition of rural. They categorized the use of the term rural into four major categories but concluded that a more precise definition was needed to make the term useful and to make research results comparable. As used in the United States, the word rural has meant "areas of low population density, small absolute size, and relative isolation, where the major economic base was agricultural production and where the way of life was reasonably homogeneous and differentiated from that of other sectors of society" (Bealer, Willits and Kuvlesky 1978, p. 339). This definition includes a demographic or ecological concept, an occupational component and a sociocultural aspect, but this is not the only definition of rural in use. For some, rural refers to anyplace that is not urban or anyplace with population densities below a specific level. Fitchen (1991) explains the difficulty of defining rural in the following manner:

> The official definition assigned to rural America is a definition by exclusion: Essentially, that which is not metropolitan America is rural America. According to the U.S. Bureau of the Census, a "metropolitan statistical area" is a central city of at least 50,000 people or an urbanized area consisting of 50,000 or more people in a city (or cities) and the surrounding counties that are economically tied to it. Rural technically refers to the "population outside incorporated or unincorporated places with more than 2,500 people and/or outside urbanized areas" (Fuguitt, Brown and Beale 1989, p. 6). Rural America,

then, is officially just a residual from urban or metropolitan, leaving it less than clear what rural really is. The very existence of a rural America is thus contingent upon an urban America (p. 247).

Some rural areas are not agricultural in nature but are merely bedroom communities for urban centers where the majority of the residents are employed in non-agricultural enterprises either in the metropolitan center or within smaller communities. As is evident, there are no standard definitions of the term rural and therefore it is important for anyone referring to a rural community to define what is meant specifically by the term in a particular context.

Within the public library world, there are two population based definitions commonly used for the term rural library. The first is that used for purposes of the Federal Library Services and Construction Act (Osbourn 1973, p. 9) which defines rural libraries as those serving communities with populations of 10,000 or less. In 1986, Herbert Goldhor suggested a further clarification of this definition for a rural library by stating that it is one which "serves fewer than 10,000 people and is located in a county which either has fewer than 150 persons per square mile or has over eighty percent of its land in farms" (p. 15). The second commonly used definition for rural library is that often used by the American Library Association. In this definition, a town or service area of 25,000 or less is considered rural. These definitions are both useful and have applications. These definitions, however, serve to illustrate the relativity of any definition of rural that might be used by social scientists.

Libraries serving populations of 25,000 or less still seem to be large to those who live in the 17 (34%) states with population densities of less than 50 people per square mile and with few metropolitan areas. These states are: Arizona, Alaska, Arkansas, Colorado, Idaho, Kansas, Maine, Montana, Nebraska, Nevada, New Mexico, North Dakota, Oklahoma, Oregon, South Dakota, Utah and Wyoming (Bureau of the Census 1994). The 25,000 designation also does not speak to the situation in another 11 states, that is, Alabama, Illinois, Indiana, Iowa, Minnesota, Missouri, New Hampshire, New York, Vermont, Washington, and Wisconsin, with higher total population densities but with a large part of their populations spread across hundreds of much smaller communities. According to *Public Libraries in the United States: 1992* (National Center for Education Statistics 1994b) which divides public libraries into eleven groups by populations served, more than 40 percent of the public libraries in even these 11 states serve populations of less than 5,000 residents. Libraries serving 5,000 or fewer residents represent almost half of the total public library (44.7%) administrative units and are scattered throughout the 50 states.

Thus, in 28 (56%) of the states, either as a function of population density or as a function of population distribution or settlement patterns, there are large numbers of small libraries serving less than 5,000 people. For these states, rural means something smaller than communities of 25,000 or even 10,000 residents. The National Center for Education Statistics (1994a) reported that in 1992 there were 4,000 central libraries with service areas of 5,000 or fewer residents. These libraries represent a high percentage of the total number of libraries in the United States, are a significant proportion of the public libraries in more than half of the states, and are more likely than the next two larger categories (those serving 10,000 or less and those serving up to 25,000 residents) to have librarians without formal graduate library science education. As a result, this project, a rural public library was defined as one having a service area of 5,000 or fewer residents. The smaller communities served by these libraries are often located at some distance from MSA's (Metropolitan Statistical Area) and at least some of the economic base is agricultural. Less than 9 percent of the librarians in these libraries have an MLS degree (National Center for Education Statistics 1994b) and most of them have little or no academic preparation for the professional responsibilities and roles they have assumed within the library and the community.

Professionalization of Librarians

Librarianship, whether technically a profession or not, has routinely been referred to as such. Particularly during the thirty years immediately following the 1951 graduate accreditation standards, librarians and sociologists engaged in ongoing debates about whether or not librarianship actually fit the definition of a profession. Some sociologists argued that it was a semi-profession typical of other semi-professions with more bureaucratic structure and less individual autonomy, a higher percentage of women than men, and a shorter training period along with a less specialized body of knowledge to be learned (Etzioni 1969). While "the 1960s marked a watershed of sociological writings on the professions" (Freidson 1994, p. 13), in more recent years, the distinctions concerning the definition of a profession or semi-profession have been less frequently debated in sociological literature. According to Elliot Freidson, the definition of the term profession and our understanding of the process by which individuals and occupational groups achieve the status of a profession is becoming more of a phenomenologically defined process rather than a dichotomy which defines an ideal against which to measure occupations. He stresses societal values, personal commitment, and client trust as important aspects of being a professional rather than the economic, political, or educational power structures which have previously been used by sociologists in defining professions. These characteristics of a professional fit rural non-degreed librarians as well as MLS librarians.

Increasingly the discussions surrounding professionalism have recognized this dynamic or phenomenological nature of professionalization. Cyril Houle (1980), in his landmark book *Continuing Learning in the Professions* noted that "the professionalizing process is complex" (p. 34) and that the process for the individual is one of *becoming* rather than one of learning how to do something. Defining professionalization as a continuing dynamic process has changed the debates from ones for or against occupations as professions to debates about the extent to which particular individuals are or are not professionals. Sociologists and educators view the process of professionalization as acculturation. This acceptance of and identification with a set of values and behaviors occurs in subtle ways resulting in a state of mind that is characteristic of a member of a particular profession. Studies on the process of identification or acculturation to a profession stress the importance of any formal pre-service educational period, the continuing education culture and other contacts with the profession (Becker and Carper 1956; Clark and Corcoran 1984; Weiss 1981; White and Macklin 1970). These illustrate the complexity of the process of professionalization and identification with a profession and its values.

Thus, while the profession continues to use the MLS degree from an ALA accredited program as the minimum qualification to enter the profession, there are thousands of smaller public libraries in the United States with librarians without such a degree. In addition, it is unlikely for a variety of reasons that the percentage of MLS librarians will improve in these libraries in the near future although the demands by the public for ever increasing and ever more sophisticated services are constantly growing. Many library educators and leaders recognize the need to find the most effective ways to assist these individuals in achieving appropriate levels of professionalization despite the caste system within the profession. The attainment of a professional identity and the resulting self-confidence within the librarian role may be one of the ways by which rural librarians achieve effectiveness. The problem is to identify the ways in which rural librarians actually do learn to define themselves as *librarians* and to function within the role of a professional so that those responsible for human resource development in libraries can implement successful strategies.

Purpose

The purpose of this study was to identify the elements in educational events, consulting encounters, or job circumstances that a selected group of rural librarians without MLS degrees believed to be significant factors contributing to the development of their professional identity as librarians. These experiences were examined to identify common factors or patterns that might assist those responsible for the education of rural librarians to design educational events and expend resources in the most effective manner. Two specific objectives were addressed in order to bring together the key elements rural librarians perceive to have affected their professionalization and identification with the profession. These were: (1) the identification of significant career events that contributed to the acquisition of a professional identify; and (2) the identification of elements in effective continuing education events that contributed to a professional identity. Additionally, personal characteristics necessary for effectiveness in the librarian role were identified by the individuals in order to clarify their definition of what it means to be a librarian.

The complexity of the library environment and the large number of individuals who have not had the acculturation and professionalization opportunities afforded by a graduate library education, make it important for library educators to identify alternate ways of providing models of professional librarianship, of enhancing professional self-confidence, and of assisting individuals in identifying with the profession in a positive manner. Issues about quality assurance for the content and delivery of continuing library education have long been concerns of the profession and the American Library Association. Within ALA, there are now more than 40 committees, round tables and other groups addressing professional education, continuing education and education delivery methods (American Library Association 1995). Regional and state library associations also devote considerable resources to educational efforts on behalf of their members and would-be members. Although there is a renewed emphasis upon both voluntary and mandatory certification for personnel in libraries of all types and sizes (Hanks 1992) and specific competencies are being defined for functions throughout the profession, the content and the operational skills needed for work in libraries are constantly changing and evolving. For those without the MLS, basic competencies are taught through a variety of programs and delivery mechanisms including conference programs, workshops and week-long resident programs and institutes.

Librarianship has an "event" based continuing education culture and tradition (Smith 1992; Stone 1974; Weingand 1992), and continuing education providers usually evaluate these individual educational events as distinct offerings rather than as part of the larger process of professionalization. Further complicating the evaluation process for these continuing education workshops, courses, or institutes is the great variation in the educational levels and library experiences of the participants. Although a series of continuing education offerings may be developed as part of a long range plan for a state, regional system, or association, evaluation of such events is focused on the delivery of each unit rather than upon the cumulative effect such offerings have had in the professional lives of individuals. Evaluations of the effectiveness of teaching and delivery methods, learning, retention, and concept implementation are sometimes conducted. In most instances, however, good speakers and popular topics and methods are identified by means of the typical one page evaluation form. Specific events or circumstances are evaluated rather than the effect these events have had upon the gradual professionalization process since the identification with the profession occurs through time rather than as a one-time event.

The identification of the elements in educational and career events or circumstances that have been effective in bringing about personal identification with the profession and professional self-confidence for those who do not have the MLS credential could provide library educators with useful information. Such information might be used in the development of educational programs, consulting models and career orientation designed to help rural librarians achieve a sense of belonging to the profession, despite their lack of an MLS. The professionalization process as outlined by Houle (1980) does not consist merely of mastery of content or competencies in operations. Such basic information is not what distinguishes successful professionals from less than successful individuals. While course content and the transfer of training to the job performance are both important, it is the professionalization process as identified by Houle (1980) and others which has long term effects upon the performance, attitudes and ultimate success of individuals. The professionalization process includes, among other things, identification with the values of the profession, critical thinking, reflection-in-action (Schön 1983, 1987, 1991), and self-enhancement or continuing education and growth (Becker and Carper 1956; Bucher and Strauss 1961; Cervero 1988; Houle 1980; Sherlock and Morris 1967). All of these aspects of the professionalization process contribute to the ability of rural librarians to be responsive and effective as leaders and change agents within an ever changing environment.

Regardless of the content, adult education plays an important role in the professionalization process and the development of self-actualizing (Maslow 1954; Rogers 1969) individuals. When one observes or participates in continuing education and basic certification training for rural librarians, it becomes clear that the most important and powerful thing being learned is often not the factual content of the specific event, but rather the powerful messages, embedded in the belief structure of the teacher (Apps 1982), about the value and role of the students. It is the affirmation of the individual in their professional role of librarian that may be the most valuable and long lasting outcome of memorable educational events. Therefore, a key aspect of educational offerings for rural librarians might be the manner in which and the degree to which the event contributes to the professional identity of the individuals. While delivering the discipline's content and using technology to solve some of the problems associated with distance and remoteness, education efforts for rural librarians might focus on issues of professional identity and personal empowerment that will have long term effectiveness within the communities they serve and within the profession. The contributions, insights and active involvement of these individual non-MLS librarians are essential to the profession in order for libraries of all sizes and in all geographic locations to be active players in the evolution of the information society.

In order to identify the elements in educational events or other circumstances that might be effectively implemented for rural librarians, one should look to what rural librarians themselves have experienced as professionalizing and important in their efforts to define their roles as librarians. The solutions to the "rural librarian problem" lie not in assuming what might be best for those in rural libraries and rural communities, but in determining what those who are effective in serving those communities believe to be elements that make a difference. Barron and Curran (1980), when discussing the assessment of the information needs of rural people, expressed ideas that might apply just as well to the library community as it assesses the needs of rural librarians:

> Too many of us mistakenly believe we know what the problems are. Too many of us really believe we know a community ... and through osmosis, learn the needs of its people. We fantasize that all small communities are about the same, just as we are sure that all big cities are about the same and share the same basic characteristics and problems. It is important to repeat that we must d-mythologize [sic] views of rural conditions and replace intuitive and impressionistic views with an understanding of real conditions. Librarians and educators are going to have to do some unlearning, some unfreezing of assumptions, if they are ever to understand rural problems. And understanding is just the first step (p. 630).

How, then, does one understand the rural librarian? How does one attempt to do some unfreezing of assumptions or some unlearning so as to better understand the situation of librarians in rural communities? If the profession is to provide opportunities for rural librarians to learn the theoretical and practical content of librarianship, as well as providing an environment where professionalization and personal empowerment is possible, then the profession must first understand the situation from the viewpoint of those involved. Busch (1990) suggests in her study of rural librarians that "studies that focus on the use of face-to-face, in-depth interviews or case studies are recommended in order to better address and identify the complexity of factors likely to influence recruitment and retention" (p. 231). Such studies may also provide a better understanding of the process of *becoming* a librarian once one has been recruited. Those who have become effective rural librarians may have insights, experiences, and observations that could enlighten continuing education providers and trainers. Jack Glazier (1992b) reminds researchers that "research is not just a top-down activity, it is also a bottom-up activity.... qualitative research is a useful bottom-up approach to research and inquiry in the social sciences" (p. 1).

This study, therefore, used a naturalistic approach to solicit the opinions and experiences of 26 individuals working as librarians in six states. The libraries are located in communities of less than 5,000 residents. The librarians were identified as appropriate rural librarians by consultants within the state library agency, by the researcher through contact with the librarians in classes, or through a combination of the two methods. Data collection was done through interviews, a personal data form and a follow-up mailing used to verify major themes in the study. The interviews were analyzed through a constant comparative method with adaptations made as appropriate and as indicated by the emerging data. The National Center for Education Statistics' national public library statistics database (1994a) was used to verify or clarify information obtained from the participants.

Definitions

The following definitions explain the meaning of key terms. Some of these definitions are the same as those used by the National Center for Education Statistics' report (1994b).

Continuing education. A credit or non-credit educational opportunity provided either beyond the formal preservice preparation for a particular function, or educational opportunities provided instead of formal preservice education. Continuing education may be a one-time event such as a workshop, a series of offerings to constitute a course, a residential institute, a program within a conference or other educational structure, or individualized instruction. A commitment to continuing education is one of the characteristics of a professional person identified by Houle (1980).

Librarian. A person who does paid work and fulfills job responsibilities to provide library services to a client group. Such "work usually requires professional training and skill in the theoretical and scientific aspects of library work, as distinct from its mechanical or clerical aspect" (National Center for Education Statistics 1994b).

Mentoring. A relationship in which an experienced, trusted person teaches, guides, and develops a novice in an organization or profession.

MLS. The MLS or Master of Library Science degree from an ALA accredited program is considered by the national, state and regional library associations to be the minimum credential for professional librarians in the United States.

Networking. The process of establishing contacts, professional and social, to provide support, information, and friendship in the context of an occupation or function. Established networks may be invoked as needed for many purposes by any member.

Population served. The number of people in the geographic area for which a public library has been established to offer services and from which the library derives income, usually through real estate and personal property tax revenues.

Professional identity. Self definition and identification with a particular professional or occupational group with characteristics defined by the group and the individual.

Public library. A local, tax-supported institution established according to state law and organized for the purpose of delivering library and information services to the general public. A public library is an entity that provides, at the very least, an organized collection of materials, paid staff to provide services, an established schedule by which such services are offered, and facilities to support such collection, staff, and schedule (National Center for Education Statistics 1994b).

Rural. A community with a population of 5,000 or less, located outside of a Metropolitan Statistical Area (MSA). This definition of rural is much more restrictive than the definition usually used to define rural libraries.

Stereotype. Learned collective perception used by society to represent and categorize a group of people. Stereotypes may be accurate or inaccurate, complimentary or derogatory. Stereotypes may have some accurate elements within an otherwise exaggerated portrayal. Elements contributing to the development and continuation of a stereotype are difficult to define and isolate.

The research reported in this study rests on a number of assumptions concerning librarians, librarianship and the research design. The first assumption is that the professionalization of rural librarians without an MLS degree is important for the public libraries and the communities where these individuals work, for the profession as a whole, and for the personal development and professional identity of the individuals themselves. Second, the qualitative research design with multi case (26) studies does not mean that the experiences of librarians in this study nor the findings reported here are generalizable to the whole population of rural librarians. Rather, it is expected that the experiences of these individuals may help to clarify the issues in the professionalization experience of rural librarians. While the study reports some of the ways in which these librarians are typical or atypical of the general population of rural librarians, this information is intended to express the degree to which these individuals might be typical or similar to the whole population. It is not intended to imply that they are statistically representative of all rural librarians without an MLS degree in communities of 5,000 or fewer residents. The population was limited by the selection process for inclusion. The six states included were selected because of convenience and because they provide a broad representation of models for certification, continuing education and commitment to rural librarian training. Because it was not the intention of this study to consider individuals without continuing education and other career experiences upon which they might reflect, no attempt was made to interview individuals judged not to be attempting to develop a professional identity. Additionally it is important to note that qualitative interviewing may provide a data memory bias due to the inability of interviewees to provide certain types of information from previous events or to articulate their experiences and opinions.

DESIGN OF THE STUDY AND DESCRIPTION OF PARTICIPANTS

Study Design

The study was carried out during 1994 and 1995. Availability and criterion-based selection was implemented to identify individuals from libraries of specific sizes and in specific states to be included. Individuals were included based upon the following criteria: (1) no formal academic preparation for librarianship (no MLS); (2) currently employed as the library director in a public library serving a population of less than 5,000; (3) considered by state agency consultants, regional system personnel or the author to be articulate, effective individuals who fulfill the role of information professional within their communities; and (4) willing to participate in a single interview of 60 to 90 minutes and to provide requested follow-up information.

The six states where interviews were conducted were Idaho, Iowa, Missouri, Montana, Nevada, and Utah. The states were selected partly because of convenience, but also because they have varied public library consulting and continuing education structures, certification requirements, and educational programs for rural librarians. The wide range of programs and expertise available to the rural librarians in these six states provided an opportunity to identify commonalities of experience despite differences in programs and resources. The librarians' perceptions of themselves and the profession were fairly consistent across the six states although the available programs and degree of commitment to rural libraries varied from state to state.

Interview Process

Whenever possible interviews were conducted at the rural library. When this was not possible, the interviews were conducted in a room or a lounge on a college campus. The interviews lasted from 50 to 110 minutes. Some interviewees appreciated the opportunity to express their opinions and to share their experiences and extended the interview period beyond the planned 60 to 90 minutes. The interviews were conducted in a private environment with only the researcher and the individual librarian as participants.

Each interviewee completed a brief *Personal Data Form* (Appendix A) in order to provide basic demographic information for the study. In addition, this form asked the participants to list at least three of the most important personal attributes needed for success as a rural librarian. Also, at various points during the interview the librarians were asked questions which related to their understanding of the effective librarian. From the responses to these questions as well as from related comments, qualities and attributes were identified that became part of a separately analyzed and reported data set of characteristics of effective librarians.

An *Interview Protocol* (Appendix B) was used to guide the interview process. However, individuals were allowed to expand upon topics of interest to them or to share events, circumstances or other information which they considered important. Each interview was audiotaped to assure accuracy. Later, the audiotapes were used to expand upon interview notes, to transcribe quotations for analysis and sorting, and to clarify facts and ideas.

The interview structure encouraged the participants to share their real life experiences rather than just theoretical beliefs about their professional roles and identities, their careers, the characteristics of effective librarians, and continuing education experiences, topics and educators. The interview questions were organized into four sections although the distinctions were not always apparent to the interviewees since their answers and comments often moved the interview from section to section naturally. The four sections were: significant career factors, educational events, professional identity, and attributes for effectiveness. The results from the first two sections of the interviews are reported here.

Compilation of Data

The Federal-State Cooperative System for Public Library Data program through the National Center for Education Statistics (1994a, 1994b) provided both a data set and a published report which were used to verify and expand the demographic, statistical and financial information provided by the librarians about their libraries. This information made it possible to identify some of the ways in which the case study libraries in this research were or were not typical of rural libraries serving the same population base. The comparison of the research libraries to the total 4,000 (National Center for Education Statistics 1994b) central public libraries serving populations of less than 5,000 residents is presented later in this section. Because statistics are not available on the individual librarians who work in public libraries, it was not possible to compare the characteristics of the individuals in this study to any national population associated with rural libraries. Upon completion of the interviews, quotations from each interview were entered into a word processing program in the form of a table that could be sorted by theme, state or specific interview. The theme or code for each quotation was selected and assigned based upon the literature and the content of the research findings. A list of five recurring themes related to the professionalization process emerged from the data.

Theme Verification

A list of five primary themes and personal characteristics were compiled and shared with participants for their verification after the initial analysis was completed. After the completion of the interviews, the list (Appendix C) was mailed to the participants with a request that they consider each in light of their own experiences as rural librarians. They were then instructed to indicate if they agreed or disagreed that the statements were representative of the experiences and/or circumstance of rural librarians. Twenty-six (100%) interviewees returned a completed *Theme Verification* form which provided a formal system for participant verification of the findings. All participants agreed with the professionalization themes. The verification of the major themes by participants and the use of the literature to further clarify the themes served as a triangulation procedure to help assure consistency and accuracy in the interpretation of the interview data.

Description of Participants

The participants are described on two levels: the individual librarians along with their personal characteristics, and the libraries and communities in which they work. The libraries are also compared to national means and percentages for libraries of similar size in similar communities. The participants are described on both the personal level and the library/community level in order to present a context for their attitudes and experiences. Comparing the 26 libraries in this study with libraries of similar size across the country does not make these libraries and the experiences of their librarians representative. The comparison does, however, provide a measure of the degree of contrast between these libraries and the universe of like rural public libraries. It is possible in this way to determine the ways in which these libraries are typical despite their unique circumstances of geography, politics, economics and culture.

The Librarians

The participating librarians disproved once again the librarian stereotype. They had varied educational backgrounds and levels. Their ages spanned four decades. Some expressed liberal political and social views, while others had ultra-conservative opinions. They were tall and short, loud and vivacious and quiet and soft-spoken, restless and calm. Most had spouses and children and some had grandchildren. The majority were natives of the area served by the library in which they worked. But, some were transplants and fit Busch's (1990) typology of the rural librarian transplant who comes to the community because of the job of a spouse or some other personal reason (p. 226). For all of their differences, though, they had some important things in common. They were all generous in their gift of time for the interviews and the research and in their willingness to share personal experiences for the benefit of others. In addition, each of these individuals was tremendously dedicated to providing the best possible library service to her or his community and to users of all ages. Their dedication transcended low salaries, limited resources of all types, long hours that include evenings and weekends, and the second class professional status imposed by their lack of the Master of Library Science degree.

The youngest of the 26 librarians who participated in this study was 30 years old and had been the library director in her community for just two years. The oldest librarian was 70 years old, but she had also been the librarian for only two years. She was an example of those individuals who come to rural librarianship as a second or third career. Often individuals who have retired from other public roles are tapped by their communities for this "public service" role which involves visibility, communication and the provision of service to all segments of the community. Because of the low pay associated with the rural library, former teachers who have retirement income are considered good candidates for the position of librarian. Such individuals have three important qualifications for the job: a college education, some experience with libraries from the perspective of a user, and supplemental income to allow them to live on the average annual salary of $15,000 (Vavrek 1992). While one individual had been at the library for 16 years and had "seen many ideas come and go" another woman had just begun her library experience and was still sorting out the vocabulary and wondering out loud if she really wanted to "get involved and excited about this stuff." The average length of time that the 26 librarians had been in their positions was 4.7 years. This may not be typical since Busch (1990) found with 492 returned questionnaires from rural librarians that the average length of service was 9 years.

The ages of the 26 individuals spanned 40 years, and their educational preparation for the role of rural librarian varied as much as their ages as illustrated in Table 1. Their educational credentials ranged from high school diplomas to graduate degrees in education and psychology. The two oldest librarians, 68 and 70 years of age, had college degrees. The average age of the librarians in this study was 48.3 years which is not different from the composite drawn by Busch (1990) of the rural librarian serving communities of less than 25,000 who is "a white female about fifty years old with a high school diploma or some college" (p. 193). One-third of the librarians in this study had baccalaureate degrees. For all but one of these 26 individuals, the role of librarian was not the first full time job they had had, nor was it their first career choice. Despite the differences, their library experiences and insights had many of the same elements.

These rural librarians worked from 16 to 40 official hours per week. The average number of paid hours of work per week was 32 with 39 percent (10) of the participants working a regular 40-hour work week. Although there was no interview question that asked about the amount of work or time devoted to their positions as librarians, every participant volunteered information about the hard work and the amount of time devoted to the job. Comments about time and work were often given in response to the last structured interview question:

Table 1.   Educational Level of Participants by Age

Educational Levels	30-39 years	40-49 years	50-59 years	over 60	Educational level totals
High school	2	3	1	1	7
Some college	2	3	2	0	7
College degree	1	2	5	2	10
Graduate degree	0	2	0	0	2
Age group totals	5	10	8	3	26

If a new librarian were to be hired in a nearby community and she or he came to you for advice, what would you tell them about their role as librarian?

Although the words varied, the theme in the answers was the same:

... but you are going to put in more hours than you get paid for. You just have to accept that. It is part of the job.

This job will consume you. It's like a blob; it's a never-ending job.

I think one of the most important things in a rural library is you have to be willing to work long hours with little pay. Just accept it, because if you don't love that library you may as well not even apply for a job like this. The library needs you, and you just have to be there to help people, and you know, to get the work done.

The message is clear. For all of the study participants, the job required more hours of work than the community could afford to employ them or other paid staff . They considered the extra hours regularly worked without pay to be an indication of their dedication to their work and their communities. This dedication or commitment to the task is one of the characteristics identified by Becker and Carper (1956) as an indication of one's professional or occupational identification and therefore represents a measure of the professionalization of these individuals.

Almost one-third (8) of the study participants had worked in this library or another library at some time prior to taking the job as library director. Those who had worked in the library where they are presently employed had mixed experiences regarding being trained for their present positions. For some, the complexity and extent of the librarian's responsibilities were a complete shock despite having been involved in the operation of this library previously. A few, however, had the advantage of working with a librarian mentor who included them in the information loop and helped them to prepare to be the librarian some day. Only one of the librarians had actually planned to be a librarian and had sought the position through a series of strategies after a short try at another career had proven unsatisfactory to her.

Table 2.   Location and Size of Participant's Libraries

Community population	IA	ID	MO	MT	NV	UT	Totals
1-999	0	2	1	1	0	0	4
1,000-2,499	2	0	3	3	1	3	12
2,500-4,999	1	1	1	4	1	2	10
Totals	3	3	5	8	2	5	26

In their interviews, the librarians spoke for themselves concerning their experiences and the themes explored in this study. Each spoke about the community, the library, the people and the meaning of being a librarian by drawing upon her or his own experiences. It is through their own words that they can best be described and represented in the report of this research.

The Communities

The communities in which the participants work as librarians vary as much as the librarians themselves. The communities are in six states and range in size from 4,702 residents to 602. The distribution of libraries across the six participating states and the size of the communities served by each are presented in Table 2. At least one of the communities is on the very fringe of the suburban/rural interface and may become a suburban library before long. Other libraries are in isolated communities which meet the definition of rural in terms of number of residents, economic basis and distance to commercial centers. Communities between 1,000 and 2,499 residents account for almost one-half of the total libraries included with only four places in the smaller category and the rest in the largest population category (2,500-4,999).

Table 3 compares the distribution of library populations for the study to those reported nationally for fiscal 1992 by the National Center for Education Statistics (1994b). The category with the most percentage of difference is the smallest population group (1-999), but the other two groups are within 5 percent of the national distribution. The participants were selected for inclusion without regard to the size of the community except for the stipulation that the total population be less than 5,000. The states were selected because of their varied models for certification and rural librarian training programs as well as for practical considerations.

The libraries where the individual interviewees are employed are of interest only in so far as they provide a context within which to consider the experiences of the librarians themselves. The communities where librarianship is practiced by these individuals frame and help to define the meaning of "being the librarian."

Nationally there are 4,000 central public libraries serving communities of less than 5,000. This number excludes both bookmobile service areas and

Table 3. Communities by Population Group

Community Population	Total Public Libraries		Public Libraries in Study	
	Total #	% of Total	Total #	% of Total
1-999	986	24.7	4	15.4
1,000-2,499	1,643	41.1	12	46.2
2,500-4,999	1,371	34.2	10	38.4
Totals	4,000	100.0	26	100.0

branch library facilities. The libraries in this study represent less than one percent of the total public libraries in this population category; however this population category (less than 5,000) represents 44.7 percent of the public libraries located in the fifty states and the District of Columbia. Table 4 shows the number and percentage of public libraries in the study by population category in each of the six states included in this study. The geography, settlement patterns, economic, and agricultural base of each state help to explain the percentage of small libraries in each instance. These numbers also help to illustrate the difference in the perceptions of what rural means. In Nevada, for example, where the population density is very low, there are only two large cities (Las Vegas and Reno), there is a great deal of both public land and uninhabited desert, and there are only 26 public libraries in the state. This number includes 12 rural libraries serving less than 5,000, or 46.1 percent of the total. In Iowa, a much more densely populated state, the settlement patterns have resulted in many very small communities so that there are 404 libraries serving less than 5,000 residents. The average percentage of rural libraries across these six states is 47.7 percent of the total number of public libraries (945) in the states. The fact that almost half of the public libraries in these six states are rural libraries by the definition used for this study again illustrates the importance of finding effective ways to assist rural librarians in the professionalization process.

Table 4. Rural Libraries within the Six States

States	Total Libraries	Population 1-999	Population 1,000-2,499	Population 2,500-4,999	Totals #	%
Idaho	107	23	25	23	71	66.4
Iowa	517	92	214	98	404	78.2
Missouri	143	3	28	26	57	39.9
Montana	83	9	26	15	50	60.2
Nevada	26	6	1	5	12	46.1
Utah	69	2	20	8	30	43.5
Totals	945	135	314	175	624	

Table 5.   Average Annual Library Expenditures

Libraries	1-999	1,000-2,499	2,500-4,999
Libraries in the Study	$10,702	$27,893	$56,741
Total Public Libraries	$10,939	$26,620	$57,958
Differences	237	$ 1,273	$ 1,217

Comparisons with Libraries of Similar Size

It is also possible to compare the 26 libraries in this study to other rural libraries of similar size with regards to budget, collection size and annual circulation. This last item serves as one measure of use and effectiveness. Such comparisons are useful to illustrate the ways in which the libraries in this study are typical or atypical of other such libraries. Table 5 compares average annual expenditures across the three population categories for the libraries in the study and all public libraries in the population category. For this measure the libraries in the study are very typical compared to libraries nationally. The figures reported are those provided by the National Center for Education Statistics for 1992 (1994a).

Tables 6 and 7 provide a similar comparison between the libraries in the study and the total public libraries in each population category. The subjects for these tables are collection size and annual circulation. In collection size, both groups are similar.

In the comparison of annual circulation transactions reported in Table 7, there is considerable difference between the libraries in the study group and the national averages. There are two possible explanations for the difference in circulation which is almost 25 percent greater for the libraries in the study. One explanation is that the response rate for this item was less than 100 percent (92.7%) in the national statistics, thus giving a lower than actual average amount. Another explanation is that the librarians in the study are those that are known and considered to be effective by their state library agencies. It may be that their effectiveness is reflected in their higher than average circulation figures. It is likely that both of these factors contribute to the higher circulation figures for the study libraries.

Table 6.   Average Collection Size

	1-999	1,000-2,499	2,500-4,999
Libraries in the Study	7001	11,595	17,334
Total Public Libraries	6830	11,208	17,241
Differences	171	387	93

Table 7. Average Annual Circulation

	1-999	1,000-2,499	2,500-4,999
Libraries in the Study	8,637	19,152	33,927
Total Public Libraries	5,676	13,875	27,129
Differences	2,961	5,277	6,798

The libraries in the study group are as diverse as the librarians who manage them. There are old Carnegie buildings with typical split-level entrances causing local library boards unique challenges in attempting to provide access to library services for all. There are new buildings still smelling of paint and carpet glue. One library was so new, that on the day of the interview, a painter was lettering the name of the library on a sign in front of the building. There are libraries sharing buildings with senior citizen centers and libraries located in the basements of courthouses. There are also libraries in buildings built during the 1960s or 1970s when grant funds for libraries were more readily available. The statistics do not convey the diversity of the libraries and the communities themselves. From tree lined streets with stately old houses in Iowa, to the open plains of eastern Montana where one can see the horizon miles away in every direction, to the lush green resort mountain regions of Idaho, these rural public libraries attest to the efforts of citizens to provide information, entertainment, education and recreation for themselves, their children, and their neighbors.

FINDINGS AND INTERPRETATIONS OF THE STUDY

This naturalistic study primarily used qualitative data to address the research objectives. The qualitative data derived from the interviews revealed many common attitudes, experiences, and views that were shared by the project participants despite their geographic and cultural differences as well as differences in personality types, educational backgrounds, job preparation, and length of time in their positions. Approximately 575 quotations related to the research objectives were identified within the interviews and these were entered into word processing tables for coding and sorting. In a few instances, statements have been modified for clarity, consolidation, or to protect the identity and confidentiality of the speaker. The meaning or sense of the statements quoted has not been altered or changed.

The research findings center around the concept of "becoming a librarian" for the participants. Their experiences in becoming librarians include the various expectations, stereotypes and definitions imposed by family, friends, communities, and others in the library community—peers, MLS librarians, consultants, and educators. Any discussion of role definition among librarians will elicit at least some remarks about the librarian stereotype prevalent in popular culture, and many were made throughout this study. The librarians' educational experiences within the library community also did much to define for them who they are as librarians and how they feel about that role. The librarians' understandings of the factors that influenced their efforts to define themselves as librarians constitute the primary findings.

The research purpose, the structure of the interview protocol, the literature, and most importantly, the participants' insights, comments and experiences resulted in the identification of broad themes and subthemes to be explored in reporting results. These themes and subthemes provide terms and concepts to define and name the research findings.

Significant Career Events for Professional Identity

Significant career events identified during the interviews fell into three general thematic areas. These themes were: the hiring narratives, examples of networking and support from others, and the first library conference or library continuing education experience. Each of these had subthemes which also emerged from the data in the process of sorting, coding and categorizing the contents of the interviews.

Hiring Narratives

The first section of the interview concerning significant career factors usually solicited the story of "how I came to be the librarian" even though no such question was asked. Each librarian enjoyed telling the story of how she or he came to be a librarian in the first place. The librarians' narratives and unique stories about their hiring, while set in different places with different circumstances, had many of the same elements. These common elements can be characterized as: accidental librarian, recruiting and compensation, not-the-stereotype, and second-class librarian. Each of these relates directly to the primary findings regarding identity and role definition. The circumstances under which they came to be librarians certainly can be interpreted to be a "significant career event" for each of them. These events contribute to their understanding of the role of librarian.

With two exceptions, the librarians in this study all came to their positions accidentally. That is, they did not set out to become librarians. Either the library position was available in or near their hometown when they were looking for a job, or they moved up as a sort of natural progression from a less responsible job within the library to the job of being library director, often without anticipating the types of changes this might mean for them. In telling their stories, the librarians emphasized the coincidences associated with finding the librarian job. For the majority of the 26 individuals interviewed, becoming a librarian was an accident of the marketplace rather than the result of a career choice.

> The girl I replaced didn't want to work that much and she told me to apply because it was so much fun. So I applied and I got the job. So that is how I got to be a librarian.

> I was working at a day care center and someone said the library was looking for someone. So I applied. I started a few hours a week and two years later became the librarian.

> The lady that had the job was moving. I used the library a lot. My kids used it. I knew the librarian. She wasn't a personal friend, but in a small town you know everyone.

None of the individuals quoted above indicated that they had any particular interest in working in the library before the job opportunity was available to them. They did not seem to have any prior knowledge of what a librarian does beyond checking out books, nor did they have any ambitions to become a librarian. Their first initiation into librarianship and what a librarian is or does came only after they were hired.

There were only two individuals in the study who actually had wanted to be librarians before circumstances placed the job in front of them. One of these librarians was a young woman who had library career ambitions and who might have gotten an MLS if her life circumstances had been different. She reported:

> I had worked in the university library when I was in college. I really liked it but after I got married and we moved away from the university, I worked in the insurance business, and I hated it. It paid better, but I had always wanted to work in a library and to be a librarian. Here I had the opportunity. I love it.

Another woman, middle-aged with grown children and a Harley-Davidson motorcycle which she rides all over the country, said that she had always wanted to be a librarian and had volunteered in school and church libraries wherever they lived while she was raising her family. Finally, she was able to move from a volunteer position to a paid position and eventually to the librarian position. Even for these two individuals who consciously wanted to be librarians, the coincidence of the availability of a library job within their rural community at a time when their personal circumstances allowed them to take the job, was a key factor in their assuming the librarian roles. The accidental quality of rural librarianship was evident in all of the narratives. This theme was one of those verified by all of the participants. On the *Theme Verification* form (Appendix C) all participants agreed with the statement:

> Rural librarianship begins as an accident of the marketplace. It is not a planned career, but results because of fortuitous circumstances.

Related to the accidental or coincidental quality of their library careers, were the common elements in some narratives that relate to issues reported by Nancy Busch (1990) concerning recruitment and retention of rural librarians. She reported that there was a tendency on the part of communities to hire known persons or only to recruit locally and to pay low wages with few benefits. The stories of the 26 individuals in this study illustrate Busch's statistical findings:

> I saw the ad posted in the grocery store and I went in and got the job, not because I had any library experience, but because I have a bachelor's degree ... and you cannot get through sixteen years of school without knowing your way around a library. I had the best qualifications of any applicant. Also, I was willing to work for $5 an hour and I'm doing that partly because I'm on Social Security.

> The librarian called one day and asked if I would be interested in working in the library to learn because she knew that I wasn't doing anything. They couldn't afford to pay me. So I went down and started. She got sick and the Board President who is a friend of mine, asked me if I would take over and they would pay me what they could. I couldn't say no.

> Even though I did not have the typing requirement originally required, they set that aside and hired me because I was from the community and I was willing to work despite the lack of benefits. I knew some people on the board and they knew me.

The stories of how these librarians were hired reflect the local focus, the limited resources of the rural communities, and the lack of understanding by local officials and others of the nature and complexity of library work.

The third common element that emerged from the stories about becoming librarians was what might be termed "not the stereotypical librarian." While librarians have been fighting the prevalent stereotype for decades, the rural librarians interviewed seemed to be particularly adverse to being identified with the dull, conservative, unattractive though intelligent, organized, persnickety and somewhat antisocial old maid portrayed as the shushing individual with sensible shoes, glasses and a bun (Wilson 1982; Carmichael 1992). When asked about how they conceptualize themselves as "librarians," a number of participants joked about the stereotype and their failure to fit it; but their concern about the prevalence of that stereotype and the need to project an image that is different from the stereotype was evident in remarks such as the following:

> I think the old stigma of the librarian and all you do is sit and read, you know, your hair in a bun, your glasses and your flat shoes, I think they still expect to see that and I think it's kind of fun to blow that away when they find out I am the librarian.

> I think everybody has a misconception of librarians. We are no longer the old librarian with the little bun and little glasses saying "shh, shh, shh, be quiet, be quiet, be quiet."

It was unclear from these comments whether the librarians themselves had this stereotypical image of a librarian before they themselves started working in the library. Another aspect of the stereotype with which these librarians did not want to be associated was that of someone who spends all day reading rather than doing. These few comments about others' ideas of what librarians do on the job are representative of comments made by everyone:

I know people think I'm reading books all day. Don't I wish!

I think my family and friends thought it was just a job where you could sit down and read a lot. No stress, no pressure. Ha!

But nobody expects librarians do anything but sit in the library in a kind of a quiet little hole.... my friend said "You'll like to work there because you like to crochet." That was her impression, you sit in a good old hidey-hole place and let the world go by!

One 35-year-old librarian with young children of her own, became quite animated when discussing the ways in which being the librarian is so much different than people seem to expect. She was particularly concerned that children should not see the librarian and library work as boring and uninteresting. This same librarian gestured broadly to the piles of books, stacks of papers, boxes of catalog cards, and other work yet to be accomplished in the over-flowing and chaotic little workroom and said:

I know I am not your typical librarian. I am not neat and tidy. I like people more than I like books and order!

These comments are not dissimilar to those made daily by thousands of librarians.

The fourth and final common element that emerged from the data concerning becoming a librarian was that of being second-class, substandard or in some way, not-quite librarians. Many of the librarians said things like the following from a very out-going and successful librarian with a new building, an expanded tax base, and a plaque from the state library association on the wall proclaiming her "librarian of the year" for the previous year:

I sometimes feel bad because my community deserves the best and all they have is me. I am not *really* a librarian but I was the best qualified person when the job was advertised. This library should have a person with an MLS. I just have to try to make everything up because I don't really know.

This attitude of being not-quite-good-enough was expressed over and over again during the course of the interviews. People who appeared to have a great deal of self-confidence about many things, expressed concern about their lack of credentials and how that made them feel. Despite their personal accomplishments, qualifications and characteristics, their dedication, or other attributes, these individuals feel that they are not good enough. They represent themselves as second-class librarians because that is the subtle (and sometimes not so subtle) message they receive from the library community.

Conclusions Regarding the Hiring Narrative Themes

The experiences of these librarians suggest that the difference between the popular concept of the stereotypical librarian and the librarians' initial views of the typical librarian may be very slight. Most (24) of these rural librarians did not indicate any prior interest in or knowledge of the role of librarian other than their experiences as library users. Their understanding of librarianship prior to assuming the role of librarian may have been no more informed than the general public's view. Such a view is largely based on the popular though inaccurate stereotype which underestimates the nature of the skills and competencies and the extent of the responsibilities required in the role of librarian even in small communities. Therefore, their identification with the values and goals of the profession did not begin until after they were hired in the position of librarian unlike those librarians with an MLS whose acculturation to the profession began in graduate school. The extent of the job responsibilities and the complexity of the role came as a surprise to most. They were adamant in denying their resemblance to the stereotypical librarian and at the same time defensive about being different from it.

These concerns are understandable when considered with Howard Becker and James Carper's (1956) four elements that individuals use to weave professional or occupational identity in order to "learn who they are and how they ought to behave" (p. 341). Two of these elements have particular significance here: the occupational title with its associated ideology and the significance for one's position in the larger society. The stereotype may interfere with the librarian's ability to assume a positive leadership role within the community. The stereotype may be an internal barrier for some librarians who waste energy worrying about being not-the-stereotype. As Griffith (1989) has admonished: "librarians need to take charge of their own image rather than to allow a stereotype to prevail especially in a small town where the image of the library will often be a direct reflection of the image of the librarian" (p. 47). A partial solution to this stereotype problem may lie in Cyril Houle's (1980) advice about the role continuing education can play by helping "practitioners know how to present themselves and their work effectively" (p. 63).

The librarians' recruitment and compensation patterns confirmed those identified by Busch (1990). They were recruited locally, they were often known by those hiring them, and many were offered substandard compensation. The process of being hired and the compensation for their work sent messages that might be understood to diminish both the importance of the work being performed and their abilities to do it. Those hiring these individuals, whether library board members or community officials, did not know what the job entailed and what skills and attributes would be most useful for the position. The messages being delivered by those in authority over the library and those who use it at the local level reinforce the second-class status imposed by the profession. From the beginning, even before the library community had an opportunity to deliver any subtle or not so subtle messages about second-class librarianship, these librarians felt their second-class status and felt less than adequate for the job.

Support from Others

The second important theme identified as significant within the career events examined was that of supportive attitudes from others. This was one of the strongest themes that emerged. Participants reported support from others, primarily other librarians, as an important component of their careers. This support took two different, although not entirely different forms—mentoring and friendship.

The concept of the mentor was explicitly mentioned by 7 participants. Four librarians talked about the value of having the support and help of the previous librarian. A librarian who had been working in the library slightly less than one year commented that:

> Because of the isolation here, the only contact I have with the profession is through phone calls, the state library association or local meetings. I learn something every time I get together with others, just talking to them.... When I talk to librarians, every time I speak with them I feel so much better about myself. I feel like a sponge. I'm always absorbing something from the other librarians. Some have sort of taken me on as their cause.

The importance of professional friends for these librarians is not unlike the importance of such connections for those at other levels of this and other professions. In speaking of librarian friends and the effect that they have had, librarians reflected upon the support and encouragement they found among such people:

> ...the librarians' friendliness, their open-mindedness, their knowledge of the outside world. Just because you live in a little place doesn't mean you have a

little mind. I'm impressed with the other librarians from small places. Their willingness to learn and their willingness to share. The sharing is really important because we are isolated.

The librarians from these small communities are an open, giving, wonderful, wonderful community. In previous jobs and through my husband's career I have been involved in other groups related through their jobs. But there's none other like the librarians. They really care.

The interview transcripts contain numerous comments in support of mentoring and friendship along with explanations of the importance these connections have had for careers and a sense of belonging to or with the librarians. All agreed with the theme statement (Appendix C) that:

Personal support from some key others (consultants, other librarians, family, community) is essential for success.

In expanding upon this theme of support and friendliness, librarians said how such connections made them feel. These feelings are also related to the personal empowerment issues discussed later in connection with effective educators.

They make me feel like I'm not the only one that has this kind of problem. I'm not the only one that has to deal with this situation. There are others in the same boat. I think knowing I'm not alone, even though I feel isolated, makes a big difference. Just knowing someone else is out there and you can talk and brainstorm and they'll know where you're coming from.

Librarians know what it all means. They cheer. That affirmation is very important to those of us who work in little libraries. It makes us feel so good to have our thoughts and plans confirmed as right or at least okay.

These two subthemes, that is, mentoring and friendship, were woven throughout the interviews.

Conclusions Regarding Support from Others

Mentoring and professional friendships were important aspects of support from others. While it is only in very recent years that librarianship has begun to investigate the role of mentoring (Grear 1990), other professions have reported that mentoring and professional friendships have been key factors in the success of individuals (Bey and Holmes 1992). The literature on professionalization indicates that mentoring, professional friendships and networking among members of a professional group are ways to reinforce professional identity and group norms (Becker and Carper 1956; Bucher and Strauss 1961; Voyt and Murrell 1990). Further, the research emphasizes the importance of the support from these others in the professionalization process. The value of mentors both in providing guidance and in serving as role models (Bandura 1977, 1978, 1986) to reflect appropriate behavior and attitudes is well documented.

The experience of these rural librarians was not noticeably different in this regard from other professional or occupational groups. The one difference that might be noted was that it was primarily other non-degreed peer librarians who served as mentors and friends who enhanced the self-confidence for these librarians in their professional roles. Librarians with more power and status within the library community did not often perform these functions. It is unclear from this research whether the division between the MLS librarians and the non-degreed librarians is so great that the non-degreed librarians either select to associate primarily with others like themselves or the profession's caste system relegates them to interaction primarily with others like themselves.

The experience of friendship within the library community is one which has been commented upon by others (Brand 1983; Brugh and Beede 1976; Dewey 1985; Hale 1994; Heim 1982; Schuman 1984; Weibel, Heim and Ellsworth 1979). The experience of professional community appears to be the same for these librarians. As one librarian said: "Librarians know what it all means. They cheer." The implication is that others do not "know what it all means" and do not understand what it means to be a librarian. The affirmation by librarian friends who understand the role and the demands seems to be particularly important as part of the role identification for these individuals. When asked about family and friends' perceptions of what it is that they do or are, few had positive comments. Those close to them do not often affirm the librarians' identities. The image the librarians have "at home" is not as affirming as the image they have with other librarians who "know what it means" and "make us feel okay and even great about what we do." The popular stereotype may be what contributes to the lack of support or appreciation from friends and family who do not understand what it means to be a librarian.

First Library Education Experience

The importance of other librarians as supporters was often discussed by the participants in the context of their attendance at their first library conference or continuing education event. All but one of the 26 participants reported having attended a state library conference or other library continuing education event within their first year on the job. From fear and apprehension to anticipation and excitement, librarians in each of the six states recalled their first big professional event. For some, even the first library education event was a very positive experience which left them energized and excited about the prospects and the possibilities. Friends were made and concepts clarified.

> It just felt good to be at that convention. It gave me energy and now it always invigorates me.

> Excitement. I learned I was on the right track. I had confidence that maybe I could do this job..

For many others the first experience was terrifying and overwhelming because of having to leave home or because of the content and strangeness. Fear of the unknown was a major factor:

> I was feeling scared. I also left feeling like everybody spoke in a foreign language. I thought, "I don't understand any of this and I never will." Now I do understand.

> I had never been to college and the whole culture seemed foreign to me.
> Well, it was kind of scary, because I thought everyone had a degree. I didn't realize that I wasn't the only one! When I found out, I relaxed.

These comments explain very real fears or apprehensions remembered about the first library conference or other library education experience.

All of the librarians were able to recall at least some of the feelings and perceptions which they associated with the first such activity, even if they could not recall the educational content of the experience. Whether the first conference or continuing education event was anticipated with dread or positive excitement, the results were reported to be much the same—networking, a positive view of themselves within a larger context that included friends like themselves for support, and new information and knowledge that could be applied back at home in the library. Other rural librarians were those most often involved in supporting the newer individuals. Only occasionally were non-rural or librarians with MLS degrees mentioned as being included in the group of caring others who served as mentors or friends.

Conclusions Regarding the First Continuing Education Experiences

The importance of providing a positive human experience in the context of professional development and continuing education is illustrated by the experiences of these individuals. Their experiences point to the importance of marketing events such as state library association conferences, system workshops, and multi-day residential institutes with complete information, without assuming that everyone knows what to expect in terms of practical circumstances, the nature of other participants, subject content, and structure. The first continuing education experience for these librarians appears to have been important in determining their attitudes towards other library continuing education events. More importantly, the first experience set the tone and expectations the librarians have for the profession and their roles within it. These experiences further reinforce the conclusion that the rural librarians lack an understanding of what their professional role is before they actually assume the position and begin work.

Significant Elements in Continuing Education

The aspects of continuing education events which the librarians identified as important or significant were varied and ranged from practical ideas about the structure and content of educational offerings to the personalities and qualifications of educators. They reported that the educational environment provided opportunities for the role of librarian to be modeled for them by other rural librarians as well as by educators. The primary themes related to the educational experiences that emerged from the interview data are: networking, relevant topics, characteristics of effective education, and characteristics of effective educators. These themes are not entirely separate nor equal aspects of the educational experience but are separated for the purposes of discussion.

Networking

The role of networking as a part of the educational process was stressed by most of the librarians and was at least mentioned by all by one of the study participants. Most of the comments about networking were made in the context of the value of networking as a component of the continuing education environment, but the theme is also appropriate as a career event. The comments about networking in the context of educational events related to the role that peers have in furthering learning for adults within the educational process.

Whether librarians were talking about their first library educational experience, the most effective class or workshop they had attended, or one that was not effective, the value of discussion with other librarians was always emphasized.

> I think that when I come to these things I learn as much from the people I come in contact with as I do in a classroom setting.

> That's where we probably learned the most—visiting with other librarians like us.

> It seems like whenever you get together with a group you learn something. I mean, even if you find out that people have problems just like you do it is valuable. They don't always have solutions for the problems either. It helps to know that.

A librarian who had taken advantage of credit and noncredit offerings presented in person and via a telecommunications network, summed up these comments about the importance of the networking and peer sharing in the educational environment:

> The most important educational factor was talking to the other librarians. I forgot most of what was actually taught in the classes and workshops, but I've remembered what I learned from the others in the classes.

Their comments indicated that the librarians considered the networking potential of educational offerings to be an important and valuable component of the educational process. One librarian got right to the point:

> We need more free time at CE things just to get together and be together as a group. We don't need as much time in class listening. We can read a lot of this.

All of the participants verified the importance of the theme of networking with others on the *Theme Verification* form (Appendix C) by agreeing unanimously with the statement:

> Networking with other librarians is one of the most important means of learning and growing as a professional.

Not only did all of the librarians indicate agreement with this theme, one librarian included a note on the *Theme Verification* form saying that this was the most important on the list.

Conclusions Regarding Networking

Within the educational context, the importance of networking and learning from others was emphasized by all of the interviewees. The librarians saw continuing education as important because it provided a venue for networking with peers rather than because it provided important information from the experts, the professional organization or the state library. The networking value of educational experiences was emphasized even in otherwise negative situations. The librarians seemed to find the affirmation they needed from peers even if they did not find it in the classroom from the educator or the consultant. It would appear from the experiences of these individuals that there are many opportunities for peer networking within continuing education offerings, but it is unclear if the experiences of these effective and articulate librarians are typical of all rural librarians, including those who are not as involved in the profession, nor as connected to their peers. Perhaps librarians who have not established networks of peers or do not attend continuing education events feel that there are insufficient networking opportunities or have had experiences without networking opportunities in the educational environment. It is important for library education providers to explore their own philosophies and to ascertain the philosophies and methods employed by educators they engage for delivery of continuing education for rural librarians to guarantee that opportunities for peer interchange and sharing are built into all presentations and event schedules or structures.

Relevant Topics

The second theme under the educational experiences that emerged from the interview data was the theme of relevant topics. The theme was also verified on the *Theme Verification* form by all of the study participants (Appendix C):

> Continuing education is valuable when it is practical and applicable to the small library situation.

One librarian included the comment that "in addition, theory and more philosophical content is valuable." The librarians all placed a great deal of importance upon educational contents that are relevant, practical and applicable for the rural library situation.

When the participants were asked about what factors would motivate them to attend an educational program or event, or what factors would discourage them from attending, the difficulties imposed by travel and time were not the key issues. For all of the librarians, the usefulness or applicability of the material or content were what made the difference. There were more than 35 specific statements expressing this theme. The message was loud and clear:

> Don't waste my time. It has to be useful. My time is too valuable.

> Information that I need, that I have been looking for. I have a chance to use it and need to know it.

> Probably the most important thing is if it is applicable to my job here.

> Having a need to learn something so that you can use it is the primary motivating factor since time and distance are major issues in our state.

> It has to be pertinent to what is happening and something I can bring back to my community and my situation and use. I need to be able to show my board that I am not just playing when I am away at these things.

The redundancy of these statements and many others illustrates the strong feelings the librarians all seemed to have about the need for practical continuing education topics that have application within rural libraries. Additionally, there were comments about the importance of covering the basics:

I still need basic subjects. I need a lot of help in just the basic everyday things.

In a small library we're busy doing so many things, and I think the state library forgets that we need basic things in addition to what is "hot" now.

I often feel as if I have missed something. Like I arrived in the middle. But it is just that they assume we know things we don't know yet.

The need for the basics of library operations is closely related to the idea of applicability.

Conclusions about Relevancy

The theme of relevance in continuing library education for rural librarians can be summed up by quoting from *The Modern Practice of Adult Education* by Knowles (1980):

> Adults tend to have a perspective of immediacy of application toward most of their learning. They engage in learning largely in response to pressures they feel from their current life situation. To adults, education is a process of improving their ability to cope with the life problems they face now (p. 53).

The librarians' emphasis upon the practical and applicable contents for educational offerings is in keeping with Knowles' theory of androgogy with its assumptions about people's need to learn what they need for real life situations in the present. The concept of the "teachable moment" (Knox 1977, 1992) is important in this regard. Matching the individuals' need to know with "hot" topics that can be applied in the rural library situation helps to emphasize the teachable moment when the most motivating forces can be brought to bear on the educational environment.

The participants suggested two separate areas for attention in regard to relevant educational offerings. One area was that of applicable topics and one was the need for basic information. They had examples drawn from their experiences to illustrate the types of topics that fit both categories. When asked about factors that contributed to their decision to attend or not attend a particular educational event, relevancy was repeatedly mentioned as the most important factor. Despite anecdotal reports and even statistics from surveys and needs assessments from state libraries, system staffs and association conference planners that contend that travel distance is the primary consideration of rural librarians in determining continuing education attendance, these librarians said that travel distance, time required away from work, and scheduling factors were not as important as relevancy of topics and the perceived competency of the presenter. The problem of staffing the library while they were away was mentioned as often as the relevancy of the program as a factor in determining attendance.

Library educators have spent considerable time worrying about the factors of travel distance, time commitment and appropriate timing for educational events. The quality and applicability of the educational experience may be able to overcome these practical barriers. The first concern of these participants was for some likelihood that the educational product to be provided would be one of quality in terms of topic and mode of delivery. The participants were concerned about having their valuable time wasted by inappropriate topics and poor delivery. The librarians' comments suggest that travel distance presents less of a problem if the expectation is that there will be a quality applicable educational experience at the end of the travel. This is not to suggest that convenience is not a factor, but it may not be the factor that ought to receive the most attention by providers. The comments by these librarians suggested that the relevancy and quality of the product is more important to effective individuals than convenience. As in other areas of marketing, quality may be more important than "cost" factors for committed individuals.

Effective Continuing Education

The characteristics of effective continuing education are difficult to isolate from the concepts of networking and relevant contents as well as from the characteristics of effective educators. However, a separate theme of effective education with many practical suggestions was evident in the interview data. The importance of various practical elements of the educational environment was emphasized in these comments. The 40 hours of interview tapes contain many practical suggestions about improving the effectiveness of continuing education. Ways to implement networking might also be considered here. The quotations below give the flavor of the suggestions made by the librarians.

> Start and end on time—no matter what!

> We like learning to be fun. It doesn't have to be drudgery.

> The courses or workshops need to be reasonable in terms of total time because we have lives outside of the library and outside of our role as librarians.

> We learn a lot working in small groups. You have to have a lot of different kinds of activities for the class—not just listening all the time to the expert.

These sample comments reflect the more general suggestions about having fun and relaxing, working in small groups, staying on schedule, and having classes of reasonable length because "we have lives..."

Conclusions Regarding Effective Continuing Education

The practical aspects of effective educational experiences mentioned by the librarians emphasized the importance of efficiency and friendliness. There were no surprises in these practical aspects of "what matters" in the educational situation, but the repeated mention of the need for schedules to be followed and programs to be run on time is an indication of the number of times that this does not happen. Although it may be an indication of the extent to which even rural librarians fit the librarian stereotype and value schedules, orderliness and a certain following of the rules, it is more likely a reflection of the demands of management in an organization with limited resources and no time to waste.

Characteristics of Effective Educators

The last continuing education theme, characteristics of effective educators, emerged from the interview data in part as the result of two questions within the *Interview Protocol* (Appendix B). The questions were:

> What characteristics do you think are most important for a consultant or library educator to have in order to work with rural librarians?

> What advice can you give a library educator like myself, about what elements ought to be designed into continuing education programs for rural librarians?

The subthemes that were identified as a result were: attitude of trust and respect, humor, motivation, relevant experience and knowledge, role modeling, and communication skills. The participant librarians provided rich insights about each of these subthemes. Two of these subthemes, an empowering attitude of trust and respect and relevant experience and knowledge, were additionally emphasized by the repeated mention of their opposites— condescending attitudes and a lack of knowledge about the rural culture and environment. One enthusiastic librarian who had only a high school education, had never traveled outside of her home state, and at least appeared to have little knowledge of broader library issues, was often able to get right to the heart of each topic. Despite her lack of official credentials, she managed to summarize all of the effective educator subthemes in one descriptive comment. She said the instructor should be:

> Someone who knows what they are talking about and knows how to put it across and has an interesting and entertaining way of presenting a class and somebody who is interested in hearing of the librarians' opinions as well.... someone who you would like to be like.

A similarly succinct comment about the negative characteristics of some educators was provided by another librarian:

> I am really put off by their attitudes. They seem to think we are stupid because we are from small places and didn't have a chance to get a college degree.

While there were some topics in this study that solicited limited comments from the participants, all of the librarians had many opinions about what it is that makes someone an effective educator. The subthemes and representative supporting quotations from the librarians are outlined in the following sections. The past experiences of the librarians gave them many examples to use to illustrate their opinions. For many individuals, the effectiveness of the educational experience was almost completely a function of the teacher/facilitator's abilities to create an empowering environment of trust and respect and then to deliver useful or appropriate content for consideration. The participants were able to give many very specific examples of good and bad experiences with educators. Their examples were more often than not accented with strong feelings of admiration, gratitude and affection for effective educators, and frustration, anger and dislike for educators who had wasted their time and sometimes their money with boring, inappropriate or ineffective classes or workshops. This was definitely not a topic about which anyone was neutral.

The first subtheme was the need for educators to create an empowering environment of trust and respect. Empowerment includes feelings of self-confidence, self-direction and positive attitudes. An empowering environment also fosters experimentation, risk taking and action. A librarian from Missouri who spoke about dignity in the educational situation also said that what matters is "the way it is delivered and how it makes you feel." The other librarians' comments agree with this sentiment. The feelings as well as the ideas of the librarians about these experiences are reflected in these representative quotes:

> I take classes from her because she helps me to feel better about what I do and how I do it. She confirms my own ability.

> Several times things were said in class and I thought "I did the right thing. I am on track." I think, "I am okay! I can do this!" This is an important part of training.

> It [education] gives me ideas that make me confident as a decision-maker...

> When I come home, I feel like I can solve problems that looked impossible before I went. I somehow feel better able to cope.

These remarks from the librarians express their personal experiences and how such experiences affected them and their feelings about themselves and their work. On the Theme Verification form (Appendix C), the librarians agreed with the statement:

> Those who work with rural librarians (consultants and educators) must be able to make the librarian feel confident about her/his ability to "be" a librarian.

While none of the interviewees mentioned the term empowered or empowerment, their comments are about the concept of personal empowerment or changing one's self perception so that one has "a greater sense of self-worth and self-confidence" (Vanderslice 1991, p. 3) and "a recognition and valuing of one's skills, knowledge, resources and personhood" (Kreisburg 1992, p. 35). Empowerment helps to conceptualize what happens when an effective educator provides an environment of trust and respect. The adult education literature strongly supports the idea that the ability of the teacher to have empathy with the students and to be an authentic person (Brookfield 1990) is essential to the teaching/learning situation. The attitude and ability of the educator to create an environment of respect and trust was the most often mentioned aspect of effective teachers. One librarian said:

> My mind and heart are more open when I have been made to feel important. I know when someone thinks I am worth the effort!

The following comments further illustrate the librarians' attention to the attitude of the educators they have encountered and the importance of trust and respect in the learning environment. The personality of the educator, while different from the value system she or he brings to the educational setting, is related to the ability to be authentic, honest and nurturing in the classroom. As the participants noted:

> The important things are a willingness to help and care. Being right there to answer my questions no matter how dumb they are. You need people who make you feel that you can ask.

> The good ones make you feel that they have really listened to you and they reveal a bit of themselves. You feel like you know them and they know you.

> You need to be able to trust these people.

> I think the quality of making a person feel comfortable in class... She brings out a lot from her students in class. It's like she draws out these things and we sort of sound off openly and try out ideas. You learn a lot.

She cares about what she is doing and she cares about the people. It makes all the difference!

While being effective as a teacher should not be viewed as a popularity contest, the ability of educators to create an atmosphere of trust and respect did matter a great deal to the librarians.

The second-class librarian status felt by those without the MLS degree was addressed by many in relation to the attitude of some educators. These rural librarians reported feeling inadequate for their responsibilities at times, and then related that library educators have occasionally reinforced these feelings of inadequacy. Twelve of the 26 librarians reported experiences with condescending consultants or educators. No questions were asked by the researcher that would have solicited these comments directly, but in sharing positive and effective educational experiences, the opposite experiences were also brought to mind and shared. The remarks quoted below serve to make the earlier quotations describing effective educators even stronger and more important. These comments were made without bitterness, but with considerable anger in some instances.

Well, it seems to me like they've just let their common sense go out the window. These educated people seem to think that other people aren't worth considering.

You don't act like your education makes you greater than everybody else the way some of these MLS librarians act...you know, I'm kind of fed up with the educated library community in many ways.

They don't speak to me; they speak at me. They don't mean to be condescending, but they are.

I am really put off by the condescending attitude or disapproval expressed by some of the teachers who present library workshops. They seem surprised that someone without a degree would bother to come to such things. They seem to think that because we don't have a degree we are incapable of getting the degree. The two things are not related. Most of us are just as smart as they are. The difference is that our lives offered different opportunities. Our paths just went in different directions.

The number of comments about negative continuing education or consulting experiences with library educators and the depth of feeling included in the telling were both sobering and saddening. As noted by Brookfield (1990), the values of educators and their attitudes towards students are communicated to the students in the context of the teaching/learning environment.

It is difficult to judge how pervasive these condescending attitudes may be, but the fact that so many remarks surfaced in an otherwise positive discussion is of interest. These remarks serve to emphasize the importance of their opposite. Respect and an empowering environment convey a sense of the value of each individual in keeping with Bookfield's (1987, 1990) belief in teacher authenticity and the communication of values within the context of the classroom environment. In addition, Bandura's (1978, 1986) concept of role modeling and self-efficacy speaks to the importance of authenticity and mutual respect in the classroom.

The experiences of the librarians in this project are compatible with Stephen Brookfield's personal empowerment philosophy, concern with authenticity, self-concept and critical thinking (1986, 1987), Mezirow's (1990, 1991) transformative learning theory, and Robert Wlodkowski's (1990) character-istics of a motivational instructor. One of the things that these writers have in common is the belief that the value systems, philosophies or belief systems of the educator have a profound influence upon the educational environment and upon the results of the educational experience. According to these theorists, the atmosphere in the "classroom" and the subtle messages about the value of individuals and the importance of their work should be conveyed in such a way that learners come away with improved self-confidence and a belief in their ability to act effectively. It is clear that the librarians here agreed that such messages have long-term effects on the development of both the careers and lives of the individuals involved.

The second subtheme related to the characteristics of educators was the ability to create a relaxed atmosphere. The value of a sense of humor and the desire for learning to be fun was frequently included in comments about the educator or the educational environment. These comments are congruent with basic adult education theory (Brookfield 1986; Cross 1981; Heimlick and Norland 1994; Verduin, Miller and Greer 1977). Some of the comments were:

> Learning should be fun!

> I prefer a lively, funny presentation rather than a serious one. And I like good stories that help me remember.

The subtheme of humor is linked directly to the subtheme of motivation. The participants felt that being able to motivate individuals was an important aspect of the teaching and learning dynamic. Scattered throughout the comments about effective education and effective educators were remarks concerning the importance of motivating individuals and groups. Further, motivation is an aspect of the empowering process. A few librarians used the term motivate, but many phrased it differently. An Idaho librarian expressed this concept by saying that educators or consultants "have to be good cheerleaders and keep us pumped up." Enthusiastic instruction seemed to be important to several of the librarians as evident in the following remarks:

> If they're people who make you feel at ease and who come across with a relaxed kind of presentation but yet they present their material in such a way that it's inspiring, it's encouraging and you go away from there thinking, "Hey, I'm going to do this. I'm going to give that a try."

> She cares about what she is doing and she is excited about it. You cannot help but be excited too. You want to know it, to go home and do it.

> It sure helps to be excited about what they're telling you. Those people make me want to go back time and time again. They're excited and they bring new ideas and they get you involved too.

These learner-librarians appeared to be in agreement with those educators who believe that "teaching is undeniably a performing art" (Lowman 1991, p. 11) and that motivating for action is essential in adult education (Cervero 1992; Cranton 1994; Wlodkowski 1990).

Although the interpersonal skills of educators received a great deal of attention in the interviews, there were also many comments about the need for teachers to have qualifications for teaching. Two types of qualifications emerged; one was knowledge of the theoretical and practical aspects of the treated topic. The second was relevant experience or knowledge of the rural library situation. Few said that educators of rural librarians need to have experience actually working in rural libraries, but everyone agreed that the educator needed to understand what the rural library environment was like and what it means to be a rural librarian. Some of the comments offered were:

> They do have to know what they're talking about or they're not going to be helping you at all, no matter how friendly and all they are. Being nice is not enough. They have to know.

> They need to be a bit of a generalist and not too specialized because the audience has to do everything and so we need to be able to ask questions related to all aspects of the subject, not just a narrow definition or one way of doing things.

> They should do their homework before they come to teach. They should know who they are teaching and what our situation is.

When asked directly if credentials such as the MLS were important for consultants or educators of rural librarians, the librarians agreed that the credentials were important but that alone they were useless. Credentials and a knowledge of the theory of library science need to be coupled with knowledge of the rural library experience and the ability to communicate what they know. As one librarian noted,

> You have to be darn sure they [educators] know something about the subject they are teaching, but that isn't the most important part.

The "most important part" may be reflected in the following comment from an older librarian who had been working in her library for more than a dozen years and still had enthusiasm and excitement about the library and the community:

> They [educators] should be open to seeing that small may be different, but small can adapt and can still be good. We may need to be drawn along a little bit slower, but we are still good!

Although the need for educators of rural librarians to understand and respect the rural library situation and environment was not specifically verified by the participants through the follow-up *Theme Verification*, every librarian mentioned this within the interview narrative. These comments about educators or consultants who are uninformed or ill-informed concerning these small rural libraries and the staffing and resource situations in them are representative:

> Sometimes I have attended workshops where they talk about small libraries, but what they mean by small is a library serving 25,000 people. These people have no idea what happens in a library our size and they don't seem to care either!

> I felt like they didn't know what a small library was. They were talking in terms of some of the biggest libraries around. I thought, we're not even a small library. We're microscopic!

The subtheme of role modeling by the educator was expressly identified by only a few of the librarians although comments illustrative of other themes, in particular motivation, could be used to support this subtheme as well. The few librarians who did identify role modeling as important made some very clear references to this function of the educator. For instance, they commented:

> The personal appearance of the presenter and the professionalism is very important. I feel like this person is not only telling me how to be a librarian but they are also showing me how to be a librarian. If they are professional I feel like I am more professional as well.

> She is the kind of librarian I want to be some day. I like her style and her attitudes.

I like the way she behaves, nice but assertive. I would like to learn that.

The librarians are "the public" for the presenters and they should be able to model the appropriate behavior. You should treat us the way you expect us to treat the public.

Another subtheme associated with the effective educator is that of communication skills. References to the importance of communication in the education process were contained in many of the comments quoted above for other subthemes. Additionally, interviewees referred to the entire communication process and its importance in the classroom, and specifically to the listening skills needed by an effective educator:

She's just real good. She has a knack of being able to make you feel like you are the one who is smart and can come up with this wonderful idea. It all boils down to being an effective communicator, a good listener, a good speaker.

I think if they would listen instead of just talk...

The ability of the educator to communicate in an appropriate and interesting manner was stressed by many and can hardly be disputed as an important characteristic for a teacher. What was a surprise was the number of examples of teachers who were unable to communicate effectively. The need for effective educators to understand the context of their students' culture and environment came through clearly as the librarians expressed strong preferences for teachers and consultants who could place theory and practical application within the context of the rural library and the rural culture.

The effective educator subthemes (i.e., an empowering attitude of respect and trust, humor, motivation, relevant experience and knowledge, role modeling, and communication) were all inter-related within the context of each individual interview. The following description by an enthusiastic first year librarian summarizes the effective educator themes:

My instructor has a great relationship with people, knows her material, has a good sense of humor, can go from one thing to another and make sense. It inspires us to be that way. I think teachers need, first of all, to be qualified, and secondly they need to have good interpersonal skills. Not defensive. Always positive. She listens. She has energy. She makes this library stuff seem exciting! She is the kind of librarian I want to be.

Conclusions Regarding Effective Educators

The subthemes that emerged in this part of the study outlined a need for continuing educators who create an empowering environment of trust and respect, infuse their teaching with humor, provide motivation, bring relevant experience and knowledge to the classroom, act as role models, and have excellent communication skills. This was the single topic that received the largest number of comments. The librarians had very strong feelings about teachers or consultants they have known.

The characteristics of effective educators as identified by the participants in this study are not surprising. They are well supported in the literature of adult education. The function of the effective educator as role model may be under represented in this study because no specific question was asked regarding the librarians' perceptions of the teacher as a role model. The research confirms the importance of the expectations of others, especially teachers in the educational situation. Adult education theorists (Brookfield 1990; Good and Brophy 1984; Wlodkowski 1985) contend that the expectations of teachers are powerful, and this seems to be no less true for adult learner librarians.

According to the librarians there is nothing that says that one cannot be entertaining, funny, animated and captivating while still providing an environment for learning. They encourage the use of humor as a tool for learning and for creating an environment of relaxed mutual respect. Appropriate humor, however, is contextual and requires knowledge of the environment within which it is placed. In the case of rural library education, this means that educators employing humor must be able to use humor that speaks to the rural librarian's experience. Wlodkowski (1985) emphasizes the qualities necessary for motivating adult learners and he believes, along with these librarians, that animation and the power of commitment are two important elements in showing enthusiasm in the educational environment. Enthusiastic instruction has a powerful influence on the motivation of learners. The comments from the participants would indicate that enthusiastic, authentic, empowering instructors are essential to provide both role models and motivation for rural librarians. They also suggest that it is possible to compensate for many less-than-perfect practical arrangements and environmental factors if the teacher is excellent. It is the teacher that defines the quality of the educational experience. Further, the comments from the librarians suggest that the ability of the teacher to empower and motivate the participants may be the most important factor in the educational experience.

The experiences and comments from the librarians indicate that consultants and instructors who are going to be working with or on behalf of rural librarians need to have knowledge about and empathy for the rural library environment. Such knowledge cannot be gained by reading the literature and compiling statistics. Gaining it requires an individual to spend time in the rural library situation to see how it "works" or fails to work. While each situation is unique, the educators or consultants must observe at least some of these organizations if they are to understand and appreciate the values, the special challenges and the rewards of working in a rural library.

The educational experiences and perceptions of these rural librarians touch upon their definitions of themselves as librarians as well as their understanding of what others believe to be librarianship. The many subthemes within them illustrate the complicated nature and subtle messages sent within the context of the educational environment. The subtle and not-so-subtle messages embedded in the educational experience through the values of the teacher/ facilitator have an effect upon those participating. The responsibility of the educator who wishes to be effective is to deliver positive rather than negative messages. The interviewees explained the value of effective continuing education by mentioning how it improved their self-confidence, their feelings of being in control of their circumstances, and their ability to more effectively act. These are all directly related to an environment of trust and respect that enhances personal empowerment. The positive educational experiences of the participants changed their self-perception, enhanced their sense of self-worth and self-confidence, and helped them recognize and value the skills, knowledge and resources that they brought to the library.

ADDITIONAL OBJECTIVE

An additional objective of this study was to understand how the participants define the role of effective librarian. Although the focus of this report does not include the details of this aspect of the study, a brief summary is provided here to provide a picture of how these rural librarians see themselves and their role.

Effective Rural Librarians

The attributes of the effective rural librarian and, therefore, the definition of the role of the rural librarian were revealed in two ways. They emerged from a direct question on the *Personal Date Form,* and at a number of points during the interview process, the participants were also asked questions which related to their understanding of the effective librarian. In addition, the librarians revealed their definition of the role of the librarian as they shared their stories about being and becoming a librarian and as they told about other librarians they had encountered. Personal attributes were identified, categorized, and summarized from the comments and lists provided by the librarians. Various patterns and schema were used to conceptualize the attributes that were identified. Two different approaches seemed to provide the best insights into the librarian's role. The first is that of the relationship of the librarian to various groups, and the second is a listing of personal attributes and abilities considered important for their success as librarians.

Relationships with Others

The first pattern that emerged from the data was that the librarians conceptualized their professional role as a series of relationships. These relationships were with society as represented by the rural community itself; the library board and the local governmental and political power structure; library employees and volunteers; library patrons, both adults and children; and, the library community as represented by the state library association, the local system or consortium, and other librarians that they had known. Attributes of effectiveness for the role of rural librarian were often expressed in terms of the librarian's connection with these various groups or entities.

Personal Attributes and Abilities

The second schema that was used to organize the various aspects of the role of rural librarian and effectiveness within that role concerned the personal attributes and abilities most often mentioned by participants as necessary for, or at least related to, effectiveness. These attributes and abilities included personal beliefs and value systems as well as personality traits and behaviors or abilities. These attributes influence the librarian's effectiveness in the relationships mentioned above. These five attributes were listed on the *Theme Verification* form (Appendix C), and all study participants agreed that the five listed attributes or characteristics were important for success in the rural librarian role. The five characteristics were: effective communication skills; willingness to work long hours (with little pay); organizational skills with people, projects and processes; self-confidence as a person; and leadership ability (which may not be obvious in new librarians, but must develop over time). Clarity about the themes and subthemes emerged after further refinement of the data, and it was possible to characterize these original themes with the following more inclusive terms: communication and people skills; dedication; organizational skills; self-confidence and assertiveness; and leadership ability. Additionally, other attributes related to self-confidence and assertiveness were mentioned by the librarians. These included being a decision maker, having tenacity, "hard-headedness" and the ability to stand up for oneself. With few exceptions, the librarians did not speak of themselves as leaders but talked instead about others who they considered leaders. Their comments about the role of the leader as change agent agree with the literature on leadership and change (Freire 1985; Hale 1994; Jarvis 1992; Nix 1976; Rogers 1982; Zaltman and Duncan 1976).

The majority of the comments by the participants, whether describing their own strengths, describing the qualities of other effective librarians, or giving advice to new librarians, fell into these five areas. However, there were a few other attributes also listed by the participants which deserve mention.

Flexibility was mentioned by five librarians. "Having a sense of humor" and "bring creative" received mention from more than one librarian. The characteristic of creativity could also be linked with flexibility. One comment about a sense of humor is worth sharing:

> You have to be able to laugh. You have to have a sense of humor and be able to sit on the floor and laugh when any sane person would be crying!

One further conclusion related to this section of the findings concerns the altruistic service attitudes so often mentioned by librarians about themselves and about effective others, real or imagined. It is possible that this dedication to service and the wishes of others contributes to or is the other side of the lack of self-confidence and assertiveness on the part of less effective librarians. There seemed to be some recognition by a few study participants that a selfless dedication to the service of others might have two sides. The altruistic attitudes described by Arlie Hochschild (1983) in her insightful study of the predominantly female service occupations that require large amounts of emotional labor, were evident in many ways throughout the interviews with these caring individuals. Many of these librarians fit Hochschild's description of the altruist who is "more susceptible to being used—not because her sense of self is weaker but because her 'true self' is bonded more securely to the group and its welfare" (p. 196).

SUMMARY AND RECOMMENDATIONS

Approximately 95 percent of the 4,000 public libraries serving populations of less than 5,000 residents are staffed by individuals without the Master of Library Science degree, a degree which is considered by the library associations to be the minimum credential for entrance into the library profession. The individuals who serve these communities in the role of librarian, administrator and leader are dedicated to their libraries and, despite limited resources and inadequate training, attempt to provide the best possible library services. While the library profession insists that everyone who works as a librarian should have an MLS, there continue to be individuals without the degree serving as librarians in communities that can neither attract nor afford to pay an adequate salary to someone with an MLS. Although technology and opportunities for distance education are expanding the possibilities for degree attainment, rural communities are still not likely to have MLS librarians because of economics. The question then, is not how to provide the MLS to rural librarians, but how to provide appropriate and effective educational and professional development experiences in order to meet the needs of rural librarians and to assure the best possible public library service given the demographic, economic, cultural and political realities of rural communities in at least half of the states.

The purpose of this study was to identify key factors which contribute to the development of professional identity for a selected group of effective rural librarians and which might assist library educators, administrators and leaders in developing appropriate experiences for other rural librarians. These 26 rural librarians shared information about their careers and their continuing education experiences that contributed to the development of their professional identity. These experiences were examined in order to describe patterns or commonalities that might provide insight into the professionalization process. The findings serve to give a conceptual frame for the shared experiences of these 26 rural librarians and to give them a voice which provides a means of naming and drawing attention to their common experiences. While the sample was small, it expands our knowledge of the experiences and perceptions of this important group of public librarians.

Three significant career events were identified along with their associated themes. These career events were the hiring narrative or story; the networking and support provided by others; and the first library education experience. Significant elements in effective educational programs identified included networking; the relevance of topics; elements for effective educational events; and the qualifications and attitudes of presenters. The findings include two schemes to define the roles and attributes of effective rural librarians. One is defined in terms of the relationships rural librarians have with others, and one is simply a listing of consistently mentioned attributes for effectiveness. Recommendations for implementation in practice and for further research are also provided.

Recommendations Related to Practice

An understanding of the rural librarian's professionalization experience provides an opportunity to appreciate that experience and to use the insights of the 26 individual librarians to provide clues to the commonalities of rural librarians. These findings point to possible applications to be considered by the library community. State library agencies, systems and consortia, state and regional library associations, graduate library schools and the American Library Association may all be able to tailor their continuing education interactions with the rural librarians to address issues identified. In addition, there are areas for practical application that do not involve the design of formal educational opportunities. Several areas are suggested for practical application of the research findings. They are not in priority order.

1. It is imperative that individuals working in rural libraries, without prior knowledge of the role of the librarian, become involved in the life of the profession as early as possible in their careers. The opportunity to observe a wide variety of librarians who may become role models and mentors

should be part of this early career experience. State libraries and state library associations or other appropriate umbrella organizations or authorities, should develop the means by which to contact and draw into the profession newly hired rural librarians within the first three to six months of their job responsibilities.

2. Formal mentoring programs should be established as a means to enhance early involvement in the profession. Such mentoring programs should match effective librarians and/or consultants with newly hired rural librarians. It is clear that the characteristics of mentors are important for success based upon the experience of these rural librarians as well as the growing literature on mentoring. Mentors should have appropriate communication skills and knowledge of the rural library experience and environment. Mentoring and role modeling should be provided early and freely.

3. One of the strongest messages that emerged from the research was that of the importance of networking with other rural librarians. The value and importance of networking as a professional development activity should be validated within the library community, and opportunities for networking should be built into all continuing education offerings. In order for this to happen, those responsible for planning and presenting educational offerings must have a philosophy of adult education that trusts and respects adult learners and recognizes the responsibility of the educator to provide the most appropriate opportunity to facilitate learning by providing structure, content and a supportive environment for learning.

4. Those providing educational opportunities for rural librarians should be aware of the role modeling element of the educational experience so that presenters or teachers are selected both for their ability to communicate appropriate values and to serve as role models. This requires that educational providers themselves be clear about what qualities they want modeled for others. Rural library educators should be able to provide a learning environment where empowerment and growth can occur. This includes the ability to motivate others to be the best that they can be. The comments by participants in this study equated the library educator's important qualities to those one finds in a good public service librarian, and this similarity is worth considering. As one librarian said: "The important characteristics for CE presenters are the same as those for the public librarian: the librarians are your public. You should treat us the way you expect us to treat the public."

5. Closely related to the role modeling and communication ability of the library educator is an attitude of professional responsibility and respect that precludes any condescension or disrespectful behavior or attitude towards individuals without the MLS degree. An environment of mutual

respect is essential in the adult learning situation. Adult education should be conducted in an environment that enhances the self image and confidence of the learner. Any educational situation that does not accomplish this is a failure. When mounting educational programs, Freire's (1970) belief that education is never neutral should be remembered. The continuing education experience will have either a positive or a negative effect. It will either provide the means for personal empowerment and professional growth or it will inhibit and diminish the individual's ability and motivation.

6. While it is unrealistic to expect that all of those serving as facilitators in continuing education programs or conference situations where rural librarians are in attendance will have actually worked in a rural library, it is appropriate that they have some real knowledge of and an appreciation for the rural library world. Rural librarians appear to be asking that, in addition to respect, there be some recognition that their world is real. Educators working with rural librarians should have some basic understanding of the realities of that world so they can provide examples and operational models that can be implemented in that setting. Public agency consultants, private consultants and educators who expect to be engaged in the education of rural librarians might visit rural libraries and spend some time in a number of them to observe what life is like. They might serve on a very limited basis as substitute librarians in rural libraries in order to improve their ability to understand the environment and the special challenges associated with rural librarianship and rural politics.

7. In relation to the topics marketed and presented for rural librarians, this study pointed to the need for relevancy and applicability for the rural situation. When topics have immediate applicability for a larger, more broadly staffed library organization, truth-in-advertising might help rural librarians select programs most appropriate to their situation and their needs so as not to waste their very limited time and resources on inappropriate offerings.

8. To accommodate turnover, basic topics need to be offered on a regular basis in some format for rural librarians, and a basic program should be produced and marketed nationally, either through ALA or from a library school rather than having each state design, fund and provide basic library skills programs. Such programs might include either a series of videos that could be viewed on an individual basis or a program that can be delivered through the use of telecommunications. The state or local system might better use its resources to provide mentoring and networking opportunities rather than in providing this kind of training. Local resources could then be used to help librarians move into the more professional aspects of librarianship rather than to deal with the development of the basic, mechanical skills required in the library.

9. The negative educational experiences reported in the study findings indicate that some tension and apprehension about educational experiences might be alleviated by placing more importance upon the "human" side of educational offerings. Clearer communication and marketing concerning the content, practical arrangements, and characteristics of the other participants, particularly for residential institutes, might be helpful in eliminating some of the apprehension associated with these events. A recognition of the possible intimidation that campus and big city situations can contribute for the first time attendee might change the way these meetings are marketed to rural librarians.

10. The profession might develop materials and programs to work more closely and directly with rural library boards and with other decision makers and officials in rural communities to help them understand the appropriate attributes for effective librarianship. A more direct and less subtle approach to countering the popular stereotype of the librarian image would assist local communities in the recruitment and hiring of individuals with the personal characteristics and values that these rural librarians identified as necessary for effectiveness. Such characteristics provide a wide range of personality possibilities but highlight the communication skills, assertiveness and political savvy essential for success rather than placing an emphasis upon passive individuals who like quiet places, read a lot and know how to use a library.

These recommendations for practice have implications for various segments of the library community. They do not require new resources so much as a reconsideration or a more directed use of current resources. They are offered as points of departure for consideration to encourage discussion and the exploration of new or enhanced models for the provision of role modeling, networking and continuing education.

Recommendations Related to Research

This study is only a small part of the research necessary to understand the needs of rural librarians and raises as many questions as it answers partly because of the limited nature of this study of 26 individual rural librarians and their experiences and partly because of the nature of research itself. Some of the related issues needing further research include:

1. The need to identify or develop an appropriate instrument to use to determine the characteristics of effective rural librarians across a broad representative sample. This would provide an opportunity to measure personal efficacy and effectiveness in the librarian role. Studies might then verify or dispute the limited findings of this study and could link

characteristics and perhaps provide rankings of importance for these characteristics. While the participants of this study verified the five primary attributes of effective librarians as presented by the researcher, a more quantifiable and specific instrument needs to be used so that finer definitions might be made. Albert Bandura's self-efficacy theory (1978, 1982, 1986) could provide a model upon which such an instrument or scale might be developed.

2. A study of rural officials and library trustees should be made to clarify the expectations these decision-makers have of the role of the rural librarian and the definitions they use to clarify how one might intervene at the recruiting and hiring stage for rural librarians. In this way it may be possible to improve the chances of success for the individual who is asked to assume the role of librarian even when that person does not have an MLS degree.

3. A systematic investigation and evaluation of state programs to support the training of rural librarians might serve to identify the most effective models, features and elements that contribute to effectiveness over time. Such a study might be designed to look at those things that contribute to long term effectiveness, to include membership in professional associations, attendance at continuing education events, leadership roles assumed over time, peer identification of individuals as role models, and library statistics measuring improved service and effectiveness.

4. A more in-depth investigation of the relationships essential for effective rural librarianship and the attributes necessary for success in each relationship might also serve to expand the findings of this study. A generalizable model of the relationship paradigm applied to rural librarians might be of help to local officials and to new librarians.

5. Because this research was a limited multi-case study, questions regarding possible differences in perceptions and identities of rural librarians in states with residential institutes compared to those in states without such programs were not addressed. Questions regarding possible differences in perceptions and identities of rural librarians in states with mandatory certification programs compared to those without such programs were also not addressed. A study specifically identifying and defining such differences would provide the basis for changes in practice.

6. One of Busch's (1990) research recommendations applies here: Another important area of the rural research agenda needing attention is that of the employers' perspectives on recruitment and retention of library personnel. Such research might include the objective and subjective qualities employers look for when recruiting RPL [rural public library] directors, how they go about recruiting new personnel, difficulties experienced in the recruitment process, and past experiences with directors who may have stayed only a short period of time. In addition,

topics such as how employers perceive optimal retention in terms of length of time in the position, their opinions on salaries, benefits and education levels, and how they perceive the role of librarians might be fruitful areas of investigation (p. 233).

7. Changes in the nature of the rural environment have resulted in an apparent increase in the demands on local rural libraries because of the growing informational and technological sophistication of residents. Research documenting the extent and nature of this phenomenon would provide information that could help rural communities plan appropriate responses.

8. The effectiveness of continuing library education planners, designers and providers should be investigated to determine what constitutes effective credentials for these responsibilities. While educators recognize that content knowledge and the ability to communicate that knowledge in a manner effective for the situation are not always related skills, the issues of quality control in library continuing education delivery continue to be debated. More research is needed to help the profession address the issues of quality in the distributed continuing education environment, including for conference offerings.

9. Additionally, the library community should examine and draw upon the literature of other professions operating within the rural environment. Their experiences in terms of credentialing, educational delivery, role modeling and retention are similar and can provide significant insights into the professionalization of rural librarians. An example pointed to by Gardner Hanks (1992) is the experience of the American social workers and their recognition of the need for professional entry and certification at levels other than the masters degree. The restructuring of their professional requirements enabled them to validate and bring practitioners into the profession. As "real" social workers they had a stronger voice in developing their professional identity. Librarianship needs to explore such models and to consider other means of empowering practitioners.

CONCLUSION

The primary problems or negative elements that emerged from the research data were the second-class status afforded non-MLS librarians by the library community, the influence of the librarian stereotype upon the professional image of the rural librarians, and the lack of quality of some continuing education. The positive elements that emerged from the research were networking, role modeling, and mentoring in the professionalization process, and the quality of the rural librarians themselves. The second-class status of librarians without the MLS degree is made manifest in the behaviors and attitudes of others. These others include library educators, consultants, MLS librarians, peer librarians, local library officials and staff, and the culture of the library profession in general. Rather than providing messages of affirmation about their abilities to fulfill their library roles, the message sent from the day of hire onward is "nothing personal, but you are not good enough." Positive and early intervention to change that message needs to occur in the careers of individual rural librarians when they are hired. It is important that they receive the information about library science and management that they need to function successfully as librarians. It is equally important that they have easy access to role models and that they receive personal empowerment messages that enhance their efficacy and verify their abilities to perform successfully as librarians. Mentoring programs, one-on-one consulting, travel grants to encourage attendance at conferences or meetings, and other means might be used to provide early career contact and opportunities for networking and identifying with the profession.

The librarian stereotype, still prevalent in popular culture, seems to have particular impact upon the careers of individual rural librarians who do not have the MLS degree. From the circumstances of their employment to their interactions with their communities, their peers and the rest of the library profession, the image of the stereotypical librarian seems to cause particular difficulty for those in rural libraries. Without the experience of a graduate education in library science and the professional identification and acculturation that occurs in conjunction with this educational experience, the rural librarian does not have an opportunity to develop an individual professional identity in advance of assuming the librarian responsibilities. Defining one's professional identity, values and role while working in the position is particularly difficult and challenging especially in isolation from other librarians. Rural librarians should be provided with role models and/ or mentors working in situations like theirs who can outline for them options for a professional identity that are congruent with their values and self-perceptions while being challenging and exciting. The librarian stereotype should not be the only option they see.

The autonomous and varied state programs for the education and training of rural public librarians appear to be uneven in a number of ways: quality of the educational content, the quality of the educational delivery, the quality of the educators, the frequency of delivery, responsiveness to the librarians, the attitudes and friendliness of providers, program design, funding, and continuing consulting services. These vary greatly from state to state. National or multi-state coordination or cooperation might provide a better end product more efficiently. Graduate schools of library science, distance education technology, Internet conferencing capabilities, and appropriate program design can all contribute to the creation and delivery of quality basic continuing or preservice education to meet the needs of rural librarians across a range of political and geographic boundaries.

The responsiveness of the 26 librarians in this study illustrates both their willingness to be involved in the life of the profession and their eagerness to be consulted about their roles and their experiences. These librarians are professionals and should be considered as such by their colleagues in librarianship. Darlene Weingand (1994) acknowledges the contributions and dedication of the rural librarians while verifying the value of the MLS:

> In the smallest situations, the notion of what is "professional" will not match the prevailing definition promulgated by library associations (i.e., a master's degree in a program accredited by the American Library Association). In these smaller towns, "professional" must rightly apply to dedication and attitude, regardless of educational preparation. This is not to discount the importance of the full master's degree; rather, it is an attempt to acknowledge both the reality of what a small community can afford and the hardworking, committed librarians who serve those communities (p. 75).

The profession might consider sanctioning other means of becoming a librarian so that individuals such as these are not placed in permanent second-class librarian status. There are a number of possible solutions available including the many models and directions for professional education that take into consideration the rapidly changing technical content and the need for accountability both within and outside of each profession (Curry and Wegin 1993). The model of the social work profession or other methods for undergraduate accreditation, national certification or peer review are all worth discussing. Distance education and technology also offer practical means to achieve a new model for what Nowlen (1990) refers to as a "holistic approach" to continuing education for the professions. The library profession is not unique in considering mandatory continuing education (Queeney, Smutz and Shuman 1990) or mandatory preservice education. In order to restructure professional education, however, the profession must be able to define what a professional librarian is and what one does allowing for differences in type and size of library.

APPENDIX A

\# _____

PERSONAL DATA FORM

NAME _____ AGE _____ SEX _____

LIBRARY _____ PHONE _____

ADDRESS _____ CITY _____ STATE _____ ZIP _____

TITLE _____ DATE EMPLOYED AS LIBRARIAN _____

YEARS IN THIS POSITION _____ \# HOURS EMPLOYED WEEKLY_____

YEARS IN OTHER LIBRARY POSITIONS _____

(continued)

LIBRARY INFORMATION:
POPULATION SERVED _____ # VOLUMES _____
ANNUAL CIRCULATION _____ # FTE EMPLOYEES _____
LIBRARY EDUCATIONAL EVENTS ATTENDED IN PAST 12 MONTHS _____
DO YOU CONSIDER YOURSELF EFFECTIVE AS A LIBRARIAN? YES ___ NO ___
DO YOU CONSIDER YOURSELF A COMMUNITY LEADER? YES ___ NO ___
WHAT PERSONAL ATTRIBUTES DO YOU CONSIDERD MOST IMPORTANT
FOR SUCCESS AS A RURAL LIBRARIAN?

APPENDIX B

_____

_____

INTERVIEW PROTOCOL

Explain that the purpose of the research is to identify characteristics of successful rural librarians and to identify effective educational events for rural librarians. Explain about the use of the recorder. Ask permission to tape the session. Give individual the option of turning the recorder off at any time. Explain confidentiality and that their comments will contribute to the study, but that they will never be personally identified as a participant nor connected to the information which they provide. Ask for questions before & during interview.

SIGNIFICANT FACTORS IN CAREER: When you remember your first few years as the librarian here, what do you remember as the most significant professional events?
What make these events significant for you?
When did each of these events occur?
How did these events help you to understand or clarify your understanding of your role as a librarian?

EDUCATIONAL EVENTS: During the time you have been librarian, you have attended meetings and continuing educational events. Tell me about one such experience that you thought was particularly effective and worthwhile for you.
What factors made it worthwhile?
What components encourage you to attend a continuing education event?
What components do you find least desirable in a continuing education offering or presentation?
Thinking back over your years as a librarian, what would you identify as the most important and positive educational event?
What made it important?
How did it make you feel?
What advice can you give a library educator like myself, about what elements ought to be designed into continuing education programs for rural librarians? (not topics)
What characteristics do you think are most important for a consultant or library educator to have in order to work with rural librarians?

PROFESSIONAL IDENTITY: When you think of yourself as a librarian, what aspects of yourself, or what personal attributes do you think of?

How do you explain your job to relatives, neighbors or others unfamiliar with the library

If you could make the same salary in your community, with the same time commitment, would you leave your library position?

ATTRIBUTES FOR EFFECTIVENESS: When you think of other effective and successful libraries you know in rural communities, what are the attributes or qualities which you think make them effective?

What three personal qualities or attributes do you think are most important for success as a librarian? (rank)

In what ways are you most effective as a librarian? If there are areas in which you do not feel particularly effective, could you tell me about them?

If a new librarian were to be hired in a nearby town and she/he came to you for advice, what would you tell them about their role as librarian?

Is there anything else about your role in the community which you would like to tell me about?

CONCLUDING REMARKS: Thank for participation, time, honesty. Ask again if there are any questions. Explain that they will receive a summary of observations from interview. Ask that they review the information and respond. Encourage them to call or write if additional ideas occur to them. Give them business card.

APPENDIX C

DATE:

TO: Participants in "Professionalization of Rural Librarians"

FR: Mary Bushing

RE: Preliminary themes

Now that the interviews have been completed, I have identified the following themes that appear in the comments from almost all of the participants. I would appreciate if you would consider these themes in light of your experiences. Then indicate to me if you think that these themes are representative of the expereince and/or circumstances of rural librarians in communities serving 5,000 of fewer people. You may return the form to me in the enclosed stamped and addressed envelope. Once again, thank you for your time, your insights and your willingness to share.

THEMES	AGREE	DISAGREE
Rural librarianship begins as an accident of the market-place. It is not a planned career, but results because of for-tuitous circumstances.		
Networking with other librarians is one of the most impor-tant means of learning and growing as a professional.		
Personal support from some key others (consultants, other librarians, family, community) is essential for success.		
Continuing education is valuable when it is practical and applicable to the small library situation.		
Those who work with rural librarians (consultants & edu-cators) must be able to make the librarian feel confident about her/his ability to "be" a librarian.		
Important characteristics for rural librarians include:		
Effective communication skills		
Willingness to work long hours (with little pay)		
Organizational skills with people, projects, processes		
Self-confidence as a person		
Leadership ability (may not be developed initially		

Thank you for your considered opinion. I truly appreciate your insights into the process of becoming librarians on the job. After you have marked the items above, please return this page to me in the enclosed envelope.

REFERENCES

American Library Association Organizational Self Study Committee. 1995. *Phase II Report.* Chicago: American Library Association.

American Library Association Planning Committee. 1989. *A Progress Report. ALA Priority Area: Personal Resources.* Chicago: American Library Association.

Apps, J. W. 1982. "Developing a Belief Structure." Pp. 25-32 in *Materials and Methods in Adult and Continuing Education,* edited by C. Klevins. San Francisco: Jossey-Bass.

Bandura, A. 1978. "Reflections on Self-efficacy." *Advances in Behavioral Research and Therapy* 1: 237-269.

————. 1982. "Self-efficacy Mechanism in Human Agency." *American Psychologist* 37(2): 122-147.

————. 1986. *Social Foundations of Thought and Action: A Social-cognitive View.* Englewood Cliffs, NJ: Prentice-Hall.

Barron, D. and C. Curran. 1980. "Assessing the Information Needs of Rural People: The Development of an Action Strategy for Rural Librarians." *Library Trends* 28(4): 619-631.

Bealer, R. C., F. K. Willits and W. P. Kuvlesky. 1978. "The Meaning of 'Rurality' in American Society: Some Implications of Alternative Definitions." Pp. 338-343 in *Change in Rural America: Causes, Consequences, and Alternatives,* edited by R. D. Rodefeld, J. Flora, D. Voth, I. Fujimoto and J. Converse. Saint Louis: C. V. Mosby.

Becker, H. S. and J. W. Carper. 1956. "The Elements of Identification with an Occupation." *American Sociological Review* 21: 341-348.

Bosak, J. and B. Perlman. 1982. "A Review of the Definition of Rural." *Journal of Rural Community Psychology* 3: 3-34.

Brand, B. E. 1983. "Librarianship and Other Female-intensive Professions." *Journal of Library History* 18: 391-406.

Brookfield, S. D. 1986. *Understanding and Facilitating Adult Learning.* San Francisco: Jossey-Bass.

————. 1987. *Developing Critical Thinkers: Challenging Adults to Explore Alternate Ways of Thinking and Acting.* San Francisco: Jossey-Bass.

————. 1990. *The Skillful Teacher.* San Francisco: Jossey-Bass.

Brugh, A. E. and B. R. Beede. 1976. "American Librarianship." *Signs: A Journal of Women in Culture and Society* 1: 943-955.

Bucher, R. and A. Strauss. 1961. "Professions in Process." *American Journal of Sociology* 66: 325-334.

Bureau of the Census. 1994. *Statistical Abstract of the United States 1994.* Washington, DC: U.S. Government Printing Office.

Busch, N. J. 1990. "Factors Relating to the Recruitment and Retention of Library Directors in Rural Public Libraries in the United States." *Dissertation Abstracts International* 51(07): 2185A.

Butler, P. 1951. "Librarianship as a Profession." *Library Quarterly* 21: 235-247.

Carmichael, J. V. 1992. "The Male Librarian and the Feminine Image: A Survey of Stereotype, Status, and Gender Perceptions." *Library and Information Science Research* 14: 411-446.

Cervero, R. M. 1988. *Effective Continuing Education for Professionals.* San Francisco: Jossey-Bass.

————. 1992. "Professional Practice, Learning, and Continuing Education: An Integrated Perspective. *International Journal of Lifelong Education,* 11(2): 91-101.

Clark, S. M. and M. Corcoran. 1984. "Professional Socialization and Contemporary Career Attitudes of Three Faculty Generations." *Research in Higher Education* 20: 131-153.

Courts, P. L. 1991. *Literacy and Empowerment: the Meaning Makers.* New York: Bergin & Garvey.

Cranton, P. 1994. *Understanding and Promoting Transformative Learning: A Guide for Educators of Adults*. San Francisco: Jossey-Bass.

Cross, P. 1981. *Adults as Learners*. San Francisco: Jossey-Bass.

Curry, L. and J. F. Wegin & Associates. 1993. *Educating Professionals: Responding to New Expectations for Competence and Accountability*. San Francisco: Jossey-Bass.

Dewey, B. I. 1985. "Selection of Librarianship as a Career: Implications for Recruitment. *Journal of Education for Library and Information Science* 26: 16-24.

Etzioni, A. ed. 1969. *The Semi-professions and Their Organization: Teachers, Nurses, Social Workers*. New York: Free Press.

Fitchen, J. M. 1991. *Endangered Spaces, Enduring Places: Change, Identity, and Survival in Rural America*. Boulder, CO: Westview Press.

Freidson, E. 1994. *Professionalism Reborn: Theory, Prophecy, and Policy*. Chicago: University of Chicago Press.

————. 1970. *Pedagogy of the Opressed*. New York: Continuum.

————. 1985. *The Politics of Education: Culture, Power and Liberation*. Hadley, MA: Bergin & Garvey.

Fuguitt, G. V., D. L. Brown and C. L. Beale. 1989. *Rural and Small Town America*. New York: Russell Sage Foundation.

Glazier, J. D. 1992. "Qualitative Research Methodologies for Library and Information Science: An Introduction." Pp. 1-13 in *Qualitative Research in Information Management*, edited by J. D. Glazier and R. R. Powell. Englewood, CO: Libraries Unlimited.

Goldhor, H. 1986. "What is a Rural Public Library?" *Library Journal* 111: 15.

Good, T. L. and J. E. Brophy. 1984. *Looking in Classrooms*, (3rd ed.). New York: Harper and Row.

Grear, R. M. 1990. *Mentoring Histories of Ohio Public Library Directors*. East Lansing, MI: National Center for Research on Teacher Learning. (ERIC Document Reproduction Service No. ED 367 364).

Griffith, L. (1989). "Political Marketing of the Rural Library." *Wilson Library Bulletin* 63: 44-47.

Hale, M. 1994. *Leadership in Small or Rural Libraries*. Presentation at the Public Library Association Conference, Atlanta.

Hanks, G. C. 1992. "Call for a New Approach Toward Educating a Librarian." *PNLA Quarterly* 55(2): 8-10.

Heasley, D. and D. Preston. 1989. "The Changes in Rural America." *Rural Libraries* 9: 1-21.

Heim, K. M. ed. 1982. *The Status of Women in Librarianship: Historical, Sociological, and Economic Issues*. New York: Neal-Schuman.

Heimlich, J. E. and E. Norland. 1994. *Developing Teaching Style in Adult Education*. San Francisco: Jossey-Bass.

Hobbs, D. J. and D. A. Dillman. 1982. "Research for the Rural United States." Pp. 1-9 in *Rural Society in the U.S.: Issues for the 1980's*, edited by D. J. Hobbs and D. A. Dillman. Boulder, CO: Westview Press.

Hochschild, A. R. 1983. *The Managed Heart: Commercialization of Human Feeling*. Berkeley: University of California Press.

Houle, C. O. 1980. *Continuing Learning in the Professions*. San Francisco: Jossey-Bass.

Jarvis, P. 1992. *Paradoxes of Learning: on Becoming an Individual in Society*. San Francisco: Jossey-Bass.

Knowles, M. S. 1980. *The Modern Practice of Adult Education: from Pedagogy to Andragogy*. Chicago: Follett.

Knox, A. B. 1977. *Adult Development and Learning*. San Francisco: Jossey-Bass.

————. 1992. *Strengthening Adult and Continuing Education: a Global Perspective on Synergistic Leadership*. San Francisco: Jossey-Bass.

Kreisberg, S. 1992. *Transforming Power: Domination, Empowerment, and Education.* Albany, NY: State University of New York.

Lowman, J. 1991. *Mastering the Techniques of Teaching.* San Francisco: Jossey-Bass.

Maslow, A. H. 1954. *Motivation and Personality.* New York: Harper and Row.

Mezirow, J. ed. 1990. *Fostering Critical Reflection in Adulthood.* San Francisco: Jossey-Bass.

_____. 1991. *Transformative Dimensions of Adult Learning.* San Francisco: Jossey-Bass.

Miller, L. 1989. "The Self-image of the Library Profession." *International Library Review* 21: 141-155.

National Center for Education Statistics. 1994a. *Public Library Data 1992* [Electronic data tape]. Washington, DC: Federal-State Cooperative System for Public Library Data.

_____. 1994b. *Public Libraries in the United States: 1992.* Washington, DC: U.S. Government Printing Office.

Nix, H. L. 1976. "Concepts of Community and Community Leadership." Pp. 313-324 in *Leadership and Social Change*, edited by W. R. Lassey and R. R. Fernández. La Jolla, CA: University Associates.

Nowlen, P. M. 1990. "New Expectations, New Roles: A Holistic Approach to Continuing Education for the Professions." Pp. 15-23 in *Visions for the Future of Continuing Professional Education*, edited by R. M. Cervero, J. F. Azzartto and Associates. Athens, GA: The University of Georgia, Department of Adult Education, College of Education.

Osbourn, S. 1973. *Library Services in Rural Areas.* Prepared on Request of the Subcommittee on Rural Development of the Committee on Agriculture and Forestry by the Congressional Research Service. Washington, DC: U.S. Government Printing Office.

Queeney, D. S., W. D. Smutz and S. B. Shuman. 1990. "Mandatory Continuing Professional Education: Old Issue, New Questions." *Continuing Higher Education Review: The Journal of the National University Continuing Education Association* 54: 11-25.

Rogers, C. R. 1969. *Freedom to Learn: A View of What Education Might Become.* Columbus, OH: Merrill.

Rogers, E. M. 1982. *Diffusion of Innovations*, 3rd ed. New York: Free Press.

Schön, D. A. 1983. *The Reflective Practitioner.* New York: Basic Books.

_____. 1987. *Educating the Reflective Practitioner: Toward a New Design for Teaching and Learning in the Professions.* San Francisco: Jossey-Bass.

_____. ed.. 1991. *The Reflective Turn: Case Studies in and on Educational Practice.* New York: Teachers College Press.

Schuman, P. G. 1984. "Women, Power, and Libraries." *Library Journal* 1091: 42-47.

Sherlock, B. J. and R. T. Morris. 1967. "The Evolution of the Professional Paradigm." *Sociological Inquiry* 37: 27-29.

Shor, I. 1993. "Education is Politics: Paulo Freire's Critical Pedagogy." Pp. 25-35 in *Paulo Freire: A Critical Encounter*, edited by P. McLaren and P. Leonard. London: Routledge.

Smith, D. 1992. "The Greening of Librarianship: Toward a Human Resource Development Ecology." *Journal of Library Administration* 17: 37-53.

Stone, E. W. 1974. *Continuing Library and Information Science Education: Final Report to the National Commission on Libraries and Information Science.* Washington, DC: American Society for Information Science.

Vanderslice, V. J. 1984. "Empowerment: A Definition in Process." *Human Ecology Forum* 14(1): 2-3.

Vavrek, B. 1989. "Educating Rural Librarians: Is the Sky Falling?" *The Bookmark* 48: 24-27.

_____. 1992. "Educating Rural Library Staff." *Library Mosaics* 31: 7-9.

Verduin, J. R., H. G. Miller and C. E. Greer. 1977. *Adults Teaching Adults.* Austin, TX: Learning Concepts.

Vogt, J. F. and K. L. Murrell. 1990. *Empowerment in Organizations: How to Spark Exceptional Performance.* Amsterdam: Pfeiffer.

Weech, T. L. 1980. "Public Library Standards and Rural Library Service." *Library Trends* 28: 599-617.

Weibel, K., K. M. Heim and D. J. Ellsworth. eds. 1979. *The Role of Women in Librarianship 1876-1976: The Entry, Advancement, and Struggle for Equalization in One Profession.* Phoenix: Oryx Press.

Weingand, D. E. 1992. "Continuing Professional Education." Pp. 343-363 in *Library and Information Science Education Statistical Report,* edited by T. W. Sineath. Chicago: American Library Association.

————— . 1994. *Managing Today's Public Library: Blueprint for Change.* Englewood, CO: Libraries Unlimited.

Weiss, C. S. 1981. "The Development of Professional Role Commitment Among Graduate Students." *Human Relations* 34: 13-31.

White, R. F. and D. B. Macklin. 1970. *Education, Careers and Professionalization in Librarianship and Information Science.* Contract No. OEC-1-7-071084-5017. Washington, DC: U.S. Department of Health, Education and Welfare. ERIC Document Reproduction Service No. 054 800.

Wilson, P. 1982. *Stereotype and Status: Librarians in the United States.* Contributions in Librarianship and Information Science, No. 41. Westport, CT: Greenwood.

Wlodkowski, R. 1990. *Enhancing Adult Motivation to Learn.* San Francisco: Jossey-Bass.

Zaltman, G. and R. J. Duncan. 1976. *Strategies for Planned Change.* New York: Wiley.

MANAGING IN THE INFORMATION AGE:
NEW RULES FOR A NEW REALITY

Ray McBeth

INTRODUCTION

Organizations in America, as well as organizations in all other parts of the world, are under increasing pressure to be more efficient and effective. This is as true in libraries and information centers as it is in manufacturing, insurance, banking, education, and other organizational environments. Unfortunately many attempts at improvement seem only to make matters worse. Tighter controls, more sophisticated tracking systems and other traditional approaches to improving productivity no longer seem to work. In part, these traditional managerial problem-solving methods do not work because the industrial era assumptions on which they are based, no longer apply. What assumptions, then, do apply? Those of an information or knowledge-based society?

It may be a cliche to say that we live in an information age, but it's important to understand what lies behind that concept. According to one source:

Advances in Library Administration and Organization,
Volume 15, pages 165-185.
Copyright © 1997 by JAI Press Inc.
All rights of reproduction in any form reserved.
ISBN: 0-7623-0371-9

Recent Government statistics in the United States indicate that at least 33 percent of new plant and equipment ... was in the information technology area. In addition, 60 percent of the increase in new plant and equipment expenditure was accounted for by information technology. These statistics support the contention that the use of information as a strategic resource is now at the heart of every major American corporate strategy (Ferrero 1991, p. 4)

It is virtually impossible to pick up a magazine or newspaper without seeing some reference to the "Information Age" or "Information Technology" and its effect on us. The Internet, cellular phones, FAX machines, CD-ROM, E-mail, voice mail, information utilities, all change the ways in which we work and interact with each other.

Stewart (1993) suggests that the information age is actually the result of four distinct revolutions that are happening all at the same time and all very fast. They cause one another and effect one another creating an overall revolution comparable in scale to the Industrial Revolution of the early nineteenth century. He says that "We all sense that the changes surrounding us are not mere trends but the workings of large, unruly forces" (p. 66). These revolutions are:

1. the globalization of markets;
2. the spread of information technology and computer networks;
3. the dismantling of hierarchy; and
4. a new information age economy.

These revolutions are especially significant because hierarchy is the structure that has essentially organized work since the mid-nineteenth century and because the fundamental sources of wealth in an information age economy are knowledge and communication rather than natural resources and physical labor.

The implications of these revolutions are staggering. We now live in a world where more people process information for a living than do any other single type of work. Many of us, regardless of background or training, are now *de facto* information specialists whether we like it or not; our primary tasks consist of managing and maintaining environments in which information, (and those who use it), form the core of our everyday operations. This new reality poses some interesting paradoxes for librarians and other information professionals. On the one hand, they have always done information work and, in many cases, were the only ones who worked primarily with information in an organization. On the other, the control that they have exercised over information services is diminished now that many others, some without formal information training, are using and processing information. In addition, new technologies, are the media of choice for many forms of information, making the librarians' "paper-based" skills increasingly obsolete.

To put the information age in perspective it is important to look at the past. The history of this country, at least in terms of primary work roles, can be described in three words: farmer, laborer, clerk (Naisbitt 1982). As recently as the turn of this past century one-third of the work force was still involved in agriculture, a significant reduction from the turn of the prior and all previous centuries. Growing industrialization continued to change the nature of the work force, and, by the 1950s, manufacturing employed the majority of workers. Today only about 3 percent of the work force is involved in agriculture, slightly more than 10 percent are involved in manufacturing and more than 60 percent are involved in clerical, professional and other information-based activities, and this percentage is growing (Naisbitt 1982). Some have suggested that in the future only 2 percent of the population will grow all the food that we eat and another 2 percent will manufacture all the things that we need (Stewart 1993). What then will the rest of us do?

These changes from an agricultural to an industrial to an information-based economy, as evidenced by primary work roles, have occurred in a relatively short period of time and are still not complete. The rapidity of the changes leaves many in the work force with industrial era values that are inappropriate for an information-based economy because of the changes that have taken place during their own work life. This failure to keep up with changing values is known as cultural lag and exists when changes in attitudes and beliefs do not keep up with changes in the material dimension of culture (Ogburn 1964). If management theory is to deal effectively with these changes, attention must be paid to the implications of managing information-based environments.

Management has been defined as "a set of activities directed at the efficient and effective utilization of resources in the pursuit of one or more goals" (Van Fleet 1991, p. 8). If we take this definition and expand it further, we can identify those activities as the four major management functions: planning, organizing, leading and controlling. Efficiency deals with resource utilization, that is doing things right, while effectiveness deals with goal orientation; that is doing the right thing. The resources available to managers include:

1. Financial Resources (the capital necessary to build the factories that formed the base for an industrial society, and tracked as return on investment)
2. Physical Resources (the plants constructed and raw materials purchased with the capital, and carefully tracked as assets and inventory)
3. Human Resources (the people that make it all happen, who have only been considered as a significant investment since the 1950s, but who are now being seen as possessors of intellectual capital)
4. Information Resources (which have historically been undervalued and viewed as secondary to the core mission of most organizations).

The resources are used to pursue one or more goals. Organizational goals have traditionally been defined as the targets or accomplishments that management expects the organization to obtain. This definition is not useful in an information age, but Drucker offers one that may have more value. He says "The essence of management is to make knowledges productive" (Drucker 1994, p. 72). His view of knowledge is not of the traditional variety. He says that there are many knowledges that are the result of the knowledge that each individual has regarding the application of his/her specialization. It is management's task to apply these knowledges to produce results.

The shift from an industrial to an information-based economy requires a similar shift in thinking regarding primary management activities. The type of shift that is needed, and which is beginning to occur, is a shift in paradigms (a concept first introduced by Thomas Kuhn in 1962). A paradigm is "a scheme for understanding and explaining certain aspects of reality" (Ferguson 1980, p. 26). A paradigm shift then is "a distinctly new way of thinking about old problems" (Ferguson 1980, p. 26). For example, our world has experienced two major paradigm shifts in our understanding of the physical universe. The first was the shift from seeing the earth as the center of the universe to seeing the sun as the center of our solar system. The second was the shift from a "Newtonian" view of physical forces to a relativistic or "Einsteinian" one. Unfortunately, as is true with most major changes, the shift to a new perspective, even though it has superior explanatory power and scope, is often not accepted easily. As Ferguson (1980) put it:

> New paradigms are nearly always received with coolness, even mockery and hostility. Their discoveries are attacked for their heresy. (For historic examples consider Copernicus, Galileo, Pasteur, Mesmer.) The idea may appear bizarre, even fuzzy, at first because the discoverer made an intuitive leap and does not have all the data in place yet.
>
> The new perspective demands such a shift that established scientists are rarely converted. As Kuhn pointed out, those who worked fruitfully in the old view are emotionally and habitually attached to it. They usually go to their graves with their faith unshaken. Even when confronted with overwhelming evidence, they stubbornly stick with the wrong but familiar (pp. 27-28).

There are significant managerial implications in the paradigm shift from an industrial to an information-based society, many of which continue to elude those involved in the day-to-day management of organizations. Traditional management activities must change as a result of that shift if organizations are to survive. If the implications do not become clear, as James Swartz suggests in his book *The Hunters and the Hunted* (1994), some managers will continue to look outside of themselves and their organizations to place blame for the current failures in which they are involved. This is a form of denial that will ultimately lead to the demise of the organization.

The managerial implications of the shift from an industrial society to a society and economy based on information are complex and often confusing. The shift has occurred rapidly but not uniformly and is therefore often confusing to managers. In practical terms this means that individuals and organizations are living through the change and adapting to it with varying degrees of success, as the shift continues to occur. For example, many individuals are now involved in information related jobs such as microcomputer support specialist, network analyst, webmaster, and the like, jobs that did not even exist a decade ago. More importantly, virtually all of us are using, or have available in our organizations, personal computers and other microprocessor-based equipment, a technology for processing information that did not exist even twenty years ago. This technology has changed and continues to change the nature of work. Assumptions regarding how work is to be accomplished that were virtually unthinkable in 1977 are now taken for granted. The existence of these new types of "jobs" and the new methods and tools for accomplishing the tasks that have emerged have significant implications for those who want to redefine what it means to manage.

Most of us grew up with an industrial perspective, that is we see "work" as something typically done only with our hands or bodies in a factory or office. That perspective has been replaced by a definition of a worker as "someone who works with hands and with theoretical knowledge. (Examples are computer technicians, x-ray technicians, physical therapists, medical-lab technicians, pulmonary technicians, and so on, who together make up the fastest-growing group in the U.S. labor force since 1980)" (Drucker 1994, p. 56). Because of this change, we may not fully recognize the managerial implications of a world in which most work involves primarily the use of our minds to create, process or distribute information.

An assessment of five major work related topics: strength, technology, strategic resources, world view, and measures of success, will demonstrate how they are changing as a result of the shift from an industrial to an information-based society.

Strength is no longer measured merely in physical terms, but it is measured more and more in mental or cognitive terms. That is, the ability to process information and make decisions is more important than the ability to manipulate things. For example, I was in a stamping plant recently. A stamping plant is a factory where large pieces of metal are turned into things like automobile fenders and door panels. On one production line, men and women were picking up pieces of metal, placing them in a press, operating the press, and then removing the newly formed pieces. On the next line, a set of robot arms was doing exactly the same thing. The robotics line had almost as many workers as the manual one. But these workers were not primarily using their muscles. Instead they were using their minds to check readouts, determine tolerances and the like. There was still work to do and people needed to do it; but, to do this work effectively, the workers had to process information rather than lift pieces of metal. This type of work substituted cognitive skills for manual strength.

The primary technology that is being used is no longer mechanical, but rather digital and electronic. Even most major mechanical devices are now electronically controlled. Anyone who has purchased a new car is well aware of this. New automobiles don't have things like points and carburetors. They have electronic ignitions and electronic fuel injection. They also have "modules" that monitor and modify the air, fuel and other mixtures to maintain top performance. Similar trends exist in home appliances, music reproduction, video and now even photography. The office also has been changed through such things as word processing, electronic mail, intranets and facsimile machines. For example, this paper was written using a microcomputer; any other way would have been inefficient. It was submitted to the editors on disk and has been published in a traditional format (paper), but the current trend is toward electronic publishing on the Internet with download opportunities for those who wish to have their own digital or paper copy.

In the past the primary strategic resource was money; it took money to build factories and buy raw materials to produce products. Today the primary strategic resource is knowledge. Just ask the programmers, accountants, consultants, attorneys and a myriad of other professionals who began successful businesses based, not so much on how much money they had but, on what they knew. As a resource, knowledge or information operates in a very different manner than most other resources. Most resources such as money, property or inventory, are "zero-sum," that is, you either have them or you do not. Information, on the other hand, is a resource that we can give away and still have. It is not exchanged, but rather shared and, therefore, is not subject to "diminishing returns." This puts it at the center of the "value added" aspect of business.

As Cleveland (1989) suggests, the inherent characteristics of information as a resource provide some clues to the rethinking we must all do to be successful in an information age. Information, for the most part, is expandable; that is, it is synergistic. As more information becomes available, we use more and as a result even more useful information is produced. Consequently, information is not scarce. Paradoxically, information is also compressible; that is it can be concentrated, integrated and summarized, as well as being compressed physically. Consequently, additional information does not necessarily require additional resources to store and maintain it. Information is substitutable; that is it, increasing, can and does replace land, labor, and capital. Consequently many who would have worked on the farm or in a factory are now working with information. Information is transportable; that is, it is available at any time and any place to anyone who wants access to it. Consequently, where you are no longer determines what kind of work you can do. Information is diffusive, that is, it is leaky and aggressive in its attempts to break the thing-oriented perspective of the past. Consequently, organizations and those who run them must assume that there are no secrets. Finally, information is sharable; that is, it cannot give rise to traditional exchange transactions but only to sharing transactions that combine resources to create new ones. Consequently, the standards, rules, conventions, and codes regarding its use will be different from those of traditional resources used to carry out "zero-sum," transactions.

When information is shared its value typically grows. This occurs because the things that others know when added to what we know, gives both of us a more complete picture of the situation or circumstance under discussion. When information is shared both parties not only retain that with which they started with, but gain additional information that can be of benefit to all parties. Treating information as if it were "zero-sum" does not work, and, in fact, it reduces the likelihood of gaining even more useful information through additional transactions. Information that is hoarded and protected is typically of little long term value, because it does not change as circumstances change. Information that is shared and opened to scrutiny can change and expand as the circumstances warrant.

Information, in its role as the primary strategic resource, does not recognize traditional political and territorial boundaries. Because of this, national perspectives are no longer adequate. The only world view that functions effectively in an information-based economy is a global one. We hear of the need for a global perspective frequently. But in contrast to that, and closer to home, we hear people ask, for example, why we do not own an "American" car? This question makes no sense. Is a Honda, built at the Marysville, Ohio plant by American workers a foreign car? What about the Chrysler product with a Mitsubishi engine? Similar changes are occurring in the service sector; your favorite hamburger, if it is a Burger King, is supplied by a British corporation. Nations can no longer behave in national or regional ways and assume that what they do should have no impact on others either economically or politically. The changes in the balance of trade, the shifts occurring in the former Soviet Union, and the conflict in the Bosnia clearly demonstrate this. As managers, we too must take a more global perspective.

Finally, different measures of success are sought in an information-based society. Organizations and the people in them have long used very objective measures of success. At the organizational level, considerations about profitability and market share, have been paramount. For individuals, salary and perks played the same role. In an information-based society we begin to ask questions about the "quality" of life. Our measures of success are less objective and more subjective. Our view is less focused on the here and now and more on the long term consequences of individual and corporate behavior. We want satisfying work that promotes not only our welfare but that of the organization in which we work and the community, country and world in which we live. These shifts in thinking and behavior have significant impact on managerial activities. An analysis of the changes that are occurring in planning, organizing, leading and controlling provides a useful indicator of the skills needed to manage effectively in the information age.

PLANNING

Planning is the first of the primary management activities. When planning, managers have focused on what the organization hoped to accomplish. Traditional planning was goal oriented. It focuses on identifying goals and determining the objectives for accomplishing them. Planning has always been about analysis. That is, the goal is broken into steps that are then formalized for implementation. This type of planning, because of its analytical nature, works always from known categories and concepts. According to Mintzberg (1994), the great fallacy in planning, especially strategic planing, as done by a planning department, is that strategic planning is in fact strategy making. The presumption that strategic planning will work is based on three fallacious assumptions: one, that prediction is possible; two, that strategists can be detached from the subjects of their strategies; and, three, that the strategy-making process can be formalized.

Prediction is rarely possible in an era in which change occurs rapidly and in which technological innovation is being explored on many fronts with little insight into which will be successful much less which will be of interest to consumers. Strategic planning cannot be separated from the day-to-day activity since that activity itself contains qualitative, and often intangible, information that has a richness of nuance and meaning that cannot be captured by aggregation; information that allows managers to see the big picture, even though it has been developed one stroke at a time. Finally, formal processes, which imply a rational sequence, can process information, but they cannot internalize it, comprehend it, or synthesize it. But, these are mechanisms which humans, with their intuitive skills, can provide. This is not to suggest that strategy formulation is not important, but only that traditional methods of "strategic planning" have not produced strategic thinking. Strategic thinking requires a different approach to planning. One approach, which was outlined more than twenty years ago but which still has not been formally institutionalized in most organizations, helps to provide the perspective necessary to manage in an information intense environment.

This approach to planning, called directional planning by McCaskey (1974), provides a useful alternative to traditional planning methods. Goal-oriented or traditional planning is appropriate when the organization can easily identify what it wants to accomplish. This rarely happens anymore. In the information age the technological, social, legal and economic environments are not stable but rather changing as new information and new ideas combine at a rapid rate to form even newer information and generate new ideas. Under circumstances like these it is difficult to know for sure what the final outcomes of any activity will be. This low level of certainty leads to high levels of organizational and personal ambiguity. When ambiguity is high and certainty is low, a strict goal orientation is untenable because outcomes are difficult to know; and, even when outcomes are known, it is often difficult to assess their impact. In these circumstances, an intuitive approach that relies on unquantifiable elements rather than an analytic approach, which relies on rational elements is more appropriate. The intuitive approach is appropriate because it relies on an intrinsic pattern of movement that the individual or organization identifies as worth pursuing.

In directional planning, the domain, or area in which the organization or individuals will work, is identified. In addition, the preferred style of acting as well as an arena for activity is identified by the organization or individuals. In this type of planning, very different modes of action are used. The focus is intrinsic, that is, it is based, not on extrinsic goals, but, on what is satisfying to the organization or individual. People interact with their organizational and social environment and through this interaction develop their goals. Strategies are formed as a result of the outcome of decisions made and implemented, not determined in advance. For these modes of action to be successful, information processing activities must be high. Managers must ascertain what others are actually doing and not assume that they know what is being done. When outcomes are unknown, more possibilities must be explored to determine what direction is appropriate, and some of these possibilities will ultimately be rejected. This approach to planning can be very stressful because it makes few assumptions about basic purposes and personal roles. This lack of a clear focus requires greater interaction and information sharing for success, and this is time and energy consuming.

More recently the concepts contained in the directional approach to planning have re-emerged as part of the discussion that focuses on learning organizations. Much planning fails because the process is assumed to be value free. It is difficult to argue with assumptions that have not been made explicit and more difficult to develop commitment to the plan when all personal thoughts, feelings and aspirations have been deliberately excluded from the process. A new form of corporate planning has been proposed to deal with the failure of traditional planning in many organizations (Senge et al. 1994).

The starting point for this kind of planning is not past decisions but every person's vision of what they want for themselves and for the organization. This is not an objective discussion, but a genuine conversation on what each person *really* feels should be done, with and in the organization, to maximize its potential. This conversation must then be extended to create a shared vision for the organization; in this process, listening to the values and concerns of each other is as important as the end product. The presence of a shared vision generates an openness that allows all to develop a realistic view of the current situation and the impediments that keep the organization from obtaining the vision that is shared for its future. Only when a shared image of the current reality has been developed can the decision makers move on to consider strategic priorities and allocate its resources in a way that will make that vision a reality. Finally, because values and direction have been brought into the process "up front" —commitment can be chosen.

One way to encourage genuine strategic thinking is to engage in what Shoemaker (1995) calls scenario planning. Scenario planning is designed to capture a whole range of possibilities in rich detail. It requires the manager to identify the basic trends and uncertainties in the field and then create a series of scenarios that will help to compensate for the usual decision making errors of overconfidence and tunnel vision.

Scenarios simplify the data available on the most important uncertainties facing the organization into a limited number of possible states, each of which outlines how the various elements might interact under certain conditions. Scenarios explore the joint impact of various uncertainties and try to capture the new state of nature that will exist after key variables shift. Their strength is that they include subjective interpretations as well as objective analyses. As Shoemaker (1995, p. 27) says:

> In short, scenario planning attempts to capture the richness and range of possibilities stimulating decision makers to consider changes they would otherwise ignore. At the same time it organizes those possibilities into narratives that are easier to grasp and use than great volumes of data. Above all, however, scenarios are aimed at challenging the prevailing mind set.

There are ten steps necessary to develop a scenario.

1. You first need to set the time frame and scope of your analysis in terms of products, markets, geographic areas, technologies or other key variables in your environment.
2. You need to identify the major stakeholders who have an interest in, who will be affected by, or who could influence the issues.
3. You need to identify the basic political, economic, societal, technological, legal or other trends that are likely to affect your issues.
4. You need to identify the key uncertainties, those events, whose outcomes are uncertain, that will affect the issues you are concerned with.
5. You need to construct your initial scenarios. One way to do this is to identify extreme outcomes by putting all positive and negative outcomes

into individual scenarios; another is to select the top two uncertainties and correlate them.

6. You need to check to see if these beginning scenarios are both plausible and consistent, eliminating those that are not.
7. You need to produce, through the process, some general themes that are tools for research and study.
8. You need to identify those additional areas of concern needed to complete your understanding of the uncertainties and trends that are of concern.
9. You should reexamine the internal consistencies of the scenarios and assess whether certain interactions should be formalized in a quantitative model.
10. You must, through an iterative process, converge on those scenarios that you will eventually use to test your strategies and generate new ideas.

The test of the "goodness" of scenarios is the degree to which they are relevant, internally consistent, archetypal, and describe an outcome that provides relatively long term equilibrium.

What planning issues are especially relevant in libraries or information centers? Some of the major uncertainties are easily identified others are probably specific to the environment. The role of technology is clearly a major issue everywhere. Crawford and Gorman (1995) provide a perspective in *Future Libraries: Dreams, Madness & Reality* in which they argue that technology will not and cannot currently replace print. The question for them then becomes "What role should technology play?" Another major concern is likely to focus on the concept of intellectual property and the value added by the information professional to the provision of information. Finally, globalization and access to information anywhere in the world will impact most library and information centers. Beyond that you must look at the other political, legal, and other trends specific to your operation to understand their implications for your future.

ORGANIZING

Organizing is the second primary managerial activity. When organizing, managers focused on how to structure the organization to accomplish its ends. Even the traditional management language sets the stage for a set of assumptions that are no longer valid. The classic perspective is that managers would determine the structure as if they somehow knew better. Traditional organizational structures have been hierarchical with a pyramid shape and typically very mechanistic in their operation. This mechanistic model follows logically from the interchangeable parts approach of the industrial revolution. In this model, workers are not seen as individuals with strengths and weaknesses that they bring to the organization but as a collection of specific skills that are purchased by the organization. In this industrial model, organizations hire engineers, accountants and secretaries to meet well-defined roles and responsibilities, not individuals. The assumption is that any engineer is the same as any other. This approach no longer seems to work because it is not subtle enough to meet current needs, particularly as organizations become more professional and technical in nature.

Bridges (1994) argues that even the concept of a job—which at its worst is typified by the expression "That's not my job"—is a social artifact that has outlived its usefulness. He claims that jobs as we know them are rigid solutions to an elastic problem. He believes that: "There still is and will always be enormous amounts of work to do, but it is not going to be contained in the familiar envelopes we call jobs" (Bridges 1994, p. 62).

So what will exist if not jobs? Drucker (1988) indicates that information-based organizations require a different structure than industrial organizations. They need to shift from a mechanistic or machinelike form that operates as designed no matter what to an organic or person-like one that interacts with the environment and adapts based on that interaction. The need for a shift from an industrial model to a more organic one occurs as both the nature of work and workers change.

In one sense, work responsibility is shifting from specialized to generalized responsibility. Fewer and fewer people work on assembly lines doing a single, boring task, and, in fact, many of those tasks have been automated. These tasks still need to be monitored, frequently requiring the use of sophisticated statistical tools that provide new forms of information to aid in decision making. Many individuals now find themselves in jobs in which they are responsible for monitoring and controlling the entire task or assembly as compared to being limited to physically accomplishing a single part of it. But, even as the work gets more generalized, the knowledge needed to accomplish the tasks gets more specialized and may even change at an astounding rate. Specialized knowledge is required as new automated equipment with new procedures and capabilities is procured to accomplish organizational tasks. As this shift in tasks occurs, the workers shift from being unskilled to being more professional. That is, they bring a specialized body of knowledge to their tasks and apply it in self-regulating ways to accomplish the goals of the organization.

In this type of environment the old hierarchical structure is not very effective. This old structure, using the principles of "Scientific Management," was designed to break tasks into smaller and smaller units until they were doable by unskilled workers. Information intense environments have highly integrated tasks that cannot and should not be broken into smaller units. These new environments require workers that approach their work as professionals. The structure that is appropriate for this type of environment is a network that allows workers access to the people and information that they need to accomplish their tasks. In addition to a network structure, changes in the work unit must occur. Departments should, perhaps, be displaced and replaced with self-directed, task-focused teams. To be effective, these teams will need to work interactively, not sequentially, in an organizational environment that is flexible, not rigid, in which people "report to each other."

It is interesting to speculate on what the new organizational structure will look like. Senge (1990) suggests that organizations that will be successful must be learning organizations. For him a learning organization is characterized by five of what he calls "component technologies" that he deems necessary to build an organization that can truly learn. The most crucial one and the one that Senge calls the fifth discipline is systems thinking; an awareness that all events in an organization, including interactions with customers and suppliers, are connected and affect each other and that we must look at the whole pattern of interaction and change. The others are personal mastery, which is a commitment to one's own lifelong learning; mental models, a willingness to examine and question the assumptions and generalizations about how we understand the world and how we take action; building shared vision, which is the capacity of the entire organization to create a picture of the future it wishes to create; and team learning, which is vital because teams are the fundamental learning unit in modern organizations, is the ability of groups to genuinely work and learn together through dialogue.

Drucker (1993, p. 95) believes that re-engineering will lead to the elimination of most management layers and a structure much like a symphony orchestra will arise where several hundred highly skilled professionals perform together with only one executive, the conductor. He also suggests that in many environments "We will increasingly see organizations operating like the jazz combo, in which leadership within the team shifts with the specific assignment and is independent of the 'rank' of each member" (p. 95). He suggests that this will create problems in the areas of motivation, reward and recognition. Davis (1987) also sees the elimination of middle management as a layer of employees between two other layers of employees, as an outcome of a more holistic model but sees a new "middle" role as the link between the provider and the customer.

Peters (1992) believes that professional service firms will be the model for future organizations. These are organizations that exist only to meet the needs of the project at hand. Examples include consulting firms of various types. These organizations are reconfiguring themselves continuously, rely extensively on expertise and specialization, and, more than anything else, they manage professional relationships.

The model that I believe will typify future organizational dynamics is one that I call the "general contractor." It is not inconsistent with Peters (1992) professional service model but assumes the existence of many relatively small (as small as one person), highly specialized organizations that work on individual contracts as the particular skills that they provide are needed. Examples of this model are evident in a variety of environments including movie-making, house-building, value-added reselling, and the like. Most of us understand this model in the arenas in which it has been successful, but we have difficulty translating that understanding to organizational environments that have not traditionally functioned that way. We understand that if we want to build a house we either act as our own or hire a general contractor who then works with and schedules many subcontractors (excavating, cement, framing, plumbing, electrical, roofing, trim, etc.) to see that the house gets built. The general contractor and each subcontractor is an independent professional who chooses to accept the "job" based on his/her expertise, time constraints and the like. It is important to note that neither the general contractor nor any of the subcontractor has any "permanent" employment. Opportunities for work are based on things like skill, reputation, and availability.

We understand this model in the environments in which it is familiar, but we tend to reject it in other environments where it is unfamiliar. How would it look in a library or information center environment? Traditional public and university libraries as the sources of information might no longer exist. A library might no longer be a place where one goes for information; instead it could be a set of services that are independent of place. A client, be he or she a student, researcher, professional, business, or the like, having exhausted his/her own information seeking strategies (which are likely to be extensive) would identify a provider of information based on reputation and experience who would then use a variety of resources to meet the specific information need. As for the role of librarians, there will always be a need for the skills of librarians in the area of cataloging and the organization of information resources. But the most important library function is likely to be reference. Finding the right information to meet the need of the "patron" in an effective and efficient manner is likely to be a skill in great demand.

LEADING

Leading is the third primary managerial activity. Traditionally, when leading, managers focused on the use of processes associated with guiding employees toward accomplishing organizational ends. The label applied to this activity has changed over the years. Management textbooks some years ago labeled this activity as "directing," but more recently the term in vogue changed to "influencing." But I believe that the concept of leading as a process directed at the shaping of behavior is more useful. This is a shift from an assumption that managers could direct behavior, that is, tell employees what to do; toward motivation, which is the set of processes that determine behavior in which conditions are created that lead to organizationally preferred choices. A leader sees him/herself as part of a team who helps members assume greater control over their own work and then use their intelligence, skills, and creativity to make the organization more effective (Zenger et al. 1993).

Changes in what it means to lead occur as managers gain a greater understanding of the essential elements of human nature. The employee is not an interchangeable part that can be substituted for any other similar employee, but a person with needs, wants and desires. To deal effectively with the employee as a whole person, the manager must support the internal motivating factors appropriate for that person. The manager as leader has the responsibility for insuring that the choices that the individual employee wants to make are compatible with the choices that the organization prefers. These choices must be consistent with the employee's values and goals and not chosen simply because the organization prefers them. Focusing on the employees' internal motivations, is vastly different from most earlier approaches which believed that external motivation was necessary, appropriate, and sufficient. Earlier perspectives assumed that the appropriate behavior would occur if sufficient managerial pressure was placed on the employee. In short, as Naisbitt (1982) suggests: "The new leader is a facilitator, not an order giver" (p. 188). Leaders must develop an environment that satisfies the needs of all who work for and with the organization.

In a managerial approach that assumes internal employee motivation, the nature of traditional leadership activities changes. The responsibility for what goes on in the organization becomes everyone's responsibility not just management's. The style of operation shifts from competition between management and employees for scarce resources, to cooperation aimed at meeting a common goal. Decisions are not made unilaterally by management but in a participatory manner with all those affected by the decision involved in the process. In order for these things to occur, there must be open communication in the organization. Information that is known by both managers and employees about the issues under discussion, must be shared and used in the decision making process. Defining the manager as a leader assumes that the ultimate success or failure of the organization, rests with all who work for it. Each manager and employee has a specific role to play in the organization and all roles are important and necessary if the organization is to be as successful as it can be.

Providing this type of effective leadership is difficult in complex organizations. It is difficult because the traditional assumptions about what a strong leader does, do not fit in complex, information intense environments. There are four elements of effective leadership that are necessary if the leader is to be truly successful. The first is a vision of the future that is valued by and takes into account the legitimate long-term interests of the parties involved in the development and management of the organization. This vision must be consistent with the purpose and mission of the organization. Second, the vision must contain a rational and intelligent strategy for moving toward that vision. This strategy has to be rooted in a broad understanding and acceptance of what additional activities must change to further achieve the goals of the organization. Third, those whose cooperation, compliance, or teamwork is necessary must support the vision and strategy. Those involved must create together a sense of shared goals and shared fate. Fourth, the core group of people whose actions are central to implementing the strategy must be motivated to be personally involved in evolving a shared agenda for the organization. They must also commit their own time and energy to the process. This can only be done if the fundamental needs and values of those involved are known and appreciated.

This type of leadership, which is almost inspirational in character, is not the same as management, which is more functional in character, although both are needed. It is required at all levels in the organization not just at the top because decision making must occur at all levels of the organization. The specific approach used must also fit the situation in which it is found.

It is clear that this type of leadership is not authoritarian but highly participatory and must build toward consensus. Leaders are very visible in the process, but they do not demand or direct; instead they help to develop, focus and articulate the vision of what the organization wants to be and energizes the network of resources necessary to make that happen. This is not a simple or easy task for it insists that conflict give way to consensus. This will require leaders to become facilitators, not isolated decision makers. It also suggests that those in authority who feel that they have to "win" to be successful will act in dysfunctional ways. In a complex and competitive organizational environment of the sort found in traditional organizations, if one wins, by definition, someone else loses. I believe that our organizations will not survive if we rely processes in which someone must lose.

We must, if we are to survive, develop cooperative environments in which the legitimate long-term interests of all of the parties involved are considered and accommodated in whatever changes are made. This is not to suggest that each gets what s/he wanted, but that the needs of all are identified, discussed and resolved with a solution that is acceptable to all. The consensual style of leadership needed to make this work requires a strength that transcends the ability to make good decisions. It requires the strength to see that good decisions get made by those who have to implement them.

According to Senge (1990, p. 340), "In learning organizations, leaders are designers, stewards, and teachers. They are responsible for *building organizations* where people continually expand their capabilities to understand complexity, clarify vision, and improve shared mental models—that is, they are responsible for learning." Notice the emphasis here. The leader does not so much create the vision or set the direction as inspire others to create a group vision and a group direction. The leader becomes a designer of the organization, and she/he is not either despised, as traditionally happens with bad leaders, or praised, as traditionally happens with good leaders. Instead, great leaders have "followers" who say, to quote an old Chinese proverb, "We did it ourselves." There is little in this design function of leadership to attract those who wish control or fame, but there is much to attract those who gain satisfaction from helping to create healthy organizations.

Leaders are also stewards. That is they are caretakers of the organization. The concept of the leader as servant (Greenleaf 1977) fits closely with this perspective. What they serve is a vision, a vision that addresses the higher order human needs of all who comprise the organization, a vision that embraces change and the risks that come with any change, a vision that is not just the leader's vision but that grows and develops out of the visions of all of those who work in the organization.

Finally, according to Senge, leaders are also teachers. That is, they help those in the organization achieve more accurate, more insightful, and most importantly, more empowering views of reality. They help the organization focus on events and patterns of behavior, which leads mostly to reactive or at best responsive behavior. But even more importantly, they help its members focus on purpose and systemic structure so that people can see the big picture and can see how the various components of the organization interact so that people can also understand both the "how," and the "why" of the organization. Leaders as teachers foster learning for everyone in the organization. They help everyone in the organization develop systemic understandings and frequently require them to give up their own past perspectives as a greater understanding of the current state of reality develops.

Senge (1990, p. 359) also suggests that what distinguishes outstanding leaders is

> ... the clarity and persuasiveness of their ideas, the depth of their commitment, and their openness to continually learning more. They do not "have the answer." But they do instill confidence in those around them that, together, "we can learn whatever we need to learn to achieve the results we truly desire."
>
> The ability of such people to be natural leaders is, as near as I can tell, the by-product of a lifetime of effort—effort to develop conceptual and communication skills, to reflect on personal values and to align personal behavior with values, to learn how to listen and to appreciate others and others' ideas. In the absence of such effort, personal charisma is style without substance. It leaves those affected less able to think for themselves and less able to make wise choices. It can devastate an organization or a society.

Huey (1994) calls this type of leader "post-heroic" and suggests that this kind of leadership only works if those in leadership positions actually give up control and abandon their past fundamental beliefs about leadership. This style, which has also been tagged virtual leadership,

> ... requires many of the attributes that have always distinguished the best leaders—intelligence, commitment, energy, courage of conviction, integrity. But, here's the difference: It expects those qualities of just about everyone in the organization. The time when a few

rational managers could run everything with a few rational numbers, it seems, was just
an anomaly, or part of an era very different from the fast-paced, continually shifting present
(Huey 1994, p. 50).

Good leadership in a library or information center will be like good
leadership in any other environment except that leaders in information specific
environments may need to be more open, more proactive and more innovative
due to the specific nature of the tasks assigned to them. Leaders will need to
encourage and support the independent decision making efforts of all in the
organization. They will need to model the information skills that they wish
others to use. They will need to be current with changes in the field and then
provide training to others regarding those changes. They will need to find ways
to give all in the organization a "stake" in the outcome of organizational efforts.

CONTROLLING

Controlling is the fourth and final primary managerial activity. When
controlling, managers traditionally focused on whether or not organizational
goals and objectives were accomplished. Managers, when involved in control
activities, attempted to answer the question: Did the organization do what it
set out to do? Historically, planning has been closely linked with controlling
in that they cycled into one another. There are three types of control.
Preliminary control monitors the quality of resources at the input stage as they
enter the system. Concurrent control monitors resources as they proceed
through the process of changing from inputs to outputs. Postaction control
monitors resources at the output or completion stage. Resources to be
controlled include money, inventory, people, and information. Most
organizations have comprehensive control systems for their financial assets as
well as their physical assets. They know what their balance sheet looks like
and have complicated inventory control mechanisms. These systems are the
natural by-products of an industrial perspective of organizations. When it took
lots of capital to start a business, what you measured was the capital itself
and the things that it purchased. Some have suggested that the old accounting
system, which focused on the costs of material and labor is not applicable in
a new economy whose chief ingredient is "intellectual capital, the intangible
assets of skill, knowledge, and information" (Stewart 1994, p. 68). Today, even
in the manufacturing sector some estimates are the 75 percent of the value that
is added derives from knowledge rather than production.

In an information intense environment, monitoring activities need to shift
from narrow production goals to broader organizational and societal goals.
If traditional planning is no longer possible, because prediction is no longer
possible, then traditional controlling activities will not provide useful
information. The question is not so much: Did the organization produce what

it set out to produce? but does what the organization produce, and the way it produces it, make a difference in the way our organization and the world works? Or, as Huey (1994) suggests control must shift from procedural issues to conceptual ones if it is to contribute to organizational success.

In looking at the major organizational resources of money, inventory, people and information, it can be seen that, in an information-based economy, the control considerations for each of them are undergoing a significant shift. In assessing financial or monetary resources managers are shifting from the use of strictly quantitative measures, such as, how much did we make? or, how much did we spend? to more qualitative measures, such as did we invest in environmentally and humanly sound equipment and services. In the control of physical resources, such as the products and services that are provided, managers are shifting from analysis of end products to an ongoing analysis of the production and delivery systems themselves. The statistical process control methods that they have been put in place in many organizations provide some evidence for this shift. With human resources, managers are shifting the focus of control from the supervisor to the individual so that each employee accepts responsibility for doing his/her work and doing it well. Finally, with information resources, managers are shifting the emphasis from compliance as measured simply by the number of key strokes entered or the number of reference questions answered to commitment, which is a genuine desire on the part of all employees to see that the needs of the organization and its customers are met. Information technology should be used to support organizational goals through more efficient processes and procedures (Walton 1989). Control activities in general are shifting from objective to subjective measures. These activities attempt less and less to answer the question how many or how much did the organization produce more and more they attempt to answer the question how well and how effectively did the organization operate?

Controlling in a library or information center is likely to consist of increased information sharing regarding the status of the organization so that all who work in it are in a position to make informed decisions. It is also likely to be interactive with an approach that does not blame but instead seeks common solutions to organizational issues. It is more likely to ask questions regarding "patron" needs and potential opportunities for service than to answer them.

PREPARING FOR THE FUTURE

To live and work successfully in an information-based society and economy, managers need new skills and attitudes. To be productive in this type of environment, McHale (1976) says that three skills are needed: a high tolerance for ambiguity, the ability to act under uncertainty, and a deliberate acceptance of error. In practical terms what do these things mean for managers? Ambiguity exists in circumstances that can be understood in more than one way; these circumstances are not clear as to their meaning or consequences. A high tolerance for ambiguity then is the ability for managers to accept and to be as comfortable as possible with this lack of clarity about the consequences of behavior. Under these circumstances, it is difficult for managers to make "right" decisions because there are no clear cut answers. The ability to act under uncertainty means that even though there is no sureness regarding the consequences of behavior, decisions still need to be made and actions still must be taken by managers if anything is to be accomplished. Finally, a deliberate acceptance of error means that, once an action is taken, the consequences of that action are likely to be discovered very quickly. These consequences are often not going to be entirely positive given the ambiguity of the environment. Acknowledgment of the reality of less than perfect decisions and an awareness that no one is to blame must be acceptable to managers as necessary in an information intense environment. The ability to learn from those decisions and continue on anyway is the only reasonable way for managers to behave in this environment and perhaps the only way for both the manager and organization to survive.

To operate in this new managerial environment there are some things that managers, and especially library and information center managers can do to prepare for the future. The first is to be aware of the changes that are occurring in organizations and the world. Today's perspectives, policies and procedures, given the changes in organizations and people, will not be effective tomorrow. Second, managers must continue to learn. New skills and insights will be needed for managers to be successful. Third, managers must become adaptable. Organizations are changing rapidly, and if managers do not change, so that they can work in different situations and under different organizational and technological circumstances, they will be left behind. Fourth, managers must be professional, that is they must gain and use specialized knowledge regarding their particular areas of responsibility to aid the organization. Library and information center managers, specifically, must use their knowledge of information processes and techniques to help the organization be more efficient and effective. In order to accomplish this they must become and remain technologically sophisticated. Managing information is no longer a simple issue associated with books and periodicals. It is now increasingly involved with more complex situations where all organizational information, regardless of medium, is treated as a common resource. Library and information center managers know how to manage those resources, but now they must learn to help their organizations see how the specific skills and insights that they bring to the organization can increase its effectiveness.

REFERENCES

Bridges, W. 1994. "The End of the Job." *Fortune* 62,64,68,72,74.

Cleveland, H. 1985. *The Knowledge Executive: Leadership in an Information Society*. New York: Dutton.

Crawford, W. and M. Gorman. 1995. *Future Libraries: Dreams, Madness, & Reality*. Chicago: American Library Association.

Davis, S. M. 1987. *Future Perfect*. Reading: Addison-Wesley.

Drucker, P. F. 1988. "The Coming of the New Organization." *Harvard Business Review* 45-53.

————. 1992. "The New Society of Organizations." *Harvard Business Review* 95-104.

————. 1993. *Post-Capitalist Society*. New York: Harper Collins.

————. 1994. "The Age of Social Transformation." *The Atlantic Monthly* 53-80.

Ferguson, M. 1980. *The Aquarian Conspiracy: Personal and Social Transformation in the 1980s*. Los Angeles: J. P. Tarcher, Inc.

Ferrero, L. P. 1991. "Using Micrographic Imaging as a Platform into the 21st Century." *IMC Journal* 4-7.

Gardner, J. W. 1990. *On Leadership*. New York: The Free Press.

Greenleaf, R. K. 1977. *Servant Leadership: A Journey into the Nature of Legitimate Power and Greatness*. New York: Paulist Press.

Heider, J. 1985. *The Tao of Leadership: Leadership Strategies for a New Age*. New York: Bantam.

Huey, J. 1994. "The New Post-Heroic Leadership." *Fortune* 42-44,48,50.

McCaskey, M. B. 1974. "A Contingency Approach to Planning: Planning with Goals and Planning Without Goals." *Academy of Management Journal* 17(2): 281-291.

McHale, J. 1976. *The Changing Information Environment*. London: P. Elek.

Mintzberg, H. 1994. "The Fall and Rise of Strategic Planning." *Harvard Business Review* 107-114.

Naisbitt, J. 1982. *Megatrends: Ten New Directions Transforming Our Lives*. New York: Warner Books.

Ogburn, W. F. 1964. *On Culture and Social Change*. Chicago: University of Chicago Press.

Peters, T. 1992. *Liberation Management: Necessary Disorganization for the Nanosecond Nineties*. New York: Knopf.

Senge, P. M. 1990. *The Fifth Discipline: The Art and Practice of the Learning Organization*. New York: Doubleday.

Shoemaker, P. J. H. 1995. "Scenario Planning: A Tool for Strategic Thinking." *Sloan Management Review* 25-40.

Stewart, T. A. 1993. "Welcome to the Revolution." *Fortune* 66-68,70,72,76,80.

————. 1994. "Your Company's Most Valuable Asset: Intellectual Capital." *Fortune* 68-74.

Swartz, J. B. 1994. *The Hunters and the Hunted: A Non-linear Solution for Reengineering the Workplace*. Portland, OR: Productivity Press.

Walton, R. E. 1989. *Up and Running: Integrating Information Technology and the Organization*. Boston: Harvard Business School Press.

Van Fleet, D. D. 1991. *Contemporary Management*, Second Edition. Boston: Houghton Mifflin.

Zenger, J. H., E. Musslelwhite, K. Hurson and C. Perrin. 1993. *Leading Teams: Mastering the New Role*. Burr Ridge, IL: Irwin.

Zuboff, S. 1988. *In the Age of the Smart Machine: The Future of Work and Power*. New York: Basic Books.

CASE STUDY OBSERVATIONS ON THE IMPACT OF COMPUTER TECHNOLOGY ON ORGANIZATION STRUCTURE IN COLLEGE LIBRARIES

Edward J. O'Hara

In her widely publicized monograph *In the Age of the Smart Machine* (1988), Shoshana Zuboff examined the process by which computer technologies were introduced into large commercial organizations. She noted that information technology not only automates, but it also "informates," a word she coined to describe how the technology generates information about the underlying productive and administrative processes through which an organization accomplishes its work" (p. 9). Zuboff observed that this new knowledge can empower workers to exploit information for fundamental business improvement as well as undermining hierarchical forms of organization. Whether the "transformative power" of the technology is successful depends "upon a series of crucial management choices" (p. 285).

Advances in Library Administration and Organization,
Volume 15, pages 187-199.
Copyright © 1997 by JAI Press Inc.
ISBN: 0-7623-0371-9

This study, completed in 1994, examined the choices that transformed three smaller academic libraries. It helps to build an empirical base from which the effects of technology on college libraries may be inferred, and in so doing, it helps library managers and researchers understand the processes occasioned by technological innovations. As a result of that understanding according to Barley (1988), they "may eventually unravel technology's multiple and often conflicting implications for the organization of work" (p. 52).

Buchanan and Boddy (1983) have similarly suggested that "it is not technology that determines organization structure, but how technology is used.... There are choices in the way work is organized and structured around technology" (p. 20). This theme of choice is echoed by Perrolle (1987) who found that the effects of computers in the workplace "depend on the choices made about how to design computers for work and how to reorganize work to facilitate the human/computer interface" (p. 150). Contending that computers both de-skill employees and enhance employee skills, Perrolle suggested that, since both phenomena occur, the issue is whether one tendency will predominate and whether "we will have a new division of labor *within* computerized work" (p. 155, emphasis in the original).

Employing a case study methodology, this investigation examined the process by which new technologies were chosen for three college library sites. At the time they were investigated, each had, as a minimum, adopted OCLC for cataloging and interlibrary loan purposes, had installed online catalogs, and had introduced online and CD-ROM databases for information retrieval. Access to the Internet had not yet become available. To explore the impact of technological innovation, the data were collected to elucidate several specific organizational issues:

1. Institutional setting for change
2. Responsibilities inherent in specific positions
3. Specialization and skills
4. Decision making
5. Professional duties
6. Managerial levels
7. Organizational planning
8. Number and size of work units
9. Leadership

The data collected in this investigation are intended to increase our understanding of the processes that accompany computerization in academic libraries that are smaller than the major university libraries whose characteristics dominate the literature of librarianship. The case study data collected for this study may be compared to the survey data collected in other studies such as Johnson's research (1991) on larger academic library organizations, Mech's observations (1990) on academic library directors, and a survey (1992) of paraprofessional status conducted by Larry Oberg and his colleagues. The findings of the investigation allow preliminary observations that suggest lines of inquiry for future study along with implications for the organizations of library work in general.

THE INSTITUTIONAL SETTING

The three libraries serving as case study sites for this inquiry are all located a prestigious liberal arts colleges: Hamilton College in Clinton, New York; Williams College in Williamstown, Massachusetts; and Connecticut College in New London, Connecticut. The parent institutions receive the designation of Liberal Arts Colleges I awarded by the Carnegie Commission on Higher Education to only 20 percent of the 719 liberal arts schools in the United States. The quality of the parent institutions is also indicated by their high ranking in the system used by *U. S. News & World Report* to evaluate colleges.

The three colleges are certainly not typical institutions of higher learning in the United States. They aim to be the best, and they seek to attract the highest caliber students. Each college accepted for admission only a minority of its applicants. In addition, each included among its freshmen a large number of students graduating in the top 10 percent of their high school graduating classes.

The ranking systems used to determine highly rated institutions do not include library data in their formulations. The three colleges nonetheless devote substantial resources to their libraries in order to support high quality education for their students. For the period studies, the annual operating budgets at the three libraries ranged from $1.6 million to $2.3 million. In addition, the percentage of institutional educational and general (E&G) expenses expended on library services reached the relatively high range of 4.5 percent to 5.1 percent, whereas the national average for private four-year colleges was 3.2 percent (Goudy 1993).

To enhance library services through computerized processes, each institution committed significant financial resources toward new technology. The most notable expenditure at each site was several hundred thousand dollars for the installation of *integrated library systems*. It is doubtful whether significant automation efforts would have occurred if the colleges had been less able to afford the high cost of these technologies. Future research may indicate whether institutional affluence is essential for college libraries to computerize their operations.

RESPONSIBILITIES INHERENT IN SPECIFIC POSITIONS

Technological change, according the Cyert and Mowery (1987), involves significant changes in the way nations, organizations, and individuals operate.

At the most fundamental level the individual worker may be required to learn new skills and may be required to seek work in new occupations and in new industries. At the three case study sites, the nature of changes in position responsibilities was explored as a first step in the research.

There is little doubt that the adoption of computers for library operations changed the character and scope of many library tasks. At the very least, staff members were required to learn how to operate advanced computing equipment and how to manipulate data and retrieve information in different ways. As computer technology was introduced into various library functions, employees at all organizational levels learned new skills to perform their jobs in a computerized environment.

The introduction of computerized processes into library functions seems to have expanded the responsibilities associated with individual positions within the organization. Repetitive chores such as catalog card filing were eliminated, and the former filers assumed broader responsibilities for analyzing cataloging data. As the number of available databases increased, reference librarians were obliged to assume broader responsibilities in determining the most appropriate strategies for helping patrons obtain information. The changing nature of library positions lends support to Zuboff's idea that computer technology has the potential to "informate" the workforce in the interest of increased organizational effectiveness.

Although the nature of tasks changed as libraries automated, there was among the case study sites only one instance in which an individual staff member's employment was terminated due to the introduction of new technology. Since this single instance occurred because of major policy differences, it does not invalidate the observation that library automation did not lead to a reduced workforce at the three sites. To avoid displacing individual workers, moreover, some changes in position requirements were implemented only after normal staff attrition had occurred. Even among the large research libraries in Johnson's (1991) survey group of universities, less than 10 percent of the libraries actually terminated employees.

SPECIALIZATION AND SKILLS

A major question for organizational research has been whether computerization leads to a de-skilling of workers. In his observations on office automation Barley (1988) suggests that "the degradation of clerical work...appears to have always rested with the choice of organizational structure rather than with the technology itself" (pp. 63-64). This view is supported by the United States Office of Technology Assessment (1985), which contended that automation can be used to either de-skill workers or to enhance their jobs and the decision to do one or the other is made consciously by managers.

What occurred at the three case study libraries? It was evident at the three sites that more specialized skills were required in an automated environment. For staff members involved in computerized work processes, additional training was necessary in order to perform their functions. To accomplish successfully jobs that utilize more complex technology, extensive experience became more important throughout the organization.

No evidence was found that individual employees were de-skilled because their functions were automated. The level of knowledge, judgment, and training required for job performance did not decrease. On the contrary, the research indicated that more skills were necessary and that the base of knowledge for individual employees had to expand if they were to succeed. Manipulating electronic data required new competencies that Zuboff (1988) described as intellective skills requiring abstraction and procedural reasoning. The increased requirement for specialized skills was also noted by Johnson (1991), who found the phenomenon especially noticeable among members of the non-professional staff. The work of Larry Oberg and his colleagues (1992) supports this view.

The need for increased skill levels in a more technologically advanced environment perhaps helps to explain why no blurring was observed in public and technical service roles played at the three case study sites. Staff members in each work unit were obliged to concentrate on the knowledge of specialized computer applications necessary to perform their own tasks. It was particularly apparent at all three institutions that the technical service units concerned with bibliographic access and control remained firmly distinct from units serving the public directly. Future empirical research may reveal whether the use of common computerized data will erode the distinction between technical services staff who focus on ordering, processing and preserving materials and public services staff who focus on providing direct service to patrons.

DECISION MAKING

In his discussion of employee skills, Barley (1988) suggests that the issue of power may be the essential consideration (p. 54). This contention is mirrored by Perrolle (1987), who notes that changes in the distribution of power are determined by "the decision-making processes with which we implement technological change" (p. 214). The key questions are whether employees can use knowledge to decide how to conduct their work and whether workers have the autonomy needed to increase the effectiveness of the organization.

In the three libraries investigated it was apparent that, as staff members gained experience with computer applications peculiar to their functions, they necessarily gained greater expertise in performing their specialized tasks. The employees shared a learning environment that required them to gain proficiency in the use of new technology, and, in turn, the staff members assumed greater importance within the library organization. Successful performance of their jobs required independent judgment which led to increased authority in deciding how their jobs should be performed.

It was apparent at the three sites that specific tasks previously performed by professional librarians were being reassigned to members of the non-professional staff. Making decisions on how staff members were to perform their duties had become more decentralized as employees at all levels gained greater freedom of action. The shift in operational control to employees more knowledgeable about complex computer processes thus enhanced the ability of librarians and support staff alike to perform their tasks independently.

A by-product of the downward thrust of decision making at the case study libraries was an apparent end to the distinction between clerical and paraprofessional employees. Tasks previously considered clerical in nature had disappeared for the most part as they were supplanted by the more complex requirements of computerized operations. Positions previously considered clerical were largely grouped together with paraprofessional positions into a single non-professional category that was given the more inclusive designation of support staff.

Similar observations regarding decision-making prerogatives were also found in Johnson's (1991) study of research libraries. Johnson found that changes had occurred in the level at which decisions were made in over half of the libraries surveyed and found that most library managers believed decision making had moved downward in the organization. Oberg (1992) also found in his study of library paraprofessionals that these workers routinely performed tasks previously assigned to professionals.

PROFESSIONAL DUTIES

If tasks were shifted downward in the organization, what were the effects of this shift on those workers defined as professionals, those whose status rests upon a mastery of technical expertise that legitimates their authority? What roles did professional librarians come to play in newly automated organizations?

As technological innovations were introduced into library departments, the need for workers to acquire new skills increased significantly at all levels. In each of the three libraries studied, cataloging was the first library operation to be computerized, and, notwithstanding an early experiment with MINI-MARC at Williams, all three libraries adopted the OCLC system for cataloging. The OCLC system, which required extensive training for catalog staffs, enabled catalogers to process new acquisitions more expeditiously, but it also required them to master the complex MARC format in order to enter or validate online bibliographic data. Knowledge of software protocols thus became necessary in addition to knowledge of the *Anglo-American Cataloging Rules* and *Library of Congress Classification* schedules.

Working with bibliographic records online, members of cataloging support staffs were able to perform many cataloging transactions previously done by professional librarians. The latter were required, in turn, to focus their efforts on the most complex cataloging transactions, transactions for which online bibliographic data were inadequate or unavailable. Despite the increased freedom to perform their cataloging duties and the need to plan for frequent changes in technology, cataloging staffs were nonetheless obliged to operate within the restrictions imposed by the MARC format.

The increased skill required for work in cataloging was mirrored in the work of interlibrary loan staffs who also were required to master OCLC computer techniques. Identifying and tracking ILL requests online required considerable technical training, but it also resulted in increased effectiveness. Improvements in interlibrary loan service through computerization led to increased patron demand at all three libraries, and this led, in turn, to increased workloads.

Changes in professional requirements were especially noticeable among the reference staffs of the three libraries. The adoption of DIALOG at all three locations represented a major commitment to a new service that only qualified librarians could provide. The extensive training necessary to retrieve data from commercial online databases meant that librarians had to mediate between their patrons and the information their patrons sought. Reference librarians thus came to spend more time on direct patron service. At times the demand was so great that reference librarians could provide the service only on an appointment basis.

Subsequent technological innovations reinforced the trend toward spending more time on direct patron service since reference librarians were obliged to assist patrons as each new information technology was introduced. Librarians were frequently required, for instance, to aid patrons in the use of online public access catalogs although these catalogs were theoretically designed to facilitate independent use by patrons. Instructional demands on reference librarians also increased as CD-ROM products and online services were adopted for public use. Each innovation also resulted in the immediate necessity for librarians to acquire additional training to develop their knowledge of the new products. Future research may show whether an increase in patron service typically results in libraries where tasks previously assigned to professionals are reassigned to support staff.

Because of the large financial commitment involved, technical expertise and judgment became critical as plans for integrated library systems were implemented at the three colleges. Hundreds of thousands of dollars were at risk at each institution, and the three library directors, though bearing ultimate responsibility, came to rely on specific members of their staffs to coordinate automation activities. At each of the three college libraries, one librarian emerged with clear responsibilities for coordinating the automation efforts. That only one individual assumed the coordinating role rather than a larger group, is perhaps not surprising since smaller libraries have fewer employees to whom additional duties may be assigned.

Size of library, according to Oberg (1992), does have significant effect on who is responsible for performing particular tasks. He observed that many large academic libraries now employ more paraprofessional staff members and fewer librarians. The issue of library size was inherent too in the study of large research libraries conducted by Johnson (1991), who found that automation complicated operational decisions. Responsibility for automation no longer devolved upon one individual but rested instead with a group described as upper level staff who collectively explored options and shared accountability. Future investigation may be useful in correlating automation activity with such factors as library size, professional/support staff ratios, and assignment of professional duties.

MANAGERIAL LEVELS

The issues raised by the introduction of new technologies relate to the future of middle managers. If the control function of managers is diminished by empowering workers, will the need for such managers decrease, and will the organizational structure of enterprises become flatter? Cyert and Mowery (1987) indicated that the evidence is unclear, but that such a phenomenon is quite possible. At the three case study libraries, the data were inconclusive.

As technological innovations got underway at the college libraries, individual work units were modified or created to accommodate changed responsibilities, though not necessarily due to the adoption of new technology. The director's managerial preference was the major factor in changes to the formal organization structures at each library. The number of managerial levels and the nature of reporting relationships were determined by a series of choices made by each director in response to changing operational requirements and institutional priorities.

At the three case study sites there was no evidence that the number of management levels had changed as a result of automation *per se*. The libraries at Hamilton and Williams became more hierarchical as new positions or functions were established. The directors retained the same number of immediate subordinates but increased the number of management levels in existing divisions or departments. In contrast, the director at Connecticut College avoided more stratification by adding to the number of subordinates directly reporting to himself. The differences in the evolution of formal structures at the three libraries support Zuboff's (1988) contention that the configuration of the organization depends on how managers choose to adapt to the new technology.

One of the choices made by the directors at Williams and Hamilton was to unify technical services units under the leadership of a single individual. The units responsible for acquisitions, cataloging, and serials work used the same bibliographic records online to perform their work, and both directors felt that greater effectiveness could be achieved under a technical services head who coordinated the three activities. At both institutions, in addition, the head of technical services was assigned responsibility for operating the computer hardware and software necessary for integrated library systems.

At Connecticut College, where the cataloging, collection development, and serials units were not formally combined, the three departments still shared the common focus of establishing and maintaining bibliographic records. Working with common bibliographic data, the staff members of each department routinely crossed organizational boundaries in order to perform their duties; but, like their counterparts at Williams and Hamilton, they operated quite apart from the staffs directly serving the public.

Johnson's (1991) survey of large libraries revealed similar results among institutions newly automated, although her survey group did exhibit a slight tendency toward a decreasing number of management levels as libraries gained greater automation experience. It is possible that a similar tendency would appear among smaller libraries as they too developed a longer automation history.

Although the formal organizational structures were ordained by the directors at the three case study libraries, it appeared that formal supervisory lines of authority were becoming less significant in the operation of the organization either by design or default. To an increasing extent, work was coordinated by staff members themselves rather than by direct supervision. Mutual adjustment among employees was particularly noticeable in technical services units, where the same bibliographic records were used to accomplish various operating tasks.

The decreasing importance of formal organizational structure was observed in the increasing use of interdepartmental committees to investigate new technologies. At two of the three sites integrated library systems were adopted only after extensive deliberations among staff members from various work units. Use of committees was especially evident in the library that shared a system with other institutions.

Using committees or task forces is perhaps a less radical substitute for matrix organizational structures in which formal work teams are created across departmental boundaries to develop specific projects. In her study of ARL libraries, Johnson (1991) also observed increased use of committees, working groups, and the like. She suggested that such groups acquired increased autonomy and power at large institutions. But this transfer of authority was not evident to as large an extent at the small college libraries employing fewer staff members.

ORGANIZATIONAL PLANNING

Technological innovation may be introduced gradually or radically into the workplace, and the effects, according to Barley (1988), may differ. He suggests that a gradual approach will have a more beneficial effect on workers since they will have an opportunity to adapt to new technology on a person-by-person or department-by-department basis.

During the years that the case study libraries were involved in planning and implementing automated library systems, their efforts were concentrated on the actual equipment and software to be adopted. Attention was focused on the specific technology under consideration and on the features that each new resource provided. The advantages of specific technological improvement were considered within the context of better service or streamlined operation.

Despite the gradual approach to adopting specific innovations, little planning was evident in anticipating the organizational response to automation: There was no master organizational plan in any of the libraries that paralleled the plans for gradual technology acquisition. Except for obvious training requirements, there appeared to. be no long range scenario for dealing with personnel issues that might arise. What occurred seemed to be a series of *ad hoc* responses to staff requirements imposed by specific technological innovations.

It appears that no systematic attention was given to issues such as the difficulty of hiring skilled staff, equity in compensating existing employees, and replacement of key workers. Nonetheless, new technologies were successfully introduced at the three libraries due perhaps to the managerial abilities of the three library directors, although other factors such as commitment of staff, quality of library systems, and institutional support could have been equally relevant.

NUMBER AND SIZE OF WORK UNITS

Buchanan and Boddy (1983) reported that the organizational structure of every firm they studied had been affected by the introduction of computers. They reported too that the organizational structure in most cases had been "ramified with the creation of new specialist groups, new management hierarchies, and new positions" (p. 245). How were libraries affected as changed tasks and jobs were combined into organizational units?

As new technology was introduced into the three libraries, the number of work units increased. Most evident in this development was the establishment of units responsible for the actual operation of centralized computer equipment, although in two cases the unit consisted of only one person. In the third case the computer operations function was performed by a staff supported by a college library and its consortium partners.

At two of the three college sites, new departments were also created to provide enhanced audiovisual services. At two of the three sites, new departments were also established temporarily for the purpose of retrospectively converting bibliographic records into machine-readable form. When observations for this present study ended, two of the three case study sites had shown a net in the number of work units.

Johnson's (1991) survey of large research libraries also reported the establishment of departments for library systems or automation. For the research libraries with over twelve years automation experience, more than half reported that such a department had developed, although the percentage diminished when libraries had fewer years of automation. A net increase in the number of work units occurred, however, at only a quarter of the large research libraries indicating that the total number of units tended to remain constant despite the addition of new functions.

Just as the number of work units changed during the automation process, the size of units at the three college libraries changed as well. During the period when retrospective conversion of bibliographic records to machine-readable form was underway, the number of people engaged in technical services work increased significantly. In the most extreme example, the effort required additional personnel working for five years. Thereafter, the number of technical services personnel decreased, particularly after the lowest level tasks had been eliminated from library operations.

The number of staff performing public services work at the college library cited remained relatively constant during the automation process. Particularly noticeable was the fact that the number of reference librarians at the sites remained constant despite their expanded responsibility for computerized information retrieval and user instruction. Johnson (1991) in her study of ARL libraries made similar observations: almost half the survey group reported a diminution in numbers of technical services staff, while two-thirds of the group reported unchanged numbers in public services. At the three college sites there was no evidence of a conscious effort to cut staff to offset computer costs, although this may have been a consequence of streamlined work processes.

LEADERSHIP

While conducting their case studies of commercial organizations, Buchanan and Boddy (1983) sought to answer the question of who decides to introduce new technology. In each case they found it was "possible to identify 'promoters,' individuals or small groups who supported technological change, often against opposition, skepticism and inertia" (p. 241). But can the same conclusion be found in the library setting?

There is little doubt that the impetus for automating the three college libraries came from the library directors at the case study sites. Each director perceived the need to provide innovative computer-based services to streamline operations and provide comprehensive information service to the college community. Each director promoted the adoption of technological innovations, led the process of selecting appropriate systems, obtained the financial support of top college administrators, and ensured the implementation of the chosen technologies. The role of the library director was critical at each of the colleges.

In Johnson's (1991) survey of the largest academic libraries, the role of the director seemed more peripheral to the automation process. In much of her survey analysis on organizational change, Johnson found the director was identified, not as a leader' but as a member of the upper management group. Especially interesting was that directors at one-quarter of the research libraries were not participants in the final decision to adopt an integrated system, although they may have given formal approval to the plan. In two-thirds of the research libraries, the directors were not involved in implementation.

In his analysis of managerial roles played by library directors at institutions of various sizes, Mech (1990) found substantial variation in the functions of the directors. At the smaller libraries the director's technical skills were considerably more significant than the technical skills of directors at larger institutions. In instituting new technology it is perhaps not surprising that the contrast between the roles played by library directors at small colleges and those at research universities was so evident.

The directors at the three smaller libraries in this present investigation were vital forces in developing and guiding the automation process at their institutions. They were compelled to weigh carefully the options for their libraries, the costs to their institutions, and the capabilities of their subordinates. The potential effects of their decisions increased in magnitude as the financial stakes grew. Despite the growing expertise among their staffs, the directors themselves bore responsibility for their library innovations and retained ultimate accountability for the success or failure of the new technology.

It appears that the directors of the three college libraries were instrumental in accomplishing two significant goals. By utilizing computer technology to streamline library operations, they increased the efficiency with which their organizations provided existing services. By introducing new technological developments to provide increased access and additional information sources, the three directors also increased the effectiveness of their libraries in providing new services. Still undetermined was whether they could achieve even greater service by using computer-generated management data in such diverse areas as collection development and allocation of personnel.

CONCLUSIONS

In adopting computer technology to enhance information services at their institutions, library directors made choices that affected the nature and scope of library organizations. The formal structure of work units, as reflected on organization charts, changed significantly as technological innovations were introduced. Less obvious were the changes affecting authority and responsibility of individual employees as well as the dynamics affecting relationships within the organizational hierarchy. The observations suggest that an appropriate managerial response was necessary at the college sites to ensure optimal library operations in a time of technological change.

As new technologies emerge, academic libraries will continue to adopt new computer applications in order to provide up-to-date information services to their campus communities. Access to information through the Internet, increasingly available to both library employees and patrons, is currently transforming ways libraries operate; and such developments suggest the continuing need to study the impact of technological innovations on library organization.

REFERENCES

Barley, S. 1988. "Technology, Power, and the Social Organization of Work." Pp. 33-60 in *Research Sociology of Organization: A Research Annual*, Vol. 6.

Buchanan, D. A. and D. Boddy. 1983. *Organizations in the Computer Age: Technological Imperatives and Strategic Choice*. Aldershot, England: Gower Publishing.

Cyert, R. M. and D. C. Mowery. 1987. *Technology end Employment: Innovation and Growth in the U. S. Economy*. Washington, DC: National Academy Press.

Goudy, F. W. 1993. "Academic Libraries and the Six Percent Solution: A Twenty-five Year Financial Overview." *Journal of Academic Librarianship* 19: 212-215.

Johnson, P. 1991. *Automation and Organizational Change in Libraries*. Boston: G. K. Hall.

Mech, T. 1990. "Academic Library Directors: A Managerial Role Profile." *College and Research Libraries* 51: 415-428.

Oberg, L., M. E. Mentges, P. N. McDermott and V. Harusadangkul. 1992. "The Role, Status, and Working Conditions of Paraprofessionals: A National Survey of Academic Libraries." *College and Research Libraries* 53: 215-238.

U. S. Congress, Office of Technology Assessment. 1985. *Automation of America's Offices, 1985-2000*. Washington, DC: U. S. Government Printing Office. ERIC Document Reproduction Service No. ED 267 293.

U. S. News & World Report. 1992. *America's Best Colleges*. New York: U. S. News & World Report.

Zuboff, S. 1988. *In the Age of the Smart Machine*. New York: Basic Books.

LIBRARIANS IN SPLIT POSITIONS WITH BOTH TECHNICAL AND PUBLIC SERVICES RESPONSIBILITIES:

THE UNIVERSITY OF ARIZONA LIBRARY EXPERIENCE

Christine E. Kollen, Nancy R. Simons and
Jennalyn W. Tellman

INTRODUCTION

In 1992 the University of Arizona Library (UAL) began a twenty-month process to redesign its organizational structure. One of the results of this redesign process was that all catalog and archival librarians, with two exceptions, were reassigned to split public/technical services positions. New responsibilities assumed by these librarians in addition to their cataloging or archival duties include collection development, faculty liaison, subject specific reference, bibliographic instruction, reference desk service and knowledge management.

Advances in Library Administration and Organization,
Volume 15, pages 201-225.
Copyright © 1997 by JAI Press Inc.
All rights of reproduction in any form reserved.
ISBN: 0-7623-0371-9

In this paper we will first present a literature survey of librarians in positions with both public and technical service responsibilities. In this paper we refer to these as split positions, but elsewhere persons in this type of position are often referred to as holistic librarians, renaissance librarians or subject specialists in the literature. Next we provide a brief history of the UAL's redesign process, an examination of the philosophy behind the new organizational structure, and a review of the assumptions that lead to the use of public/technical services split positions. We describe how these positions were implemented and report on both the positive and negative experiences of librarians currently working in these split positions. Finally, we discuss some of the changes that have occurred during the past two and a half years since the reorganization and briefly describe the actions of a group attempting to address some of the special challenges associated with these split positions.

LITERATURE SEARCH

For many years there have been articles lamenting the weaknesses of a library structure in which reference librarians and technical service librarians do not understand each others' responsibilities and constraints. Many of these articles refer to feelings of competition and sometimes resentment between public services librarians and their technical services counterparts. Most of the articles have suggested ways to ameliorate the resulting problems by giving multiple responsibilities to librarians, making them holistic librarians. Commonly mentioned benefits include an enhancement of the librarians' skills, better use of individual's talents, flexibility in staffing and increased job satisfaction. Some articles have reported the results from libraries that have moved away from narrowly defined specialties for librarians to more generalized or holistic positions. These results have been mixed.

A Call For Subject Specialists

As early as 1942, Lund (1942) proposed reorganizing functions for greater efficiency so that the ordering, accessioning, and descriptive cataloging processes might be organized as a unified division and so that subject cataloging and reference service likewise might be organized as a unified division. This early article did not address issues that later writers discuss such as miscommunication and competition. Rather it provided a practical suggestion for dealing with inefficiencies and redundancies.

Thirty years later, Gration and Young (1974) also recommended that libraries use subject specialists who would have responsibilities for reference, bibliographic instruction, and selection. The authors drew on their experience with a staff of subject specialists at a predominantly undergraduate college library during the period of 1969-1972 and concluded that it was important to put the selection staff in public areas in order to receive user feed-back about collection needs, thus enabling the selectors to make better collection development decisions.

Avery (1977) built on Lund's ideas by suggesting that reference librarians would become much better acquainted with the collection if they participated in the organization of it, and, consequently, they would be better able to assist users. At the same time, regular interaction with users would put subject catalogers more in tune with readers' expectations of the subject catalog. She also noted that increased familiarity with the collection from many angles would increase the librarians' awareness and aid in collection development. She suggested that reference librarians' experience with bibliographic verification would enable them to be integrated into the cataloging process without a radical change of skills or perspective. Avery also suggested that people who feel uncomfortable doing two jobs at once might consider rotating positions. She believed that she had become a better cataloger because of her work in the reference department and that her cataloging experience had been useful at the reference desk.

The University of Illinois was an early library to move librarians towards multi-functioning roles. Gorman (1979, 1983) has written in favor of the subject specialist approach. He spoke of the tremendous subject knowledge of catalogers which is seldom used in reference work and of reference librarians who are proud of their lack of knowledge of cataloging. Gorman referred to the idea that there are public services types and technical services types as absurd and damaging. He believed that all librarians need to comprehend the importance of reader services, the intricacies of library automation, and the nature and structure of bibliographic control. They must also possess a keen and analytical appreciation of the materials libraries collect. He proposed creating groups of librarians formed around services or languages or combinations of the two. Librarians in these groups would perform all appropriate professional functions including selection, collection development, reader advisory and reference services, original cataloging (when copy is not available) and bibliographic instruction. He noted that this is a traditional model for small and specialized libraries.

Breaking Down Public/Technical Services Barriers

A common theme that runs through the literature about holistic librarians is that there is a misunderstanding between public service and technical service librarians. Gorman (1983) described some disadvantages of traditional organizational structures such as a lack of communication and mutual trust, inefficiencies and redundancies. Peele (1974, 1980) referred to these misunderstandings, suggesting that technical service librarians serve at the reference desk. In an April Fool's article he suggested that all members of reference sections of libraries know that they are the only ones in the library who do real professional work. They do not understand catalogers who are described as a phlegmatic breed who seem to become excited only if someone touches their catalog.

Both McCombs (1985, 1986) and Altmann (1988) also expressed concern about a lack of understanding between librarians who work in technical services and those in public services. One suggestion McCombs offered for improved communication was to create split positions. She proposed a renaissance librarian who would understand the totality of librarians' roles.

Bechtel (1994) advocated a holistic, nontraditional approach to staffing. She believed that improved relations within the library would be accomplished as a result as well as gains in organizational flexibility. She believed that increased knowledge of the whole of librarianship overcomes traditional antipathies, misunderstandings, and divisions among departments or functions of the library and promotes cooperation rather than competition and greatly improves service to students and faculty. Buttlar and Garcha's (1992) study indicated that a majority of the respondents agree that staff sharing allows technical and public services librarians to learn and appreciate each others' roles.

An article by Walbridge (1992) suggested creating librarians with holistic views. This has the advantage of combining the cataloger's knowledge of the bibliographic record structure with the reference staff's understanding of user needs. Walbridge did not suggest that librarians become generalists, but rather that catalogers should spend less than a majority of their time cataloging. Their focus should be on cataloging the most difficult materials and managing cataloging processes and work flow. They should ensure that cataloging decisions are made with the user in mind.

Other Reasons For Holistic Librarianship: Automation, Downsizing

Gorman (1979, 1983) stated that the online catalog does away with the rationale for the distinction between public and technical services professional librarians. Cargill (1989) suggested that technology is blurring the lines between traditional areas and that there is a scarcity of librarians in some functional areas. Multi-tasking of responsibilities will help libraries bridge this skills gap. Economy may also dictate that positions be redesigned in order to maintain effective service. Cargill also contended that there would be numerous benefits from this integration of roles; however, it might be easier for new staff to assume them than for older staff.

Better Service and Other Benefits

Many writers tended to concur with Bechtel (1994) that librarians with more general responsibilities can provide all services at a higher level of competence. A reference librarian who understands cataloging is better able to help the students and faculty use the catalog. A cataloger who performs reference services can better apply cataloging rules. Librarians who know the classification scheme as well as the reference collection are better able to assist users. Bechtel noted an increase in job satisfaction among those with split responsibilities while indicating that some librarians may initially find the need to be generalists daunting. She stated that acquiring breadth and depth of skills liberates librarians from a narrow focus and releases new energies. Bechtel wrote that multi-trained librarians result in greater flexibility in staffing. Altmann (1988) also noted that advantages accrue to the library, including greater control over the collection, enhanced service to clients, increased the library's flexibility, reduced polarization between functional units, and enhanced the library's capacity to recruit good people.

Surveys

Linsley (1984) conducted a survey of 100 academic libraries to determine the incidence of dual job assignments, the positive and negative aspects of dual assignments, and the personality or job traits which contribute to the success or failure of those working in these assignments. Positive comments from her survey included better communication, cooperation, and understanding between departments, increased job satisfaction, more flexibility, and the belief that the librarian does a better job. Fifty-three percent of the libraries surveyed had dual job assignments. While these assignments were quite varied, the most common was a split between reference and collection development. Even when there was no formalized dual job assignments, the sharing of job duties was occurring in these libraries on an informal basis. Two reasons cited often for these assignments were staff cuts and the need to utilize the subject expertise of librarians. It was noted that dual assignments have a better chance of success if the assignments are complementary. Seventy-nine percent of the library directors surveyed indicated satisfaction with this arrangement.

In another survey, Eskoz (1991) asked academic libraries how many catalogers were involved in work outside their department and how these assignments worked out. She noted a variety of benefits of assignments in more than one department. These included: heightened job interest, better use of individual abilities, increased understanding between technical and public services, more flexibility for emergencies, catalogers more attuned to users' needs and reference librarians using their cataloging experience to better assist patrons. At campuses with more than 30,000 students, 90 percent of the catalogers had shared responsibilities outside the catalog department. However, at medium sized campuses, only 50 percent had shared responsibilities. Smaller campuses showed percentages between that of the very large and the medium sized libraries. In general, this outside activity was limited to a few hours per week. The survey suggested that there is an increasing number of libraries with catalogers with assignments outside their departments.

Buttlar and Garcha (1992) tried to determine how the work of academic libraries is structured and the extent to which there has been a departure from the traditional pattern of dividing activities between public services and technical services departments in recent years. They also analyzed the attitudes of library administrators towards this type of reorganization. Of the 93 libraries studied, 65.2 percent were organized along traditional lines with separate technical services and public services functions, 32.6 percent reported some partial integration of these two functions, and 2.2 percent had no separation between technical and public services functions. Seventy-three percent of directors allowed opportunities for staff sharing. Catalogers participated in reference desk service in 42.4 percent of the libraries, on-line searching in 15.2 percent, bibliographic instruction in 25 percent, circulation in 4.5 percent, and selection and collection development in 43.5 percent. However, reference librarians participated in monographic cataloging in only 7.5 percent of the libraries, in serials cataloging in 4.5 percent, in acquisitions in 16.1 percent and in bibliographic searching in 22.6 percent. Directors in organizations that have some degree of integration tended to view this holistic approach more positively than directors in more traditional organizations. The directors of re-organized libraries perceived that there was more stress placed on staff than did directors in traditional organizations. Most respondents agreed that the technical services librarians' experiences working with the public definitely helped them to catalog materials in a way that would ultimately better serve the public. According to Buttlar and Archa, the most common crossover activity for catalogers is to work a percentage of their time at the reference desk on an optional basis while still spending the majority of their time performing the task for which they were hired.

Reports From Some Librarians Who Have Implemented a Holistic Approach

Jenda (1994) has provided a very thorough argument to support having holistic librarians, a discussion of the benefits and drawbacks of this approach, and a summary of the many implications of such an organization. She examined the structure of the University of Botswana Library which adopted a subject-centered library organization in 1981. Professional librarians perform a combination of technical and public service functions. Like other authors, she writes that the staff from any one section often do not appreciate the problems of other sections. In the University of Botswana Library's new structure, subject librarians perform a variety of functions including collection development, cataloging and classification, both subject-specific and general reference and information services, bibliographic instruction, and library orientation. In addition, each subject librarian has liaison duties with the appropriate teaching departments. There are librarians who are not subject specialists but are responsible for managing technical components such as acquisitions, cataloging and circulation. Jenda listed both positive and negative aspects of this kind of organizational structure. The positive aspects that she enumerated are the same as those mentioned by other writers. They include closer interaction among staff and departments; a greater variety in work assignments and in the utilization of professional skills; a more dynamic, flexible, and responsive staff; and improvement in the quality of library service. Negative aspects enumerated have also been mentioned by other writers. They include increased fragmentation of staff workloads with resulting time management problems, work management problems, a lack of consistency in cataloging, and work overload. Jenda also concluded that librarians with subject responsibilities perform their tasks in a highly fragmented manner and waste more time than do librarians working in other libraries.

Smith (1993) discussed the planning and implementation of the holistic approach at the University of Tulsa. It was modeled after the subject divisions used at the University of Illinois at Urbana-Champaign and at Pennsylvania State University. Professional catalogers were transferred to various subject libraries and reference librarians were trained to catalog. In their planning discussions, the University of Tulsa's library administration addressed the problems associated with individuals having two supervisors and the difficulty of developing appropriate expertise in multiple areas. Despite their planning, Smith noted that the supervision of professional librarians has been problematical. Some individuals have had difficulty in organizing their time for two sets of responsibilities, and some supervisors have had difficulty when cooperation with another supervisor was required.

Difficulties and Challenges

Null (1988) discussed the tensions that are created when assignments are split between collection development and reference. As with others who discuss multiple assignments, Null expressed a major concern with managing competing demands on the librarian's time. He pointed out that collection development rarely has the immediacy of reference work and that it often gets shoved into a lower priority. Null suggested that formal reporting lines and job descriptions allow librarians to know which criteria are being used to evaluate them and what they must do to meet their supervisors' expectations.

He wrote that role conflict and role ambiguity, where expectations are in conflict and there are unclear expectations, adversely affect job satisfaction. Null also noted that the literature of time management does not focus on how to juggle two or more primary tasks. He referred to Patricia Swanson's concern that, although all of us do not do everything equally well and probably do not want to do everything, we often are expected to do so, and that we are, (or can be) evaluated as if we do.

Gration and Young (1974) commented on the necessity for appropriate time limits for reference work that can assure that there will be adequate time available for other responsibilities in a multi-tasked environment. Avery described her experiences as a "multi-roler" at Duke and referred to the difficulties of trying to balance the amount of time spent on each task. In a survey conducted by Linsley (1984), 32 percent of the respondents indicated that the librarians working in their libraries had trouble pleasing two supervisors. Many respondents indicated that librarians have a greater chance for success in dual job assignments if they have complementary jobs and an appreciation for student and faculty service regardless of the department in which they work. Eskoz (1991) noted some problems with multiple work assignments including the fragmentation of time, a lack of consistency in cataloging, difficulties with staff being able to develop expertise in multiple areas, and lower cataloging production. Shared duties are often not reciprocal: catalogers may assist at the reference desk, but as noted above, reference librarians do not share in cataloging nearly as often, and, if they do, quality control may be a problem and cause interdepartmental friction. Altmann (1988) noted other disadvantages of assigning multiple responsibilities, to include a loss of productivity in the transitional stage, a reluctance or inability of some staff to fit into the new organization, stress caused by rapid change, new job responsibilities, a proliferation of committee and project work, and a complex reporting structure. She also noted that not all of us do everything well and that it may be good to nurture individual talents and strengths.

Suggestions for Effective Holistic or Split Positions

Moeckel (1993) referred to the difficulties of dual staff assignments while maintaining that dual assignments are the wave of the future. She indicated some procedures which are necessary for multi-tasking to be successful. Moeckel contended that it is necessary to have well defined jobs to prevent unreasonable workloads. It is also important to match the person to the job; people who enjoy the challenge and conflict of a complex assignment are essential. When people are forced into such assignments, there may be an increase amount of stress and burnout, and the morale of the organization may suffer. Training is critical to ensure that people have the necessary and appropriate skills for all of the tasks assigned to them. There are also problems of role conflict, time pressures and greater amounts of stress for people in dual assignments than there are for people who serve in more traditional positions. It is important that individuals with dual assignments have time management skills, organizational skills, and the ability to deal with ambiguity. Bechtel (1994) agreed that the process of making the staff into generalists takes time and planning to allow for training and for new assignments of responsibilities.

Hardin (1993) reported on his experience as a holistic librarian and had some suggestions for both managers and employees who are dealing with this kind of structure. Both should be flexible, build in buffers to allow for tasks taking more than their allotted time, allow for a longer learning period, learn to shift gears smoothly, take advantage of being focused on the big picture, and have fun.

HISTORY OF SPLIT POSITIONS AT THE UNIVERSITY OF ARIZONA LIBRARY

Prior to October 1, 1993 and the implementation of the redesigned organization at the University of Arizona Library (UAL), split positions between technical and public service departments had been employed on a limited basis (Fore and Knight 1989). In 1985, the UAL administration created a half-time Science Cataloger/half-time Science Reference Librarian position. Both departments had demonstrated a need for additional staff with science expertise, and only one position was available. In addition to the Science Cataloger/Reference position, the Middle East Librarian was split between the Catalog Department and the Oriental Studies Collection (OSC), a public service department. This librarian cataloged materials in the vernacular while carrying out collection development and reference duties in OSC.

It should also be noted that there were three other split positions at the UAL. These positions included a Science Reference/Maps Reference Librarian, and two staff positions, one split between the Catalog Department's Authority Section and Computer Operations and the other between the Catalog Department and OSC. Historically, split positions, although not used extensively, were seen as a means of addressing the problem of limited resources. As a side benefit, UAL administrators valued the increased communication between departments and staffing flexibility that split positions offered.

Additional strategies to ease the shortage of reference staff included the use of several technical services staff who volunteered their services for two to four hours per week at both the Main Library and Science-Engineering Library reference desks. In an effort to partially repay the technical services staff for their reference desk time, two science-engineering reference librarians and one humanities reference librarian assigned subject headings to University of Arizona (UA) theses and dissertations.

BRIEF HISTORY OF UA REORGANIZATION

A brief review of the philosophy surrounding the UAL's organizational design process is necessary to understand the Library's decision to increase its use of split positions, especially positions split between technical and public service units. For those interested in the organizational design process itself, a number of articles are available that provide greater detail on this topic (Fore, Knight and Russell 1993; Giesecke 1994).

During the fall of 1991, a number of factors converged to precipitate a review and redesign of the UAL's entire organizational structure. Among those factors influencing the decision to reorganize were economic conditions including continuous state budget problems and serials inflation, the impending implementation of the UAL's first integrated library information system (SABIO), the changing information technology, and the recent arrival of Carla Stoffle, the new Dean of Libraries. An additional catalyst for change was the October 1991 report of the UAL Taskforce on Access/Ownership (Jones 1991). Many of the assumptions and recommendations of this report were instrumental in shaping a new organizational structure that could accommodate an increasing emphasis on access to rather than ownership of materials (Brin 1994).

The nineteen month review of the UAL's organizational structure and the resulting creation of a new organizational structure began as a self-study facilitated by the Office of Management Services of the Association of Research Libraries in March 1992. All library staff members were invited to participate in the redesign process. Approximately one quarter of the staff participated directly in the process, and everyone had numerous opportunities to provide feedback. It should be noted that in 1992-1993, the UAL had three strategic goals that it accomplished: the redesign of the organizational structure; the implementation of SABIO; and the completion of a $700,000 serials cancellation project.

From the beginning, the UAL's organizational redesign process was planned to review the library as a whole rather than focusing on one or two areas or departments. Another important aspect of the early design phase was the identification of institutional values for the new organization and the development of working assumptions to shape the restructuring process. These values and working assumptions were compiled into a four page document distributed to all library staff by the Organizational Design Project Steering Committee. Several of the key assumptions are summarized and listed below.

1. The library will be user-focused, not collection focused and needs assessment will be critical in determining user needs.
2. Self sufficiency of library users and expansion of access are major goals for the Library.
3. There is no perfect organization, and this redesign will not solve all problems. However, the UAL will be better structured to fulfill its mission at the end of the process. Change will become a constant.
4. Continuous learning is valued and will be a key to our organizational success.
5. We will be working in a team based environment.

As the organizational design work was completed, and teams and work activities were identified, UAL moved into the implementation phase where personnel and resources were allocated to the newly designed teams. Figure 1 shows the four main divisions of the new structure with the focus of each of these divisions. Within each division, the figure lists each team and the activities for which this team is responsible.

Two major activities occurred during the implementation phase. The first involved the assignment of staff to their new teams based on a checklist of their knowledge, skills and abilities as well as their stated team preferences. The other activity necessary to begin functioning in the redesigned organization was the selection of team leaders for the newly created teams. Both the reassignment of staff and the selection of team leaders occurred during the summer of 1993, and people began reporting to their new teams October 1, 1993.

Assumptions Influencing Use of Split Positions

As mentioned and identified earlier, throughout the reorganization process, assumptions and priorities were established and developed to help guide the process. The assumptions and priorities that led to the utilization of split positions fell into three areas. The first assumption was that the Library would be structured to allow greater flexibility in staffing in order to better fulfill its mission. Insufficient staff was available to work on the front lines, and this presented a critical problem as the Library's emphasis was shifting to a customer focus. To compound the problem, state economic conditions and university budget problems made it evident that no additional staff could be added in the foreseeable future.

The second assumption was that split job assignments would provide staff with greater opportunity for advancement. A corollary assumption was a commitment to retain current staff and provide them with the necessary training to develop the skills needed in the new organization. Split positions would allow staff the opportunity to try working in new areas and begin developing new skills while still using their current skills.

October 1, 1993-

Direct Access Services interacts with the user primarily through the product of their work.
- Information Access Team (IAT)
     Activities: acquire library materials (e.g. acquisitions, ILL, document delivery)
- Bibliographic Access Team (BAT)
     Activities: receive and process materials (e.g. receiving & cataloging of materials, database maintenance)
- Materials Access Team (MAT)
     Activities: provide access to materials (e.g. circulation, stack maintenance, reserve)

Mediated Access Services provides reference assistance to all users of the UAL. All staff (classified and professional) contribute 20% of their team time to support this service.
- Undergraduate Services Team (UST)
     Activities: coordinate mediated access services (e.g. staff the information and reference desks, e-mail reference, general library tours and instruction sessions, handicapped services access)

Integrative Services integrates the needs of the user with the activities of the library organization.
- Fine Arts/Humanities Team (FAH)
- Science Engineering Team (SET)
- Social Sciences Team (SST)
- Research Archives Manuscripts Special Collections (RAMSC)—(Special Collections, Southwest Folklore Center and Center for Creative Photography)
     Activities: needs assessment, faculty contact, bibliographic instruction, collection development, in-depth reference consultation and knowledge management.

Library Support Services provide support for all teams, allowing them to focus on the user.
- Library Support Team (LST)
     Activities: team facilitation, library-wide planning, staff development, diversity, development.
- Business Operations Team (BOT)
     Activities: budget, accounting, payroll, building management.
- Library Information Support Team (LIST)
     Activities: support for staff computer, training staff to use new technologies, computer support for SABIO, cd-rom lans

Figure 1.   Organizational Structure University of Arizona Library

A third assumption that supported the use of split positions was that, as staff spent more and more of their time interacting with computers, a variety of other work activities would be desirable.

Assumptions Leading to Split Positions for Original Catalogers

The three assumptions above set the stage for the use of split positions in the redesigned organization. During the reassignment phase of the reorganization, it was assumed that all original cataloging and archivist positions would be split. Librarians performing original cataloging were assigned 25 percent or 50 percent to an integrative (public) services team. There are five assumptions that lead directly to the splitting of catalog librarians' assignments.

1. Librarians would be working directly with faculty.
2. There would be a direct benefit for customers to have available and to use the subject expertise of catalog librarians.
3. The Library would be able to purchase catalog records in the future.
4. Working directly with the customers to see how they view and use the records that they had created would provide a direct benefit to catalog librarians.
5. A large amount of the catalog librarian's time was spent acting as a resource person for staff in the catalog department rather than in producing original catalog records.

Before we begin a discussion of the implementation of split public/technical service positions, we need to define the activities for which such a position is responsible. Figure 2 is a generic position description for someone holding a 50/50 split between the Original Catalogers work team of the Bibliographic Access Team (BAT) and an integrative services team. In addition to being responsible for all activities on both teams, all staff at the UAL contribute time to support mediated access services (see Figure 1) and participate in library-wide cross functional project teams.

IMPLEMENTATION OF THE PHILOSOPHY

The Library's reorganization, purposely reduced the number of FTEs assigned to original cataloging. Before the reorganization, there were 16.25 FTE librarians who were either in the Catalog Department or who had original cataloging or arrangement and description responsibilities. Some librarians working with special formats or non-roman languages, although not assigned to the Catalog Department, did have substantial original cataloging or arrangement and description responsibilities. Most of these librarians spent about half of their time on cataloging (see Table 1).

Prior to the reorganization, the Chinese and Japanese Librarians were assigned full-time to the OSC, the Map Librarian was assigned full-time to the Map Collection, the Manuscripts Librarians were assigned full-time to the Special Collections Department, and the Photographic Archives Librarians were assigned full-time to the Center for Creative Photography (CCP). However, the Middle East Librarian was assigned half-time to the Catalog Department and half-time to the OSC, and one of the Science Librarians was assigned half-time to the Catalog Department and half-time to the

Original Cataloger's Work Team/Integrative Services Team
50/50 Split

Original Cataloger's Work Team (a work team within the Bibliographic Access Team)
- *perform original descriptive cataloging and subject analysis of monographs and/or serials in subject/language/format assigned.*
- *serve as a resource person for the Copy Cataloging and Authority Work Teams.*
- *participate in the ongoing management of the SABIO database, assisting with problem solving and decision making regarding issues of quality and accuracy.*
- *serve as liaison/resource contact with other teams as appropriate.*
- *participate in library-wide cross functional project teams.*

Integrative Services Team
- *establish communication links with faculty, staff and students in assigned academic departments (usually 1 to 2 departments for a 50% FTE person).*
- *elicit feedback from faculty, staff and students on their information needs and library services that support those needs.*
- *develop and provide course-related educational sessions for assigned academic department(s).*
- *provide in-depth reference assistance in area of subject specialization.*
- *select locally owned material and the tools to access remote material for assigned Library of Congress classification area(s).*
- *participate in library-wide cross functional project teams.*

Contribution to the Undergraduate Services Team
- *4 to 6 hours per week staffing a reference desk, providing e-mail reference, and/or teaching general instruction classes.*

Professional Responsibilities
- *contribute to the University and the Profession through involvement in university committees and professional associations.*
- *contribute to the profession through scholarly endeavors.*

Figure 2. Generic Position Description

Science-Engineering Department. There was a lack of consistency as to whether librarians with both original cataloging or archival and public service responsibilities were assigned to one department or were split between two. The new organization attempted to use logic in assigning staff to teams and eliminate any inconsistencies as to how staff members were assigned.

After the reorganization, 8.55 FTE librarians were assigned to BAT. All librarians who have original cataloging or arrangement and description responsibilities are assigned to BAT and, except for two, they are assigned to split positions with integrative services teams. The two positions that currently are not split with an integrative services team were originally designed to be split positions but were not divided due to special circumstances. This may change in the future.

In analyzing why the number of catalog librarian positions in the library was reduced, two key points emerged. Both of these have their basis in the

Table 1. Comparison of FTE for Catalogers and
Archivists in the Old and New Organization

Position	Organization Old	New	Split with Integrative Services Team
Principal Cataloger	1.0	0.00	
Catalog Management	1.0	0.75	0.25 Science Engineering Team (SET)
Spanish/Portuguese+ & Social Sciences	1.0	0.75	0.25 Social Sciences Team (SST)
Other W. European Literature, Humanities & Social Sciences	1.0	0.50	0.50 Fine Arts/Humanities Team (FAHT)
Russian Language	1.0	0.0	
Arabic Language	0.5	0.5	0.50 SST
Chinese Language*	0.5	0.5	0.50 FAHT
Japanese Language*	0.5	0.5	0.50 FAHT
Sciences/Social Sciences	1.0	0.75	0.25 SET
Sciences+	0.5	0.5	0.50 SET
Music	1.0	0.75	
Media	1.0	0.25	
Maps*		0.5	0.50 SST
Serials	1.0	1.0	
Serials	1.0	1.0	
Serials	1.0	0.0	
Photographic Archives*	0.50	0.50	Research Archives and Special Collections (RAMSC)
Photographic Archives*	0.50	0.55	0.45 RAMSC
Photographs (Historical)*	0.50	0.25	0.75 RAMSC
Manuscripts*	0.75	0.50	0.50 RAMSC
Manuscripts*	0.50	0.50	0.50 RAMSC
TOTAL FTE	**16.25**	**9.55**	

Notes: * In the old organization, these positions were assigned to a public services department, such as Oriental
Studies Collection, Map Collection, Center for Creative Photography, or Special Collections.
+ After two years these positions changed, the Spanish/Portuguese position changed to 0.25 BAT and
0.75 SST; the Science position changed to 0 BAT and 1.0 SET.

assumptions and priorities of the reorganization. First, vacant librarian positions that were originally assigned to the Catalog Department were reassigned in the new organization to other teams in the Library, especially integrative services teams (see Table 1). The basis for this reassignment was the assumption that there was insufficient staff available to work on the front lines, as discussed above. Second, the responsibilities of the positions that were reassigned from the Catalog Department to integrative services teams shifted to positions that remained in BAT. For example, the Russian language, media, and two serials catalog librarian positions were all open positions that do not exist *per se* in the new organization. The responsibilities for Russian language cataloging moved to a paraprofessional position in BAT, with some material outsourced; responsibilities for media cataloging moved to the music catalog librarian position; and the three serial catalog librarian positions were consolidated into one.

A review of some of the assumptions outlined in the previous section will explain these moves. One of the assumptions was that it will be possible to purchase more catalog records in the future. Even though we have not fully utilized the potential of purchasing catalog records, we are moving in this direction. So far, we are using Blackwell North America (BNA) to provide catalog records for most American imprint books received from that vendor and TECHPRO (available through OCLC) for original cataloging. This will have a profound impact on both copy and original cataloging. Another assumption was that a large amount of a catalog librarian's time was spent acting as a resource person for staff in the Catalog Department and was not spent producing original catalog records. Several factors affected the amount of time that catalog librarians would need to spend acting as a resource person for staff. In the new organization, the Library would be able to purchase more catalog records, so copy catalogers would be producing less. Staff who in the past would consult with catalog librarians for call numbers would now be able to use SABIO, the new online catalog as a reference to facilitate their work. As mentioned earlier, SABIO was implemented at the same time as the reorganization. In addition, there were certain activities that librarians did in the old organization that staff could be trained to do, activities that were perceived not to require a librarian's attention. These changes meant that the impact of decreasing the number of catalog librarians would be somewhat ameliorated as the new organization was implemented.

As noted above, all librarians assigned to the Catalog Department in the old organization, with two exceptions, were reassigned to positions split between BAT and an integrative services team. The majority of librarians who are members of integrative services teams provide reference desk service, including librarians split between BAT and an integrative services team. Librarians in split positions provide reference desk service as part of their integrative services time, so it does not come out of their BAT time or decrease the amount of time available to do cataloging. Librarians on the Research Archives Manuscripts, and Special Collections Team (RAMSC) provide reference service by appointment. This also comes out of their RAMSC time and not out of their BAT time.

Two related assumptions explain why it was perceived that it was important for catalogers to provide reference desk service. First, there will be a direct benefit for customers to use the subject expertise of catalog librarians. Second, there will be a direct benefit for the individual to work directly with the customers to see how they view and use the records created by the catalog librarians. In total, it is believed that BAT will be able to be more responsive to its customers, to directly use the expertise of catalog librarians, and to help the user become self-sufficient.

Librarians originally assigned to departments in the old organizations where they had both original cataloging or archival and public services responsibilities were reassigned to BAT and an integrative services team, usually with a 50/50 split. These departments included: the Center for Creative Photography, the Map Collection, the Oriental Studies Collection, and Special Collections. All of these librarians were responsible for either a special format, such as manuscripts or maps, or a non-roman language, such as Chinese or Japanese. Both before and after the reorganization, these librarians functioned much like "special librarians." In the old organization each worked in a specialized area, such as Chinese librarianship, with responsibilities for original cataloging, reference, collection development, instruction, and faculty liaison. After the reorganization, they were still responsible for the same activities although now they were assigned to two separate teams, such as BAT and the Fine Arts Humanities Team so that they had twice the meetings, twice the team responsibilities, and substantially more library wide responsibilities.

One of the problems identified early by the "special librarians" split between BAT and RAMSC were that their activities, and the issues and problems associated with them were very different from the "mainstream" catalog librarians. The activities of an archivist in describing a manuscript collection goes beyond the mere creation of a bibliographic record. The bulk of the arrangement and description activities ends in the creation of finding aids to manuscript or photographic archival collections instead of bibliographic records. Although an archivist provides access to a manuscript collection and a catalog librarian provides access to books or serials, the ways in which each is accomplished and the underlying issues and problems are very different. Therefore these librarians were placed together on the Research Archives Manuscripts work team in BAT (RAMBAT). The rest of the "special librarians", including the Chinese, Japanese, Middle East, and map cataloging librarians, were placed on the Original Cataloging work team in BAT.

EXPERIENCES

The authors of this paper interviewed 13 librarians who presently have responsibilities in integrative services teams and BAT. The questions were developed from comments by members of the Original Catalogers work team in a brainstorming session and from experiences and predictions reported in the literature. A copy of the questions asked are in the Appendix.

How Work in One Area of Responsibility Influences Work in Another

Librarians' experiences as catalogers or archivists affect how they retrieve information. Catalogers believe that their understanding of the database construction enables them to find information in the online catalog more effectively and also makes it easier to translate reference questions into LC subject headings. It enables catalogers or archivists in specialized collections to know their collection better and thus provide better reference or research assistance.

Conversely, experience providing reference service affects how cataloging is done. Catalogers report that they add subject headings or table of contents information as notes based on questions asked at the reference desk. Interactions with researchers also impact how archivists provide access to their collections. Seeing how researchers use finding aids influences how these aids are constructed. Catalogers are inclined to report errors or see that errors are corrected that are found while working on the reference desk. An example of this kind of modification of the catalog came shen a former catalog librarians working at the reference desk noticed that users were having problems finding journal titles. As a result, a separate index was created in the online catalog for journal titles.

In general, catalogers did not find that their cataloging experiences affected their material selection, although some reported that experience as a cataloger may make them aware of what's being received and can influence what is selected in the future as a result. However, their work at the reference desk or with researchers may make them more aware of the gaps in the collection and the materials they select may serve to fill those gaps. Some librarians with cataloging responsibilities may also decline to purchase material if they know it will be backlogged.

Bringing Librarians Together

Most librarians feel that the quality of the interactions between technical services and public services librarians has improved as a result of split assignments. Catalog librarians feel that they understand the issues affecting integrative services librarians. However, they feel that integrative services librarians do not understand the issues relating to cataloging any more than they did in the past. In contrast, librarians and archivists in specialized collections feel that the interactions have not changed.

Being on two teams increases the number of people with whom each librarian interacts and provides an opportunity to know members of each team and to understand each team's concerns. In addition, librarians and staff throughout the Library are working on projects together much more often than in the past.

Precedence and Excellence

All 50/50 splits, with one exception, feel that integrative services takes precedence over BAT. The 75/25 splits feel that their 75 percent split takes precedence. Most of the librarians surveyed felt that the area in which they had the most experience prior to the split was the area in which they excelled. However, one respondent felt that one could not excel in anything in the new arrangement because there was not enough time available to develop expertise.

Time Management

In the past, those who had separate desks for each of their activities found it easier to manage their time. Now, however, only one split has two desks, and those who have only one desk find it very difficult to balance their time between two separate teams. Some of the strategies used to address this problem include: blocking time to concentrate on one activity, not attending meetings, and developing time management skills. Some of those surveyed commented that: in the new situation, it is a challenge to manage time; they feel fragmented; they spend a disproportionate amount of time on integrative services responsibilities; they feel that everything is mixed up; and it takes longer to learn things when they don't have the time to devote to them exclusively.

Split Position Differences and Supervisor Expectations

Some of those surveyed felt anxious and uncertain that the work they are doing will be satisfactory to both of their team leaders. Being split between BAT and an integrative services team requires that the person be flexible enough to move from the activities of one team to the other. There may also be a sense of not belonging to either team in some cases. Not only do people in split positions have two sets of meetings to attend and two sets of e-mail messages to read, but they also must allow preparation time for meetings, respond to e-mail, take responsibility for team objectives, and feel that they have become an unofficial conduit for information from one team to another. Some people experience an information overload. Some may not be able to take on challenging projects and can barely keep up with what is essential in their job. They do not feel that they can work to their highest potential.

Expectations are now centered more on the team rather than the individual. In some situations, teams may expect 100 percent devotion, commitment, and involvement for those assigned to a team even though that assignment is only supposed to consume part of their time.

Training

Most librarians interviewed reported that the training for most new activities was not adequate, and too little time was provided to practice new skills for them to become proficient.

Job Satisfaction

Several people reported greater satisfaction with their job. They like the variety provided in the new organization. But others feel that they were doing the bare minimum and that they are not doing a good job. Split positions seemed to work better if the combination creates a logical whole, such as in area studies or in dealing with special formats. Otherwise, the person may come to feel that he or she has two separate discrete positions.

"Whole Library" Approach and Greater Flexibility

There was a mixed response to questions relating to how split assignments affect people's view of the library as a whole. During team meetings, library-wide issues may be discussed, and many librarians with split assignments feel that project teams are more apt to facilitate an understanding of the whole library than is likely to occur when a person is assigned to two teams.

Other Benefits and Drawbacks

There is more opportunity in the new organization for individuals to make changes and to learn new things. Individuals have an opportunity to work with colleagues they would not ordinarily have a chance to interact with on a regular basis. The new structure gives catalogers an opportunity to learn new skills that help them cope with changing organizational plans. There is variety and no boredom. One person interviewed said that the old way was like planting only cabbage in the garden. Another felt that the change has allowed the library to consider new ways of doing things. The reorganization gave a window of opportunity for individuals to try new jobs in a way that otherwise would not have been possible.

Some people feel scattered in split positions and feel pressured to learn many, diverse functions. One person made the analogy of a tent with no center pole but lots of stakes or poles around the edges. Some people are not as adept or comfortable as others in juggling multiple responsibilities, and these people feel that they may be forced into doing something they are not good at or do not like. People on split teams may feel uncomfortable or defensive when one team complains about the other and may feel that they are being used as a wedge to change or affect the other team. People are losing specialties and becoming generalists.

Where Are We Now?

It has been two and a half years since the reorganization. Implementing the vision of the new organization is an interesting process. The vision was mainly based on theory, although there was an attempt to gather and use as much data as possible within time constraints. The following sections address some of the issues and concerns regarding split positions that we anticipated as well as those we did not anticipate.

Continued Downsizing of BAT

During last year's budget process, BAT was asked to return $200,000 in salaries in order to support the Library's strategic plan. As a result, several staff positions and one FTE librarian were permanently moved from the Original Cataloging work team to integrative services teams. The two individuals involved provided original cataloging for Spanish and Portuguese and science monographs. Please refer to Table 1.

Outsourcing

Two things are happening to relieve catalog librarians of old responsibilities and permit them to assume their integrative services responsibilities. The Library has begun using OCLC TECHPRO to catalog books that can no longer be handled in-house. Books with OCLC records that lack call numbers or subject headings or are in a foreign language that copy catalogers can not read are outsourced. This removes the responsibility for catalog librarians to serve as resource persons for staff. Books that need original cataloging, (primarily in European languages other than English) are being outsourced. This frees up some additional time for catalog librarians.

Process Improvement

During the past two years it has become apparent that the workflow as designed during the implementation phase and further refined at the beginning of the reorganization needs to be redesigned. In response a process improvement team was formed to examine how the Information Access Team (IAT) and BAT function. This team is examining what happens to an item from the moment an order is placed in IAT until it appears on the shelf. The process improvement team has selected high volume, main stream material to examine, including government documents. This redesign study was necessary because the initial restructuring of the Library was done while we were in the process of migrating to an online environment and without a prior process improvement study. It is not clear what impact the results of this study will have on the librarians in BAT.

Split Position Group

Soon after the reorganization two library-wide sessions were held in order to discuss and clarify issues related to split-team assignments. No resolution or next steps were identified at that time. A group of seven staff and librarians in split-team assignments began meeting in August 1995 to determine ways to deal with the extra challenges and barriers to being highly successful and effective library employees. So far, they have revisited the theory and practice of split-team positions. They have discussed and collected input on why split positions were created. A few members of the group collected time data over a period of five weeks. A common theme that emerged from this data was that these positions are extremely fragmented. The group met with a member of the University's Human Resources Department, and it was confirmed that, when people are in split positions, their work increases exponentially, not linearly. After the five-week data collection period, two group members used this data in teams to successfully manage other expectations of their work loads. The group's future plans are to identify the most significant barriers to being effective and successful. In addition, they are planning on several more data collection periods that will involve a large number of staff both in split and non-split assignments.

CONCLUSION

Split positions at the UAL have had mixed success. There have been many benefits noted, challenges identified, and drawbacks experienced. The findings at UAL are congruent with what is reported in library literature. Most of the literature reported that holistic librarians take on new responsibilities as when catalog librarians take turns providing reference desk service. The UAL is unusual in that catalog librarians in split positions became members of two teams with all of the responsibilities of both teams including collection development, faculty liaison, subject specific reference, bibliographic instruction, reference desk service and knowledge management, as well as cataloging responsibilities. Some librarians in split positions at the UAL would prefer to be unsplit. Others appreciate the benefits of split positions and find their position enjoyable and rewarding even though they feel that these positions have some drawbacks. The success of individuals in split positions is influenced by factors such as an individual's personality and temperament, their teams' expectations, and whether their split assignments complement each other. There also seems to be some movement in the Library for librarians in split positions to negotiate an appointment to just one team as positions become available. Clearly the results of the reorganization have been mixed.

APPENDIX

Questions asked of former catalog librarians for this study:

1. How do you feel that your experience as a catalog librarian has impacted your service at the reference desk?
2. How do you think that your experience as a catalog librarian has impacted your material selection?
3. How do you feel your experience on the reference desk has impacted the way that you catalog?
4. Do you think that there has been closer interaction between public and technical services librarians?
5. How have you managed your time?
6. What are the expectations of your supervisors?
7. How do you perceive your role in a split position as different from someone not in a split position?
8. Of all of your job responsibilities for both positions, which take precedence?
9. Do you think that you excel in one are of your responsibilities over another area? How long have you had these responsibilities?
10. What can you tell us about training for your new responsibilities?
11. How has increasing the variety of job responsibilities impacted your job satisfaction?
12. Do you feel that your experience being on an integrative services team has facilitated a "whole library" approach?
13. Do you think that the library has benefited by greater flexibility in staffing?
14. What other benefits can you describe?
15. What other drawbacks have you experienced or observed?

ACKNOWLEDGMENTS

We would like to thank our colleagues on the Bibliographic Access Team at the University of Arizona Library.

REFERENCES

Altmann, A. E. 1988. "The Academic Library of Tomorrow: Who Will Do What?" *Canadian*

Library Journal 45: 147-152.

Avery, C. L. 1977. "New View: Combining the Worlds of Reference and Cataloging." *Michigan Libraries* 43: 9-11.

Bechtel, J. M. 1994. "Librarian Generalists: Holistic Librarianship." *College & Undergraduate Libraries* 1: 9-22.

Brin, B. and E. Cochran. 1994. "Access and Ownership in the Academic Environment: One Library's Progress Report." *Journal of Academic Librarianship* 20(4): 207-212.

Buttlar, L. J. and R. Garcha. 1992. "Organizational Structuring in Academic Libraries." *Journal of Library Administration* 17(3): 1-21.

Cargill, J. S. 1989. "Integrating Public and Technical Services Staffs to Implement the New Mission of Libraries." *Journal of Library Administration* 10(4): 21-31.

Eskoz, P. A. 1991. "Catalog Librarians and Public Services--A Changing Role?" *Library Resources and Technical Services* 35(1): 76-86.

Fore, J. S. and R. C. Knight. 1989. "Interdepartmental Cooperation: Making the University of Arizona Library Stronger." *Crossing Borders: New Territories in the 90's, ASLA-AEMA Contributed Papers* 49-52.

Fore, J. S., R. C. Knight and C. Russell. 1993. "Leadership for User Services in the Academic Library." *Journal of Library Administration* 19(3/4): 97-110.

Giesecke, J. R. 1994. "Reorganizations: An Interview with Staff from the University of Arizona Libraries." *Library Administration & Management* 8(4): 196-199.

Gorman, M. 1983. "Reorganization at the University of Illinois Urbana/Champaign Library: A Case Study." *Journal of Academic Librarianship* 9(4): 223-225.

Gorman, M. 1979. "On Doing Away with Technical Services Departments." *American Libraries* 10: 435-437.

Gration, S. U. and A. P. Young. 1974. "Reference-Bibliographers in the College Library." *College & Research Libraries* 35: 28-34.

Hardin, S. 1993. "The Servant of Two Masters." *Technicalities* 13(7): 11-12.

Jenda, C. A. 1994. "Management of Professional Time and Multiple Responsibilities in a Subject-Center Academic Library." *Library Administration & Management* 8: 97-108.

Jones, D., J. T. Leach, S. Bosch, B. Brin, E. Cochran, L. Greenfield and M. Parish. 1991. *Report of the Task Force on Access/Ownership Policy.* Tucson, AZ: University of Arizona Library.

Linsley, L. S. 1984. "The Dual Job Assignment: How it Enhances Job Satisfaction." *Academic Libraries : Myths and Realities: Proceedings of the Third National Conference of the Association of College and Research Libraries* 146-150.

Lund, J. J. 1942. "The Cataloging Process in the University Library: A Proposal for Reorganization." *College and Research Libraries* 3: 212-218.

McCombs, G. M. 1985. "The Reference Librarian as Middleman: Conflicts between Catalogers and Reference Librarians." *The Reference Librarian* 12: 17-28.

McCombs, G. M. 1986. "Public and Technical Services: Disappearing Barriers." *Wilson Library Bulletin* 61: 25-28.

Moeckel, L. E. 1993. "Managing Staff with Dual Assignments: Challenge for the 1990s." *Library Administration & Management* 7(3): 181-184.

Null, D. G. 1988. "Robbing Peter ... Balancing Collection Development and Reference Responsibilities." *College & Research Libraries* 49: 448-452.

Peele, D. 1974. "Overdone: Dumping Your Thing and Converting Catalogers into Useful Members of Society in Four Steps." *Wilson Library Bulletin* 48(8): 648-649.

Peele, D. 1980. "Staffing the Reference Desk." *Library Journal* 105: 1708-1711.

Smith, D. R. 1993. *Integration of Public and Technical Services.* Tulsa, OK: University of Tulsa.

Swanson, P. K. 1984. "Traditional Models: Myths and Realities." *Academic Libraries: Myths and Realities: Proceedings of the Third National Conference of the Association of College and Research Libraries* 89-92.

Walbridge, S. L. 1991. "New Partnerships Within the Library." *Journal of Library Administration* 15(2): 61-72.

MEASURING THE EFFECTS OF CHANGE IN A LIBRARY WORK ENVIRONMENT FOLLOWING A CLIENT-FOCUSED REENGINEERING EFFORT

Kathleen M. Webb and Kerrie Moore

INTRODUCTION

During the last fifteen years, academic libraries have undergone sweeping changes that are altering the way they do business. The first of these changes relates to technology. The integration of computer technology into every functional area, the proliferation of CD-ROM resources, and the evolution of the Internet from a communication medium to a vital research tool are just some of the shifts that have occurred. While many of these changes have enabled libraries to better serve their patrons, they have also sometimes been difficult to integrate into day-to-day operations given the traditional organizational structures of libraries.

Advances in Library Administration and Organization,
Volume 15, pages 227-247.
Copyright © 1997 by JAI Press Inc.
All rights of reproduction in any form reserved.
ISBN: 0-7623-0371-9

There are also financial challenges. Libraries have been faced with soaring serial costs and information and publishing explosion (Drake 1993). However, funding for libraries has not kept pace because colleges and universities are dealing with financial problems as a result of cutbacks in public funding and demographic changes that brought fewer students to college. Michalko (1993), the president of the Research Libraries Group has said, "All of these forces have made reorganization, reallocation, and retrenchment the 'three Rs' of the 1990s" (p. 11). It is no wonder that libraries all over the country are evaluating their organizational structures.

Roesch Library of the University of Dayton has not been immune to the changes occurring within the library workplace. In recent years a variety of circumstances has led the library and the university administration to institute changes in the library's organizational structure. This article describes the situation at the university, the process undertaken, and an application of the Work Environment Scale (WES), a quantitative measurement tool that was used to assess the impact of the changes on the library staff.

LITERATURE REVIEW

A brief look at the literature pertaining to academic libraries over the last ten years illustrates a focus on the decision making process and organizational structures. Terms such as Total Quality Management (TQM) and matrix, collegial, teams, participatory, and client-centered management predominate. A search limited to the last 10 years in H.W. Wilson's *Library Literature* index using the subject "College and University libraries—Administration of" yielded 360 citations. A search for "Staff participation in administration" yielded 104 citations. An evaluation of the articles shows that two or three of the more popular themes in recent years are team structures or participatory workplaces and client- or user-centered organizations.

Team Management in Academic Libraries

One of the most prolific areas of academic library management literature is team or participatory management. Terms often associated with this type of management structure include teams, participation, empowerment, and collegiality. Characteristics of the model include group decision making, peer evaluation, mutual respect, and equality of power (Alghamdi 1994). Some literature differentiates between participative and empowered management, stating that a participative management structure seeks input before a decision is made, while an empowered organization actually provides for sharing in the decision-making process between managers and those they manage (Lubans 1996). These two structures represent a continuum; (Martell 1987) however, for the purposes of this review, the literature will be grouped together.

Participative management structures are not new to libraries. As early as 1970 David Kaser was arguing that librarians who were trained in all areas of the profession should have greater participation in the decision making process. Also in 1970, Maurice Marchant completed his dissertation entitled, "The Effects of the Decision Making Process and Related Organizational Facets on Alternative Measures of Performance in University Libraries." He found a strong positive relationship between the extent to which librarians participate in the decision process and performance variables such as job satisfaction and long-range planning (Marchant 1976). Burckel's (1984) article, "Participatory Management in Academic Libraries: A Review," contains an excellent and thorough review of the literature on participatory management in libraries from 1971 to 1980.

The reasons for developing participative structures are many. One of the most important is that "participatory management tends to break down institutional barriers, forcing us to become knowledgeable about other areas of libraries, while building a greater understanding of organizational constraints" (Webb 1988, p. 50). Other features of collegial management models include the ability of staff to make suggestions and have their ideas heard, the likelihood of better decisions since all parties affected participate in the decision making process, more communication among departments, better problem solving, and an environment that promotes innovation (Alghamdi 1994; Towler 1993; Bechtel 1994).

While much of the literature describes the positive aspects of a more participative or collegial workplace, there are some drawbacks. Boisse (1996) addresses problems that could occur from flattening the organization. He identifies eight issues to be aware of when considering a less hierarchical organization. They include career considerations, performance appraisal systems, accountability, communication, turf wars, conflict between the old and the new, education of all library staff, and letting go of control from the top. Alghamdi (1994) echoes some of these considerations and adds the issue of time. He notes that, in some cases, decisions in organizations with collegial structures take longer than in a traditional hierarchical organization. Webb (1988) points out that there could be "frustrations created by the different skill levels of participating employees, dilemmas of trying to reach a consensus with diversified groups, and reluctance of employees to accept the responsibilities for their decisions" (pp. 50-51). Finally, White (1985) cautions against viewing participative management as "an obviously good thing" (p. 62). While he favors employee involvement in the decision process, he maintains that participative management is only one possible method that should be considered.

While these problems do exist in some cases and should be considered, there are many examples of successful team management and participatory structures. Bechtel (1994) describes the Dickinson College Library's collegial management structure. This excellent article provides a detailed look at the principles and missions that underlie that library's structure as well as the procedures and policies that have been put into practice there.

Lubans (1996) details the Duke University Library's shift to self-managing teams. He describes the role of a manager in this type of organization as one that includes: coaching—"Challenging teams to question assumptions" (p. 34); consulting—"Investigating new ways of doing things and bringing this information to teams" (p. 35); encouraging—"Recognizing and celebrating good work and calling attention to high performance" (p. 35); and leading— Eliminating barriers" (p. 35). Articles relating to experiences at Harvard (Clack 1993; Lee 1993; Lee and Clack 1996), at Clemson University Libraries (Boykin and Babel 1993), and at the University of Arizona (Fore et al. 1994) also provide useful information and evidence that participative structures can work.

Client-Centered Literature in Academic Libraries

A look at the titles of the articles cited earlier shows how the TQM literature has contributed greatly to the increased emphasis on teams and participation. It has also contributed to a focus on client-centered organizations. Sirkin (1993) describes the basic element of TQM as customer satisfaction. Brewer (1995) defines a client-centered organization as "guided by customer wants and needs ... A customer-driven organization treats its frontline employees as representatives of the organization and gives them the authority and training to handle problems" (p. 208).

A client-centered or client-driven focus has been a goal of successful for-profit organizations for years, but libraries have been slower in adopting that type of focus. This may be due in part to a reluctance to view our users as customers (Kovel-Jarboe 1996). However, Butler (1993) states in her introduction to *Libraries as User-Centered Organizations: Imperatives for Organization Change*, "As librarians move away from the current paradigm of library as storehouse of information packages collected "just in case," to a new paradigm of library as gateway and network connector to needed information "just in time," they must also shift their focus from the information product to the user of information, a profound change in vision that affects nearly every assumption we make about our work and our profession" (p. 1).

There is increased evidence of this mode of thinking in the literature. Waters (1990) writes about client-driven reference collections at the University Research Library at UCLA. Her article is a case study detailing the steps taken to identify their primary clientele and to base their collection management decisions on that population's needs. The strategies they employed illustrate how tough choices can be made somewhat easier when a clear definition of primary client is available.

Harloe (1989) describes a collection development model that incorporates the principles of a client-centered library collection. He details a process for moving to a collection development process that involves librarians as well as teaching faculty. Brewer (1995) explains the necessary planning processes for moving to a customer-driven library. Libraries have recognized the necessity for all staff members to examine how a shift to a client-centered library will affect how they do their jobs. Goleski (1995) describes a training program for library staff at the Vanderbilt University library. This workshop, called "Learning to Say 'YES,'" was primarily for units in the library that did not generally see themselves as serving the library's clients. The workshop explained that units such as technical services, automation, and networks are serving internal clients. By educating these units on the benefits of considering coworkers as clients they found that, not only are their coworkers better served, but the library's primary clientele benefits as well. Wilson (1995) describes the efforts of the staff at the University of Washington Libraries to define and implement a user-centered approach to services and budget allocations. Finally, Sirkin (1993) provides an excellent list of specific changes made and services offered by libraries who have improved customer service.

In a time of declining budgets and increased technological capabilities on the part of users, it only makes sense to set priorities and goals based on the needs of the client (Stuart and Drake 1993). In order to fully evaluate those needs it is necessary to allow the employees interacting with clients more input into the decision process. The literature clearly indicates that academic libraries should continue to incorporate strategies such as collegial management and client-focused service into their structures. Consequently, in 1995 the University of Dayton's Roesch Library began a process to redesign its organizational structure based on these principles.

CONTEXT FOR THIS STUDY

Founded in 1850, the University of Dayton is a comprehensive, Catholic university with a student body of 6,400 full-time undergraduates and approximately 3,400 graduate students. Roesch Library is the largest of the three campus libraries and employs twelve full-time librarians and twenty-six support staff. When reorganization was first considered in 1995, the management structure that was in place was a hierarchical arrangement that had been in place since 1986 (see Appendix A). It was led by the Dean, Associate Director for Technical Services, and Associate Director for Public Services. Departments reporting to the Associate Director for Technical Services included Acquisitions, Bibliographic Control, Preservation/Conservation, Periodicals, and University Archives. Departments reporting to the Associate Director for Public Services included Reserve/Periodicals, Access Services, Reference, and Government Documents. The Administrative Office and the Systems Department reported directly to the Dean. A Coordinators Committee comprised of the various department heads functioned as the communication vehicle for the library and dealt with areas of policy.

The external forces affecting Roesch Library were similar to those affecting academic libraries across the country. Decreased funding and higher material costs had resulted in continued realignment of the serials and book budgets. Increased technological developments had resulted in higher patron expectations such as access to the World Wide Web and fulltext printing, while, the library had received only limited increases in funds that were not sufficient to allow the library to fully implement these changes. Budget cuts kept some staff positions empty with little hope that they would be filled. Partnerships with other libraries were changing and expanding. As a member of OhioLINK, a consortium of Ohio academic libraries, Roesch Library has benefited from the increased services and resources it provides, but this membership has also increased the workload of many library staff members.

The internal forces affecting the workload and work environment of the library included:

- a changing collection development model in which librarians would be assuming the role of subject selector for one or more disciplines, an action taken to improve an uneven undergraduate collection.
- an acknowledged split between staff working in the technical service and public services areas that caused communication problems and interrupted the work flow within the library.
- work being done by librarians that the support staff could accomplish, with the support staff not taking full advantage of their individual abilities.
- an acknowledged division in the staff resulting from varying reaction to the Dean's leadership style (Simons 1996).

These factors led the university administration to agree with the Dean of Libraries and Information Technologies that the library would benefit from a reorganization.

TIME LINE/PROCESS

The first official move toward the library reorganization can be traced to early Spring 1995 and an all-staff meeting led by the University Provost. He stated that the library's reorganization was inevitable and that the concept was fully supported by the university administration. Also during this meeting, the results of the Dean's Performance Evaluation, conducted between December 1994 and February 1995, were discussed. Employee comments during the evaluation process showed that factions had grown along organizational lines and that the library exhibited a schism among staff members (Simons 1996).

It was assumed that a reorganization would effectively eliminate the divisions that had appeared among staff and result in better communication and increased productivity.

On May 17, 1995 the Restructuring Advisory Taskforce (RAT) was formed. Taskforce members included the Head of Information Services, the heads of the Periodical and Bibliographic Control Departments, and a Reference Librarian/Interlibrary Loan Supervisor. An E-mail message from the Dean to all staff outlined the role of the RAT team. "The Advisory Taskforce, consisting of four librarians appointed by the Provost and led by the Dean, is charged with guiding a reflection and discussion process which will provide an opportunity for all staff associates and library faculty to offer advice and suggestions relative to the attainment of an organizational structure which will be more client-focused and attuned to the challenges and realities which are presently facing the University Libraries. The Taskforce, by September 15, 1995, will draft a set of recommendations relative to a preferred organizational future. These recommendations will be forwarded to the Provost at that time. The Dean may, at his discretion, attach other observations or recommendations to the Taskforce recommendations" (Garten 1995c).

Linda Simons, a member of the RAT team, further described the role of the team as the vehicle that, in addition to designing an organizational structure the Dean and Provost could accept, also would act as the facilitators of the process. The RAT team would provide the staff with the opportunity and the means to offer insights and ideas regarding the restructuring. The university administration and the Dean believed that it was important that the staff had ownership of the process employed during the organizational change. The RAT team members had credibility and the respect of the staff, especially those staff members from the departments that they represented (Simons 1996).

In June the Dean and the RAT team held several staff and faculty luncheons to explain and discuss the concept of a "Client Focused Model." Background material for these meetings included articles about collegial management principles (Bechtel 1994), customer service programs (Goleski 1995), and the difference between teams and committees (Quinn 1995). The main purpose of the meetings was to obtain reactions and recommendations from the faculty and staff regarding the ideas presented in these articles and the proposed organizational changes. According to Simons (1996), these initial meetings were not very helpful. At the time it was too early in the process for people to have confidence in the process, and many staff members were reluctant to speak frankly.

The most important opportunity for employee participation came during a two-day workshop led by Richard Dougherty of Dougherty & Associates, entitled "Transforming Visions into Realities: A Team Approach to Reengineering Library Services and Managing Change." The goal of the workshop was to develop " ... further clarification of a preferred organizational future and the creation of a practical 'action plan' supportive of both restructuring and the recently completed Library Vision 2005 document" (Garten 1995b).

This workshop was a watershed event in the reorganization process (Simons 1996). Dougherty designed the workshop to bring out issues that were important to library staff members. After two days of intense discussions and debate the library employees identified seven Action Initiatives:

- We are committed to the creation of a flexible, client-oriented organizational structure that represents and includes input from all library staff.
- We are committed to client-focused collection development using subject selectors who are given full responsibility and authority within their designated areas.
- We are committed to conducting "market research" on our clients' information needs as a means of becoming a more effective and responsive library.
- We are committed to initiating an ongoing staff training and orientation program.
- We are committed to seeking ways and means through which to improve communication between and among all staff members.
- We are committed to exploring a range of personnel issues, that is, tenure/promotion requirements vs. client-services obligations, pay issues, and classification issues.
- We are committed to exploring ways and means through which to increase the Libraries' advocacy with the University Administration.

An intended result of these initiatives was the movement away from a more polarized organizational structure to one with a clear client-focus and an explicit collegial atmosphere. These initiatives were important to the process because the staff gained a sense of ownership. Most staff members were excited to move forward with the process, hoping that they would have the opportunity to use their individual skills and talents to their fullest potential.

In order to maintain the momentum brought on by the success of the workshop, the Dean and the RAT team solicited volunteers to serve on taskforces addressing issues outlined in four of the initiative statements. The taskforces were asked to look at Market Research, Training, Communication, and Personnel issues. Seventy percent of the staff members chose to participate. These taskforces were critical to the change process. The opportunity to participate regardless of rank or department resulted in the collapse of the dividing lines between technical services and public services departments, and between support staff and faculty (Simons 1996).

During the months of August and September the new organizational structure was developed further. The RAT team continued to request feedback from all staff as well as the taskforces and entered into individual discussions with staff members who would be directly affected by some of the organizational changes (Simons 1996). They also requested, and were granted, an extension of the deadline for the recommendations to be presented to the Provost.

The newly formed taskforces were busy during the latter part of 1995 and early 1996. Their major accomplishments were:

- The Market Research Taskforce obtained funds and commissioned a series of surveys and focus groups using the University of Dayton's Center for Business and Economic Research and the Social Sciences Resources Center, to pinpoint exactly in which areas we were or were not meeting our clients' needs.

- The Communication Taskforce established a monthly newsletter, "The Online Grapevine," to highlight new personnel, procedural changes, and announcements. The taskforce also initiated a monthly birthday coffee and a lecture series designed to improve communication skills and employee relations.

- The Training Taskforce began a series of classes for staff members. Classes included Internet training and an introduction to the World Wide Web, as well as training on equipment like the newly purchased scanner and a deluxe photocopy machine.

- The Personnel Taskforce initiated and facilitated a process to update all job descriptions and personnel forms held by the university's Human Resources Department. The taskforce also requested that an evaluation of support staff salaries be conducted which led to some equity adjustments.

NEW MANAGEMENT STRUCTURE

In mid-September the RAT team presented to library personnel the final draft of the new organizational model. The Dean explained the proposed model to the library staff as building upon "the earlier discussed client-services focus," and "the use of relatively autonomous teams working within a flattened organizational structure" (Garten 1995a).

The Dean further explained that, "The model incorporates a new manner in which to do collection development, employs the notion of 'responsibility portfolios' for librarians, and vests primary direction for the library in a governing council on which all librarians and two elected support staff members sit" (Garten 1995a). The new governing body, the Services and Resources Council, would be the vehicle through which library policy would be developed. During the next few weeks, staff members responded to the draft, and many recommended changes were incorporated into the plan. The final recommendations were sent to the Provost's Office on October 10, 1995 and were approved soon thereafter.

The new organizational model that emerged (see Appendix B) consisted of the Dean and three leadership positions, recommended by the Dean and ratified by the newly formed Services and Resources Council. These positions are a Head of Client Services, a Coordinator and Head of Collection Management, and a Head of Bibliographic Management. Appointments are for four years. Also, persons giving leadership to these positions would receive a stipend over and above their regular salary, similar to faculty department heads.

Eight information access and support teams were also created. Each team is empowered to make managerial decisions as to how to most efficiently manage their own areas. The teams do, however, report to the person holding the appropriate leadership position. The largest and most encompassing leadership position is the Head of Client Services. Four teams report to this person; the Information Desk, Circulation/Reserve, Building Services, and Interlibrary/Document Delivery. This person is also in charge of the Libraries in the Dean's absence.

Because one of the main focuses of the library reorganization was the emphasis on serving our clients' information needs, the library made several fundamental changes to identify and serve those needs. Some examples include:

- two reference desk assistants hired to provide increased staff during the busiest times in the Reference Room.
- the Reserve and Circulation desk functions combined into one area and Current Periodicals, previously part of the Reserve unit, converted from a closed to an open area in response to complaints from students who used the service regularly.
- a Building Services team created to oversee stack maintenance, mail, and the coordination of the student assistant program and budget.
- the Interlibrary Loan Unit and OhioLINK delivery services combined to form the Interlibrary/Document Delivery Team to better meet our clients' needs for materials not owned by Roesch Library.

Although not directly responsible for providing client services, the remaining teams are essential to a client-centered model. The Collection Development Support Team is responsible for the acquisition of books and periodicals, and reports to the Coordinator and Head of Collection Management who is also responsible for the coordination of the new collection development model. In this new model each librarian is the liaison to one or more academic departments and is responsible for selecting material in the department's subject areas. The Head of Bibliographic Management is responsible for the Copy Cataloging and Materials Preparation Teams. The eighth team, Systems

Support, as well as the Administrative Assistant to the Dean and the Accounts Control Clerk, report directly to the Dean. Lastly, The Marian Library, which in the previous model had been part of Roesch Library's structure, was singled out and made a separate entity.

MEASURING THE EFFECTS OF THE CHANGE

During the reorganization process the authors began to consider the possibility of measuring the impact this organizational shift would have on individual and departmental perceptions of their work environments. A study was proposed to measure the staff's perception of the library's work environment, both immediately preceding the announcement of the new structure, and again six months later. The hypothesis upon which the study was based was that the planned organizational changes would positively affect staff perceptions of the work environment. It was based upon several assumptions. The anticipated organizational change clearly was going to affect many areas of the library. The chain of command was evolving as was the Services and Resources Council, the policy making body. While some staff job responsibilities and physical locations would change, others would see little change at all in their day-to-day work. Since not everyone was going to be affected in the same way, it was decided that the survey should focus on measuring the perceptions of the workplace as a whole and not an individual's job satisfaction. The instrument selected for this study was the Work Environment Scale (WES) developed by Moos and Insel (1974). The WES has three forms: the Real form used to measure the existing environment, an Ideal form used to measure an ideal environment, and an Expectations form used to measure a person's expectations of their work environment. In this study the Real form, Form R, was used. This instrument was selected for a variety of reasons. First, the WES can "describe workplace social environments" (Moos 1994a, p. 5), the primary reason for selecting it. Second, the WES has "adequate internal consistency and test-retest reliability" (Sheehan 1995, p. 1123). This was very important since we would be administering the test twice. Third, the test is easy to administer with a series of 90 statements to which a response of "True" or "False" is given. Finally, the WES provides normative data in the form of the General Work Group averages, enabling ust to compare Roesch Library results with other organizations (Moos 1994a).

The WES measures an employee's perception of their coworkers and their jobs by evaluating three dimensions: Relationship, Personal Growth, and System Maintenance and Change (see Table 1).

Table 1.   WES Subscales and Descriptions

Relationship Dimensions

1.	Involvement	the extent to which employees are concerned about and committed to their jobs
2.	Coworker Cohesion	how much employees are friendly and supportive of one another
3.	Supervisor Support	the extent to which management is supportive of employees and encourages employees to be supportive of one another

Personal Growth Dimensions

1.	Autonomy	how much employees are encouraged to be self-sufficient and to make their own decisions
2.	Task Orientation	the emphasis on good planning, efficiency, and getting the job done
3.	Work Pressure	the degree to which high work demands and time pressure dominate the work milieu

System Maintenance & Change Dimensions

1.	Clarity	whether employees know what to expect in their daily routing and how explicitly rules and policies are communicated
2.	Managerial Control	how much management uses rules and procedures to keep employees under control
3.	Innovation	the emphasis on variety, change, and new approaches
4.	Physical Comfort	the extent to which the physical surroundings contribute to a pleasant work environment

Source: Moos (1994b, p. 1).

All dimensions were important to the study. It was hoped that the organizational changes being made would help to eliminate the departmental divisions. Also, allowing two elected Support Staff to serve on the Services and Resources Council would allow all staff to participate in the decision making process, lessening the division between support staff and faculty even further. The combined effect of these changes would improve the Relationship Dimension. The change to work teams with decision making responsibilities would positively effect the Personal Growth as well as the System Maintenance and Change Dimensions. Finally, it was assumed that all staff would feel more confident about bringing ideas for improving work in their areas to their team leaders, also raising the System Maintenance and Change Dimension.

At an all-staff meeting the authors explained the purpose of the survey and requested that everyone attend one of three scheduled survey times. All staff members agreed to participate. At each session the participants were each given a test booklet and answer sheet, and the authors were available to answer questions. The first time the instrument was administered was early December,

Table 2.   Comparisons of Means and Standard Deviations for the WES

WES Subscales	Total Staff Test #1 Mean	Total Staff Test #1 SD	Total Staff Test #2 Mean	Total Staff Test #2 SD	Statistics— One-tailed t
Involvement	6.08	2.59	7.0	1.80	-1.74*
Peer Cohesion	5.51	2.13	6.42	1.70	-1.99*
Supervisor Support	5.68	2.83	6.48	2.22	-1.34
Autonomy	5.86	2.13	6.76	2.02	-1.80*
Task Orientation	5.97	2.35	6.64	1.87	-1.31
Work Pressure	4.22	2.50	3.48	2.36	1.26
Clarity	5.81	2.17	5.94	2.44	-0.23
Control	4.24	2.14	3.52	2.15	1.42
Innovation	4.59	2.67	6.18	2.27	-2.69*
Physical Comfort	2.86	2.14	2.70	1.96	0.34*

Note: * indicates mean changes significant at the 0.05 level

four weeks before the organizational shifts were to begin taking place. The second was early June, six months later. There was a total of thirty-seven respondents for the first time and a total of thirty-three respondents for the second. The lower number was due to a retirement, a sabbatical leave for one librarian, and two positions that had been vacated and not yet refilled.

In order to compare the first and second administration of the survey, the means, standard deviations, and one-tailed univariate t-tests were calculated for each subscale. Significant differences were computed at the 5 percent level (see Table 2). The means for each of the WES subscales were graphed to enable comparisons between Time 1 and Time 2 (see Figure 1).

The Results

The three WES dimensions were examined and a comparison was made of the staff means for T1 and T2, as well as, a comparison between T2 and the General Work Group averages. The General Work Group averages were based on scores from respondents in many work environments including retail food employees, office workers, teachers and other education professionals, nurses, hospital administrators and other health care professionals, and maintenance workers (p. 21).

Relationship Dimension

The Relationship Dimension measures Involvement (job commitment), Peer Cohesion (coworker support), and Supervisory Support. There was a significant improvement in the Time 2 score for two areas of this dimension, Involvement and Peer Cohesion.

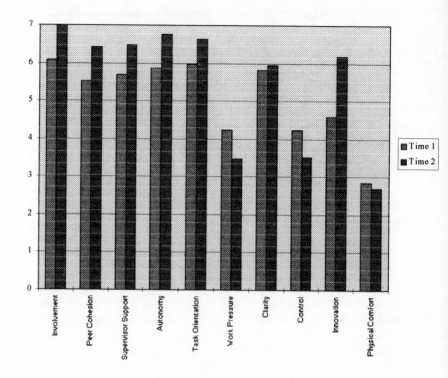

Figure 1.

The improvement of the Involvement score which related to the employees' interest in and commitment to their jobs, may be attributed, in large measure, to the Dougherty workshop and the taskforces. The workshop gave staff members ownership of the organizational change and encouraged employee input as to how best to use their individual interests and talents to improve the library's work environment. As a result, job responsibilities were modified to enable staff members to work to their fullest potential. The development of a policy making committee, the Services and Resources Council, also increased the staff's sense of involvement since support staff are encouraged to suggest agenda items for the council and the minutes of its meetings are posted to all staff via e-mail.

The improvement of the Peer Cohesion score, which measures how well the staff relates to one another, is a positive sign of the achievement of the initial goals of the organizational change. As stated earlier, there was a morale problem within the library at the beginning of the reorganization caused by factions that had grown along departmental lines. This had caused serious communication and work flow problems. The modification of the

Table 3. Comparison Means for the Work Environment Scale

WES Subscales	Total Roesch Staff Mean Time 2	General Work Group Means (N=3,267)
Involvement	7.0	6.13
Peer Cohesion	6.42	5.95
Supervisor Support	6.48	5.73
Autonomy	6.76	5.88
Task Orientation	6.64	6.09
Work Pressure	3.48	4.80
Clarity	5.94	5.52
Control	3.52	4.79
Innovation	6.18	4.37
Physical Comfort	2.70	4.95

previous organizational structure and simultaneous formation of taskforces allowed for the development of a more collegial atmosphere within the organization. Comparing the Time 2 scores to the normative data reported by Moos (1994a), it can be seen that Roesch Library scored higher than the General Work Group averages on all subscales of the Relationship Dimension (see Table 3).

Personal Growth Dimension

The Personal Growth Dimension measures Autonomy, Task Orientation (the emphasis on getting the job done), and Work Pressure. While there was no significant change in the Task Orientation and Work Pressure scores, there was a significant change in the Autonomy score. This improvement can be directly attributed to the development of the eight information access and support teams. These teams were designed to be independent and were given the opportunity to make managerial decisions.

The Roesch Library Time 2 scores are higher than the General Work Group average for Autonomy and Task Orientation. Interestingly, Roesch Library staff measures of Work Pressures are well below the average scores for the General Work Group population. This could be due in part to the professions represented in the normative sample.

System Maintenance and Change Dimensions

The System Maintenance and Change Dimensions measures clarity, that is how well rules and policies are communicated; Control, that is how much control management uses in the workplace; Innovation, and Physical Comfort. The area that experienced significant change was Innovation. Roesch Library scored well above the General Work Group average on this subscale. This positive result can be attributed to two factors. First, the efforts of the RAT team ensured that the entire staff was involved in the restructuring. Throughout the process staff members were encouraged to participate and offer suggestions on how to improve library services. Second, the development of the teams and placing the decision making powers in the hands of the team leaders have encouraged a willingness to try new approaches for increasing productivity and improving the work environment.

The library scored higher than the General Work Group average on Clarity and Innovation, while scoring lower on Managerial Control and Physical Comfort. The most significant difference between the Roesch Library scores and the General Work Group averages is in Physical Comfort. Roesch Library's extremely low scores can be attributed to environmental concerns with the building. The library experiences continual problems with the heating and cooling systems creating hot and cold zones throughout the building. The building also has asbestos in the ceilings. As a result, the university must hire an outside contractor to fix burned out fluorescent lights, light ballasts, and malfunctioning air control valves. This often results in a significant delay in completing necessary work.

Nonetheless, it appears that the work environment of Roesch Library is improving. Although only four of the nine WES subscales showed significant improvement, those that did were some of the problem areas which led to the reorganization. Moreover, it was encouraging to see that Roesch Library tends to score above the General Work Group averages on all Dimensions.

CONCLUSION

In the Fall of 1996 Roesch Library was preparing to start its first full academic year under the new organizational structure. As students, faculty, and staff begin visiting the library some changes will be immediately apparent, such as the combined Circulation/Reserve desk, the open Current Periodicals area, and increased staffing at the Reference desk. Faculty will see additional changes. They will now be working with the librarian assigned to their subject areas to schedule bibliographic instruction sessions and to order materials.

Other changes are more subtle but no less important. The Building Services Team is devising methods of keeping the stacks in order and reshelving materials as quickly as possible. The Collection Development and Bibliographic Management Teams are working on streamlining the materials acquisition process to reduce the time between ordering and availability. The Document Delivery Team is in the final phase of making an Interlibrary Loan

Form available on the campus Web site to allow people to request materials from an office or dormitory room. The librarian selectors are beginning a process to evaluate the periodicals in their subject areas to determine if money is being spent on the resources our clients need. Finally, policy issues of all types are being discussed by the Services and Resources Council in order to obtain as many points of view as possible before committing resources of time, personnel, or money.

These changes and others like them are all a direct result of the reorganization and highlight its positive impact. The results of the Work Environment Scale are also evidence that the reorganization has improved the work atmosphere. While not every measure increased enough to be considered statistically significant, the ones that did are certainly elements associated with a successful collegial, client-focused organization: involvement or job commitment, coworker cohesion, autonomy, and innovation.

As the new structure evolves some positions continue to be redefined. Departmental divisions are not as apparent as they once were, and the new collection development model has been introduced to and accepted by the faculty. It appears that the library staff are feeling better about their jobs, working more effectively with each other, feeling capable of making their own decisions, and are willing to try new ways of doing things. Finally, some support staff members have been promoted and given more responsibility, freeing librarian time for collection development duties.

Appendix to Follow

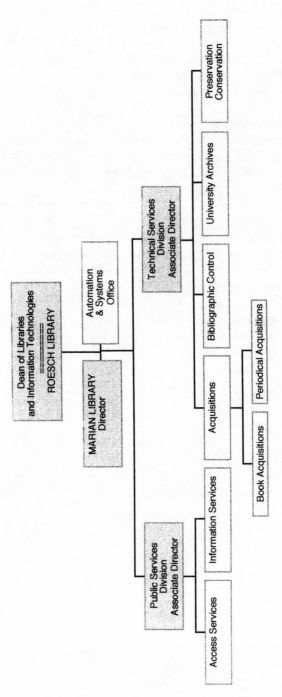

Boxes in the organizational chart:

Dean of Libraries and Information Technologies
ROESCH LIBRARY

MARIAN LIBRARY
Director

Automation & Systems Office

Public Services Division
Associate Director

Technical Services Division
Associate Director

Access Services

Information Services

Acquisitions

Bibliographic Control

University Archives

Preservation Conservation

Book Acquisitions

Periodical Acquisitions

Appendix A

244

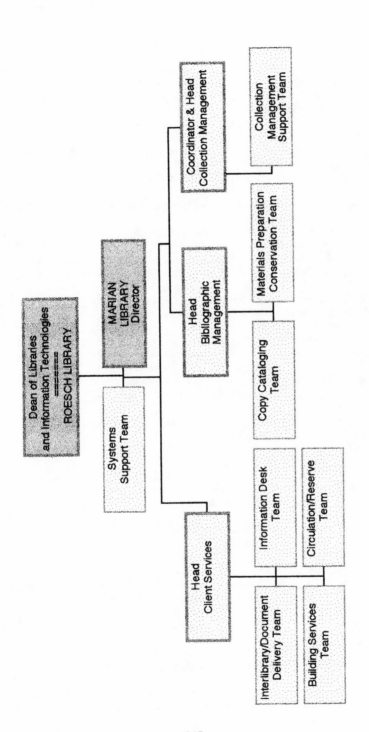

Appendix B

245

REFERENCES

Alghamdi, F. A. 1994. "The Collegial Model: Its Applications and Implications for Academic Libraries." *Library Administration & Management* 8(1): 15-20.

Bechtel, J. M. 1994. "Collegial Management: Principles and Practice." *Library Administration & Management* 8(1): 21-33.

Boisse, J. A. 1996. "Adjusting the Horizontal Hold: Flattening the Organization." *Library Administration & Management* 10(2): 77-81.

Boykin, J. Jr. and D. B. Babel. 1993. "Reorganizing the Clemson University Libraries." *Journal of Academic Librarianship* 19(2): 94-96.

Brewer, J. 1995. "Service Management: How to Plan for It Rather Than Hope for It." *Library Administration & Management* 9(4): 207-210.

Burckel, N. C. 1984. "Participatory Management In Academic Libraries: A Review." *College & Research Libraries* 45(1): 25-34.

Butler, M. A. ed. 1993. *Libraries as User-Centered Organizations: Imperatives for Organizational Change*. New York: Haworth Press.

Clack, M. E. 1993. "Organizational Development and TQM: The Harvard College Library's Experience." In *Integrating Total Quality Management in a Library Setting*, edited by S. Jurow and S. B. Barnard. New York: Haworth Press.

Drake, M. A. 1993. "Technological Innovation and Organizational Change." In *Libraries as User-Centered Organizations. Imperatives for Organizational Change*, edited by M. A. Butler. New York: Haworth Press.

Fore, J. S., R. C. Knight and C. Russell. 1993. "Leadership for User Services in the Academic Library." In *Libraries as User-Centered Organizations. Imperatives for Organizational Change*, edited by M. A. Butler. New York: Haworth Press.

Garten, E. 1995a. Message from Fr. Heft. *E-mail to Administration.*

——. 1995b. Process Being Employed. *E-mail to Administration.*

——. 1995c. Role of the Advisory Taskforce. *E-mail to Administration.*

Goleski, E. 1995. "Learning to Say 'Yes': A Customer Service Program for Library Staff." *Library Administration & Management* 9(4): 211-215.

Haka, C. H. 1996. "Organizational Design: Is There An Answer." *Library Administration & Management* 10(2): 74-76.

Harloe, B. 1989. "Achieving Client-centered Collection Development in Small and Medium-sized Academic Libraries." *College & Research Libraries* 50(3): 344-353.

Kaser, D. 1970. "Modernizing the University Library Structure." *College & Research Libraries* 31(4): 227-231.

Kovel-Jarboe, P. 1996. "Quality Improvement: A Strategy for Planned Organizational Change." *Library Trends* 44(3): 605-630.

Lee, S. 1993. "Organizational Change in the Harvard College Library: A Continued Struggle for Redefinition and Renewal." *Journal of Academic Librarianship* 19(4): 225-230.

Lee, S. and M. E. Clack. 1996. "Continued Organizational Transformation: The Harvard College Library's Experience." *Library Administration & Management* 10(2): 98-104.

Lubans, J. 1996. "I Ain't No Cowboy, I Just Found This Hat: Confessions of an Administrator in an Organization of Self-Managing Teams." *Library Administration & Management* 10(1): 28-40.

Marchant, M. P. 1976. "Participative Management in Academic Libraries". Contributions in *Librarianship and Information Science*, edited by P. Wasserman. Westport, CT: Greenwood Press.

Martell, C. 1987. "The Nature of Authority and Employee Participation in the Management of Academic Libraries." *College & Research Libraries* 48(2): 110-122.

Michalko, J. 1993. "Higher Education, the Production Function, and the Library." In *Libraries as User-Centered Organizations: Imperatives for Organizational Change*, edited by M. A. Butler. New York: Haworth Press.

Moos, R. H. 1994a. *A Social Climate Scale: Work Environment Scale Manual*,. 3rd edition. Palo Alto, CA: Consulting Psychologists Press.

————— . 1994b. *The Social Climate Scales: A Users Guide*, 2nd edition. Palo Alto, CA: Consulting Psychologists Press.

Moos, R. H. and P. N. Insel. 1974. *Work Environment Scale, Form R*. Palo Alto, CA: Consulting Psychologists Press.

Quinn, B. 1995. "Understanding the Differences Between Committees and Teams." *Library Administration & Management* 9(2): 111-116.

Sheehan, E. P. 1995. "Review of the Work Environment Scale, 2nd Edition. In *The Twelfth Mental Measurements Yearbook*, edited by J. C. Conoley and J. C. Impara. Lincoln, NE: The Buros Institute of Mental Measurements, The University of Nebraska-Lincoln.

Simons, L. 1996. Interview by Kerrie Moore. Dayton, Ohio.

Sirkin, A. F. 1993. "Customer Service: Another Side of TQM." *Journal of Library Administration* 18 (1/2): 71-83.

Stuart, C. and M. A. Drake. 1993. "TQM in Research Libraries." *Special Libraries* 84(3): 131-136.

Towler, C. F. 1993. "Problem Solving Teams in a Total Quality Management Environment." In *Integrating Total Quality Management in a Library Setting*, edited by S. Jurow and S. B. Barnard. New York: Haworth Press.

Waters, M. B. 1990. "Client-Driven Reference Collections for the 1990s." *Reference Librarian* (29):93-102.

Webb, G. 1988. "Preparing Staff for Participative Management." *Wilson Library Bulletin* 62(9): 50-52.

White, H. S. 1985. "Participative Management is the Answer, but What Was the Question?" *Library Journal* 110(13): 62-63.

Wilson, L. A. 1995. "Building the User-Centered Library." *RQ* 34(3): 297-302.

A CONTINGENCY APPROACH TO EXPLORE THE RELATIONSHIPS AMONG STRUCTURE, TECHNOLOGY, AND PERFORMANCE IN ACADEMIC LIBRARY DEPARTMENTS

Hweifen Weng

Organization design has become an issue that managers of all types of organizations must consider as they face massive societal and technological change. The best-seller status of management books such as *In Search of Excellence* (Peters and Waterman 1982), *The Change Masters* (Kanter 1983), *Reinventing the Corporation* (Naisbitt and Aburdene 1985), or *Thriving on Chaos* (Peters 1987) all indicate managers' interests in new forms of organization. Corporate managers increasingly recognized organizational structure as a source of sustained competitive advantage and a critical success factor. Many new organization design and redesign experiments are being attempted. Management literature also abounds with works on the new forms

Advances in Library Administration and Organization,
Volume 15, pages 249-317.
Copyright © 1997 by JAI Press Inc.
All rights of reproduction in any form reserved.
ISBN: 0-7623-0371-9

of corporate structure, for example lateral organizations (Galbraith 1994), learning organizations (Hodgetts, Luthans and Lee 1994), or team-based structures (Mankin, Cohen and Bikson 1996).

Managers of academic libraries are certainly facing the issue and responding with some redesign experiments. However, many of them still arrived at the normatively prescribed organization design via a trial-and-error process. As the tasks and functions of the organization become increasingly more complex, such an approach may become a liability (Lewin and Stephens 1993). As librarians confront change, studies are needed to answer a crucial question for organization design: what form or forms of structure might characterize organizations of the future?

Early in 1983, Willard and Teece (1983), in their study of the impact of automation in Australian libraries, had already suggested a research agenda centering on finding the most appropriate types of library structures to provide effective services using the new technologies. However, in the early stages of library automation, librarians paid more attention to the technical issues of developing systems or issues concerning library patrons' experience (Johnson 1991a). Not until the mid-1980s did the attention gradually shift to the personnel aspects of library automation, regarding the impact on not only those who use libraries, but also those who work in libraries and those who manage libraries (Kirkland 1989).

One of the major issues was the blurring of the distinction between technical and public services, and the effectiveness of functional structures (Cline and Sinnott 1983; ARL 1985; Myers 1986; de Klerk and Euster 1989). For example, Kaplan (1989, p. 308) observed in her summary of technical services automation, that the most significant issue of the year was the ongoing merger of technical and public service functions. It was argued that using online catalogs, sharing databases, and employing the services of bibliographic utilities have called the traditional separation of public/technical functions into question.

In practice, however, most of the reports of reorganization in library literature were case studies of single libraries, the descriptions of which may not be generalizable as patterns of organizational change in academic libraries. As a matter of fact, several comparative studies found that most libraries were still organized around traditional functions (de Klerk and Euster 1989; ARL 1991; Johnson 1991a; Buttlar and Garcha 1992). Hence, before seeking answers to future organization forms, more research is needed with respect to the current patterns of library structures and how they affect the achievement of organizational goals.

In the sociology and business school literatures, the dominant approach to understanding organizational structures has been structural contingency theory (Pfeffer 1982, p. 147). The central theme of the theory states that organizations with a structure that closely matches the requirements of its context, for example, size, technology, environment, are more effective than those that do not.

In the research literature, one of the most studied relationships in structural contingency theory is that between technology and structure. However, in empirical studies, few researchers have seriously examined how contingency factors such as technology link with structure to affect performance. In addition, most researchers have studied manufacturing or product-processing organizations, while few have studied service or people-processing organizations, such as government agencies or hospitals (Reimann and Inzerilli 1981, p. 245). Rarely did studies on the technology-structure relationship focus on information organizations such as academic libraries that have recently been undergoing great technological changes and have expressed increasing concern about organizational change since the mid-1980s.

PURPOSES OF THE STUDY

Hence, this study was conducted to pursue two agenda. First, the study attempted to assess the applicability of structural contingency theory to understand organizational structure in a different organizational setting, for example, academic libraries. Second, using the framework of structural contingency theory, this study attempted to explore the relationships between structure and technology in library departments in search of rules of organization design that may assist managers to develop guidelines for the future.

Specifically, this study intended to apply structural contingency theory to describe structure and technology of library departments and to explore what patterns of structural design were appropriate for achieving the highest performance in consideration of their technological characteristics.

THE ASSUMPTIONS

The study used structural contingency theory as the theoretical framework to guide the research. Underlying the theory is a deterministic orientation toward social structure and behavior, assuming that organizational structure and behavior are constrained by external causal forces (Van de Ven and Astley 1981). Structural elements are assumed to be interrelated in such a way that they instrumentally serve the achievement of organizational goals. Managers were assumed to have a reactive role to fine-tune organizational structure according to the exigencies it confronts.

LITERATURE REVIEW

Structural Issues in Librarianship

In the mid-1980s, after two decades of applying computer-related technologies to library operations, librarians started dealing less with the introduction of technology and more with its results, among them, the impact of automation on library structure. Intner and Fang (1991) observed that as integrated online bibliographic systems have matured, the responsibilities of librarians will cut through the strict line between public and technical services. A number of writers argued for the integration of public and technical service functions and for abolishing the strict division between technical and public services (Gorman 1984; Adan 1988; Cotta-Schönberg 1989; Drabenstott and Burman 1994).

Recognizing the need to restructure to make the best of technology, some of them described what a future structure might look like. In principle, Shaughnessy (1982) recognized that there would be no one best design, and suggested that an open, adaptive, and organic structure would offer more advantages than a closed, stable, or mechanistic structure. Cotta-Schönberg (1989) proposed a "service structure" that would fully orient towards service, and would be "shaped and reshaped as a flexible framework for concrete strategy to obtain the particular objectives of any given library" (p. 61). Reviewing library literature, Drabenstott and Burman (1994) concluded that the library of the future would be flatter than traditional libraries, and that staff may no longer permanently connect with a particular department based on library operations or functions.

In the meantime, some libraries were trying out new structures to adapt to the impact of computerization, and numerous reorganization efforts in response to automation were reported in the literature.[1] For an overall change, Gorman (1979, 1984, 1985, 1987) and Martell (1983) proposed specific models that are widely cited and discussed. In practice, Adams (1986) and Johnson (1991b) both observed the increasing use of a matrix approach or of committees and task forces in which each individual played several roles and was responsible for more than one person. Overall, these experiences conform to the trends depicted in the literature: service- or user-oriented structural design, matrix approach of job assignments, de-specialization of professional librarians. However, most libraries remain hierarchical with divisions of public and technical services. Flatter structure occurs only in a few libraries.

On the other hand, several empirical and comparative studies examining a mass of libraries found that there was still no sweeping change in academic library structure. In brief, studies conducted in the 1980s found that some forms of functional integration have been attempted, for example, the uses of project committees, librarians with dual functions. However, the effects of library automation on library structure as a whole remained minimal; that is, most libraries continued to organize along the traditional pattern of public and technical services divisions no matter what the library size is, large or small.

The findings from studies in the early 1990s exhibited the same patterns. In 1990, ARL conducted another survey to follow up the extent of change since 1984 (Association of Research Libraries 1991). The analysis of 71 organizational charts sent by the member libraries indicated few significant changes in library organizational structures trends. Similar results of no change were also reported in Johnson's 1991 study (Johnson 1991a). Another study (Buttlar and Garcha 1992) was conducted in 1992 and found that a majority of the libraries surveyed (65% of 93 libraries) were organized traditionally and 30 (32.6%) reported some partial integration.

The consensus in the literature is that there is a need for change. Evidently, computerization has blurred the traditional functional division between public and technical services. What is less evident, however, is whether the future depicted in numerous writings will hold true. There is still not yet a clear pattern of reorganization, and no one style of organization has definitely been accepted as a norm. Librarians continue to experiment based on their library's personnel, organizational, technological, and environmental features.

Some observations can be concluded from this literature. First, library units are becoming increasingly interdependent, thus blurring the line between public and technical services. Hence, interdependence—one of the dimensions of technology in structural contingency theory—between library units appears to be an important factor influencing library structure nowadays. Secondly, the most common change in library structure reported in the literature is the decrease in departmental specialization accompanied by a high degree of automation. This phenomenon contradicts the evidence in structural contingency theory that computer usage is positively related to structural complexity, namely vertical and horizontal differentiation measured by professional and personnel specialization. Because most of the studies in librarianship are limited in generalizability, the agreement and disagreement of current structural conditions of academic libraries with structural contingency theory need to be tested further.

Contingency Approach to Study Departments or Work Units

The dominant approach to explaining organizational structures during the past three decades has been structural contingency theory (Pfeffer 1982, p. 147; Van de Ven and Drazin 1985, p. 334). Figure 1 represents the components of the theory. It implicitly assumes that there is an effectiveness or efficiency-seeking orientation on the part of organizational managers, which acts to produce congruence between organization designs and contextual factors to achieve maximum organizational outcomes.

Drawn primarily from large-scale empirical studies, structural contingency theory is not a theory in the conventional sense. It is not a well-developed set of interrelated propositions; but rather is more of an orienting strategy or metatheory that suggests ways to conceptualize a phenomenon, or an approach to explaining the phenomenon (Schoonhoven 1981, p. 350). The central theme of the theory is that an organization's efficiency depends on the relation between

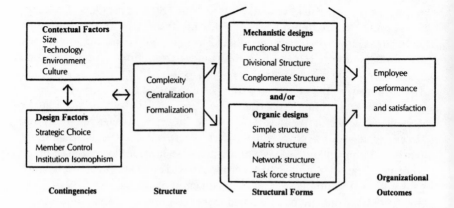

Figure 1. A Contingent Approach to Organizational Structure

the state of the environment, for example, technological uncertainty, and the form of the organization (Grandori 1987, p. 1). Two conclusions are drawn from these studies. First, there is no one best way to organize; and second, any way of organizing is not equally effective under all conditions (Galbraith 1973, p. 2). That is, a wide range of organization forms may be equally effective. Burns and Stalker (1961) classified them into mechanistic and organic forms. The former are characterized as being high in specialization, formalization, and hierarchy of authority while the later are low in specialization, formalization, and hierarchy of authority (Robbins 1983). The theory then explains what factors the choice of organizational forms depends on.

Contingency theorists recognized that there is no single explanation for the forms taken by organizations; rather, multiple explanations are needed to understand organizational structures because some factors may operate together in a correlated or even conflicting manner. There are two major categories of factors affecting structure (Hall 1987, p. 101): contextual factors that include size, technology, the environment, as well as cultural conditions, and design factors that include strategic choice, member control, as well as institutional isomorphism.

In the present study, the emphasis is placed on the relationship between technology and structure in organizations and how they interact to enable organizations to achieve their highest performance. Researchers in this field have in common not only an interest in the role of technology in organizations, but also a commitment to the use of technological variations as a contingency variable. They all agree that there is no one best way to structure organizations—that structure should and often does vary with particular technological conditions.

Conceptualizations of Technology

In structural contingency studies, conceptions of technology have tended to be broad rather than narrow. Few analysts have restricted the term to its colloquial meaning of hardware, for example, tools, equipment, machines. Most researchers include such artifacts as work procedures and techniques in their conceptions of technology. Others incorporate workers' skills, know-how, and knowledge. Broad definitions also include the characteristics of the objects or materials on which work is performed. The broadest conceptions encompass the task environment within which the organization operates (Scott 1990).

In spite of this diversity of conceptions, there has been considerable consensus among contingency theorists on which aspects or dimensions of technology are most significant for predicting organizational structure. Building on the work of Woodward (1965), Perrow (1967, 1970), and Thompson (1967), most researchers have emphasized the following three dimensions of technology.

1. TECHNICAL COMPLEXITY (Woodward 1965). Based on the empirical study of management organizations in British industry initiated in 1953, Woodward (1965) categorized her findings of organizational technology into three categories: unit production, mass production, and process production, which were further divided into eleven subgroups. The resulting categories are seen as a scale of technical complexity that indicates how controllable the production process is or how predictable its results are.

2. ROUTINE-NONROUTINENESS (Perrow 1967, 1970). Perrow conceptualized technology as the actions "that an individual performs upon an object, with or without the aid of tools or mechanical devices, in order to make some change in that object" (Perrow 1967, p. 195).

He proposed that two aspects of technology were directly relevant to organizational structure: the number of exceptions encountered in the work (p. 195), and the nature of the search process undertaken by the individual when exceptions occur (p. 196). If there is a large number of exceptions and the search is neither logical nor analytic, the technology is described as nonroutine. Few exceptions and analyzable search procedures describe a routine technology.

Using this cognitive concept of technology, Perrow (1970, p. 78) placed organizations at various points in the two-dimensional space created by the two variables—the number of exceptions and the analyzability of search, as illustrated in Figure 2. For example, a research and development firm may be very nonroutine; whereas a continuous-processing industry, such as those that produce oil or chemicals may be very routine.

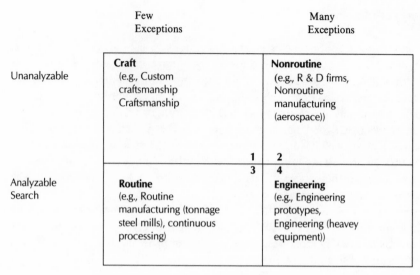

	Few Exceptions	Many Exceptions
Unanalyzable	**Craft** (e.g., Custom craftsmanship Craftsmanship)	**Nonroutine** (e.g., R & D firms, Nonroutine manufacturing (aerospace))
	1	2
	3	4
Analyzable Search	**Routine** (e.g., Routine manufacturing (tonnage steel mills), continuous processing)	**Engineering** (e.g., Engineering prototypes, Engineering (heavey equipment))

Source: Perrow (1970, p. 78).

Figure 2.   Perrow's Conception of Technology

3.   INTERDEPENDENCE (Thompson 1967). Thompson conceptualized technology as interdependence of work flow that can exist between units and suggested that it be measured by focusing on the flow of work, materials, and objects among unit personnel (pp. 54-65).

Three patterns of interdependence were identified, as illustrated in Figure 3. Pooled interdependence represents an absence of work flow between units. Work units are interdependent in the sense that each of them "renders a discrete contribution to the whole [organization] and each is supported by the whole" (p. 54). Sequential interdependence represents a unidirectional exchange pattern where each work unit's inputs are the outputs from another unit. Direct dependence exists between work units, and the order of that interdependence can be specified. Reciprocal interdependence represents a contingent pattern in the work flow when an output from each unit becomes an input to the other. Thompson believed that "the types of interdependence form a Guttman-type scale: all organizations have pooled interdependence; more complicated organizations have sequential as well as pooled; and the most complex have reciprocal, sequential, and pooled" (p. 59).

In addition to these three dimensions, with the development of new technologies, computers in particular, the degree of automation or computerization has emerged as one of technological dimensions in technology-structure research. However, there is still no dominant approach to measuring automation.

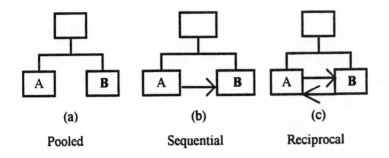

	(a)	(b)	(c)
	Pooled	Sequential	Reciprocal

Source: (Adopted from McCann and Galbraith 1981, p. 63).

Figure 3. Types of Interdependence

Conceptualizations of Structure

Organizational structure is concerned with the arrangement of people, departments, and other subsystems in the organization. It serves three basic functions: (1) to produce organizational outputs and to achieve organizational goals; (2) to minimize or at least to regulate the influence of individual variations on the organization; and (3) to provide settings in which power is exercised, decisions are made, and organization's activities are carried out (Hall 1987, p. 99).

The concept of structure has achieved some degree of agreement over three decades of development, despite differences in operationalization (Fry 1982; Miller and Dröge 1986). It is made up of three components: complexity, centralization, and formalization (Robbins 1983).

Complexity is defined as the degree of formal structural differentiation within an organization (Price and Mueller 1986, p. 100). A highly complex organization is characterized by many occupational roles, subunits (divisions and departments), levels of authority, and operating sites. The word formal in the definition signifies that this differentiation is officially established by the organization, not part of the informal structure of the organization. It is usually broken down into three parts: vertical differentiation, spatial dispersion, and horizontal differentiation (Hall 1987; Robbins 1983). The former two aspects are usually measured at the organizational level by institutional measures, while the later is usually measured at the subunit, or departmental, level by perceptual measures.

Vertical, or hierarchical, differentiation refers to the depth of the hierarchy. Differentiation increases, and so does complexity, as the number of hierarchical levels in the organization increases (Robbins 1983, p. 50). Relationship between vertical differentiation and technology is tested only in studies conducted at the organizational level.

Spatial dispersion refers to the degree to which an organization's activities and personnel are dispersed geographically. It is measured by counting the number of geographical locations, and the distance of these locations from the organizational headquarters as well as the number of people in these separate locations (Hall 1987, p. 64).

Horizontal differentiation is the major dimension tested in the subunit or work group level of analysis (Fry 1982). It refers to the degree of differentiation between units based on the orientation of members, the nature of the tasks they perform, and their education and training. There are three aspects in the concept of complexity: professional specialization, the level of professional qualifications (Gerwin 1981, p. 14), and personnel specialization (Van de Ven and Ferry 1980). Professional specialization is usually measured by the number of different classes of functional activity, such as the number of job titles in an organization (Van de Ven and Ferry 1980). The second aspect, the level of professional qualifications or expertise, is usually measured by actual rather than prescribed conditions (Gerwin 1981, p. 14). In research, actual qualifications of job holders are used more frequently than the qualification requirements of the jobs themselves (Hage and Aiken 1967). In their study, Van de Ven and Ferry (1980) identified another aspect of complexity, personnel specialization, which referred to the interchangeability of jobs among unit personnel. Interchangeability, or the converse, personnel specialization, means the degree to which A can perform B's job at short notice and B can perform A's, even when A and B have different job titles or different functional assignments. In a department with high personnel specialization, job rotation is very difficult because personnel roles are not interchangeable in the near term (p. 164).

Centralization is concerned with how power is distributed and how decisions are made in an organization. Robbins (1983) defines centralization as "the degree to which the formal authority to make discretionary choices is concentrated in an individual, unit, or level (usually high in the organization), thus permitting employees (usually low in the organization) minimum input into their work" (p. 78). There are two theoretical dimensions of centralization of interest in technology-structure research: the hierarchy of authority and the degree of participation in decision-making (Hage and Aiken 1967; Fry 1982). Van de Ven and Ferry (1980) define hierarchy of authority as the distribution of influence on various decisions by various groups of people within an organization (p. 426). Degree of participation refers to how much an individual participates in decisions that affect the organization, for example, the hiring of personnel, the promotions of personnel, the adoption of new organizational policies, and the adoption of new programs or services such as those in Hage and Aiken's study (1967, p. 510).

Formalization refers to the degree to which the norms of an organization are explicitly formulated. It is usually measured by the extent to which rules and procedures are used in organizations (Gerwin 1981, p. 16) and operationalized by the presence of rule manuals (Hage and Aiken 1967), and the degree to which rules, procedures, instructions, and communications are recorded (Van de Ven and Ferry 1980).

The Structure-Technology Relationships

Applying these concepts, organizational researchers have carried out a considerable number of empirical studies over the past three decades to assess the relationships between technology and structure. In general, the effect of technology has been found to be greater when an organization is small and when structural characteristics are close to the work flow. The effect of technology is also greater at the department level (Daft 1986).

Miner (1982, p. 243) indicated that measures of Perrow's routine-nonroutine dimensions have shown consistent relationships to structural factors. Alexander and Randolph (1985) agreed that there has been some acceptance of the definition of technology provided by Perrow (1967) and defined operationally by Lynch (1974).

Gerwin (1981) observed that the empirical results of studies focusing on the job level supported the structure-technology relationship. Specifically, it was determined that the qualifications required of line personnel decreased, rule following became more prevalent, and employee participation in decision making diminished as technology became more routine (p. 13). A similar conclusion was derived in Reimann and Inzerilli's review (1981) of the organizational subunit structure. They found that, "as the transformation process of the work group becomes less routine, or more uncertain and complex, its structure becomes more organic, with increased participation, autonomy, and informality of relationships in the groups" (p. 249). Fry (1982) also found that there are remarkably consistent findings using the routine-nonroutine technology conception despite several different operationalizations of the construct. It is widely supported that subunits will adopt less formalized and centralized structures as technology moves from routine to nonroutine (Hrebiniak 1974; Van de Ven, Delbecq and Koenig 1976; Comstock and Scott 1977).

If technology is conceptualized as interdependence, significant relationships likely exist among interdependence and measures of division of labor, specialization, and differentiation (McCann and Galbraith 1981, p. 66). Fry's review (1982) revealed that as subunits became more interdependent, they became less formalized, the hierarchy of authority decreased and the degree of participation increased (p. 537).

However, reviews done by Dewar and Werbel (1979), Dalton et al. (1980), Argote (1982), Fry and Slocum (1984) indicated that many early studies were in fact congruency theories, which merely hypothesized the relationship between organizational context (e.g., technology) and structure without examining whether this context-structure relationship affected performance. Studies failing to measure performance directly cannot conclusively indicate that variation in designs has serious consequences for performance and provides only indirect tests of contingency theory. Therefore, Fry and Smith (1987) suggested that "the nature of the relationship between congruence and effectiveness must be explored further" (p. 123). It is argued that if organization theory and research are to be relevant to practitioners, emphasis must be placed on organizational effectiveness, a criterion that apparently matters most to managers (Van de Ven 1981, p. 249).

Contingency Propositions.

In a congruent proposition, a simple unconditional association is hypothesized as existing among structural and technological variables in the model; for example, the greater the task uncertainty, the more complex the structure. On the other hand, a contingency proposition hypothesizes a conditional association of two or more independent variables with a dependent outcome, for example, task uncertainty interacts with structural complexity to affect performance.

There are alternative perspectives of contingency propositions in structure-technology studies (Van de Ven and Drazin 1985; Venkatraman 1989). The type of contingency propositions adopted in structural contingency research is central and critical to both theoretical discussions and empirical research. Nevertheless, few scholars have seriously examined its implications; but they have postulated relationships using phrases and words such as matched with, contingent upon, consistent with, fit, congruence, and co-alignment. Precise guidelines for translating these verbal statements to the analytical level did not appear until the 1980s.

Venkatraman (1989) identified six perspectives of "fit" in strategy research: fit as moderation, mediation, profile deviation, matching, gestalts, and co-variation. These categories are based on the degree of specificity of the theoretical relationships and on whether the relationship is anchored to a particular criterion, for example, performance, or whether the relationship adopts a criterion-free specification. Among the six perspectives, fit as moderation, mediation, and profile deviation explore the relationship between structure and contextual variables and explicitly examine the effect of the relations on performance variables. The other three are criterion-free propositions, which are specified without reference to a criterion variable, although, subsequently, its effect on a set of criterion variables could be examined. For each perspective, there should be a link between theoretical arguments and accompanied analytical schemes.

As to studies of structure-technology relationships, there is no dominant approach or perspective as yet. Nevertheless, researchers suggested that adopting multiple approaches as competing theories or models can greatly aid the development of midrange theories (Van de Ven and Drazin 1985), and can lead to more useful and powerful operationalization, data collection, data analysis, and interpretation (Venkatraman 1989).

In the following pages, some studies explicitly investigating the effect of structure-technology relationships on performance will be reviewed in light of Fry and Smith's suggestion that, if organizational research is to be relevant to practitioners, emphasis must be placed on organizational effectiveness and its determinants (1987, p. 123).

Dewar and Werbel (1979) conducted one of the earliest study explicitly focusing on the relationships among structure, technology, and performance in 52 departments of 13 companies. In their study, conflict and satisfaction were dependent variables that were found to be predicted by technology, structure, and the fit between the two. They found that frequent use of rules and regulations when work was routine led to a decline in satisfaction. That is, formalization associated with routine technology tended to decrease job satisfaction.

Schoonhoven (1981), in a study of the quality of surgical care in hospitals, proposed a causal model of organizational effectiveness predicted from three technology-structure interactions: $Y = a + X_1X_2 + X_1X_3 + X_1X_4 - X_1 + X_2 + X_3 + X_4 + X_5 + e_y$, where Y = effectiveness, X_1 = work flow uncertainty, X_2 = de-standardization, X_3 = decentralization, X_4 = professionalization, and X_5 = resources. Among all the relevant studies, this model presented the best result, $R^2 = .81$. In terms of the three interaction terms, Schoonhoven found that in lower uncertainty subunits, de-standardization reduces effectiveness; on the other hand, in greater uncertainty subunits, de-standardization increases effectiveness. For interaction between uncertainty and decentralization, she found that in lower uncertainty subunits, decentralization decreases effectiveness; while in greater uncertainty subunits, decentralization increases effectiveness. For interaction between uncertainty and professionalization, she found that the greater the technological uncertainty, the greater the positive impact of professionalization on effectiveness.

Argote (1982) conducted a study in 30 hospital units in six states. In terms of the relationship between technology and structure, she found that the higher the input uncertainty, the lower the use of authority for organizational coordination. In terms of the interaction between technology and structure, she found that programmed means of coordination with low uncertainty increased effectiveness and that nonprogrammed means of coordination with high uncertainty also resulted in high effectiveness.

Fry and Slocum (1984), studying 35 police units, found that only the fit between search behavior and specialization significantly predicted effectiveness. In addition, technology alone predicted performance while structure did not. That is, high-performance work groups faced fewer exceptions, engaged in analyzable search behaviors, and were more highly interdependent than low-performance work groups.

Alexander and Randolph (1985), in a study of the quality of care provided by 27 nursing units, found that the fit between technology and structure was a better predictor of work group performance than either technology or structure alone, and better than technology plus structure. For performance, the variance explained by technology and structure was .35, while the variance explained by technology, structure, and the fit between structure and technology was .59. Nevertheless, fit alone can explain 50 percent of variance. In conclusion, these researchers found that, in nursing subunits where tasks and patient diagnoses varied widely, personnel were highly involved in decision making and in defining tasks. In regards to the relationship between uncertainty and formalization, they found that the fit between variability and horizontal participation and the fit between uncertainty and formalization were important. Therefore, they suggested that subunits with more complex problems should require relatively more rules and procedures to provide quality care, and that subunits with little uncertainty should use relatively little formalization.

Drazin and Van de Ven (1985), in testing alternative forms of fit between technology and structure, proposed three approaches: managerial selection, interaction, and system. In their analysis, they found that managerial selection and system approach to fit exhibit evidence to support the hypotheses that the fit between technology and structure would determine performance and job satisfaction. However, the interaction approach to fit was not supported by their data.

| | | TASK UNCERTAINTY | |
		Low	High
HORIZONTAL DEPENDENCE	Low	**Type 1** No conflicting contingencies Fit with both is possible Higher performance	**Type 3** Some conflict in contingencies Greater design variation One misfit likely Lower performance
	High	**Type 2** Conflicting contingencies One misfit inevitable Lower performance Equifinality of design	**Type 4** No Conflicting contingencies Fit with both is possible Higher performance

Source: Gresov (1989).

Figure 4. Patterns of Context with Two Contingency Factors

David, Pearce, and Randolph (1989) examined the link among technology, structure, and performance in five large banks in the southeastern United States. They found that, for group performance, the variance explained by two fit variables—analyzability-vertical differentiation and predictability-horizontal differentiation—was .228. However, technology alone was not a significant predictor. In addition, interdependence-horizontal differentiation was a better predictor than interdependence-connectedness.

Gresov (1989, p. 435), using Van de Ven and associates' 1975 data, examined the effects of task and dependence on unit design and efficiency. A multiple-contingencies (i.e., task uncertainty and horizontal dependence) model of work unit design was proposed in this study, illustrated in Figure 4.

This model and the empirical data suggested that work units were usually organized to respond to multiple contingencies, for example, task uncertainty and horizontal dependence. Work units facing consistent contingencies, that is, both low or both high in task uncertainty and horizontal dependence as in Type 1 and Type 4, were likely to design organizational structure accordingly, that is, an organic structure for Type 1 situations and a mechanistic structure for Type 4 situations. They would perform better on the average than units facing conflicting contingencies as in Type 2 and Type 3. However, when units faced low task uncertainty and high horizontal dependence, no design was optimal. On the contrary, for units facing high task uncertainty and low dependence (Type 3 units), the appropriate pattern of design was the same as for units facing high task uncertainty and high horizontal dependence, that is, organic structure; deviation from this pattern would be negatively related to unit efficiency.

In conclusion, five types of relationship were tested in the above studies:

1. S = (T) (Argote 1982; Drazin and Van de Ven 1985; Fry and Slocum 1984);
2. P = (T) (Alexander and Randolph 1985; David et al. 1989; Dewar and Werbel 1979);
3. P = (S) (Alexander and Randolph 1985; Argote 1982; David et al. 1989; Dewar and Werbel 1979; Fry and Slocum 1984);
4. P = (S, T) (Alexander and Randolph 1985); and
5. P = (S, T, S * T) (all of the studies reviewed);
   where S = structure, T = technology, and P = performance.

In the first test of the relationship between technology and structure, findings are inconsistent. With regards to the relationship between technology and complexity, Drazin and Van de Ven (1985) found that as task uncertainty increased, specialization and personnel expertise increased; whereas Fry and Slocum (1984) found no relationship among specialization, search behavior (i.e., task analyzability in Drazin and Van de Ven's measure), and interdependence, but they found a negative relationship between exceptions and specialization. With regards to the relationship between technology and formalization, Drazin and Van de Ven (1985) concluded that standardization decreased as task uncertainty increased. Nevertheless, in Fry's analysis, there was a positive correlation between formalization and exceptions but a negative correlation between formalization and search behavior. Finally, with regards to technology and centralization, Argote (1982) and Drazin and Van de Ven (1985) found that the higher the uncertainty, the less supervisory discretion was used. However, Fry and Slocum (1984) found that there was no correlation between technology and participation.

In the test of the relationship between performance and technology, Dewar and Werbel (1979) found that technological routineness decreased satisfaction, and Alexander and Randolph found that technology alone made a significant contribution to the quality of care (R^2 adjusted $= .40$). On the contrary, David, Pearce, and Randolph (1989) found that technology variables (task predictability, problem analyzability, and interdependence) did not make a significant contribution to group performance.

As to the relationship between structure and performance, Fry and Slocum (1984) and Alexander and Randolph (1985) all found that structure alone was not a significant predictor of unit performance. However, Dewar and Werbel (1979) and Argote (1982) found that formalization relates to performance; while David, Pearce, and Randolph (1989) found that structural complexity, both horizontal and vertical differentiation, explained a significant proportion of the variation in group performance (mean $R^2 = .228$, $F = 5.03$, $p < .01$).

Alexander and Randolph (1985) also found that technology and structure together explained 35 percent of the variance in group performance ($F = 3.34$, $p < .05$).

The last sets of tests reviewed are the focus of all the studies cited, that is, the test of the fit between technology and structure as a predictor of work group performance. Two studies applied a system approach to examine multiple contingencies and performance relationship. Their findings were consistent (Drazin and Van de Ven 1985; Gresov 1989). However, most of the studies that have been conducted examine pair-wise relationships among technology, structure, and performance. In spite of the differences in the operationalization of fit variables, the findings of the fit between technology and centralization and the fit between technology and complexity are consistent. That is, when unit technology is nonroutine, that is, when it exhibits characteristics of high uncertainty or high variability, it is indicated that unit structure should be decentralized, professional, and highly differentiated, both horizontally and vertically to achieve high performance.

However, the fit between technology and formalization yields inconsistent effects on group performance. Schoonhoven (1981) found that high uncertainty coupled with de-standardization resulted in high effectiveness and that low uncertainty coupled with de-standardization resulted in low effectiveness. On the contrary, Alexander and Randolph (1985) found that high uncertainty coupled with high formalization increased the quality of nursing care.

One possible explanations for all the inconsistent findings may be that the measurements and conceptualizations of variables in these studies are so diverse that meaningful comparisons are difficult. Therefore, the present study was designed as an exploratory study, instead of a hypotheses testing study since there seems not enough ground for hypotheses formulation yet.

RESEARCH DESIGN

This study was designed to explore the structural and technological characteristics of departments or work units in academic libraries, and the impact of the structure-technology relationships on library department performance. It was conducted within the framework of an exploratory, comparative organizational study.

In the research, the dependent variable was library department performance, which included two dimensions—subjective evaluation by respondents and objective data from library statistics. The independent variables were library department structure and technology, both of which were multidimensional variables and were operationalized accordingly.

The survey method was utilized to collect comparative department or unit level of data on structure, technology, and subjective dimension of performance. Data from the *Integrated Postsecondary Education Data System* (*IPEDS-L*), *Academic Libraries Surveys* (U.S. Department of Education 1992, 1994, 1996) were the source of objective dimension of performance. Subgroup analysis was the primary statistical techniques used in exploring interrelationships among variables.

Sample Selection and Data Collection

Three criteria were set to define the population from which the study sample was drawn:

1. libraries serving institutions listed in the 1992 IPEDS Academic Libraries survey (U.S. Department of Education 1994). There are 3,274 libraries in the 50 states and District of Columbia;
2. libraries with no branches, that is, the value for the variable A01 (number of branch libraries) in the data file equal zero (U.S. Department of Education 1994). A total of 2,405 or 73 percent of the total libraries listed met this criteria.

3. libraries with 11 or more full-time equivalent (FTE) employees. Based on the survey instruction, the total FTE staff included librarians and other professional staff, all other paid staff, contributed services staff, and student assistants from all funding sources. The number of libraries fulfilling all three criteria was 1,080 or 33 percent of the libraries tested in the IPEDS survey.

In the structural contingency studies literature, there are no clear guidelines on how large the work group size should be to qualify as an appropriate sample for study. Based upon Dewar and Werbel's definition of departments (1979), the criterion in the study was set for a minimum of 11 FTE employees in a library, assuming that, in addition to the library director, there would have to be an average of five persons in charge of either technical or public service functions in a library for it to form a certain kind of formal organizational structure. Dewar and Werbel followed the procedure used by Dewar and Hage (1978), and defined departments as units of at least five persons having at least two levels and organized to deliver a specific service, apply a functional expertise, or serve a geographic area (p. 432). They felt that five was the minimal number for the provision of reliable data.

As a result of the three criteria, only small and medium-sized academic libraries serving mainly four-year public institutions were included in the study.

Sampling Procedures

The unit of analysis in this study was the functional departments or units in academic libraries, including technical and public services which are usually divided further into acquisitions, cataloging, serials control, circulation, interlibrary loan, and reference services. It was assumed that each library would have at least two units involved in the study, that is, public and technical services. For a large library, the units of analysis may include all six departments.

As to the sample size, there are various rules of thumb for selecting an optimal size even though there are no absolute specifications. In the present study, Pedhazur's suggestion was followed (1982, p. 148): the ratio of the number of independent variables to the size of the sample be 30 subjects per independent variable for conducting multiple regression analysis.

There are 10 independent variables in the study as discussed below. Therefore, 300 units were needed in the sample to obtain results that, if significant, could be generalized to other libraries. However, due to the usually high non-response rate of mail questionnaires (Bailey 1994, p. 149), the number of cases was increased. As Babbie (1973, p. 165) suggested, a 50 percent response rate can be considered adequate. Therefore, this study doubled the minimum to 600 library departments or work units. Assuming that each library may provide at least two units for study, it was decided to sample 300 libraries in order to obtain the required 600 units of analysis.

A two-staged procedure was conducted to select the sample. At the first stage, a stratified random sample of 303 libraries were selected from the pre-defined population and verified against the *American Library Directory, 47th edition* (Bowker 1994) for addresses and names of library directors. At the second stage, a letter was sent to library directors of the sampled libraries to request their participation in the research. The letter explained the purpose of the study, and requested the names of persons in charge of the following activities for questionnaire distribution: public services, technical services, acquisitions, cataloging, circulation, interlibrary loan, serials control, and reference services. After two follow-ups, a total of 159 (52.48%) library directors agreed to participate in the research, and they provided names of 766 people to whom questionnaires were distributed; 117 (38.61%) were unable to participate, and 27 did not respond (8.91%). For those unable to participate, 38 indicated that their libraries were not suitable sites for this study due to inadequate staff size, that is, the total FTE employees size less than 11. a third follow-up letter was sent to nonrespondents requesting their reasons for not responding. No obvious bias was found.

Data Collection

The instrument used to collect data on structural and technological characteristics of library departments was a mail questionnaire, which was pretested through three iterations and is included here as an Appendix. The questionnaires were then distributed to the 766 contact persons suggested by their directors.

In the structural contingency literature, studies conducted at the subunit or work group level generally adopted perceptual measures by sending questionnaires to all staff members of the work group and aggregating individual scores to work group scores. Inevitably, this method limited the number of organizations to be studied. As a result, many of these studies were conducted within a very limited number of organizations, for example, Fry and Slocum's study of only one large metropolitan police department, which consisted of 61 work groups (1984), or Alexander and Randolph's study of three hospitals, which consisted of 27 nursing subunits (1985). Even though their sample size may have been adequate to test the structural contingency theory, their findings could not reveal the general patterns of the structure-technology relationship of the profession studied.

Due to the sample size requirement, a minimum of 300 units, the study used department heads or unit supervisors as informants of departmental or unit characteristics. It was assumed that department heads or unit supervisors would be able to report or at least estimate the structural and technological

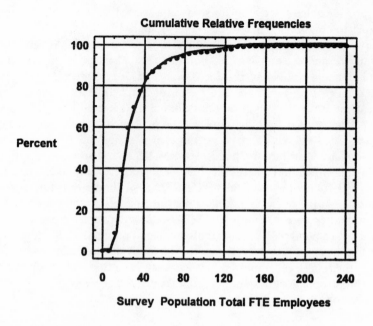

Source: (Data based on *IPEDS Academic Library Survey, 1994*)

Figure 5.   Cumulative Frequency of Total FTE
Employees for Survey Population

characteristics of the department because their positions are close to their
subordinates. As shown in Figure 5, 80 percent of the survey population had
a total of fewer than 40 FTE employees. Therefore, most of the respondents
in the study may not supervise more than 20 persons, and their report should
be representative of the situations of the department. However, it was still
recognized that such measures evaluated only the designed structure, that is,
the managerial choice of organization design, and the reported behavior
represented the manager's reporting rather than the actual behavior of their
subordinates in the department.

A total of 766 questionnaires were sent out in the first mailing, followed
by one postcard reminder, and, second mailings of questionnaires for non
respondents. Excluding 58 undelivered questionnaires, the final response rate
for the questionnaire distribution was 52.54 percent (372 responses) from 136
libraries. Eliminating some of questionnaires with ambiguous responses, 355
responses (50.14%) were usable.

A letter and a reply postcard were sent to a random sample of 60 of the
254 nonrespondents (24%) for reasons of not responding. Twenty-seven
postcards were returned, and no obvious bias was found.

Table 1.   Summary of Variables for the Study

Variables	Concepts	Dimensions	Measures
Dependent Variable:			
Performance	Library Dept. Effectiveness	Subjective Objective	Perception of performance Department outputs: vary by functions
Independent Variables:			
		1. Unit specialization	Number of job titles in the department
Structure	Complexity	2. Professional qualification	The average years of education by department members
		3. Personnel specialization	Degreed of interchangeability of job among departmental personnel
	Centralization	4. Hierarchy of authority	How much say or influence different levels of personnel on certain decisions
		5. Degree of participation	Frequency of dept. members' involvement in decision-making
	Formalization	6. Formalization	Degree of norms in the department explicitly formulated or written
Technology	7. Routiness	Variability	Number of exceptions encountered in work by dept. members
	8. Intradepartment Dependence	Analyzability	Dependence between department members in accomplishing tasks
	9. Interdepartment Dependence		Dependence on personnel outside the department for task accomplishment
	10. Degree of computerization	Time Extent System integration	Length of computerized operation Extent of computer usage Degree of system integration for the unit or department

Variables and Measurement

The variables for the study are summarized in Table 1. A 36-item instrument was developed to measure structure, technology, and subjective dimension of department performance[2]. Statistics from the *IPEDS Academic Libraries* surveys provided the data for objective dimension of department performance.

Measures of Library Department Performance

Organizational performance as a dependent variable in structural contingency theory has been envisioned and measured in various ways. Dalton, Tudor, Spendolini, Fielding, and Porter (1980) classified them into hard performance criteria, such as sales, gross profit, production, commissions, and services rendered (nonprofit sector), as well as soft criteria, such as supervisor appraisals, self-perceptions (p. 50). They argued that hard performance criteria are better indicators of bottom line organizational performance.

In studies of structural contingency theory, the concept of performance includes effectiveness and efficiency. The measurement depends on the research settings, as discussed above. For many studies, researchers adopt both institutional and perceptual measures (see Alexander and Randolph 1985; Drazin and Van de Ven 1985).

In studies of library organizations, most reports of improved services were qualitative statements without quantitative evidence. The few researchers who measured performance quantitatively operationalized the concept differently. In their study of public libraries, for example, Damanpour and Evan (1984) used 11 performance indicators and categorized them into five types of measures. The first four types were objective measures based on data from annual statistical reports of public libraries published by the separate states, including measures of efficiency (turnover rate: circulation/holdings, circulation/total expenditure, and circulation/number of staff), service (number of staff/population served, holdings/population served, and material expenditure/population served), input (library income/population served), and output (circulation/population served). The final type was a subjective measure of three indicators: overall library performance, extent of services, and quality of services, which were based on assessments made by the library directors. The level of analysis for their study was organizational. The objective criteria were based on published library statistics.

For studies of academic libraries, Lynch and Verdin (1986) measured performance by respondents' assessment of two questions: (1) how has the utilization of computer technology in general affected the quality of work? and (2) how has the utilization of computer technology in general affected productivity? Similarly, Johnson (1991a) asked the following question: How do you feel the quality of records created after automation compares with those created before automation in terms of errors in records, records conforming to AACR2, and records consistency across the unit. However, the validity and reliability of the measures were not soundly tested. Both studies were conducted at the organizational level and measured only subjective dimensions of performance.

Besides library organization studies, there is a large body of literature conceptualizing performance in a variety of approaches in studies focusing on library effectiveness. They can be categorized by (1) the level of analysis, including the organizational-level (McDonald and Micikas 1994), subunits of organizations (Van House, Weil and McClure 1990), or the level of the individual; (2) activity, program, or service, for example, evaluation of reference services, catalog use, document delivery capabilities, technical services (Lancaster 1977; Baker and Lancaster 1991); (3) criteria chosen as either measures or indicators of effectiveness, for example, outcomes (desired results), input or resources (budget, library staff, materials, facilities), and programs (ongoing activities) (Cronin 1985), output measures (e.g., materials availability and use, attendance, facilities use, reference transactions) (Van House, Weil and McClure 1990); and (4) assessment techniques, for example, evaluation by reputation, value-added method, applying existing performance measures, (Shaughnessy 1990), library operations research (McDonald and Micikas 1994).

As for library administrators, the collection and use of statistics is also of significance as part of their efforts to accurately describe their libraries' performance, evaluate and enhance effectiveness, and plan for the future (Association of Research Libraries 1987b). In the ARL report, statistics collected by the various libraries were grouped into five general categories: (1) measures of activity and workload, for example, reference questions asked/answered, books circulated; (2) measures of holdings, for example, volumes owned, serials subscriptions; (3) measures of facility use, for example, turnstile count; (4) measures of resources generated and expended, for example, annual expenditures, staff size; and (5) other measures, for example, user satisfaction.

Summarizing the literature, McDonald and Micikas (1994) indicated that very little theoretical justification was presented in the literature for most criteria proposed assessing library effectiveness. Furthermore, the terms used to denote performance were confusing: performance measure, measurement, evaluation, efficiency, and effectiveness (p. 44). In addition, multiple models of organizational effectiveness have existed, and there was no known best criteria for assessing organizational effectiveness. Nevertheless, they suggested that the only way to deal with definition and assessment problems is to make choices that limit the construct space so that the investigator can focus on a limited set of criteria (p. 39).

In the present study, the concept of performance was limited to three aspects. First, the level of analysis for the performance measures in the study was departmental. That is, performance measures in the study referred to the performance of a department as a unit rather than the performance of individuals within the department.

Second, performance measures in the study referred to library effectiveness. Lancaster (1977) suggested that effectiveness should be measured in terms of how well a service satisfies the demands placed upon it by its users. Such an evaluation can be either subjective (e.g., based on opinions via questionnaires) or objective (e.g., based on the measurement of success in quantitative terms) (p. 1). Van de Ven and Ferry (1980), recognizing the difficulty of operationalization for studies conducted at the subunit or work group levels, suggested that different units within a complex organization should strive to attain, and should be held accountable for different effectiveness goals. Therefore, library department effectiveness was operationalized based on the services expected of that department.

The last and foremost consideration for operationalization required performance data in the study to be comparable across libraries for the same departments. Specifically, measurement techniques, unit definitions, and time periods had to be identical.

Library department performance in the study was measured by how effectively a department or a unit achieved its expected services. Two types of library department performance data were collected: subjective evaluation by respondents and objective data from statistics. The subjective approach was commonly used and was similar to evaluation by reputation. The data were collected in the questionnaire by asking respondents to do a self-evaluation on three aspects of performance in relation to other departments of similar size of FTE employees: (1) the quantity of work produced; (2) the quality of work produced; and (3) the efficiency of the department's operation. A 5-point scale was designed to collect the data (Appendix, Item 33).

However, subjective measures are soft criteria (Dalton et al. 1980) and may be biased by the respondents. Therefore, there is a need to collect objective dimensions of performance measures, the hard criteria. The hard criteria are the services or products delivered by each department (Dalton et al. 1980). In academic libraries, there is no commonly accepted hard criteria for each department. However, libraries do collect management statistics for line departments as part of their efforts to evaluate effectiveness (Association of Research Libraries 1987b). Therefore, statistics collected by academic libraries can be viewed as hard criteria for library performance.

The study used the *Integrated Postsecondary Education Data System (IPEDS-L), Academic Libraries Survey* as the source for objective performance measures. IPEDS statistics were chosen for three reasons. First, this is the only source containing a national sample of academic libraries. Second, a majority of the ARL member libraries use IPEDS (then HEGIS) definitions and instructions for collecting library management statistics (Association of Research Libraries 1987b). In addition, designers of the new measures for ARL attempted standardization with the IPEDS survey and instructions (Shapiro 1991, p. 58). That is, we can assume that most academic libraries in the survey present the same dimensions of data following the instructions. Third, data from the survey are used widely by librarians and others as a basis for increased support for individual libraries and by the American Library Association and other interested entities as a basis for increased support of libraries in general (Conley 1981, p. 20). In brief, the data from the IPEDS survey should be reasonably comparable across libraries. To further ensure the reliability of the IPEDS data, data sets from two time periods were used: Academic Library data files 1992 and 1994 (U.S. Department of Education 1994, 1996). However, it was recognized that not all measures for all dimensions of library unit effectiveness were available in the IPEDS survey. Nonetheless, it was not the intention of the current study to develop a

Table 2. Objective Performance Measures for
Public Service Functions Selected from IPEDS Surveys

Functions	Indicators
Circulation	Circulation transactions for general and reserve collections in 1992 and 1994
Interlibrary Loan	Interlibrary loans provided to and received from other libraries in 1992 and 1994
Reference	Reference transactions per typical week in 1990[a] and 1994, Public service hours per typical week in 1992 and 1994, Number of presentations per typical week in 1992 and 1994, Number of persons served in presentations per typical week in 1992 and 1994

Note: [a] No data available for 1992 but 1990.

comprehensive list of measures for each department but to select useful measures for the purpose of the study.

In the study, three steps were taken to develop department performance measures. First, six basic measures were developed to represent six functions identified as the major responsibilities of library departments: circulation, interlibrary loan, reference services, acquisitions, cataloging, and serials control. Second, the six measures were standardized using a 10-rank scale. Third, a composite of functional measures was developed based on the functions of the department to operationalize department performance. The following sections detailed the three steps.

First, six functions were identified as the major responsibilities of library departments. For each function, a set of measures was developed. For public services measurement, Cronin (1985) and Van House et al. (1990) suggested an array of possible measures. Many of them are statistics collected constantly in libraries. Table 2 summarizes the indicators for public service functions.

For circulation functions, circulation transaction is a basic indicator of the extent of usage of library collections (Van House et al. 1990, p. 55). In the IPEDS survey, circulation transactions referred to the number of items lent from the collections for use usually outside the library. The transactions referred not only to the initial charges, either manual or electronic, but also to the renewals.

For interlibrary loan functions, the number of requests sent and received are two common indicators of the activities in the department (Cronin 1985). In the IPEDS data file, they referred to the number of filled requests for material provided to and received from other libraries or document delivery services. The materials reported included both originals and copies and those sent by telefacsimile or other forms of electronic transmission.

For reference services functions, there are a number of approaches to measuring reference effectiveness, including unobtrusive or intrusive observation, and evaluation by peers, users of the services, or trained proxies

(Association of Research Libraries 1987a). Traditionally, library administrators have relied on quantitative data for decision making in reference services due to the difficulty of qualitative measurement. Three types of data are usually collected: reference desk service, public services hours, and instructional services. A typical indicator for reference desk services is the tallying of number and types of reference transactions that transpire at a service point during a specified time period (Association of Research Libraries 1987a). This type of data gathering gives a fairly accurate reading of the quantity of service being provided. For instructional services, two sets of statistics are constantly collected: the number of presentations per typical week and the number of persons served in presentations per typical week.

The data for reference transactions was based on IPEDS 1990 (U.S. Department of Education 1992) because no data were available for IPEDS 1992. Reference transactions in IPEDS files referred to information contacts that involved the knowledge, use, recommendations, interpretation, or instruction in the use of one or more information sources by a member of the library staff. The time period specified for the data collection was per typical week, which was defined as a week in which the library was open for its regular hours and contains no holidays. It was seven consecutive calendar days, from Sunday through Saturday, or whatever days the library was normally open during that period. Presentations to groups in IPEDS data file referred to information contacts in which a staff member or person invited by a staff member provided information intended for a number of persons and planned in advance. The services may be either bibliographic instruction of library use presentations, or it may be cultural, recreational, or educational presentations. Presentations on and off library premises were both included as long as they were sponsored by the library.

For technical services, the study focused on evaluating performance of activities conducted in each function. The indicators for acquisitions, cataloging, and serials control are summarized in Table 3.

Table 3.   Objective Performance Measures for Technical Service
Functions Selected from IPEDS Surveys

Functions	Indicators
Acquisitions	Total volumes or units added for books, bound periodicals, newspapers in 1992 and 1994; Total volumes or units added for other library materials in 1992 and 1994
Cataloging	Total volumes and titles added during fiscal year for books, serial backfiles, and government documents that are cataloged in 1992 and 1994
Serials Control	Total number of paid and unpaid subscriptions held at end of fiscal year 1992 and 1994; Total number of serials titles added during the fiscal year 1992 and 1994

For acquisitions function, the major demands placed upon it by its users are to "provide the first of a library's obligations to its public, to gather collections of materials" (Intner and Fang 1991, p. 58). This function is central to technical services, and includes the procedures that bring materials into the library. In its broadest sense, the tasks are related to obtaining all kinds of library materials—books, periodicals, newspapers, government documents, CD-ROMs, media kits, sound recordings, and so on (Heitshu 1991). Therefore, the measures for acquisitions performance were operationalized as the number of volumes added in the fiscal year for an array of materials (Table 3). In the study, serials were excluded from the acquisitions as a separate function. The units of analysis for the measures were volumes instead of titles because for acquisition operations each volume needs to be obtained and processed individually no matter whether it is a single volume title or a volume in a set. These indicators assumed that all the materials added to the collections were obtained through acquisitions and can be indicators of the efforts of the department to provide services to the users.

The central responsibility of the cataloging functions is to organize library materials so that someone can identify a desired item quickly and easily from among the thousands of titles in the collection. In essence, the final products of cataloging are materials ready for use by the public. Therefore, we can measure cataloging performance by the total number of materials cataloged and added to the collections regardless of the procedures taken to achieve the final stage. In the IPEDS data file, the number reported for cataloging activities included the volumes and titles of any printed, mimeographed, or processed work contained in one binding or portfolio, hardbound or paperbound, which has been cataloged, classified, or otherwise made ready for use. Government documents that were accessible through the library's catalog regardless of whether or not they were shelved separately were also included.

In the study, the serials control function was treated separately because of the unique problems associated with the processing of serials, including acquisition and cataloging. Differences in book and serials processing are primarily due to the continuing life of a serial (Cline and Sinnott 1983), which results in the need for constant monitoring of receiving and possible cataloging changes. That is, we can assume that the operations of serials control involved all the titles in the collection. The objective of serials control was to provide access, physically and bibliographically, to all those titles. Therefore, the number of serial subscriptions held and added during the year was selected as indicators of the efforts of the serials control operation. In the IPEDS data file, serial subscriptions referred to both those received that were paid for and those without payments.

The six measures developed from IPEDS surveys used different units of measurement. However, to ensure the comparability of department performance, the standardization of units of measurement was required.

Table 4. Ten Percentile Groups for Circulation
Transactions for General Collections in 1992

Group	Percentile	Value	Group	Percentile	Value
1	9.09	13.316	2	18.18	18.649
3	27.27	22.256	4	36.36	28.338
5	45.45	35.535	6	54.55	45.687
7	63.64	63.900	8	72.73	80.355
9	81.82	109.477	10	90.91	178.310

The original scores from IPEDS data, therefore, were transformed into 10 ranks using SPSS RANK procedures. The ranking was based on the percentiles of the scores. For scores falling within the first percentile group, the ranking value was assigned one; for scores falling within the second percentile group, the ranking score was assigned two, and so forth. For example, for circulation transactions for general collections in 1992, the original scores were divided into 10 percentile groups as illustrated in Table 4. For libraries with fewer than 13,316 transactions, the rank score was assigned one. For each functional measure, the final score was derived from averaging the rankings of the indicators.

The third step used to operationalize department performance was to develop a composite score based on department functions. The assumption was that each library department or unit might have single or multiple functions. Therefore, a list of department or unit functions was first compiled based on respondents' descriptions of job titles and names of departments in the questionnaire. For each case in the study, then, an average ranking score was derived from the composite of the functional measures. For example, if a unit's functions included circulation and interlibrary loan, its department performance was measured as the average of circulation and interlibrary loan rankings.

Measures of Structure

Structure is a multidimensional variable that includes the concepts of complexity, centralization, and formalization.

Complexity at the work group level was defined as horizontal differentiation, which referred to the degree of differentiation between units based on the orientation of members, the nature of the tasks they perform, and their education and training. It was operationalized as unit specialization, level of professional qualifications of expertise, and personnel specialization.

Unit specialization was defined by Van de Ven and Ferry (1980) as "the number of different tasks or jobs delegated to an organizational unit; it refers to the degree of functional differentiation within a unit" (p. 163). It was usually measured by counting the number of job titles in a department. In the questionnaire, respondents were asked to list all the job titles in the department

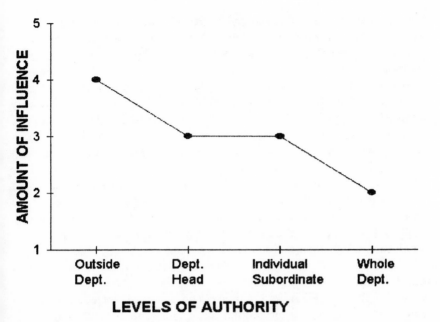

LEVELS OF AUTHORITY

Outside Dept.: People in line management outside of your dept.

Individual Subordinate: Your subordinates individually

Whole Dept.: You and your subordinates as a group in dept. meetings

Figure 6. Hypothetical Control Graph

with a brief description of the job contents (Appendix, Item 8). The qualitative descriptions served as a checkpoint to standardize different job titles for the same job contents.

Level of professional qualifications of expertise referred to the actual qualifications of job holders rather than the qualification requirements of the jobs themselves and was measured by the average years of education of departmental members. In the questionnaire, respondents were asked to count the number of persons holding a certain degree in the department (Appendix, Item 9). Howard's scheme of degree of education was adopted with slight modification for the study (Howard 1977). Personnel specialization was measured by the degree of interchangeability of jobs among unit personnel, or conversely, the degree and easiness of job rotation in the department. In the present study, Van de Ven and Ferry's 4-item scale from the Organization Assessment Instrument (OAI) (1980) was adopted (Appendix, Item 10-13)[3]. However, the time frame was changed to 6 months to make it consistent in the present study.

Centralization was defined as the degree to which decision making was concentrated at a single point in the organization. Two aspects of centralization were measured in this study: the hierarchy of authority and the degree of participation.

To operationalize the hierarchy of authority, a "control graph" approach developed by Tannenbaum and colleagues (Tannenbaum 1968) at the University of Michigan was adopted. The control graph distinguishes two important aspects of the perceived authority structure in organizations: (1) the distribution of authority, which refers to the degree of influence exercised by people at different hierarchical levels; and (2) the total amount of authority, which refers to how much influence is exercised at all organizational levels. The horizontal axis of the graph is the level of hierarchy, and the vertical axis is a rating scale of the degree of influence, as illustrated in Figure 6. In the hypothetical control graph, people in line management outside of the department have the largest amount of influence, which implies a centralized structure.

In addition, Price and Mueller (1986) suggested that there is a need to measure centralization by dimensions of decisions. In the study, Pungitore's decisions schemes (1983) were adopted and modified, including decisions relevant to the hiring and promotion of personnel, to departmental budget matters, to departmental policy changes, to departmental procedural changes, to the institution of new services, to the acquisition of materials/equipment, to publicity for departmental activities, and to automation-related decisions.

Four levels of hierarchies were identified in the study: people in line management outside of the department, the respondent as the department head, the subordinates in the department individually, and the department head and subordinates as a group in department meetings. In the questionnaire, respondents were asked to rate how much say or influence each of the levels have in those specified decisions. A 5-point scale was used to measure the hierarchy of authority (Appendix, Item 15).

For each level of authority, for example, upper management, department head, department members as a group, and individual members, the amount of influence was derived by summing the scores for the eight decision areas. For each dimension of decision, on the other hand, the degree of influence was analyzed by the level of hierarchy. To test hypotheses and explore the research questions, an overall score was obtained by averaging the scores for authority from upper management, department heads, individual subordinates, and department members as a group.

The degree of participation was operationalized as the frequency of department members' involvement in decision-making in the dimensions specified above. Respondents were asked to evaluate the frequency on a 5-point scale (Appendix, Item 16). The scale score was derived by adding the number for each decision involvement.

Formalization referred to the degree to which the norms of an organization were explicitly formulated. One way to explicitly formulate the norms of an organization was to reduce them to formal written documents. In the present study, respondents were asked to indicate what types of formal documents were used in the department (Appendix, Item 17).

Measures of Technology

Conceptions of technology have tended to be broad rather than narrow, as discussed above. In the present study, four aspects of technology were measured: task routineness, task dependence within the department, and with other departments, as well as degree of computerization.

Routineness of tasks referred to the variability and analyzability of tasks. The former measured the number of exceptions encountered in the work and the later measured the ease and clarity of knowing the nature and order of tasks to be performed. In this study, Van de Ven and Ferry's 4-item scale from the Organization Assessment Instrument (OAI) (1980) were adopted to operationalize the concept of variability (Appendix, Item 18-21), while Withey, Daft, and Cooper's scale (1983) was adopted and modified to measure task analyzability (Appendix, Item 22-25).

One issue arises when we adopt two different scales for measurement: the number of points on answer scales. In the OAI instrument, a 5-point scale was used while the Withey, Daft, and Cooper scale used seven numbered responses. The effect of the number of scale points on the reliability of measures has received considerable attention and much empirical investigation. However, conflicting research conclusions have been drawn on the question of how many scale points are optimal (Van de Ven and Ferry 1980, p. 62). It is argued that if a scale has too few response categories, each will be very diverse, grouping people with quite different opinions into the same category. On the other hand, if too many categories are used, the respondents will not be able to distinguish between adjacent categories and may get frustrated and refuse to answer (Bailey, 1994, p. 129). Therefore, it is up to the researcher to decide how many points to use. In this study, a 9-point response was used to measure routineness to allow for greater variance of scores. The results of pretesting indicated that respondents had no problems reacting to the scale.

Interdependence of tasks referred to the degree to which department members depended on and supported others in task accomplishment. There are two aspects of interdependence, intradepartment and interdepartment.

For task dependence within the department, Van de Ven and Ferry's work flow interdependence index was adopted for the present research (1980, pp. 166-168). The first scale was a Guttman scale, measuring intradepartment dependence, which was a hierarchy of increasing levels of task interdependence between departmental personnel, operationalized by whether the work flow was in (1) independent, (2) sequential, (3) reciprocal, or (4) team arrangements (Appendix, Item 27). In addition, two questions based on Mohr's (1971) index were included to measure intradepartment task interdependence in a different approach (Appendix, Item 26, 29).

As to the measurement of interdepartment dependence, few studies were available to provide guidelines on conceptualizations. Van de Ven and Ferry's OAI interunit relations module was applied to develop measures for interdepartment dependence (Van de Ven and Ferry 1980). In their study, they measured interunit relationships in terms of "context (the degree of dependence, awareness, consensus, and domain similarity among the parties involved), process (the transactions of resources and information between the units), structure (the formalization and complexity of the relationships, and the distribution of influence among the parties in the dyad), and outcomes (the perceived effectiveness of the relationship)" (p. 406). For each dimension, they provided a set of measures and definitions for operationalization.

In this study, a six-item scale (Appendix, Item 30) was developed to evaluate the relationships between library departments based on Van de Ven & Ferry's operationalization in the *Organization Assessment Instrument* (1980). The scale measured resource dependence among units, the awareness between departments, and the interunit influence on department operations.

Degree of computerization refers to the extent to which computers were used for task accomplishment. Since the development of computer technology is so fast, most early operationalization of the degree of computerization seems outdated. Therefore, we used the most recent studies available as a reference to construct a new scale to measure the concept. In 1984, Carter operationalized the extent of computer usage by asking newspaper production managers to indicate the extent of computer usage on a 6-point scale ranging from "not at all" to "all the time" for a list of tasks (Carter 1984).

Another scale was the one used in a library study: Pungitore's Library Automation Scale (1983, 1986). The level of analysis for her study was the organizational level, that is, the information collected regarding automation pertained to the whole library. This instrument measured five dimensions of the level of automation in libraries: years automated, pieces of hardware, method of software development, number of functions automated, and number of data processing specialists. To collect data on the pieces of hardware, Pungitore's survey asked respondents to indicate whether and how many pieces of the following computer equipment was on-site in the library: large computers, minicomputers, microcomputers, word processors, terminals, printers, data sets, tape drives, disk drives, and others (Pungitore 1983, p. 80).

The software component of level of automation was operationalized to ask respondents to indicate what functions were automated. Eleven functions were considered in measuring software development: acquisitions, serials control, audio-visual control, cataloging, reference (use of an online public access catalog), literature searching, circulation, interlibrary loan, payroll, word processing, budget, and management (Pungitore 1986, p. 74). For each function, respondents were further asked to indicate the approach of software development: in-house development, lease or purchase of a commercially produced software package, or online shared access to a system such as OCLC via terminal. Her study assigned a higher score to in-house development assuming a greater commitment of resources by libraries.

The fourth dimension of the level of automation measured the presence of computer specialists, which was defined as the number of employees engaged at least half-time in computer-related activities. This variable was measured through a checklist of 14 possible activities. "Yes" responses to the items were summed to arrive at a specialist score. A high score was perceived as an indication that the use of computers was extensive enough within the organization to require persons with specialized skills.

The composite variable, (i.e., the level of automation), therefore, was measured as the sum of the hardware, software, and specialist scores. The total number of items for the scale was 35, with a Cronbach's alpha value of .9114 (Pungitore 1986, p. 77).

An examination of both studies revealed that Pungitore's scales were out-dated. The use of three dimensions to measure hardware, software, and data processing specialists was obviously obsolete given the rapid development of computer technology. In her scale, two dimensions were not influenced by the development of technology: the number of years automated and the number of functions automated. By contrast, Carter's measures (1984) are more applicable because the evaluation of the usage was independent of the development of computer technologies, but both measures had value. Hence, in this study, we will combine both measures with modifications.

Three aspects of the degree of computerization were measured in the study: (1) the length of computerization, measured by the number of years using computers for task accomplishment (Appendix, Item 31), (2) the extent of computer usage, and (3) the degree of system integration. For aspects 2 and 3, respondents were first asked to list what activities were automated in the unit. For each activity, respondents then indicated the extent of computer usage, the types of software/systems used, and whether the software/systems were shared with other departments inside or outside the library and the names of those departments (Appendix, Item 32).

The last question, systems sharing, measured the degree of system integration, which was a measure unique to the study. Adan (1988) implied that the degree of systems integration had an impact on library structure, stating that the more fully integrated a library's automated system, the more fully integrated the library. The measure assumed that the most computerized operations in a library unit were those integrating all activities into one computer system instead of stand-alone systems for each activity.

Exploratory Questions

To facilitate the study, three questions were posed as follows:

1. What were the structural characteristics of library departments in terms of complexity, centralization, and formalization?
2. What were the technological characteristics of library departments in terms of routineness of operations, interdependence, and degree of computerization?
3. What were the relationships among structure, technology, and performance? In what matters did technology connect with structure to affect department performance?

Delimitation and Limitation of the Study

The methodology outlined here posed some delimitation and limitation on the study. First, only small and medium-sized academic libraries serving mainly four-year institutions were included in the study.

Second, the study focused on only six functional departments or work units in academic libraries: acquisitions, cataloging, circulation, interlibrary loan, reference, and serials control. Other departments, such as preservation, special collections, or collection management, were excluded.

Third, only department heads or unit supervisors were selected as informants on department or unit characteristics. Therefore, it was recognized that such measures evaluated only the designed structure, that is, the managerial choice of organization design, and the reported behavior was the manager's reporting of, not the actual behavior of their subordinates in the department.

DATA ANALYSIS AND FINDINGS

Libraries and Library Departments in the Study

Three hundred and fifty-five department heads or unit supervisors from 136 academic libraries responded to the questionnaire. On the average, two to three department heads in a library participated in the study, as expected in the research design. These libraries were either small or medium-sized, compared by three indicators of library size: the number of total full-time equivalent employees, the size of collections, including both the number of monographs and the number of serials subscriptions, and the population served (see Table 5).

The 355 respondents in the study worked at the current position for an average of 9 years, with a range from 3 months to 34 years. Thirty-six of them worked for less than or equal to one year, among them 28 for one year.

Table 5. Profile of Partipating Academic Libraries[a]

Library Characteristics, 1994	50th Percentile	Minimum	Maximum	Mean
Total FTE staff	26	7	147	34
Librarians & other professionals	7	2	44	9
All other paid staff	10	1	66	13
Student assistants	7	1	55	11
Monographic Collections	88,358	1,924	986,554	134,233
Current Serial Subscription	930	10	22,158	1,687
Population Served: FTE Student Enrollment, 1991[b]	2,846	379	25,299	4,544

Notes: [a] Data are computed from IPEDS 1994 Academic Library Survey unless noted otherwise.
　　　　　[b] Data are computed from IPEDS 1992 Academic Library Survey.

One hundred and thirteen respondents, 31.8 percent, worked for more than 10 years, with the longest for 34 years. We can assume, then, that they knew their department or unit and their responses would be close to the situations in their departments. Three hundred persons responded to the questions about their educational background. A majority of them, 95.36 percent, had a master or a M.L.S. degree.

Department heads or unit supervisors from a variety of library departments participated in the study. Based on the names of their departments and their job titles, 47 percent of these departments were multi-functional. When asked to indicate whether their department belonged to public or technical services, 52.1 percent grouped their departments as belonging to public services, and 40.6 percent as technical services (Table 6). None of the remaining twenty-three indicated that their departments belonged to both public and technical services.

The size of departments ranged from 1 to 90 people, with an average of 13.37 persons in a department, including professional librarians, support staff, and student assistants (Table 7). However, the majority of the departments were relatively small in the number of professional and support staff. The mean for the number of professional librarians in a department was 2.74, and for support

Table 6. Grouping of Departments by PS/TS

PS/TS	Frequency	Percent	Cumulative Percent
PS	185	52.6	52.6
TS	144	40.9	93.5
Others	23	6.5	100.0
	3	Missing	
Total	355	100.0	

Table 7. Library Departments Characteristics

	Mean	Standard Deviation	Minimum	Maximum	Valid N
Dept. Size # of Persons in a Dept.	13.37	12.98	1	90	347
Professional	2.74	2.60	1	15	273
Support Staff	3.67	3.34	1	30	316
Student Assistants	10.59	11.59	1	80	258
Performance Ratings Self-Evaluation on					
Efficiency	3.90	0.86	1	5	333
Quantity	3.98	0.84	1	5	333
Quality	4.12	0.75	1	5	333
IPEDS Rankings	5.79	2.12	1.25	10.00	355

staff, 3.67. As can be seen in Table 7, student assistants constituted the major workforce for academic library department operations, with a mean of 10.59 student assistants in a department.

Overall, respondents rated their department performance highly in terms of the quantity and quality of work produced, and the efficiency of department operations as can be seen in Table 7. On a scale of 1 to 5, with 1 equal to far below average and 5 equal to far above average, the means of the ratings were close to 4. However, data from IPEDS Academic Library Surveys indicated that their performance level was slightly above average on a scale of 1 to 10. a correlation test indicated that subjective and objective dimensions of performance were not associated ($r = .037$).

Structural Characteristics

Structurally, academic library departments exhibited neither mechanistic nor organic characteristics. In terms of complexity, previous structural contingency studies maintained that complex work units exhibited characteristics of low unit specialization, evidenced by a greater number of job titles; high professional qualifications (Drazin and Van de Ven 1985); and high personnel specialization, that is, low job interchangeability (Gresov 1989).

However, results of this study presented an inconsistent picture of complexity in academic library departments or working units, as can be seen in Table 8. The average number of job titles in a department was 4.71.

For professional qualifications of the department, the average year of education received was counted. A modification of Howard's weighting system was used to re-scale this variable (Howard 1977, p. 267). Answers to the questions were weighted by multiplying the response to high school diploma

Table 8.   Structural Characteristics of Complexity

Characteristics	Mean	Standard Deviation	Minimum	Maximum	Valid N
Unit specialization: # of job titles	4.71	2.48	1	19	343
Professional Qualifications: Average Level of Education	4.89	1.62	1	8.67	346
Professionals	3.25	0.61	1	5	273
Support Staff	1.66	0.50	1	3	315
Student Assistants	1.09	0.30	1	3.40	258
Personnel Specialization: Job Interchangeability	11.99	4.24	2	20	337

by 1, college degrees by 2, master degrees by 3, dual masters by 4, and doctoral degrees by 5. The final score for professional qualifications was derived by summing the average degrees of education for professionals, support staff, and student assistants. The score for the sample's average level of education was 4.89 within a range of 1 to 8.67. The average educational level for professionals was 3.25, meaning that they usually possessed a master degree or dual-master degrees. For support staff, the average educational level was 1.66, meaning that they possessed high school diplomas with many having either a BA or some other college degree.

The average level of job interchangeability was 11.99, within a range of scores from 2 to 20 where a high score meant high personnel specialization, that is, low job interchangeability. The data indicated that department members rotated jobs sometimes but some of them might need retraining to perform other's tasks.

In summary, examining the means against the range of the scores, departments or units in the study had a low number of job titles, that is, a high level of unit specialization, a slightly high level of professional qualifications, and a medium level of personnel specialization. That is, in academic library departments, moderately or highly educated professionals and support staff worked with a limited number of tasks that could be, and were occasionally, rotated if the persons were retrained.

Centralization is concerned with the degree to which decision making is concentrated at a single point in the organization. Two dimensions were examined in the study: the hierarchy of authority and the degree of participation. The hierarchy of authority included three aspects: levels of authority, amount of influence, and dimensions of decisions. The results in Table 9 indicated that department heads or unit supervisors had the largest total amount of influence on decision making, followed by persons in upper

Table 9.   Hierarchy of Authority

	Upper Management	Dept. Head	Individual Members	Members as a Group
Total Amount of Influence				
Mean	29.72	31.35	23.23	23.77
Minimum	6	8	7	8
Maximum	40	40	40	40
Average Degree of Influence by Decision Areas (Range 1-5)				
Personnel	3.90	4.11	2.82	2.73
Budget	4.50	3.19	2.03	2.24
Policy	3.67	4.32	3.30	3.36
Procedures	2.91	4.51	3.69	3.42
New Services	3.89	4.10	3.09	3.32
Equipment Acq.	3.97	3.93	2.92	2.99
Publicity	3.21	3.87	2.99	2.97
Automation	4.28	3.95	2.82	3.16

management outside the department or the working unit, department members as a group, and individual members in the department.

For each level of hierarchy, the degree of influence varied depending on the area of decisions (Table 9). Persons in upper management positions had the most say on budget matters and automation-related decisions, but the least influence on department procedural changes. For department heads, the influence was almost even across decision areas except on budget matters. Individual members in a department usually had the least influence except in decisions regarding policy, procedures, or instituting new services. When department heads and members of the department came together as a group in a department meeting, the group tended to have a more influence than did individuals.

As to department members' degree of participation in decision-making, it also varied by decision areas. As can be seen in Table 10, they participated mostly in decisions regarding departmental procedural changes, followed by the institution of new services. However, they were seldom involved in decisions regarding budget matters. This pattern was consistent with the results of the levels of influence by decision areas.

Examining both dimensions of centralization together, we observed that the decision-making power in academic library departments was concentrated at the department head level. Department members might participate in the decision-making processes sometimes; nevertheless, the department heads usually had the final say on these decisions. In terms of decision areas, department members had a higher degree of participation in matters concerning daily operations, such as procedural changes or department policy. However, decisions concerning the whole library, such as budget matters, were seldom made at the departmental level.

Table 10.   Degree of Participation by
Decision Area (Range of Scores: 1-5)

Decisions	Mean	SD	Valid N
Procedure	3.50	1.15	337
New Services	3.20	1.31	312
Policy	3.19	1.21	330
Automation	3.11	1.28	333
Acquisitions of Equipment	3.10	1.27	336
Publicity	2.80	1.29	284
Personnel	2.71	1.46	286
Budget	2.42	1.24	320

Table 11.   Types of Documents Used in Library Departments

Types of Documents	Number of Depts. Using the Document	Percent
Job Descriptions for Support Staff	300	84.51
Procedures operating manual	251	70.70
Job Descriptions for Professionals	208	58.59
Department Policy Manual	169	47.61
Staff Manual	156	43.94
Statement of Dept. Goals & Objectives	138	38.87
Organization Chart	111	31.27

In terms of formalization, the concern here was with the degree to which the norms of an organization were explicitly formulated. There was an average of four written documents used regularly in library departments. The most common documents were procedural manuals and job descriptions for professional librarians and support staff (Table 11). Organizational charts for departments and statements of department goals and objectives were seldom used.

Technological Characteristics

Four dimensions of technology were investigated in the study. Task routineness was concerned with the number of exceptions encountered in department work and the ease and clarity of knowing the nature and order of tasks to be performed. A nine-point eight-item scale was used to measure the concept. High scores meant high task routineness.

Results in Table 12 indicated that tasks in library departments exhibited a slightly high level of routineness, with a mean score (54.71) close to the maximum score of routineness (72). The analysis of tasks variability and analyzability further indicated that library departments sometimes encountered exceptional situations; however, they usually had sufficient knowledge or well-established procedures to deal with such problems.

Table 12. Library Department Technological Characteristics

Dimensions of Technology	Mean	Standard Deviation	Minimum	Maximum	Valid N
Routiness	54.71	8.60	26	72	339
Variability	13.06	4.85	4	28	343
Analyzability	27.75	5.30	8	36	347
Intradepartment Dependence	11.78	2.81	4.99	18.96	317
Interdepartment Dependence	31.69	7.05	11.00	54.00	343
Dept. 1	34.35	8.14	12	54	341
Dept. 2	30.68	8.44	9	54	327
Dept. 3	29.58	9.59	6	54	290
Computerization	18.84	6.29	5.60	37	270
Years	12.25	6.01	1	31	314
Extent	4.07	.82	1	5	338
Systems Integration	2.34	1.23	1	6	291

In terms of task interdependence, the means for intra and interdepartment dependence fell around the mid-point of the range of scores (Table 12). The results indicated a medium level of dependence within the department and with other departments. Most respondents in the study were able to identify at least two departments or work units in the library with which they interacted closely. However, the importance of these three departments decreased slightly by the order of reporting.

Table 13. The Most Often Identified Other Key Departments

ACQ		CAT		CIR		ILL	
Others	%[a]	Others	%	Others	%	Others	%
CAT	24.4	ACQ	29.6	REF	17.2	CIR	21.7
REF	14.4	CIR	14.3	ADMN	12.1	REF	15.9
ADMN	11.1	REF	11.2	TS	11.5	ADMN	14.5
CIR	7.8	SYS	8.2	SYS	10.9	SER	8.7
SER	7.8	ADMN	7.1	CAT	9.2	TS	8.7

REF		SER		PS		TS	
Others	%	Others	%	Others	%	Others	%
ACQ	15.3	ACQ	19.0	TS	17.8	CIR	19.8
CIR	12.4	CAT	17.5	ADMN	15.0	REF	17.6
SYS	12.4	REF	17.5	CAT	8.9	PS	13.9
CAT	10.2	CIR	14.3	ACQ	8.3	ADMN	11.8
ADMN	9.5	SYS	7.9	SYS	8.3	SYS	9.1

Note: [a] The chance of being identified as a key department.

Table 14.   Degree of System Integration

	Score Assigned	Frequency	Percent	Cumulative Percent
Stand alone	1	81	27.8	27.8
Only within the department	2	78	26.8	54.6
Partial integration with other departments	3	70	24.1	78.7
Systems shared by all library departments	4	54	18.6	97.3
Systems shared within the campus	5	5	1.7	99.0
Systems shared outside the institution	6	3	1.0	100.0
		64	Missing	
Total		355	100.0	

Departments with different functions identified other different departments as can be seen in Table 13. For example, departments with acquisition functions often identified cataloging, reference, and administration as the other departments with which they had close contact. Departments with cataloging functions identified acquisitions, circulation, and reference departments as key departments.

In terms of the degree to which operations were computerized, library departments exhibited a medium level of computerization, as can be seen in Table 12, with the mean falling at the midpoint of the range of the score. The results indicated that there was a great variation among library departments in the number of years they had been automated. The average length of time that units had been computerized was 12.25 years.

However, no matter how long they had been computerized, library departments used computers extensively, with a mean of 4.07 on a 5-point scale with 1 equal to no automation and 5 equal to complete automation. The results of systems integration, on the other hand, indicated that most systems were either used primarily within the department or partially shared with other departments in the library (Table 14). Rarely was the systems accessible campuswide. The average degree of systems integration for library departments was 2.34 on a 6-point scale with 1 equal to a stand-alone system and 6 equal to a system shared outside the institution.

The Relationships among Structure, Technology, and Performance

At first glance, the correlations among structural, technological and performance variables (Table 15), indicate that technology is correlated with structure and that structure is correlated with performance. Nevertheless, there

Table 15. Correlations Among Department Structure, Technology, and Performance Variables

	1	2	3	4	5	6	7	8	9	10	11	12	13
1. Unit Specialization	1.000 (343)												
2. Professional Qualifications	.254*** (338)	1.000 (346)											
3. Personnel Specialization	.173*** (326)	.097* (329)	1.000 (337)										
4. Hierarchy of Authority	.135** (320)	.168*** (322)	.065 (314)	1.000 (329)									
5. Participation	.232*** (335)	.190*** (336)	.018 (329)	.532*** (323)	1.000 (344)								
6. Formalization	.166*** (343)	.061 (346)	-.061 (337)	.092* (329)	.142*** (344)	1.000 (355)							
7. Routiness	-.050 (329)	-.149*** (331)	-.090 (322)	-.062 (316)	-.141*** (330)	.064 (339)	1.000 (339)						
8. Intra-dept. Dependence	.158*** (308)	.034 (310)	-.192*** (304)	.134** (301)	.275*** (310)	.247*** (317)	-.037 (307)	1.000 (317)					
9. Inter-dept. Dependence	.169*** (331)	.115** (334)	-.070 (325)	.233*** (319)	.345*** (333)	.149*** (343)	.025 (331)	.354*** (308)	1.000 (343)				
10. Computerization	.225*** (264)	.165*** (264)	.076 (257)	.188*** (252)	.179*** (265)	.007 (270)	-.016 (261)	.097 (243)	.093 (267)	1.000 (270)			
11. Subjective Performance	.007 (323)	-.004 (325)	-.130** (316)	.116** (310)	.153*** (323)	.222*** (333)	.084 (319)	.039 (300)	.033 (325)	.294 (262)	1.000 (333)		
12. Objective Performance	.367*** (343)	.159*** (346)	.037 (337)	.056 (329)	.033 (344)	.119** (355)	-.036 (339)	.072 (317)	-.006 (343)	.199*** (270)	.037 (333)	1.000 (355)	
13. Performance Overall	.257*** (323)	.101* (325)	-.060 (316)	.112** (310)	.129** (323)	.238*** (333)	.027 (319)	.083 (300)	.028 (325)	.156** (262)	.716*** (333)	.724*** (333)	1.000 (333)

Notes: ᵃ Correlations computed using pairwise deletion option of SPSS, N in parentheses.

*p < .10;
** p < .05;
*** p < .01.

290

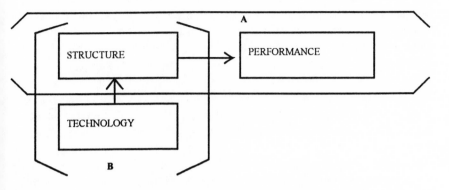

Figure 7.   The Relationships between Structure,
Technology, and Performance

is no direct relationship between technology and performance. As can be seen in Table 15, technological dimensions are not statistically correlated with department performance, except for degree of computerization.

However, as illustrated in Figure 7, there was some type of linkage between structure, technology, and performance variables. This section focuses on exploring that linkage.

As discussed previously in the literature review section, structural contingency researchers have adopted alternative perspectives to investigate the linkage between structure and technology and its impact on performance. The perspectives adopted will affect not only the formulation of theoretical propositions but also the choice of statistical techniques for data analysis. In this study, moderation and matching perspectives of structure-technology relationships were examined to determine which of them could better explain library department performance.

Some researchers believe that technology serves as a moderator in developing a relationship between structure and performance. Those holding the view of moderation have hypothesized that structure determined performance, as illustrated in Figure 7, Bracket A; but that the effect of structure on performance depended on technology. Therefore, researchers tried to investigate how structure interacted with technology to explain performance.

To explore the moderating effect of technology on the structure-performance relationship, we need to differentiate the form and strength of moderation. Arnold (1982) outlined the distinction as "testing the *degree* of relationship between two variables (measured by the magnitude of the correlation coefficients *r*) and the *form* of that relationship (indicated by the coefficients of the regression equation)" (p. 144).

If a researcher hypothesized that the predictive ability of structure on performance differed across different levels of technology, this hypothesis reflected the strength (or degree) of moderation and could be tested using subgroup analysis by examining whether there were statistically significant differences in predictor-criterion correlations for different subgroups (Venkatraman 1989). On the other hand, if a researcher hypothesized that the performance outcome was jointly determined by the interaction of the predictor and the moderator, then the hypothesis reflected the form of moderation and could be tested using moderated regression analyses (Venkatraman 1989, p. 426).

Another group of researchers hold a matching perspective and have hypothesized that there is a theoretical match between structure and technology that exists without reference to a criterion variable, such as performance, as illustrated in Figure 7, Bracket B. This group of researchers assume that the theoretical match between structure and technology will affect performance. Venkatraman (1989) identified three statistical schemes to operationalize the match between structure and technology: deviation score analysis, for example, match as Technology-Structure (Alexander and Randolph 1985); residual analysis, for example, match as the residuals from the regression of structure on technology (Dewar and Werbel 1979); and analysis of variance (ANOVA) (Joyce, Slocum and Von Glinow 1982).

In this study, both moderation and matching perspectives were adopted for data analysis. When technology was treated as a moderator between structure and performance, the strength and the form of moderation were both explored, tested by subgroup analyses for the former and multiple regression analyses for the latter. When a theoretical match between structure and technology was hypothesized, two statistical schemes were used to operationalize the match between structure and technology: residual analysis and ANOVA. Findings of the study indicated that those who see technology as a moderator appear to be on firmer ground than those who accept the matching perspectives when trying to explain the relationships among structure, technology, and performance in academic library departments. Moreover, the data collected in the study supported more strongly the degree (not the form) of technology's role as moderator on the relationships between structure and performance. That is, the correlations between structure and performance were different across different levels of task routineness, interdependence, and computerization. In this section, only the results of subgroup analyses are discussed since it is the most promising perspectives to understand the relationships among structure, technology and library department performance. Please refer to Weng (1997) for analyses of other perspectives.

*Technology as a Moderator on the Relationship between Structure
and Performance*

In this study, subgroup analyses were conducted to explore technology's effects as moderator on structure-performance relationships. For subgroup analyses, each dimension of the technological characteristics was divided into three groups using SPSS Ranking procedures. For each group, the correlations between structural characteristics and performance were computed and compared. To compare whether there were statistical significance among the correlation coefficients, Arnold (1982, p. 151) suggested using Cohen and Cohen's χ^2 (chi squared) distribution (1975) for k-1 degrees of freedom where k was the number of independent subgroup coefficients being compared:

$$\chi^2 = \sum_{i=1}^{k} (n_i - 1)\, r_i^2 - \frac{\sum_{i=1}^{k} (n_i - 1)\, (r_i)}{\sum_{i=1}^{k} (n_i - 1)}$$

where
n_i = sample size for subgroup I,
r_i = correlation regressions for subgroup I.

Task Routineness as the Moderator.

Table 16 summarizes the results of the differences of correlations between structure and performance across low, medium, and high routineness of technology. Except for personnel specialization, the correlations between structural characteristics and performance showed a statistically significant difference in three levels of task routineness.

Three aspects of the results should be noted from the data: (1) the dimensions of structure that are correlated with performance, (2) the direction of correlation, and (3) the magnitude of correlations. First, when task routineness of a department was low, performance was correlated with unit specialization, professional qualification, hierarchy of authority, and degree of participation. When task routineness was either medium or high, performance was correlated only with unit specialization and formalization.

Second, except for the hierarchy of authority, the directions of the correlations between structural characteristics and performance are consistent across three levels of task routineness. Specifically, most of the structural characteristics are positively correlated with performance. In terms of

Table 16. Significant Differences among Correlations of
Structural Characteristics and Performance for
Low, Medium, and High Task Routiness Subgroups

Structural Characteristics	Low (N = 118)	Medium (N = 109)	High (N = 112)	χ^2
Unit specialization	.31**	.29**	.23**	25.92***
Professional qualifications	.23**	.04	.10	7.35**
Personnel specialization	-.04	-.08	-.02	2.70
Hierarchy of authority	.17*	-.01	.11	4.64*
Degree of participation	.24**	.13	.03	8.53**
Formalization	.11	.25***	.35***	21.55***

Notes: * $p < .10$;
** $p < .05$;
*** $p < .01$.

complexity and performance, high performance tended to be associated with high complexity while low performance was associated with low complexity. That is, high-performing departments tended to have more job titles and more highly educated staff, while low performing departments tended to have fewer job titles and a less well educated staff. A similar pattern was observed for the correlation between centralization and performance. High-performing departments also tended to be decentralized, and low performing departments tended to be centralized, when task routineness was either high or low.

Third, the magnitude of correlations between performance and structural characteristics differs in three subgroups. As tasks became more routine, the correlations between performance and unit specialization, degree of participation decreased; on the contrary, the correlations between performance and formalization increased. Nevertheless, the magnitude of performance's correlations with professional qualifications and hierarchy of authority was highest under low routineness and lowest under medium routineness.

Intradepartment Dependence as the Moderator.

In terms of the moderating effect of intradepartment dependence on the structure-performance relationship, the results indicated that it only moderated the degree of association between performance and unit specialization, formalization, as can be seen in Table 17. The positive direction of correlations suggested that high performance was associated with a high number of job titles, that is, with high complexity and high formalization.

The magnitude of the correlations was less straightforward. The correlation between performance and unit specialization was higher under the conditions of low intradepartment dependence, followed by low and medium levels of dependence. The correlation between formalization and performance, on the

Table 17. Significant Differences among Correlations of
Structural Characteristics and Performance for
Low, Medium, and High Intradepartment Dependence Subgroups

Structural Characteristics	Low (N = 106)	Medium (N = 106)	High (N = 105)	χ^2
Unit specialization	.29***	.22**	.26**	20.69***
Professional qualifications	.14	-.00	.17	4.96*
Personnel specialization	-.02	-.18*	-.03	3.61
Hierarchy of authority	.12	.08	.02	2.15
Degree of participation	.01	.14	.08	2.66
Formalization	.24**	.32***	.14	18.60***

Notes: * $p < .10$;
      ** $p < .05$;
      *** $p < .01$.

other hand, was higher under the conditions of medium level of intradepartment dependence, followed by low and high dependence.

Interdepartment Dependence as the Moderator

Results in Table 18 indicate that interdepartmental dependence moderates the relationship between structure and performance. Similarly, three aspects should be noted for the effect of interdepartment dependence as the moderator. First, when the level of dependence was low, library department performance was correlated with many dimensions of structural characteristics. However, the number of correlated dimensions decreased as library departments depended more on other departments for task accomplishment. Specifically, when the dependence was medium, performance was correlated with unit specialization and formalization; when the dependence was high, performance was correlated with unit specialization, degree of participation, and formalization.

Second, as to the directions of correlations, the results indicate that interdepartmental dependence moderated the positive correlations between performance and complexity, centralization, and formalization. That is, high-performing departments tended to exhibit characteristics of high complexity, that is, a high number of job titles and a high degree of education; they tended to decentralize their decision-making power to department members; and they tended to be formalized. Conversely, low-performing departments tended to be less complex and formalized, but more centralized. However, the direction of correlation between degree of participation and performance was opposite under conditions of medium dependence. That is, when interdepartmental dependence was lower, high performing departments tended to be centralized and low-performing departments tended to be decentralized.

Table 18. Significant Differences among Correlations of
Structural Characteristics and Performance for
Low, Medium, and High Interdepartment Dependence Subgroups

Structural Characteristics	Low (N = 113)	Medium (N = 115)	High (N = 115)	χ^2
Unit specialization	.26***	.24**	.26***	21.58***
Professional qualifications	.18*	.04	.10	4.84**
Personnel specialization	-.12	.06	-.13	4.01
Hierarchy of authority	.18*	.01	.12	5.18**
Degree of participation	.17*	-.02	.23**	9.19**
Formalization	.23**	.20**	.34**	23.41***

Notes: * $p < .10$;
        ** $p < .05$;
        *** $p < .01$.

Third, in terms of the magnitude of correlations, the correlation between unit specialization and performance was high for both low and high levels of interdepartmental dependence. The correlation between professional qualifications and performance was higher under conditions of low interdepartmental dependence than under conditions of high dependence. However, the moderating effect of interdepartmental dependence on the correlation was different for these two dimensions of centralization. For hierarchy of authority, the correlation with performance was higher under conditions of low dependence; on the contrary, for degree of participation, the correlation was higher under conditions of high dependence. For the correlation between performance and formalization, the magnitude was higher under conditions of high interdepartment dependence than under low dependence. Overall, all the moderating effects of interdepartment dependence were least under medium conditions of interdepartment dependence.

Degree of Computerization as the Moderator

Data in Table 19 again support technology's effects as a moderator in structure-performance relationships. First, in terms of the dimensions of structure that were correlated with performance, when library departments were less computerized, unit specialization, hierarchy of authority, degree of participation, and formalization all correlated with performance. However, when departments became more computerized, structural characteristics correlated less well with performance. In departments of medium computerization, performance was only correlated with unit specialization. In highly computerized departments, performance correlated with unit specialization and personnel specialization.

Table 19. Significant Differences among Correlations of
Structural Characteristics and Performance for
Low, Medium, and High Degrees of Computerization Subgroups

Structural Characteristics	Low (N = 90)	Medium (N = 90)	High (N = 90)	χ^2
Unit specialization	.28***	.19*	.19*	13.18***
Professional qualifications	.15	.07	-.01	2.38
Personnel specialization	.10	-.01	-.25**	6.51**
Hierarchy of authority	.32***	-.06	.03	9.42***
Degree of participation	.34***	-.07	.03	10.70***
Formalization	.31***	.12	.17	12.21***

Notes: * $p < .10$;
** $p < .05$;
*** $p < .01$.

Second, in terms of the direction of correlations, only unit specialization and formalization were positively correlated with performance across three levels of computerization. That is, high performing departments tended to have more job titles and to be more formalized and low performing departments tended to have fewer job titles and were less formalized.

For centralization, the correlations were positive when the use of technology was either low or when departments were highly computerized; however, the correlations were negative when the computerization was in the middle range. That is, for library departments with either low or high computerization, high performance tended to be associated with a high degree of participation and high authority at department level; and low performance tended to be associated with low degree of participation and high degree of authority from upper management. Nevertheless, for departments with a medium degree of computerization, the directions were the opposite; that is, high performance was associated with low degree of participation and departmental authority while low performance was associated with high degree of participation and departmental authority.

Third, as the magnitude of performance's correlation with structure increased, the data indicated that the correlation was higher under a low degree of computerization than under conditions of high computerized technology. That is, when activities were computerized, it was less evident that structure correlated with performance, but the correlation was higher in less computerized departments.

CONCLUSIONS

In comparison with findings of previous subgroup analyses, for example, Argote (1982), this study confirmed some previous findings. For example, the correlation between performance and formalization is higher under conditions of high task routineness than under low routineness, and the correlations between the degree of participation and performance is higher under conditions of low routineness than under high routineness. However, findings of the study did not support the interaction effect, that is, the product term of structure and technology on performance. These findings can be viewed as tentative since generalization is not appropriate due to the assumptions and scope of the study previously discussed.

These results, however, provide valuable clues on the relationships among structure, technology, and performance in academic library departments, and they also provide grounds for future testing of these relationships. In brief, findings of the study supported that library department structure and performance are correlated; however, the pattern and degree of correlations will be affected by departments' technological characteristics. In addition, different technological characteristics will have different moderating effects.

Based on these findings, the following contingency propositions are recommended for future hypotheses testing:

Recommended Hypothesis 1. The correlation between complexity and performance is higher under conditions of low routineness than under conditions of high routineness.

Recommended Hypothesis 2. The correlation between decentralization and performance is higher under conditions of low routineness than under conditions of high routineness.

Recommended Hypothesis 3. The correlation between formalization and performance is higher under conditions of high routineness than under conditions of low routineness.

Recommended Hypothesis 4. The correlation between unit specialization and performance is high under conditions of low intradepartment dependence than under high dependence.

Recommended Hypothesis 5. The correlation between formalization and performance is high under medium level of intradepartment dependence than under conditions of high or low dependence.

Recommended Hypothesis 6. The correlation between professional qualifications and performance is high under conditions of low interdepartment dependence than under conditions of high dependence.

Recommended Hypothesis 7. For hierarchy of authority, the correlation with performance is higher under conditions of low dependence. For degree of participation, the correlation is higher under conditions of high dependence.

Recommended Hypothesis 8. For the correlation between performance and formalization, the magnitude is higher under conditions of high interdepartment dependence than under low dependence.

Recommended Hypothesis 9. The correlation between structure and performance is higher under a low degree of computerization than under conditions of high computerized technology.

Implications of the study

Two problem areas were pursued in this study. First, the study assessed the applicability of structural contingency theory in different organizational settings, namely, academic libraries. Second, using the framework of structural contingency theory, this study explored the relationship between structure and technology in library departments in search of principles of organization design that may assist managers in choosing the most appropriate organizational structure to achieve the highest performance using new technologies.

Overall, structural contingency theory provides a useful framework to describe and to understand structure and technology of academic library departments and how these factors interact to influence departmental performance. Findings of the study indicated that describing library departments simply as bureaucratic, mechanistic, or organic agencies is inadequate in an evaluation of the effectiveness of organizational structure in achieving organizational goals. Only through the detailed analyses of structural characteristics in terms of complexity, centralization, and formalization, as well as their relationships with performance and contingency factors such as technology can we generate guidelines for organization design.

For instance, Duncan (1979), and Baligh, Burton, and Obel (1990) depicted how data such as those collected in this study can be used to design specific organizational structure. Duncan suggested a decision tree analysis approach to help managers pick the appropriate design. To proceed with the design process, nevertheless, managers first need to understand the characteristics of the environment, to include the technological characteristics of organizational units and the interdependence of organizational units in carrying out their objectives (Duncan 1979, p. 62). Once the organization's environment has been diagnosed, managers can then decide what type of structure is appropriate. The instrument developed in this research (Appendix), therefore, can serve library managers as a tool to collect data on their structural and technological characteristics and to aid them in diagnosing the appropriateness of their department structure.

Baligh, Burton and Obel (1990), on the other hand, illustrated how to devise an expert system of organization design, incorporating the relationships found in studies such as this one to encompass the knowledge base of the system. Specifically, they translated these relationships into "if-then" statements, and recommended specific structural properties accordingly. In their knowledge base, for example, they would have such statements as: "If task variability is high and the tasks well defined, then formalization should be low and centralization should be high" (p. 40). The expert system would then ask the user about the facts of the size, technology, and so forth, apply the rules in the knowledge base to these facts, and then make a specific recommendation on the structure and properties. For example, the system may recommend that the organization should be functional with high formalization, narrow span of control, and lots of rules.

From the data found in this study, certain patterns of library department structure may be emerging. With caution due to the study's scope and assumptions, it is suggested that findings of the study may lend themselves to distinguish those library departments needing reorganization from those that do not. For example, within the restrictions noted above, library departments may need reorganization if they exhibit characteristics of either nonroutine tasks coupled with low complexity and high centralization or routine tasks coupled with low complexity and low formalization. On the other hand, library departments may not need to worry about reorganization if they exhibit characteristics of nonroutine tasks coupled with high complexity and low centralization.

The ultimate aim of any research is the provision of accurate and reliable information for decision making. To that end, this study is a small first step in exploring what form or forms of library department might be appropriate to achieve department goals. Especially when we are confused by all those so called "management fads" (Fisher 1996), what the field needs are more systematic studies on what principles of organization design may work for libraries.

To further our understanding of the effectiveness of library structures, the following are suggested for future research. First, this study focused only on one contingency factor, for example, technology and its effect on structure-performance relationships. Even though the findings indicate that technology is a significant factor in moderating the relationships, a large proportion of variance of performance is not explained. As illustrated in Figure 1, technology is just one factor affecting the choice of organizational forms. The findings of the study indicate the need to explore the effects of other contingency factors, such as organizational size or the environment on library structure.

Second, this study focused only on pair-wise relationships among structure, technology, and performance. That is, the study analyzed only how single contextual factors, such as task routineness, affected single structural characteristics, such as formalization, and how these pairs of context and structural factors interacted to explain performance. This reductionism may explain why so many relationships were found to be statistically nonsignificant in the study. The systems approach advocated by Van de Ven and Drazin (1985) as well as Gresov (1989) should be the next step to better understand organization design by examining multiple contingencies and multiple structural elements together.

APPENDIX

Academic Libraries Structure and Technology Study Questionnaire

Date: September 18, 1995

To: Participants, Academic Libraries Structure and Technology Study
From: Hweifen Weng, Doctoral Candidate, School of Communication, Information and Library Studies, Rutgers University

As part of my doctoral research on organizational design for academic libraries, I am investigating the organizational characteristics of structure and technology in selected college and university libraries in the United States.

Your library, with your Director's consent, is one of the libraries which will be part of the study. Your name was provided to me by your library director. I am asking your support in completing the attached questionnaire which is a survey of the characteristics of structure and technology of *your department/ working unit*. Please make an effort to respond to *all* of the items on the questionnaire. Circle or write down the answer which best suits your particular situation. *All responses are strictly confidential.* No individual person or library will ever be identified in any report from this study.

Please provide a copy of your most recent *organizational charts* and *annual statistics reports* as background materials for your department/working unit.

Please return the questionnaire in the enclosed postage-paid envelop by *October 18, 1995*.

Your time and participation is truly appreciated and a copy of the summary of the study's findings and conclusions is yours by simply checking the following box.

☐ Organizational charts enclosed.
☐ Annual statistics report enclosed.
☐ Please send me a copy of the study's findings and conclusions.

1. Name and **Title** : _____

2. Name of Department : _____ (Please check if
   your ***department/working unit*** belongs to : ☐ Public, ☐ Technical Services or ☐Other
   _____)

3. Whom do you report to (please just list the title)? _____

4. How many people do you supervise in ***your department/ working unit ?***

	Full-Time	Part-Time
Professional	_____	_____
Support Staff	_____	_____
Student Assistants	_____	_____

5. What is the total size of the student body? FTE _____ ; Head count _____

6. Please list all graduate degrees you hold (e.g. MA, MLS, Ed.D., Ph.D., etc.) _____

7. How many years have you worked in your present position? _____

DEPARTMENTAL STRUCTURE

In this section, I would like to know some of the structural characteristics of ***your department/working unit.***

8. Please list all the positions, professional and clerical, by functions, not classification alone in
   your department/working unit. In addition, please write down a brief job description.

JOB TITLES	JOB DESCRIPTIONS
1. _____	_____
2. _____	_____
3. _____	_____
4. _____	_____
5. _____	_____
6. _____	_____
7.	

Please add pages as necessary.

9. This question requests the average level of education received by the individuals in *your department/working unit*. Please think about the highest degree held and write down the number of persons holding the specified degree. Individuals are to be counted only once.

HIGHEST DEGREE HELD	NUMBER OF INDIVIDUALS IN EACH CATEGORY		
	PROFESSIONALS	SUPPORT STAFF	STUDENT ASSISTANTS
High school diploma			
BA, BS, or other college degree			
BLS			
MA, MS, or equivalent			
MLS or equivalent			
Dual-Masters			
Ph.D. in subject or Ed.D.			
Ph.D. in library or information science			
Do not know			
Other (please specify)			

The following questions address the job rotation in *your department/working unit*. Please circle the numbers which best describe your situation.

10. During the past 6 months, how many of the individuals in your department/working unit rotate their jobs by performing different tasks?

N/A	NONE	ONLY A FEW	ABOUT HALF	MANY	ALL OF THEM
0	1	2	3	4	5

11. How many of the individuals in your department/working unit are qualified to do other department member's jobs?

N/A	NONE	ONLY A FEW	ABOUT HALF	MANY	ALL
0	1	2	3	4	5

12. How easy would it be to rotate the jobs of the individuals in your department/working unit, so that each could do a good job performing the other's tasks?

N/A	VERY DIFFICULT. MOST MEMBERS WOULD NEED EXTENSIVE RETRAINING	QUITE DIFFICULT. SOME MEMBERS WOULD NEED EXTENSIVE RETRAINING	SOMEWHAT DIFFICULT. A FEW MEMBERS WOULD NEED RETRAINING.	QUITE EASY. SOME MEMBERS WOULD NEED MINOR RETRAINING.	VERY EASY. NO MEMBERS WOULD NEED RETRAINING.
0	1	2	3	4	5

13. During the past 6 months, how often did the individuals in your department/working unit rotate their jobs by performing one another's work?

N/A	NEVER	SEVERAL TIMES	ABOUT EVERY MONTH	ABOUT EVERY WEEK	ABOUT EVERY DAY
0	1	2	3	4	5

14. Please explain briefly your response to the above question :

_____

_____

15. In *your department/working unit*, how much say or influence do each of the following have on those decisions? (Please write down the number which best characterizes your department/working unit with **1= none; 2= little; 3= some; 4= quite a bit; 5= very much.**)

DECISIONS	PEOPLE IN UPPER MANAGEMENT OUTSIDE OF YOUR DEPARTMENT / WORKING UNIT	YOU, AS THE DEPARTMENT HEAD	OTHER INDIVIDUALS IN YOUR DEPARTMENT/ WORKING UNIT	YOU AND YOUR COLLEAGUES/STAFF AS A GROUP IN DEPARTMENT MEETINGS
a. Hiring, promoting personnel	___	___	___	___
b. Departmental budget matters	___	___	___	___
c. Departmental policy changes	___	___	___	___
d. Departmental procedural changes	___	___	___	___
e. Instituting new services	___	___	___	___
f. Acquisition of materials/ equipment	___	___	___	___
g. Publicity for departmental activities	___	___	___	___
h. Automation-related decisions	___	___	___	___

16. During the past six months, how frequently did your colleagues/staff participate in the following types of decisions for *your department/working unit* ?

DECISIONS	N/A	NEVER	SELDOM	SOMETIMES	OFTEN	ALWAYS
a. Hiring, promoting personnel	0	1	2	3	4	5
b. Departmental budget matters	0	1	2	3	4	5
c. Departmental policy changes	0	1	2	3	4	5
d. Departmental procedural changes	0	1	2	3	4	5
e. Instituting new services	0	1	2	3	4	5
f. Acquisition of materials/ equipment	0	1	2	3	4	5
g. Publicity for departmental activities	0	1	2	3	4	5
h. Automation-related decisions	0	1	2	3	4	5

17. What types of formal documents are used in *your department/working unit?*

☐ ORGANIZATION CHART   ☐ JOB DESCRIPTIONS FOR PROFESSIONAL LIBRARIANS

☐ DEPARTMENT POLICY MANUAL   ☐ JOB DESCRIPTIONS FOR SUPPORT STAFF

☐ STAFF MANUAL   ☐ OTHER JOB DESCRIPTIONS (PLEASE SPECIFY)

☐ PROCEDURES OPERATING MANUAL   ☐ OTHER (PLEASE SPECIFY) _____

☐ STATEMENT OF DEPARTMENT GOALS AND OBJECTIVES   ☐ OTHER _____

DEPARTMENTAL TASKS

In this section, please think about all the normal, usual, day-to-day tasks performed in *your department/working unit* and mark the appropriate answers to the following questions.

Example: How much	VERY MUCH THE SAME	MOSTLY THE SAME	QUITE A BIT DIFFERENT	VERY MUCH DIFFERENT	COMPLETELY DIFFERENT
	1————|————|————|————|————|————|————|————9				

18. How much the same are the day-to-day situations, problems, or issues your colleagues/staff encounter in performing their major tasks?

VERY MUCH THE SAME	MOSTLY THE SAME	QUITE A BIT DIFFERENT	VERY MUCH DIFFERENT	COMPLETELY DIFFERENT
1————|————|————|————|————|————|————|————9				

19. How many of the tasks in your department/ working unit are the same from day-to-day?

ALMOST NONE	SOME	ABOUT HALF	MANY	ALMOST ALL
1————|————|————|————|————|————|————|————9				

20. During a normal week, how frequently do exceptions arise in your colleagues/staff's work which require substantially different methods or procedures for doing it?

VERY RARELY	OCCASIONALLY	QUITE OFTEN	VERY OFTEN	CONSTANTLY
1————|————|————|————|————|————|————|————9				

21. How often do your colleagues/staff follow about the same work methods or steps for doing their major task from day to day?

VERY RARELY	OCCASIONALLY	QUITE OFTEN	VERY OFTEN	CONSTANTLY
1————|————|————|————|————|————|————|————9				

22. To what extent is there a clearly known way to do the major types of work your colleagues/staff normally encounter?

VERY LITTLE	SOME	ABOUT HALF	MANY	VERY GREAT
1————|————|————|————|————|————|————|————9				

23. To what extent is there a clearly defined body of knowledge of subject matter which can guide your colleagues/staff in doing their work?

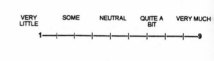

24. To what extent is there an understandable sequence of steps that can be followed in doing the work in your department/working unit?

25. For your colleagues/staff to do their work, to what extent can they actually rely on established procedures and practices?

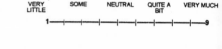

The next questions are about the **internal flow of work** among the individuals in *your department/working unit*. Please circle the appropriate responses.

26. My colleagues/staff have one-person jobs; they have little need to check or to work with others.

HIGHLY ACCURATE	FAIRLY ACCURATE	BORDERLINE	RATHER INACCURATE	VERY INACCURATE
1	2	3	4	5

27. Listed and diagrammed are four common ways that the work can flow in a department. Please indicate how much of the normal work flows among the individuals in *your department/working unit* in a manner as described by each of the following cases:

	ALMOST NONE OF THE WORK	LITTLE	ABOUT 50% OF ALL THE WORK	A LOT	ALMOST ALL OF THE WORK
a. **Independent Work Flow Case**, where work and activities are performed by your colleagues independently and do not flow between them. Work Enters Unit / Work Leaves Unit	1	2	3	4	5

	ALMOST NONE OF THE WORK	LITTLE	ABOUT 50% OF ALL THE WORK	A LOT	ALMOST ALL OF THE WORK
b. Sequential Work Flow Case, where work and activities flow between your colleagues, but only in one direction. Work Enters Work Leaves	1	2	3	4	5
c. Reciprocal Work Flow Case, where work and activities flow between your colleagues in a reciprocal "back and forth" manner over a period of time Work Enters Work Leaves	1	2	3	4	5
d. Team Work Flow Case, where work and activities come into your department/working unit and your colleagues diagnose, problem-solve and collaborate as a group at the SAME TIME to deal with the work. Work Enters Work Leaves	1	2	3	4	5

28. Please go back and circle the one method listed above which best describes *your department/working unit's* work flow (Circle a or b or c or d).

29. To do their jobs properly, my colleagues/staff must collaborate extensively with others.

HIGHLY ACCURATE	FAIRLY ACCURATE	BORDERLINE	RATHER INACCURATE	VERY INACCURATE
1	2	3	4	5

30. The following questions are concerned with **external relationships** *your department/ working unit* maintained with other departments/units, e.g. administration, acquisition, systems, etc., in the library during the past six months. Please write down the names of three of the most important other departments/ units that your department/working unit had to coordinate with during the past 6 months. Think about your relationship with that department/unit and mark the line which best describes your contact with them.

Example: How much ....

| VERY MUCH THE SAME | MOSTLY THE SAME | QUITE A BIT DIFFERENT | VERY MUCH DIFFERENT | COMPLETELY DIFFERENT |

1----|----|----|----|----|----|----|----9

A. NAME OF FIRST KEY DEPARTMENT/UNIT

a. How important was this department in attaining the goals of your department/ working unit in the past 6 months?

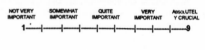

b. For this department to accomplish its goals and responsibilities, how much does it need the services, resources, or support from your department/working unit?

c. For your department/working unit to accomplish its goals and responsibilities, how much do you need the services, resources, or support from this department?

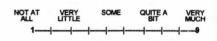

d. How well informed are you about the specific goals and services of this department?

e. How much say or influence does this department have on the internal operation of your department/working unit?

f. How much say or influence does your department/working unit have on the internal operations of this other department?

B. NAME OF <u>SECOND</u> KEY DEPARTMENT/UNIT

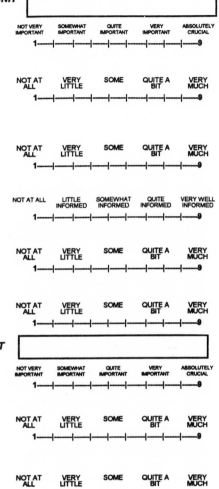

a. How important was this department in
   attaining the goals of your department/
   working unit in the past 6 months?

NOT VERY IMPORTANT   SOMEWHAT IMPORTANT   QUITE IMPORTANT   VERY IMPORTANT   ABSOLUTELY CRUCIAL
1—|—|—|—|—|—|—|—9

b. For this department to accomplish its goals
   and responsibilities, how much does it need
   the services, resources, or support from your
   department/working unit?

NOT AT ALL   VERY LITTLE   SOME   QUITE A BIT   VERY MUCH
1—|—|—|—|—|—|—|—9

c. For your department/working unit to
   accomplish its goals and responsibilities,
   how much do you need the services,
   resources, or support from this department?

NOT AT ALL   VERY LITTLE   SOME   QUITE A BIT   VERY MUCH
1—|—|—|—|—|—|—|—9

d. How well informed are you about the
   specific goals and services of this
   department?

NOT AT ALL   LITTLE INFORMED   SOMEWHAT INFORMED   QUITE INFORMED   VERY WELL INFORMED
1—|—|—|—|—|—|—|—9

e. How much say or influence does this
   department have on the internal operation of
   your department/working unit?

NOT AT ALL   VERY LITTLE   SOME   QUITE A BIT   VERY MUCH
1—|—|—|—|—|—|—|—9

f. How much say or influence does your
   department/working unit have on the internal
   operations of this other department?

NOT AT ALL   VERY LITTLE   SOME   QUITE A BIT   VERY MUCH
1—|—|—|—|—|—|—|—9

C. NAME OF <u>THIRD</u> KEY DEPARTMENT/UNIT

a. How important was this department in
   attaining the goals of your department/
   working unit in the past 6 months?

NOT VERY IMPORTANT   SOMEWHAT IMPORTANT   QUITE IMPORTANT   VERY IMPORTANT   ABSOLUTELY CRUCIAL
1—|—|—|—|—|—|—|—9

b. For this department to accomplish its goals
   and responsibilities, how much does it need
   the services, resources, or support from your
   department/working unit?

NOT AT ALL   VERY LITTLE   SOME   QUITE A BIT   VERY MUCH
1—|—|—|—|—|—|—|—9

c. For your department/working unit to
   accomplish its goals and responsibilities,
   how much do you need the services,
   resources, or support from this department?

NOT AT ALL   VERY LITTLE   SOME   QUITE A BIT   VERY MUCH
1—|—|—|—|—|—|—|—9

d. How well informed are you about the specific goals and services of this department?

e. How much say or influence does this department have on the internal operation of your department/working unit?

f. How much say or influence does your department/working unit have on the internal operations of this other department?

The following questions are about the degree of automation in *your department/ working unit*.

31. When did *your department/working unit* install its first computer application which is directly related to the achievement of your functions? _____ .

32. The following questions address the approach and the extent of computer usage for all the activities in *your department/working unit*. Please :

   (1) write down the names of all the activities your department/working unit carries on on a regular basis in the following space;

   (2) indicate the extent of computer usage for that activity by the following scale:
   1 = no automation at all; 2 = most manually, some automation; 3 = half manually, half automation; 4 = most automation with some manually; 5 = all automation;

   (3) if it is automated, write down the types of software/systems used for the activity;

   (4) indicate whether this is a shared software/system with other departments inside or outside your library and the name of that department.

ACTIVITIES	EXTENT OF COMPUTER USAGE	SOFTWARE/SYSTEMS	SHARED SYSTEMS WITH ......
Example 1. pre-order searching	5	*RLIN*	CAT DEPT.
Example 2. serials check-in	3	*INNOPAC*	ACQ, CIR, CAT

1. _____   _____   _____   _____

ACTIVITIES	EXTENT OF COMPUTER USAGE	SOFTWARE/SYSTEMS	SHARED SYSTEMS WITH ......
2.			
3.			
4.			
5.			
6.			
7.			
8.			

33. In relation to other similar library departments of equivalent size and FTE staff, how would you rate *your department/working unit* on each of the following factors during the past year?

	FAR BELOW AVERAGE	SOMEWHAT BELOW AVERAGE	ABOUT AVERAGE	SOMEWHAT ABOVE AVERAGE	FAR ABOVE AVERAGE
Quantity of work produced	1	2	3	4	5
Quality of work produced	1	2	3	4	5
Efficiency of department operations	1	2	3	4	5

34. Please comment on your responses to question 33.

_____

_____

_____

_____

_____

35. Please comment on how computer-related technologies affect your department's structure.

_____

_____

_____

_____

_____

_____

_____

36. Please provide other comments.

_____

_____

_____

_____

_____

_____

_____

Completed questionnaire can be mailed in the enclosed, stamped envelop, addressed to :
   Hweifen Weng / Office of the Ph.D. Program / School of Communication, Information and
   Library Studies / Rutgers University / 4 Huntington Street / New Brunswick, NJ 08903

THANK YOU VERY MUCH FOR YOUR COOPERATION.

ACKNOWLEDGMENTS

This paper is based on the author's dissertation (Weng 1997). I am greatly indebted to the guidance provided by my Dissertation Committee: Dr. Betty Turock, who served as my dissertation chairwoman, and Dr. Donald King, Dr. Daniel O. O'Connor, and Dr. Thomas W. Shaughnessy. Their encouragement and support are crucial for me to complete this project.

NOTES

1. Please refer to Weng (1997) for a detail review of library reorganization reports and empirical studies.
2. Please refer to Weng (1997) for detail analyses of the reliability, validity, and scoring procedures for the measures.
3. Dr. Van de Ven granted the permission to use OAI measures for the present study on a letter to the author dated 4/11/1994.

REFERENCES

Adams, R. J. 1986. *Information Technology and Libraries: A Future for Academic Libraries.* London: Croom Helm.

Adan, A. 1988. "Organizational Change in Law Libraries: The Impact of Automation on Traditional Library Structure." *Law Library Journal* 81: 97-102.

Alexander, J. W. and W. A. Randolph. 1985. "The Fit Between Technology and Structure as a Predictor of Performance in Nursing Subunits." *Academy of Management Journal* 28(4): 844-859.

Argote, L. 1982. "Input Uncertainty and Organizational Coordination in Hospital Emergency Units." *Administrative Science Quarterly* 27: 420-434.

Arnold, H. J. 1982. "Moderator Variables: A Clarification of Conceptual, Analytic, and Psychometric Issues." *Organizational Behavior and Human Performance* 29: 143-174.

Association of Research Libraries. (ARL). 1985. *Automation and Reorganization of Technical and Public Services.* SPEC Kit no. 112. Washington, DC: ARL, Office of Management Studies.

_____ . 1987a. *Performance Evaluation in Reference Services in ARL Libraries.* SPEC Kit no. 139. Washington, DC: ARL. Office of Management Studies.

_____ . 1987b. *Planning for Management Statistics in ARL Libraries.* SPEC Kit no. 134. Washington, DC: ARL. Office of Management Studies.

_____ . 1991. *Organization Charts in ARL Libraries.* SPEC Kit no. 170. Washington, DC: ARL. Office of Management Studies.

Babbie, E. R. 1973. *Survey Research Methods.* Belmont, CA: Wadsworth.

Bailey, K. D. 1994. *Methods of Social Research*, 4th edition. New York: Free Press.

Baker, S. L. and F. W. Lancaster. 1991. *The Measurement and Evaluation of Library Services*, 2nd edition. Arlington, VA: Information Resources Press.

Baligh, H. H., R. M. Burton and B. Obel. 1990. "Devising Expert Systems in Organization Theory: The Organizational Consultant." Pp. 35-77 in *Organization, Management, and Expert Systems*, edited by M. Masuch. Berlin: Walter de Gruyter.

Burns, T. and G. M. Stalker. 1961. *The Management of Innovation*. London: Tavistock.

Buttlar, L. J. and F. Garcha. 1992. "Organizational Structuring in Academic Libraries." *Journal of Library Administration* 17(3): 1-21.

Carter, N. M. 1984. "Computerization as a Predominate Technology: Its Influence on the Structure of Newspaper Organizations." *Academy of Management Journal* 27(2): 247-270.

Cline, H.F. and L. T. Sinnott. 1983. *The Electronic Library: The Impact of Automation on Academic Libraries*. Lexington, MA: Lexington Books.

Cohen, J. and P. Cohen. 1975. *Applied Multiple Regression/Correlation Analysis for the Behavioral Sciences*. Hillsdale, NJ: Erlbaum.

Comstock, D. E.and W. R. Scott. 1977. "Technology and the Structure of Subunits." *Administrative Science Quarterly* 22: 177-202.

Conley, B. H. 1981. *A Study of Performance as Measured by Selected Indicators and its Relationship to User Satisfaction and Resource Allocation*. In Five 1980 Land-Grant Institution libraries Doctoral Dissertation, Rutgers University.

Cotta-Schönberg, M. von. 1989. "Automation and Academic Library Structure." *Libri* 39(1): 47-63.

Cronin, M. J. 1985. *Performance Measurement for Public Services in Academic and Research Libraries* Occasional Paper Number 9. Washington, DC: Office of Management Studies, Association of Research Libraries.

Daft, R. L. 1986. *Organization Theory and Design*, 2nd edition. St. Paul, MN: West Publishing.

Dalton, D.R., W. D. Tudor, M. J. Spendolini, G. J. Fielding and L. Porter. 1980. "Organizational Structure and Performance: A Critical Review." *Academy of Management Review* 5: 49-64.

Damanpour, F. and W. M. Evan. 1984. "Organizational Innovation and Performance: The Problem of 'Organizational Lag.'" *Administrative Science Quarterly* 29: 392-409.

David, F. R., J. A. Pearce II, and W. A. Randolph. 1989. "Linking Technology and Structure to Enhance Group Performance." *Journal of Applied Psychology* 742: 233-241.

De Klerk, A. and J. R. Euster. 1989. "Technology and Organizational Metamorphoses." *Library Trends* 374: 457-468.

Dewar, R. and J. Hage. 1978. "Size, Technology, Complexity, and Structural Differentiation: Toward a Theoretical Synthesis." *Administrative Science Quarterly* 23: 111-136.

Dewar, R. and J. Werbel. 1979. "Universalistic and Contingency Predictions of Employee Satisfaction and Conflict." *Administrative Science Quarterly* 24: 426-448.

Drabenstott, K. M. and C. M. Burman. 1994. *Analytical Review of the Library of the Future*. Washington, DC: Council on Library Resources.

Drazin, R. and A. H. Van de Ven. 1985. "Alternative Forms of Fit in Contingency Theory." *Administrative Science Quarterly* 30: 514-539.

Duncan, R. 1979. "What is the Right Organization Structure? Decision Tree Analysis Provides the Answer." *Organizational Dynamics* 59-80.

Fisher, W. 1996. "Library Management: The Latest Fad, A Dismal Science, or just Plain Work?" *Library Acquisitions: Practice & Theory* 201: 49-56.

Fry, L.W. 1982. "Technology-structure Research: Three Critical Issues." *Academy of Management Journal* 253: 532-552.

Fry, L.W. and J. W. Slocum, Jr. 1984. "Technology, Structure, and Workgroup Effectiveness: A Test of a Contingency Model." *Academy of Management Journal* 21: 221-246.

Fry, L.W. and D. A. Smith. 1987. "Congruence, Contingency, and Theory Building." *Academy of Management Review* 12(1): 117-132.

Galbraith, J. R. 1973. *Designing Complex Organizations*. Reading, MA: Addison-Wesley.

Galbraith, J. R. 1994. *Competing with Flexible Lateral Organizations*, 2nd edition. Reading, MA: Addison-Wesley.

Gerwin, D. 1981. "Relationships Between Structure and Technology." Pp. 3-38 in *Handbook of Organizational Design*, Vol. 2, edited by P. C. Nystrom and W. H. Starbuck. New York: Oxford University Press.

Gorman, M. 1979. "On Doing Away with the Technical Services Departments." *American Libraries* 107: 435-437.

_____ . 1984. "The Ecumenical Library." *Reference Librarian* 9: 55-64.

_____ . 1985. *The Impact of Technology on the Organization of Libraries*. London: CLSI Publications.

_____ . 1987. "The Organization of Academic Libraries in the Light of Automation." *Advances in Library Automation and Networking* 151-168.

Grandori, A. 1987. *Perspectives on Organization Theory*. Cambridge, MA: Ballinger Publishing.

Gresov, C. 1989. "Exploring Fit and Misfit with Multiple Contingencies." *Administrative Science Quarterly* 34: 431-453.

Hage, J. and M. Aiken. 1967. "Program Change and Organizational Properties: A Comparative Analysis." *American Journal of Sociology* 72: 503-519.

Hall, R. H. 1987. *Organizations: Structures, Processes, and Outcomes*, 4th edition. Englewood Cliffs, NJ: Prentice-Hall.

Heitshu, S. C. 1991. "Acquisitions." Pp. 101-145 in *Library Technical Services: Operations and Management*, edited by I. P. Godden. San Diego, CA: Academic Press.

Hodgetts, R. M., F. Luthans and S. M. Lee. 1994. "New Paradigm Organizations: From Total Quality to Learning to World-Class." *Organizational Dynamics* 223: 5-19.

Howard, H. A. 1977. *The Relationship Between Certain Organizational Variables and the Relate of Innovation in Selected University Libraries*. Unpublished doctoral dissertation, Rutgers University.

Hrebiniak, L. 1974. "Job Technology, Supervision and Work Group Structure." *Administrative Science Quarterly* 19: 395-410.

Intner, S. S. and J. R. Fang. 1991. *Technical Services in the Medium-Sized Library: An Investigation of Current Practices*. Hamden, CT: Shoe String Press.

Johnson, P. 1991a. *Automation and Organizational Change in Libraries*. Boston: G.K. Hall.

_____ . 1991b. "Technological Change in Libraries." Pp. 327-345 in *Encyclopedia of Library and Information Science*, Vol. 48, edited by A. Kent. New York: Marcel Dekker.

Joyce, W., J. W. Slocum, Jr. and M. A. Von Glinow. 1982. "Person-situation Interaction: Competing Models of Fit." *Journal of Occupational Behavior* 3: 265-280.

Kanter, R.M. 1983. *The Change Masters: Innovations for Productivity in the American Corporation*. New York: Simon and Schuster.

Kaplan, D. P. 1990. "The Year's Work in Technical Services Automation, 1989." *Library Resources & Technical Services* 34(3): 299-312.

Kirkland, J. ed. 1989. "The Human Response to Library Automation." *Library Trend* 374: 385-542.

Lancaster, F. W. 1977. *The Measurement and Evaluation of Library Services*. Washington, DC: Information Resources Press.

Lewin, A. Y. and C. U. Stephens. 1993. "Designing Post Industrial Organizations: Combining Theory and Practice." Pp. 393-409 in *Organizational Change and Redesign: Ideas and Insights for Improving Performance*, edited by G. P. Huber and W. H. Glick. New York: Oxford University Press.

Lynch, B. P. 1974. "An Empirical Assessment of Perrow's Technology Construct." *Administrative Science Quarterly* 19: 338-356.

Lynch, B. P. and J. A. Verdin. 1986. *Relationship of Technology and Characteristics of Library Functional Units: Report to the Council on Library Resources*. Report No. CLR 799A; PGC Library Resources 2-5-36859. Washington, DC: Council on Library Resources, Inc. ERIC ED 278 427.

Mankin, D., S. G. Cohen and T. K. Bikson. 1996. "Teams and Technology: Fulfilling the Promise of the New Organization." Boston: Harvard Business School Press.

Martell, C. 1983. *Client-centered Academic Library: an Organizational Model*. Westport, CT: Greenwood Press.

McCann, J. and J. R. Galbraith. 1981. "Interdepartmental Relations." Pp. 60-84 in *Handbook of Organizational Design*, Vol. 2, edited by P. C. Nystrom and W. H. Starbuck. New York: Oxford University Press.

McDonald, J. A. and L. B. Micikas. 1994. *Academic Libraries: The Dimensions of Their Effectiveness*. Westport, CT: Greenwood Press.

Miller, D. and C. Dröge, C. 1986. "Psychological and Traditional Determinants of Structure." *Administrative Science Quarterly* 31: 539-560.

Miner, J. B. 1982. *Theories of Organizational Structure and Process*. Chicago: The Dryden Press.

Mohr, L.B. 1971. "Organizational Technology and Organizational Structure." *Administrative Science Quarterly* 16: 444-459.

Myers, M. 1986. "Personnel Considerations in Library Automation." Pp. 30-45 in *Human Aspects of Library Automation: Helping Staff and Patron Cope*, edited by D. Shaw. Urbana-Champaign, IL: Graduate School of Library and Information Science, University of Illinois at Urbana-Champaign.

Naisbitt, J. and P. Aburdene. 1985. "Reinventing the Corporation: Transforming Your Job and Your Company for the New Information Society." New York: Warner Books.

Pedhazur, E. J. 1982. "Multiple Regression in Behavioral Research: Explanation and Prediction." Fort Worth, TX: Holt, Rinehart and Winston.

Perrow, C. 1967. "A Framework for the Comparative Analysis of Organizations." *American Sociological Review* 32: 194-208.

―――――. 1970. *Organizational Analysis: A Sociological View*. Belmont, CA: Wadsworth.

Peters, T. J. and R. H. Waterman. 1982. *In Search of Excellence: Lessons from America's Best-run Companies*. New York: Harper and Row.

Peters, T. 1987. *Thriving on Chaos: Handbook for a Management Revolution*. New York: Knopf.

Pfeffer, J. 1982. *Organizations and Organization Theory*. Marshfield, MA: Pitman.

Price, J. L. and C. W. Mueller. 1986. *Handbook of Organizational Measurement*, 2nd edition. Marshfield, MA: Pitman Publishing Inc.

Pungitore, V. L. 1983. *Effects of Automation on the Organizational Design of Public and Academic Libraries: an Exploratory Study*. Unpublished doctoral dissertation, University of Pittsburgh.

―――――. 1986. "Development and Evaluation of a Measure of Library Automation." *Library and Information Science Research* 8(1): 67-83.

R. R. Bowker Company. 1994. *American Library Directory*, 47th edition. New York: Author.

Reimann, B. and G. Inzerilli. 1981. "Technology and Organization: A Review and Synthesis of Major Research Findings." Pp. 237-274 in *The Functioning of Complex Organizations*, edited by G. England, A. Negandhi and B. Wilpert. Cambridge, MA: Oelgeschlager, Gunn and Hain.

Robbins, S.P. 1983. *Organization Theory: The Structure and Design of Organizations*. Englewood Cliffs, NJ: Prentice-Hall.

Schoonhoven, C. B. 1981. "Problems with Contingency Theory: Testing Assumptions Hidden Within the Language of Contingency 'Theory.'" *Administrative Science Quarterly* 26: 349-377.

Scott, W. R. 1990. "Technology and Structure: An Organizational-Level Perspective." Pp. 109-143 in *Technology and Organizations*, edited by P. S. Goodman, L. S. Sproul and Associates. San Francisco: Jossey-Bass.

Shapiro, B. J. 1991. "Access and Performance Measures in Research Libraries in the 1990's." *Journal of Library Administration* 15(3/4): 49-66.

Shaughnessy, T. W. 1982. "Technology and the Structure of Libraries." *Libri* 322: 149-155.

―――――. 1990. "Assessing Library Effectiveness." *Journal of Library Administration* 12(1): 1-8.

Tannenbaum, A. S. 1968. *Control in Organizations*. New York: McGraw-Hill.

Thompson, J. D. 1967. *Organizations in Action*. New York: McGraw Hill.

U.S. Department of Education. 1992. *Academic Libraries: 1990* [Machine-readable data file]. Washington, DC: National Center for Education Statistics Producer & Distributor.
_____ . 1994. *Academic Libraries: 1992* [Machine-readable data file]. Washington, DC: National Center for Education Statistics Producer & Distributor.
_____ . 1996. *Preliminary 1994 Academic Library Data File* [Machine-readable data file]. Washington, DC: National Center for Education Statistics Producer & Distributor.
Van de Ven, A. H. 1981. "The Organization Assessment Perspective: The Organization Assessment Research Program. Pp. 249-298 in *Perspectives on Organization Design and Behavior*, edited by A. H. Van de Ven and W. F. Joyce. New York: John Wiley & Sons.
Van de Ven, A. H. and W. G. Astley. 1981. "Mapping the Field to Create a Dynamic Perspective on Organization Design and Behavior." Pp. 427-468 in *Perspectives on Organization Design and Behavior*, edited by A. H. Van de Ven and W. F. Joyce. New York: John Wiley & Sons.
Van de Ven, A. H., A. Delbecq and R. Koenig. 1976. "Determinants of Coordintion Modes within Organizations." *American Sociological Review* 41: 322-338.
Van de Ven, A. H. and R. Drazin. 1985. "The Concept of Fit in Contingency Theory." *Research in Organizational Behavior* 7: 333, 365.
Van de Ven, A. H. and D. L. Ferry. 1980. *Measuring and Assessing Organizations*. New York: John Wiley & Sons.
Van House, N. A., B. T. Weil C. R. McClure. 1990. *Measuring Academic Library Performance: A Practical Approach*. Chicago: American Library Association.
Venkatraman, N. 1989. "The Concept of Fit in Strategy Research: Toward Verbal and Statistical Correspondence." *Academy of Management Review* 14(3): 423-444.
Weng, H. 1997. *A Contingency Approach to Explore the Relationships among Structure, Technology, and Performance in Academic Library Departments*. Unpublished doctoral dissertation, Rutgers University.
Willard, P. and V. Teece. 1983. *Public Libraries and Automation: Four Case Studies*. [Kensington, N.S.W.]: School of Librarianship, University of New South Wales.
Withey, M., R. L. Daft and W. H. Cooper. 1983. "Measures of Perrow's Work Unit Technology: An Empirical Assessment and a New Scale." *Academy of Management Journal* 26(1): 45-63.
Woodward, J. 1965. *Industrial Organization: Theory and Practice* . London: Oxford University Press.

ABOUT THE CONTRIBUTORS

Mary C. Bushing is an active library educator and consultant in the area of collection development and library management. She is on the faculty at Montana State University in Bozeman, Montana and serves as Collection Development Librarian for the University Libraries. She is the author of numerous publications and holds a BA from George Williams College, Downers Grove, Illinois; an M.L.S. from Rosary College, River Forest, Illinois; and a Doctorate in Adult and Higher Education from Montana State University in Bozeman, Montana.

Frances Haley is the Executive Director of the Ohio Library Council. She served as project coordinator for "Measuring Library Services" and will coordinate the second phase of the project in fiscal year 1997-1998. Haley also served as project coordinator during the development phase of the Ohio Public Library Information Network (OPLIN).

Christine Kollen is currently in a split position at the University of Arizona Library. She is on the Bibliographic Access Team with responsibilities for original cataloging of cartographic materials and the Social Sciences Team with responsibilities for collection development, bibliographic instruction, knowledge management, needs assessment, faculty liaison, and general reference. She started a the University of Arizona Library in 1987. Her interests are in instruction and Geographic Information Systems. She holds a B.S. from the University of Washington and a M.L.S. from the University of Arizona.

Raymond R. McBeth is the Associate Dean of Graduate and Adult Education at Wheeling Jesuit University. He has been a frequent presenter and consultant in the area of information and records management, the impact of technology on organizations, and organizational development. He was also one of the co-founders of the Notari Systems Group, which was a firm that specialized in solving a variety of information management problems for small and medium-sized businesses.

Kerrie A. Moore is the University Archivist and Psychology Subject Selector, Roesch Library, University of Dayton, in Dayton, Ohio. She received a M.A. in History from Wright State University, Dayton, Ohio in 1990. Ms. Moore is a founding member of the Miami Valley Archivists Round Table and currently serves on the Program Committee. She is also chair of the Roesch Library Market Research Task Force.

Edward J. O'Hara received his bachelor's degree in International Relations from American University in Washington, DC., and after a stint in the Army, embarked on a career in the business world while also pursuing his master's degree in history from New York University. He received his M.L.S. from Rutgers and then worked as a bibliographer at Boston University and later as head of collection development at the University of Kentucky before becoming the library director, first, at Sacred Heart University in Fairfield, Connecticut, and, then, at Manhattanville College in Purchase, New York. After receiving his D.L.S. from Columbia University, O'Hara was appointed library director at the College of Mount Saint Vincent in New York City.

Elizabeth L. Plummer is the librarian at Mercy College of Northwest Ohio, Toledo, Ohio. Associated with the Religious Sisters of Mercy, the college awards Associate Degrees in Nursing and Pharmacy Technology. She is responsible for Reference and Technical Services. Her research interests are customer service, library automation, and library space planning. She received her Master of Library Science from Kent State University, Kent, Ohio in 1996; Master of Arts from Bowling Green State University, Bowling Green, Ohio in 1976; and a Bachelor of Arts from Heidelberg College, Tiffin, Ohio in 1975.

Nancy Simons is a member of the Science-Engineering Team at the University of Arizona. In 1990, she was hired into a position split 50/50 between the Catalog Department and the Science-Engineering Library and remained in that position until 1995. Prior to coming to the University of Arizona, she served as a science reference librarian at Oklahoma State University. She holds a M.L.S. from the University of Arizona.

Jennalyn Tellman has two positions at the University of Arizona Library. She is a member of the Bibliographic Access Team with responsibilities for cataloging and she is a member of the Fine Arts and Humanities Team with responsibilities for collection development, advanced reference, bibliographic instruction, knowledge management, needs assessment, and general reference. She has been at the University of Arizona Library since 1990. Her previous experience is in special libraries. She has interests in the areas of instruction and in split positions. She holds a B.A. from Wellesley College and a M.S.L.S. from Simmons College.

Connie Van Fleet is an Adjunct Associate Professor in the School of Library and Information Services at Kent State University and has also served on the faculty at Louisiana State University. Dr. Van Fleet is the author of numerous publications and is the former co-editor of *RQ*. She is the recipient of the 1996 Reference and User Services Association Margaret E. Monroe Library Adult Services Award.

Kathleen M. Webb is the Government Documents Librarian at the Roesch Library at the University of Dayton in Ohio. She received her M.L.S. from the University of California, Los Angeles. Previously she was a Reference Librarian at the Dayton & Montgomery County Public Library and Sinclair Community College. Her professional interests include library web page design and Bibliographic instruction.

Hweifen Weng received her bachelor's degree in Library Studies at National Taiwan University before pursuing her MLS at Rutgers University as a Mary Elizabeth Wood Foundation fellow. She then completed her Ph.D. in Library Studies while working as a Graduate Assistant in East Asian Cataloging, Technical and Automated Services and as a Project Assistant in the Serials Department at Rutgers.

Marilyn Domas White holds a Ph.D. from the University of Illinois and is an Associate Professor at the College of Library and Information Services, University of Maryland, College Park, Maryland. She has recently completed research funded by the Special Library Association on measuring service quality in special libraries and the Council on Library Resources on document use over the life of a research project. She is currently working with Eileen G. Abels and Karla Hahn on a user-based process for designing Web pages, funded by Disclosure, Inc. Her publications have appeared in *Library Quarterly, Special Libraries, RQ*, and *The Reference Librarian*.

INDEX

J
A
I

Advances in Library Administration and Organization

Edited by **Delmus E. Williams,** *Dean,*
University Libraries, University of Akron and
Edward D. Garten, *Dean of Libraries and*
Information Technologies, University of Dayton

Volume 14, 1996, 277 pp. $78.50/£49.95
ISBN 0-7623-0098-1

P
R
E
S
S

Also Available:
Volumes 1-13 (1982-1995) $78.50/£49.95 each

JAI PRESS INC.
55 Old Post Road No. 2 - P.O. Box 1678
Greenwich, Connecticut 06836-1678
Tel: (203) 661- 7602   Fax: (203) 661-0792

Advances in Library Automation and Networking

Edited by **Joe A. Hewitt,** *Associate Provost for University Libraries, University of North Carolina, Chapel Hill*

The purpose of this series is to present a broad spectrum of in-depth, analytical articles on the technical, organizational, and policy aspects of library automation and networking. The series will include detailed examinations and evaluations of particular computer applications in libraries, status surveys, and perspective papers on the implications of various computing and networking technologies for library services and management. The emphasis will be on the information and policy frameworks needed for librarians and administrators to make informed decisions related to developing or acquiring automated systems and network services with special attention to maximizing the positive effects of these technologies on library organization.

Volume 5, 1994, 282 pp. $73.25/£46.95
ISBN 1-55938-510-3

Edited by **Joe Hewitt**, *Associate Provost for University Libraries, University of North Carolina, Chapel Hill* and **Charles Bailey, Jr.** *Assistant Director for Systems, University of Houston*

CONTENTS: Introduction, *Joe A. Hewitt.* Next-Generation Online Public Access Catalogs: Redefining Territory and Roles, *Carolyn O. Frost.* Full-Text Retrieval: Systems and Files, *Carol Tenopir.* What Can The Internet Do for Libraries, *Mark H. Kibbey and Geri R. Bunker.* Electronic Document Delivery: An Overview with a Report on Experimental Agriculture Projects, *John Ulmschneider and Tracy M. Casorso.* Campus-Wide Information Systems, *Judy Hallman.* Use of a General Concept Paper as RFP for a Library System Procurement, *Mona Couts, Charles Gilreath, Joe Hewitt, and John Ulmschneider.* Research on the Distributed Electronic Library, *Denise A. Troll.* Notes on the Contributors.

Also Available:
Volumes 1-4 (1987-1991) $73.25/46.95 each

J
A
I
P
R
E
S
S

J A I

P R E S S

Prize. Crafoord Prize in Mathematics. Dantzig Prize. Rollo Davidson Prize. De Morgan Medal. Richard C. DiPrima Prize. Dirac Medal. Distinguished Public Service Award. Fermat Prize for Mathematical Research. Fields Medal. Fondation Carriere de Mathematiques. Fondation Elie Cartan. Fondation Emil Picard. Fondation Francoeur. Fondation Henri Poincare. Fondation Poncelet. Lester R. Ford Award. Forder Lectureship. Leslie Fox Prize in Numerical Analysis. Fulkerson Prize. Geometry Prize. Godel Prize. Guggenheim Fellowhips. Yueh-gin Gung and Dr. Charles H. Hu Award for Distinguished Service to Mathematics. Deborah and Franklin Tepper Haimo Award for Distinguished College or University Teaching of Mathematics. Israel Halperin Prize. Hardy Lectureship. Merten M. Hasse Prize. Louise Hay Award for Contributions to Mathematics Education. Hedrick Lectureship. Dannie N. Heineman Prize for Mathematical Physics. Interntional Congress of Mathematicians, Plenary Lectures, 45 minutes. International Congress of Mathematicians, Plenary Lectures, 60 minutes. International Giovanni Sacchi Landriani Prize. Jeffery-Williams Lectureship. Joint Policy Board for Mathematics Communications Award. Junior Berwick Prize. Junior Whitehead Prize. King Faisal International Prize in Science. Thomas Rankin Lyle Medal. MacArthur Fellowships. Monroe Martin Prize. Frank and Brennie Morgan Prize for Outstanding Research in Mathematics by an Undergarduate Student. National Academy of Sciences, Elected Members. National Academy of Sciences Award in Applied Mathematics and Numerical Analysis. National Academy of Sciences Award in Mathematics. National Medal of Science. Naylor Prize and Lectureship in Applied Mathematics. Frederic Esser Nemmers Prize. Rolf Nevalinna Prize. Nihon Sugakukai Iyanaga Sho. Ostrowski Award. George Polya Award. George Polya Prize. Polya Prize. Vasil Popov Prize in Approximation Theory. Premio Bartolozzi. Premio Caccioppoli. Premio Tricerri. Presidential Faculty Fellow Award. Prix Charles Lagrange. Prix Eugene Catalan. Prix Francois Deruyts. Srinivasa Ramanujan Medal. W.T. and Idalia Reid Prize. Salem Prize. Ruth Lyttle Satter Prize. Alice T. Schafer Prize for Excellence in Mathematics by an Undergraduate Woman. Hans Schneider Prize in Linear Algebra. Rolf Schock Prize in Mathematics. Senior Berwick Prize. Senior Whithead Prize. SIAM Activity Group on Linear Algebra Prize. SIAM Prize for Distinguished Service to the Profession. Spring Prize. Leroy P. Steele Prizes. Simion Stoilow Prize. Swedish Mathematical Society Fellowship. Sylvester Medal. John L. Synge Award. TWAS Award in Mathematics. Oswald Veblen Prize in Geometry. Theodore von Karman Prize. John von Neumann Lecture. Alan T. Waterman Award. Norbert Wiener Prize in Applied Mathematics. James H. Wilkinson Prize in Numerical Analysis and Scientific Computing. Wolf Foundation Prizes. SOURCES FOR FURTHER INFORMATION. LIST OF SPONSORS. INDEX TO PRIZE ABBREVIATIONS. INDEX TO RECIPIENTS. SUBJECT INDEX.

J A I

P R E S S

J A I   P R E S S

Advances in Serials Management

Edited by **Cindy Hepfer,** *Head Serials Department, Health Sciences Library, State University of New York at Buffalo,* **Teresa Malinowski,** *Serials Coordinator, University Library, California State University, Fullerton,* and **Julia Gammon,** *Head Acquisitions Department, Bierce Library, University of Akron*

Volume 6, 1997, 252 pp. $73.25/£46.95
ISBN 0-7623-0101-5

CONTENTS: CD-ROMS, Surveys, and Sales: The OSA Experience, *Frank E. Harris and Alan Tourtlotte.* Management and Integration of Electronic Journals into the Serials Department, *Barbara Hall.* A Collaborative Approach to Conversion: The University of Washington Serials Control Project, *Diane Grover and James Stickman.* Serials Vendor Service Quality Evaluation: An Ongoing Performance Review Process, *Ruth H. Makinen and James L. Smith.* Bibliometric Tools for Serials Collection Management in Academic Libraries, *Katherine W. McCain.* The Integration of Science Serial Collections into a Consolidated Science Library, *Kathryn Kjaer, Sally C. Tseng, and Barbara Lucas.* Compact Storage — A Part of the OhioLINK Strategy and a Solution to Shelving Needs for Journal Collections, *Pat Salomon and Barbara Shaffer.* The Impact of the Faxon Company on the Serials Community, 1881-1996, *Constance L. Foster.*

Also Available
Volumes 1-5 (1986-1995) $73.25/£46.95 each

JAI PRESS INC.
55 Old Post Road No. 2 - P.O. Box 1678
Greenwich, Connecticut 06836-1678
Tel: (203) 661- 7602   Fax: (203) 661-0792